A READER IN CULTURAL ANTHROPOLOGY

NORMAN ALGER
Moorpark College

Many Answers

WEST PUBLISHING CO.
St. Paul • New York • Boston
Los Angeles • San Francisco

Library of Congress Cataloging in Publication Data

Alger, Norman, comp.

   Many answers: a reader in cultural anthropology.

   1. Ethnology.   I. Title.

GN315.A47   301.2   73–23106

ISBN 0–8299–0006–3

Alger—Cult.Anthropology WC

PREFACE

The human experience has been a varied one and different cultures have found many ways to solve the many problems of life faced by all men. The articles selected for this reader in cultural anthropology have been chosen to illustrate some of these many answers. An understanding of the vast range of variation in human behavior is not only desirable in terms of human survival but can often provide us with new insight into our own culture.

The articles selected for this reader were chosen for their readability and for their appeal to the students. Students in my cultural anthropology classes were asked what they would like to see in a reader and every attempt has been made to meet their suggestions.

Earlier versions of this reader were reviewed by William S. Evans, Jr., Don Layton and R. Dennis Ringer and I am grateful to each of them for their constructive criticisms.

I would like to thank my editorial assistant Veronica Ramirez for her part in the formulation of this reader. Not only did she handle all of the many details of the manuscript's preparation, but she also made many valuable suggestions as to the selection of articles.

I would also like to thank Clyde Perlee, Jr. of West Publishing Company for invaluable assistance and encouragement. The freedom given to me by Mr. Perlee made the editing of this reader an enjoyable experience.

N.T.A.

Oxnard, California
February, 1974

*

TABLE OF CONTENTS

†

Many Answers:

A Reader in

Cultural Anthropology

*

I. Anthropology
and
Anthropologists

Anthropologists are frequently called upon to explain their roles in research and teaching. To merely define anthropology as "the study of man" does not adequately answer such questions as there are many other professionals who also study man. The first article in this section by Sol Tax answers some of these questions by comparing anthropology to other academic disciplines and by telling something of the work and research interests of different types of anthropologists. The second article by Walter Goldschmidt explains in some detail what types of anthropologists there are and what their more specific interests are likely to be. Both of these articles should give the reader a good background to appreciate the vast diversity of interests reflected by the other articles in this reader. The final article of this section, by Mario D. Zamora examines the social significance of cultural anthropology, and ethical problems related to the field of cultural anthropology.

What Do Anthropologists Do? † *

I T has been said that anthropology is what anthropologists do, and that anthropologists do what they please. While this may seem somewhat facetious, it does reflect some truth about the nature of the field. Anthropology seeks to reach insights into the nature of man that cannot be reached through other disci-

† By Sol Tax, Professor of Anthropology and Dean of the University Extension at the University of Chicago. He is also editor of Current Anthropology.

* Social Education—Vol. 32, #2 (Feb. 1968): 132–134 National Council for Social Studies 1201–16th Street N.W. Washington, D. C.—20036.

plines that study him.   Therefore, anything related to man—including monkeys—is fair game for anthropologists.

How is anthropology different from other disciplines?   There are at least two ways that a discipline can reach new insights. One is to study *material* not studied by other disciplines.   Like every discipline, anthropology has always done this.   But instead of finding a space between two others—as in the case of biochemistry—it skirts the edges of many.   Since anthropology chooses the subject of mankind as a whole—including man biologically, socially, and culturally at all times everywhere—it appears to some as an academic garbage can which picks up odds and ends that other people do not want to study.

The other way to reach new insights is to study the material of other disciplines from a different point of view.   Thus anthropologists may study the same material as geneticists, paleontologists, sociologists, or psychologists.   But because they have a different frame of reference, they may arrive at useful new conclusions.   Whether by chewing at the edges of other disciplines, or studying old material in a new frame of reference, or both, anthropologists have developed a substantial new body of knowledge.

What is the substantive content of anthropology?   Let us take a closer look at some areas that anthropologists find relevant to the study of man.   Because man is the only animal with language, the study of speech and of languages is important to understanding what man is and how (evolutionally speaking) he got where he is.   Since communication through language is essential to the maintenance of society and to the transmission of ideas from one generation to the next, the study of language is indeed central to the entire study of man.

Although chimpanzees and other animals may fashion and use very simple tools, man is uniquely a technologist.   Studying man's tools is central to anthropology; but so is the study of art, games, music, dance, literature, and all other products of human invention.

Whether thought of as cultural inventions or social necessities, the variety of social relationships lies at the heart of anthropology.   Tribes, chiefs, war, clans, classes, the family; the cycle of ritual with birth, puberty, marriage, and death are a few examples of such social relationships.

History is always anthropology. History and anthropology seek to investigate many of the same questions. When did man start wearing clothing and why? When and how did man drift into the Americas? Were the ancient civilizations developed independently in the Near East, the Far East, and in America? How has the function of religion changed in the last 7,000 years? Since the answers to many of these questions can be found in what man put down as he recorded his own history, studying history can also be studying anthropology.

Of course, psychology can help the anthropologists explain some of the behavior of man. Anthropologists as well as psychologists must ask how peoples differ and why—in their perceptions, their personalities, and the character of their cultures.

What are the different interests of anthropologists? Anthropology studies a wide variety of topics; but, of course, anthropologists themselves are all specialized. Because they are specialized within a widely diversified field, they are generally very different from one another.

Anthropologists can be classified roughly into four major interest areas: physical anthropology, prehistoric archeology, cultural or social anthropology, and linguistics are the names most commonly employed.

Archeologists, linguists, and physical anthropologists often find their problems in far-off lands. However, it is more than just a matter of interest that has led the cultural anthropologist to study cultures other than his own. Cultural anthropologists must study cultures other than their own in order to insure their own scientific objectivity. Thus today, English, American, Japanese, and Indian anthropologists, among others, study one another's national character through field work in small communities and the evidences of their literary traditions.

Who employs anthropologists? Who is it that pays anthropologists to dig up fossil men or to study the music of American Indians? Universities are the largest employers of anthropologists. In the universities anthropologists teach and do research, with the research supported by grants from the government (in most countries) and private foundations (in some). Museums and research institutes are the second largest employers of anthropologists. In museums, anthropologists curate the collections, prepare the exhibits, and usually devote more time to research than is possible for university teachers.

Some anthropologists work as advisers to government (or to business or industry); but anthropology is almost wholly a scholarly profession. Universities and research institutes are themselves supported by governments (in some countries entirely); but unless they are actually working for a department of government administration, anthropologists tend to be free agents responsible in their research only to the academic community.

How are anthropologists alike? I have been using the word anthropology in its inclusive sense. In Northern and Eastern Europe, the word refers specifically to the biological aspects of the study of man. Ethnology and ethnography, philosophy and linguistics, archeology and prehistory are treated as separate disciplines. In most of the English-, French-, Spanish-, Portuguese-, and Italian-speaking countries—and in Asia and Africa generally—the prehistorians, ethnologists, linguists, and human biologists call themselves, and feel some kinship as, anthropologists.

This feeling of kinship dates back to at least 1839 when there was formed in Paris a society of scholars from many disciplines for the explicit purpose of gaining together an understanding of all aspects of man. The movement spread rapidly to London, New York, Moscow, and other capitals, so that soon there was a self-conscious international community whose goals and values separated it from any of the component disciplines from which its members had come (or to which they were still also attached). The anthropologists of today are those individuals who still maintain the spirit of this society and who communicate with the other individuals throughout the world who also are involved in its aims.

Anthropologists, wishing thus to construct a picture of the whole of man, cannot think of man as here and now: "here" is to be compared with a world of "theres," and "now" is the effect of complete history. Anthropologists cannot study man without considering both his biological limitations and capacities and the way these are qualified by his cultural environment. This was the new frame of reference that led to the unusual openness to all sources of knowledge that is characteristic of anthropology. In this especially, anthropology is unique.

Academic disciplines jealously guard their subject matters. Special languages develop strong boundaries, and intercommunications between related disciplines are often severely limited. The original anthropologists were people who were willing to cross these boundaries for a common purpose. Anyone who shared that purpose could be an anthropologist. Since this is still true, many anthropologists are *also* (for example) geneticists, geologists, anatomists, sociologists, psychologists, or musicologists, who work with colleagues in their special disciplines, but are different from these colleagues because they also communicate with the main body of anthropologists and with the diverse specialists who share their interest in the broader study. These "dualists" serve the purpose of anthropology particularly well, bringing to it from related disciplines the newest relevant knowledge.

Anthropology is general, but anthropologists are all specialists; the generality is the product of their continuing intercommunication in an organic and changing network. Necessary to this result is the interest of anthropologists in other anthropologists. They are self-selected for mutual interest, since each is always free to retreat into his specialty alone.

By selection of profession also, anthropologists tend to be people who are interested in people. Since anthropology emphasizes the wholeness of man, this interest cannot be just remote and analytical. One who is interested in people is likely also to be interested in their welfare. Thus, it is not surprising that anthropologists tend to become involved in social issues, especially those which relate to native peoples. In fact, the first anthropologists' society was formed through the efforts of an English "Society for the Protection of Aborigines."

However, an anthropologist can also defeat his purpose by becoming too involved with people. There is the extreme case of the young anthropologist who becomes so immersed in the culture of the group he studies that he becomes a member of the tribe, no longer able—or perhaps willing—to contribute what he learns to the common pool of anthropological information.

The more general experience is only a loss of objectivity which threatens the usefulness of his data unless he has the benefit of continuing contact with other anthropologists. The anthropologist is left straddling a strange fence. He must become involved enough with the people he studies so that he can be sure that he understands them, but not so much that he cannot. Antropologists must be both scientists and humanists, and yet neither completely scientists nor humanists.

Because of the diversity in the subject matter, anthropologists are people who have a high tolerance for a variety of tools and subjects. And even then, if they are to encompass all of their subject matter at once, they must be able to live with some ambiguity in their conclusions. It is simply impossible to look at all the minute details and to perceive the scope of the whole at the same time.

Like all disciplines, anthropology has its jargon. However, this jargon is not so "tight" in most anthropology as it is in many other disciplines. This looseness, or ambiguity, makes for openness; but it also makes anthropology perhaps less of a science. While cumulative or systematic progress in the field is thus slowed, fatal intellectual blood clots are kept from clogging the interdisciplinary flow.

How do anthropologists work? Almost every anthropologist, however general his interests, usually—when he is engaged in a research—works on a particular problem. The method he uses to arrive at a solution depends upon the topic of research he chooses. Sometimes the anthropologist works in the laboratory or the library. More characteristically he works in the field.

The original anthropologists, exploring a distant territory to which a scientist might not soon return, did a very diversified kind of research. They made physical observations and measurements of the people, recorded the language, and studied all aspects of material and non-material culture.

Even now in places where people, cultures, and languages are rapidly changing or disappearing (due to so-called "modernization") anthropologists hurriedly salvage as much data from the area as possible. But most research now is oriented to very specific problems within human biology, prehistory, ethnography, or linguistics, or bridges two or three of these.

When the anthropologist goes to the field, he brings with him the generalized type of knowledge characteristic of his discipline. As quickly as possible, he appraises the whole culture in which his problem is set, then begins to test particular hypotheses for which the field situation is especially suited. A "field season" lasts anywhere from three months to two years and the anthropologist tends to return again and again to his people, and to maintain contact between field trips through correspondence.

The anthropologist in the field must apply the knowledge of any of the disciplines—geology, botany, medicine, psychology, and any others that become relevant.

No matter what his problem, an anthropologist needs mainly to learn from people; so the anthropologist's main concern in field work is developing rapport with a community of complete strangers of an alien culture, who have no interest in being disturbed for a purpose not their own, or even within their understanding. If the anthropologist is wise, he accepts the role of the ignorant person he is, and enlists the interest that the parent or the teacher has in the innocent child excited to learn.

Since the outsiders previously encountered by the community were probably less educated and more arrogant, the anthropologist may be a refreshing change. Whether administrators, teachers, employers, business people, or even missionaries, these outsiders usually have tried to get the local people to do or be what they do not wish. The anthropologist, however, respects them, learns from them, and puts his knowledge of the outside world at their disposal. The anthropologist makes his way in a strange culture, not by "tricks of the trade" but by falling into some slot where both he and the natives are comfortable. His "slot" might be in a small social circle, but it is genuine.

It is both harder and easier to study a human group than, say, a troop of baboons; but the general principle is the same. The successful anthropologist hopes to do as well as Dr. Phyllis Jay, who made her way into the social life of a band of monkeys in India, and wound up second from the bottom in the group's pecking order.

The romance of field work, however, is only the visible part of the iceberg; the other eight-ninths is hard clerical labor, with mapping and digging tools; card indexes and long rolls of paper for genealogies and charts; notebooks and copying and calculating; and doing most things the hard way. The second season in any location, however, gives the anthropologist all of the pleasure of homecoming to old friends. He returns with clearer knowledge of what tools to bring to solve problems which he can now foresee.

The Fields of Anthropology † *

ANTHROPOLOGY is usually divided into four basic fields of study, and each anthropologist specializes in one of these. Indeed, as our knowledge increases, it is necessary for the individual anthropologist to specialize more narrowly within these fields.

Biologic or Physical Anthropology. The physical anthropologist is concerned with man as a biological being. He is concerned with the relation between the human species and other animals, with the gradual evolution of man, with the biological features that distinguish the races, and with the relation between man's biological well-being and his culture.

Some physical anthropologists study man's relation to other animals, particularly the apes and monkeys. Biologists classify man together with these animals as primates, and man is closer to these animals in behavior, as he is in biology, than he is to any other animal. Physical anthropologists are concerned with the origin of man—where and when did it take place, and what caused man to become different from other creatures. They are also interested in understanding ape behavior, for it may lead to knowledge of how man once behaved, before he acquired language and culture. Very many have watched the behavior of troops of monkeys and apes for hours to study the relationships between the old and young, the males and females.

Some physical anthropologists are most interested in the study of fossil man, to understand the evolution of man from his beginning when he was quite different in appearance and structure to the time when the modern races of man developed. They must find these ancient remains in places like Olduvai Gorge in Tanzania, from which the earliest known types of men come, and then study every detail of the bones they find. From such information they can determine whether the individual walked erect, whether he used tools, and many details of his appearance. They cannot know, of course, what his hair looked like or what color his skin and eyes were, for only the bones remain of these

† By Walter Goldschmidt.

* On Becoming an Anthropologist 1970—American Anthropological Association pp. 3–6. Reproduced by permission of the American Anthropological Association and the author.

earlier and extinct species of men, but they can reconstruct many details of hominid evolution.

Other physical anthropologists are interested in modern man as he differs in different parts of the world. They have classified man into "races" on the basis of careful examination of differences in structure, skin, hair, eyes, etc. Nowadays, there is less concern with the racial differences than with the way in which these features are inherited. Many physical anthropologists are thus doing work that is very close to the field of genetics, which is a part of the science of biology. As a matter of fact, they often work in departments of biology or in schools of medicine, as well as in departments of anthropology.

Archeology. Archeology is the study of man's past, based on the things that people have left in the ground. In a way it is a part of the study of history, and many history departments have archeologists working in areas where man had writing, such as in ancient Egypt and Greece. Archeological investigations also support more recent historical research, as for instance in Colonial America. But most archeologists study the remains of peoples who had no writing and were therefore not known to history. These archeologists must know anthropology, for they interpret what they find by comparing it with what is known about primitive cultures.

The first task of the archeologist is to dig up the remains that give evidence of man's past behavior. Whether he digs up an Indian camp near his town, or a cave in Europe in which men lived tens of thousands of years ago, or a city in Mesopotamia at the dawn of man's knowledge of writing, he must dig with meticulous care and preserve every evidence of how the people lived. He is not so much interested in the artifacts, as he calls the things that he finds, as he is in the evidence of how man lived and how that life changed through time. Scraps of bone tell him what the people ate. Fossil pollen from plants tells him not only what men ate but what kinds of plants existed in the area at the time. Details of the arrangements within a site tell him things about the social organization. Therefore he must record precisely where each item came from and preserve everything made or used by man—even samples of the soil.

The second task of the archeologist is to analyze his finds; to use these scraps of evidence to show what the climate was, whether the people had domestic animals and engaged in farming, what kind of religious beliefs they had, how their society was organized. Ultimately, from many such careful studies the archeologist will give us a complete picture of the unfolding of human history from when man first came onto the earth up to modern times.

Linguistics. The one thing that most clearly separates man from all other animals is his use of language. Not only is speech important in distinguishing man from other beings, but it is also critical in the understanding of other parts of culture, for it is largely by means of language that men learn the culture they become part of. For these reasons, linguistics is a very special branch of anthropology—so special and important that it has become a science of its own. Still, many linguists are anthropologists.

Every people has the ability to speak, and this means not only that they have words for things but that they have a grammar, even though their language was never written down. The first task of the linguistic anthropologist is to make dictionaries and grammars of the languages of primitive peoples. They do this through detailed questioning of the native speakers of the language.

There are many things that we learn from studying languages of people in different parts of the world. First of all, we can find out what languages are related to one another. We learned long ago that English and German are fairly closely related, that these are more distantly related to French and Spanish, and that ultimately most of the European languages and many of those from India are all part of the same "family." Linguists have made studies of the historical relations of other families of languages and thus contributed to our knowledge of the history of the people who speak them. The second thing we learn by the study of language is to see how the language people use influences the way they think about things. The words a people use classify the things and events around them, but the principles of classification vary and therefore things do not fall into the same categories. Navaho grammar emphasizes the verb, in contrast to ours which emphasizes the noun, so that they think more in terms of process while we think more in terms of actors. Such differences have been shown to affect the native speakers' way of seeing and understanding things. Third, by studying different languages, the linguist hopes to show how language works; what it is that makes man a speaking animal when all other creatures do not talk. The linguistic anthropologist is also interested in the place of linguistics in the lives of people; their beliefs and attitudes about language and its use, the relation of language to other modes of communication, the patterns by which one or another language, or variety of a language, is chosen, depending on situation and purpose. Some are working on the relation of these kinds of knowledge to problems of education and social development in the contemporary world.

Cultural Anthropology. By far the greatest proportion of anthropologists devote themselves to the study of the customs, the culture and the social life of living peoples. These are generally called cultural or social anthropologists.

For about three quarters of a century, anthropologists have gone out to study peoples in various parts of the world: the Australian aborigines in the "outback," the Eskimo in the Arctic, the native tribes of America and Africa. They have recorded the legends, the beliefs, the daily life and the social relationships that they found. The description of the way of life of a people is called an ethnography. In former times, when travel was difficult and there were very few anthropologists and many tribal peoples to study, the cultural anthropologist tried to study every aspect of native life. Nowadays, he generally specializes in one or another part; perhaps he is most interested in the economy, or the religious ceremonies, or the way the people take care of their infants. In such research he examines these events as they relate to the total culture.

Many people believe that anthropology is the study of primitive people. Though most cultural anthropologists do study tribal or peasant societies, some have always been interested in customs and behavior patterns in our own society. Many anthropologists have studied modern American communities; they have even studied the customs of doctors in hospitals and the conduct of teachers and children in schools. An increasing number of students enter anthropology with such interests.

Anthropologists study cultures in order to make a record of how man lives in different times and places. But this is only the beginning, for the anthropologists seek to explain why people behave different ways in different places. In order to try to answer this very difficult question, the anthropologists compare the behavior of peoples, to see how they vary and what can explain the differences that they find. The more that the anthropologist has pondered this basic question, the more he has felt he needed to know about the details of human behavior in different societies. Even though the number of tribal societies is dwindling rapidly, there is much that still remains to be discovered about how people live in those that remain; there is still much work to be done.

All living races or varieties of man belong to a single species, *Homo sapiens* (although other species and even other genera are found in fossil form). It is not surprising that, despite differences in culture, human behavior has a degree of similarity wherever it is found, and these consistencies are also important. We have already pointed out that all men have language, though the *form* of the language varies. Similarly, we can say that all peoples live in social groups, and organize their social life according to customary rules, though the rules vary. All peoples, for instance, recognize the importance of kin and regulate much of their behavior according to the relationship that exists among them, just as we do—though, again, how they feel about particular relatives may differ from our sentiments. All people have some form of marriage, some kind of legalized union for procreation, and all people consider marriage between kin to be incestuous—though once again, just what degree of relationship is to be considered incest will vary from one people to another. All peoples exhibit religious beliefs; all have notions of gods or spirits and all engage in ceremonies concerning these supernatural events, but it is not necessary to point out that they do not all believe the same thing. The uniformities and consistencies are as important to understand as the differences.

Moral, Immoral Science: The Case for Cultural Anthropology † *

I. Introduction

THIS paper attempts to review in a broad and somewhat generalized fashion the scope, significance, and ethics in cultural anthropology. Specifically, it seeks to answer the following fundamental questions: (1) What is the *scope* of the science of cultural anthropology? (2) What is the *significance* of cultural anthropology to the contemporary problems of mankind? and finally, (3) What are the *ethical* questions related to the field of cultural anthropology?

II. Scope of Cultural Anthropology

Cultural anthropology is one of the subdisciplines of general anthropology, the science of man and his achievements as well as his body, behavior, and values in time and space. The subdiscipline of cultural anthropology deals with one key concept in the social sciences which has far-reaching significance in theory, technique, and application—the key concept of *culture*. Culture, in the scientific sense, is the way of life of a people which has been learned, shared, and transmitted from one generation to another by means of language and symbols. The term "culture" is often equated with "social heritage," "design for living," "conventional understanding," and "the super-organic," among others. Two eminent anthropologists, Alfred Louis Kroeber and Clyde Kluckhohn wrote a monumental and classical book on CULTURE: A CRITICAL REVIEW OF CONCEPTS AND DEFINITIONS which tells us more about the concept, its history, implications, significance and application. Suffice it to say in this discussion that culture means the totality of human life. It includes man's religion, politics, economy, education, health, philosophy, aesthetics and other facets of human existence in their functional unity and integration.

† Remarks by Mario D. Zamora, Visiting Foreign Professor Eastern Montana College, before the Biology and Society Lecture Series of the Eastern Montana College, Billings, Montana, U.S.A. on March 12, 1973, 7:15 p. m. Library 148.

* The Indian Historian, Vol. 6, No. 2 (Spring 1973): 24–28. By permission of the editors.

The late Felix Keesing, an anthropologist from Stanford University, further divides cultural anthropology into three divisions: (1) ethnography; (2) ethnology; and (3) social anthropology. Keesing says that ethnography is the description of the way of life of a people; ethnology is the comparison and contrast of such a lifeway; and social anthropology is the formulation of abstract laws, principles, and generalizations about human behavior and values based on the ethnographic data and ethnological analysis.

We can, thus, see the broad scope of the discipline of cultural anthropology. It encompasses almost every department of human life. Cultural anthropologists are interested in the politics of a nation, in its religious harmony or strife, in its health and vitality, in its education system and philosophy, in the way people see beauty and ugliness in man, nature and personality, and in the national and local economy of a country. All these concerns preoccupy the time and efforts of our cultural anthropologists in their search for the universal and the particular, the general and the unique, the broad as well as the specific detail of human custom and tradition.

Cultural anthropologists are likewise involved in *human engineering* or in the improvement of the human condition—in poverty programs, in liberation movements, in human rights for minorities and for women, in clean and honest government, in safe unpolluted environment; in sum, in the elevation of the quality and style of human life. Thus we can see the broad and far-ranging scope of the subdiscipline of cultural anthropology in the lives and fortunes of humans everywhere.

III. The Significance of Cultural Anthropology

Cultural anthropology is important in four interrelated ways: (1) It promotes cross-cultural understanding; (2) It serves as a guide to sociocultural change; (3) It offers broad liberal education; (4) It enhances unity and progress; and finally, (5) It enriches man's freedom and justice. Let me now discuss each one.

A. *Cross-cultural understanding:*

"Cultural anthropology enhances inter-ethnic and cross-cultural understanding. The concept of *cultural relativism* which states that cultures have their own dignity and morality and therefore no culture is more superior than another could be the key concept in unlocking the door to smooth and harmonious relations between/among peoples of different cultural background and traditions. Cultural uniqueness and cultural differences should not be mistaken for backwardness or for having a "lower" culture. Moral judgments such as these reflect a lack of understanding and objectivity in viewing other peoples and their cultures." (Zamora: 1972:9).

B. *Sociocultural change:*

"A knowledge of general principles of cultural anthropology can be very useful to understanding guided sociocultural change, especially in societies undergoing rapid changes such as many nations in Asia, Africa, Latin-America and in many tribal and peasant societies. Factors such as values, communication, sociocultural and historic base, social structure, vested interest groups, cost and risk, innovator, appraiser, and innovation among others can guide planners and agents of change in directing the process toward what is considered "for the better." (Zamora: 1972:9).

C. *Liberal education:*

"Cultural anthropology, like the other branches of general anthropology, offers tremendous amount of information and insight on the lifeways, and values of hundreds of cultures and societies, already studied by anthropologists. One clearing house of such studies that have had far-reaching impact on intellectual and educational centers of learning in the U.S., Europe, and in other countries is the Human Relations Area Files (HRAF) of Yale University, conceived and developed by Dr. George Peter Murdock, an eminent U.S. anthropologist from Yale University who later moved to the University of Pittsburgh. Hundreds of books and monographs in cultural anthropology dealing with all sorts of societies and cultures offer limitless insights into the lifeways of many ethnic groups different from us. These data, information etc. can enhance the educational outlook of one who is genuinely interested in broader human concerns that cultural anthropology can give to mankind." (Zamora: 1972:9–10).

D. *Unity and progress:*

"Time was when man lived in isolated caves, almost completely independent from other caves, other ethnic groups.

Cultural anthropological findings about these caves and ethnic groups have been collated and put together to give us a broader national or international framework with which to view the isolated units. This kind of outlook and thought is necessary if we are to promote unity and harmony not only in the relations between small groups but also among nations. It is important for the group and the nation to identify themselves tenaciously to a bigger loyalty—to the nation and the world—in order to foster one world. Division, factional strife, revolutions and wars are not conducive to promoting and enhancing the quality of human life on earth. We cannot go ahead and succeed in socio-economic development, in technological programs, in educational uplift, and in the attainment of political and social stability unless there is unity and peace among us. Otherwise, we channel our productive resources, our funds, and manpower to armaments and defense—a phenomenon now common among some nations, especially the big powers like USA, Russia and others." (Zamora: 1972:10).

E.   *Freedom and justice:*

"One of the fundamental problems that preoccupies the time, efforts, and funds of the United Nations is the decolonization of a number of societies that are still subjects of other nations. A nation's freedom, a nation's striving for justice and equality—these are not yet fully attained in this 20th century although the United Nations is exerting serious efforts to make men and nations free. One good example is the case of *Apartheid* in South Africa where the colored peoples have been subjected to indignities by white peoples. In the United States, the Negroes are gradually obtaining freedom and justice. In many countries, the minority groups have been very articulate about their rights and their hopes for a richer life in larger freedom." (Zamora: 1972:11).

"A comprehensive knowledge about these peoples' values and behavior, their philosophical view of the world, their psychological make-up can help immensely not only in dealing with them but also in helping them attain for themselves a life of dignity, unity, and sovereignty." (Zamora: 1972:11).

IV. The Ethics of Cultural Anthropology

A. *Perspective:* Before raising several pointed ethical questions related to cultural anthropology, it is useful to give a brief summary of the background of the involvement of many anthropologists in problems related to professional ethics, particularly before, during and after the second world war. Anthropologist George M. Foster of the University of California (Berkeley) is my main source for this summation:

"Until little more than a generation ago anthropologists were guided by a simple, unwritten ethical code: "An anthropologist is a gentleman (lady)." We saw ourselves in much the same position as the physician, the lawyer, or the minister: privy to a great deal of confidential information that if carelessly handled, might cause embarrassment and hardship to our informants. We took it for granted that we would no more violate the confidence of our informants than of our friends, and we did our best to make sure that none of our actions, including publication, would adversely affect the people we studied. This simple code worked well; the tribal and peasant peoples then studied by anthropologists were so far removed from the middle and upper classes of their countries that it seemed highly unlikely that harm could come to them because of what an anthropologist might do. Without question, and in the interests of scientific accuracy, we gave the names of, and pertinent facts about, our principal informants, and we went to great effort to be thorough in recording geographical information." (Foster: 1973:256).

In England before the 1930s, a number of anthropologists served the British Empire by carrying on field research in colonial Africa in an effort to understand more clearly the customs and traditions of the natives for effective colonial administration. The anthropologists, who probably meant well, could not see their subtle role and image: they reinforced colonial rule—a view espoused eloquently by educated Africans in British universities, especially in the late 1930s. This discovered educated African image of British anthropologists led many of them to abandon their role in applied anthropology for the vast and far-flung British Empire. (Foster: 1973:256).

According to Foster, the American anthropologist did not encounter the delicate and even dangerous ethical position of their British colleagues in colonial societies. However, there is one U. S. colonial possession that can more or less approximate the British dilemma: the Trust Territories of Micronesia after the second world war. The American anthropologists, however, who took part in colonial affairs believed that the U. S. administration of the territory was humane and that they were free to work and to publish their findings. The anthropologists also felt that their research served the cause of the Micronesians. (Foster: 1973:256–257).

During World War II, the services of many anthropologists were enlisted by the U. S. government in order to defeat allied enemies, notably Germany and Japan. The U. S. anthropologist who served as researchers and consultants to the U. S. Army research units did not have qualms of conscience in doing so in the belief that they were serving their country and the cause of democracy. (Foster: 1973:257).

The Foreign Morale Analysis Division and the Office of War Information had in its rolls such eminent anthropologists as Clyde Kluckhohn, Ruth Benedict, Alexander Leighton, Morris E. Opler and others. (Foster: 1973:257).

With the end of the war, links were established by anthropologists with major governmental branches such as the Defense Department and the U. S. Technical Assistance programs abroad. Anthropologists served as researchers and consultants in defense projects as well as technical assistance programs abroad in fields like agriculture, community development, social research and other fields of endeavor. (Foster: 1973:257).

In the early 1960s, however, the conditions were somewhat altered, due mainly to certain circumstances which brought the problem to sharper focus. Dr. George M. Foster tells the rest of the story:

". . . The Department of Defense, which had long supported social science research in a variety of ways, stepped up its level of support, and anthropologists and other social scientists and their universities as well were drawn into contractual arrangements with government for increasingly dubious purposes. Matters came to a head with Project Camelot, instigated in 1964 by the Army's Special Operations Research Office. Through the mechanism of what was apparently a sham university contract, American social scientists (including an anthropologist) were sent to Chile in early 1965 to enlist the cooperation of Chilean social scientists in survey research to study the general question of identifying criteria for predicting possible revolution, and to find means of dealing with such situations. Chile seems to have been selected, not because of the imminence of revolution, but rather because it seemed a logical scientific site for such a project." (Foster: 1973:258).

"Although Project Camelot was in no sense a secret in Chile, Department of Defense support apparently was concealed. When the U. S. Army's interest in the project was revealed in May, 1965, "Chile was the scene of wild newspaper tales of spying and academic outrage at being recruited for spying missions" (Horowitz 1967:11). The project canceled, American personnel were called home, and the academic community has never been the same since. Insofar as anthropology was involved the import was clear: Research involving at least one American anthropologist was being used as a cover for military purposes." (Foster: 1973:258).

Many U. S. anthropologists were deeply concerned with Project Camelot. They felt that the mistake of one man should not jeopardize the whole anthropological profession. And so, moving swiftly, the American Anthropological Association assigned Dr. Ralph Beals, a distinguished ex-President of the Association, to prepare a draft code of ethics. The work led to what is now known as the "Statement on Problems of Anthropological Research and Ethics," which was endorsed overwhelmingly by the Fellows of the Association in 1967. (Foster: 1973:258).

The statement stresses "the ethical imperative of a full and frank disclosure of all research support, and the right of anthropologists to publish their research findings without government censorship. Except in times of war formally declared by Congress . . . anthropologists should undertake no work not related to their usual teaching, research, and public service functions nor should they engage in clandestine activities." (Foster: 1973:258).

During the Vietnam War, according to Dr. Foster, "Some anthropologists continued to serve as government consultants during this time, including service on panels and committees with Department of Defense and military personnel. The extent to which anthropologists have been involved in Southeast Asian affairs as a consequence of the Vietnam War and whether any have violated the letter or spirit of the Statement on Problems of Anthropological Research and Ethics, is unclear. Charges and countercharges . . . have shaken the American Anthropological Association since 1970, but we do not know all of the facts, and perhaps we never will." (Foster: 1973:259).

With this brief background on ethics and the role of the anthropologist, let me now consider some of the controversial issues and problems in the profession.

B. *Ethical issues:* The principal focus of study, research, and investigation of the cultural anthropologist is the human being wherever he lives, regardless of his creed, race, color, ethnicity or ideology. This human being is studied in his totality—his body, his behavior and his values as they are related to complex factors of ecology, society and personality. This human being is both unique and universal, static and dynamic. He is very sensitive and tolerant, patient and impatient, glorious or ignominious, depending on the issues or problems that confront him at a given time and space as well as other factors or variables that affect his total life.

This human being—the hero as subject of anthropological research—is sensitive on three levels or dimensions of relationships: (1) man to man relations; (2) man to land relations; (3) man to supernatural relations. Each relation will now be considered.

(1) *Man—man relations:* The main issue in man to man relations is actually the issue of why and how an anthropologist as a human being studies another human being or beings without debasing his culture and the integrity of his personality. What right do we as anthropologists have to make other human beings the objects of our continuous study and research? What right do we have to probe into their intimate lives in the name of advancing anthropological knowledge? What right do we have to serve not only as recorders and interpreters of change but also as active agents of change for what we consider to be "a better life"? But what is a "better life"? Does better life mean an advanced technology that has led to the manufacture of nuclear bombs? Does better life mean the establishment of powerful regimes and rotten governments that degrade rather than enhance the dignity of man? Does better life mean prosperity for some but poverty, disease and ignorance for millions?

What right do we have as anthropologists to be utilized by government or other private and public agencies for all sorts of ends and means—including enhancing the effectiveness of colonial powers in Africa and Asia or systematizing data and knowledge for victory in war against an enemy? These are serious questions that the members of the anthropological discipline have been asking within the professional societies such as the American Anthropological Association and in learned journals such as *Current Anthropology* (the world journal of the sciences of man) and the *Journal of Asian Studies*.

(2) *Man—land relations:* The relationship of the anthropologists to the environment he lives in is another crucial question. To what extent should the anthropologist concern himself with the land—where his subjects (the human beings) are born, live, and die? To what extent should he gather data and information in the name of anthropological science and feed such data to some agencies for exploitative ends? To what extent should he be utilized by units or entities for the ultimate destruction or extinction of all the "blessings" of the environment? Should he or should he not participate fully in any serious move to ensure the safety and survival of the environment? These questions lead us to the third type of relations: the man—supernatural relations.

(3) *Man—supernatural relations:* What are the ethical issues related to the anthropologist and the supernatural power or powers? Should anthropologists serve as agents to change the native or indigenous peoples' religion on the ground that they are mere "superstitions"? Should he or should he not respect their god or gods on the ground that they are just different? Should he not maintain an attitude of detachment, of what is known as cultural *relativism* (i. e., each culture has its own dignity) or should he fight and crusade for an ethnocentric feeling that the scientistic western culture and religion are better and therefore should dominate over the traditional religious systems? Should he regard traditional religious systems such as what is labelled "paganism" or "spirit-worship" or "ancestor worship" as deterrents to what he believes to be a modern, industrial, urbanized and even "civilized" religious life? In sum, should the traditional religious idol or God or Gods be destroyed in the name of science, in the name of Mohammed, Christ, Ram or Zoroaster on the ground that these modern religious systems are the correct answers to socio-economic and political developmental plans and programs?

These are moot questions that all human beings are confronted with, especially in the world-wide effort to change the so-called "underdeveloped" or "backward" third world of Asia, Africa and Latin-America by the western world. There are direct or indirect cultural clashes and confrontations between indigenous beliefs, behavior and values with what is supposed to be a scientific, modernistic industrial and urbanized western model. The cultural clashes occur in all realms of human endeavor: In sociology, in ecology, in religion, in economy, in health, in education, in aesthetics, in philosophy, and in virtually all aspects of the totality of human concerns—in short, in culture.

V. Concluding Remarks

I have presented very briefly the scope, significance, and ethics of cultural anthropology in a somewhat broad manner. I have raised controversial issues which will be asked again and again in a world torn between science and superstition, between the seeming clashes of values and traditions among nations in contact.

You can perhaps raise the crucial question: Is anthropology then a moral or immoral science? That question is very difficult to answer; it all depends on one's cultural definition of *morality* as well as other varied factors involved in our own capacity to make judgments of man, nature, and ideas. But from my discussion, one can see the many positive efforts and blessings that cultural anthropologists can bring. On the other hand, there are also serious ethical questions which need to be raised in the process of making anthropological science effective and useful.

I leave you with one great comforting thought from the mind of a mighty Harvard anthropologist, Clyde Kluckhohn; who once said that anthropology is the study of man in his infinite variety. Every human being is *different* and deserves *dignity* and *respect*.

References and Suggested Readings

Foster, George M. 1973. Traditional Societies and Technological Change. New York: Harper and Row Publishers.

Keesing, Felix M. 1959. Cultural Anthropology. New York: Holt, Rinehart & Co.

Kluckhohn, Clyde. 1949. Mirror for Man. New York: McGraw-Hill.

Kroeber, A. L. and Kluckhohn, C. 1952. Culture: A Critical Review of Concepts and Definitions. Harvard University: Peabody

Museum of American Archaeology and Ethnology Papers, Vol. XLVII, No. 1.

Linton, Ralph. 1945. The Science of Man in the World Crisis. New York: Columbia University Press.

Spicer, Edward H. (ed.). 1952. Human Problems in Technological Change: A Casebook. New York: Russell Sage Foundation.

Zamora, Mario D. and Salazar, Zeus A. (eds.). 1969. Anthropology: Range and Relevance (a reader for non-anthropologists), Quezon City: Kayumanggi Publishers. 751 pp.

Zamora, Mario D. et al. (eds.). 1971. Themes in Culture (Essays in honor of Morris E. Opler), Quezon City: Kayumanggi Publishers, 424 pp.

Zamora, Mario D. 1972. Cultural Anthropology: Its Dimensions, Its Limitations, Its Applications. Manila: MCS Enterprises, Inc. 120 pp.

*

II. Human and Other Behaviors

Although anthropologists do have a great diversity of interests there is one unifying theme that runs through the study of anthropology. This central theme is the study of human behavior and, more specifically, those learned, shared and transmitted behaviors that are classified under the rubric of culture. In recent years it has become obvious that learned behavior in itself is not a unique capability of man, but that it is, in varying degrees, exhibited by many non-human animals. The first selection in this section, by Hans Kummer, shows how important learning is to one group of non-human animals—the Japanese macaques. The short newspaper article—"Monkey See, Monkey Do"—that follows suggests that sexual behavior is not a simple "instinct," but rather that it is influenced by learned behavior. The last selection in this section by George Peter Murdock carefully analyzes the concept of culture and discusses its various characteristics.

Adaptation By Tradition *

Japanese Macaques: Feeding Traditions on Koshima Island

THE little island of Koshima is a wooded, precipitous mountain surrounded by sandy beaches and the sea. Until recently only the mountain and its forest had any ecological significance for the group of Japanese macaques (Macaca fuscata) inhabiting the island; they had so far not foraged on the beach and they had never entered the water. In 1952, however, the researchers of the Japan Monkey Center began to feed the troop on the beach of the island and thus triggered an ecological expansion that provided some fascinating insights into the adaptive potential of primates. The following description is based on a detailed report by Kawai.

* "Reprinted from Hans Kummer, Primate Societies (Chicago: Aldine Publishing Company, 1971); copyright © 1971 by Aldine Publishing Company. Reprinted by permission of the author and Aldine."

The artificial feeding consisted of throwing sweet potatoes onto the beach. The group soon got used to leaving the forest and to eating potatoes as free of adhering sand as possible. The beach became not only a new foraging ground, but also the breeding ground of what the Japanese researchers call a "preculture." One year after the feeding was started, a nearly two-year-old female named Imo was observed carrying a sweet potato to the edge of a brook. With one hand she dipped the potato into the water while she brushed off the sand with the other. In the years to follow, the technique slowly spread throughout the group. In addition, the washing was gradually transferred from the brook to the sea. Today potato-washing in salt water is an established tradition which infants learn from their mothers as a natural adjunct of eating potatoes.

The new habit was transmitted from monkey to monkey in two distinct forms. "Individual propagation" first transmitted the habit from the young to the adults of the existing generation. The ease or resistance with which a monkey took to potato-washing in this phase was partly a function of sex and age. The class to learn most readily was that of the juveniles between one and two-and-a-half years, Imo's own age class. Male and female juveniles learned with equal readiness. Five years after Imo started the behavior, nearly 80 per cent of the younger group members in the age class of two to seven years washed their potatoes. The adults above the age of seven were more conservative. Only 18 per cent of them had acquired the new behavior and all of these were females. The remaining adults never adopted the habit.

These results, however, could not be explained by adult and male conservatism alone. A close social relationship with a performer was also essential. Potato-washing was not acquired by observing some distant group member, but only when feeding with an intimate companion. Thus, mothers readily learned from their children and older siblings from younger brothers and sisters. Subadult and young males, on the other hand, had few opportunities to feed side by side with potato-washers; they stay mostly on the periphery of the group, whereas the youngsters and their mothers live in the central part.

By the time a male returns to the center as a leader, he is apparently too old and inflexible to change his ways. But lacking the opportunity to feed with performers is hardly the only cause

of male resistance to the new behavior. One year after Kawai's
report, Menzel published a study on the response of feral (wild)
Japanese monkeys to strange objects placed on one of their trails.
Juveniles responded much more frequently to a yellow plastic
rope, for example, than did adults. Up to the age of three years,
males reacted as often as females, but among adults, the females
responded in 48 per cent of the cases, adult males only in 19 per
cent. A typical "nonresponse" of adult males was an almost
imperceptible angling off from the line of travel and a mere
glance sideways toward the rope. Obviously, detectable responses to the yellow rope and readiness to adopt the new habit of potato-washing are similarly distributed among the sex and age classes, although the first is an individual action that does not require
a close social affiliation with a model. Some as yet unknown factor in the behavioral setup of the adult male seems to suppress responses to novel stimuli regardless of their social context. Among
Japanese macaques, at least, the adult male shows little disposi-
tion to be an active promoter of new behavioral adaptations.
The apparent acceptance of such a role by the human male may
be a result of the neoteny of our species, that is, of the tendency
to preserve juvenile traits of behavior into adulthood.

At Koshima, potato-washing mothers passed the behavior to
all their infants born after they had themseves acquired the
habit and thus initiated the second phase, which Kawai calls the
"precultural propagation." At this stage, expansion reversed its
direction and began to pass from the old to the young. In addition, the behavior was now acquired in a new way. Whereas
juveniles and adults had so far picked up the complete washing
behavior at once, the infants now learned bit by bit. Earlier
generations had never entered the water, but the new babies were
now taken into water clinging to their mothers' bellies. By the
time they began to eat solid food, they were fully habituated to
the medium that their ancestors had avoided. At the age of six
months, they began to pick up from the water, pieces of potato
which their mothers had dropped. The complete washing behavior developed by one to two-and-a-half years, also the age
that had proved most accessible to the new behavior at the stage
of individual propagation.

The second way of acquiring the behavior had an interesting
secondary effect: All potatoes that the new infants ate were
seasoned with salt water, and the taste of salt apparently became

associated with potatoes. Many of the new generation now not only washed their potatoes, but also seasoned them by dipping them into the sea between bites.

The Koshima group had still more in store. When the scientists began to scatter wheat on the beach, the female Imo, now four years old, invented another trick. Instead of picking the grains singly out of the sand, she carried handfuls of mixed sand and wheat to the shore, threw the whole mess into the water, and waited for the sand to sink and the wheat to float; then she collected the wheat and ate it. Again, the habit spread among juveniles and their mothers, and again the adult males would have nothing to do with it. There was, however, one interesting difference: Potato-washing had been most readily acquired by one to two-and-a-half-year-old monkeys. In contrast, most of the monkeys who acquired the wheat trick were of the age class between two and four years. Note that Imo herself was one-and-a-half years when she invented potato-washing and four years when she introduced wheat-washing.

Perhaps, then, new behaviors are most readily copied from peers. There is, however, another possible explanation that must remain speculative but that raises significant implications. The main component of potato-washing is brushing the tuber with one hand or, in another form, rolling it between the hand and the ground. These are the same movements baboons use when removing dirt or bristles from a fruit. Apparently these behavior patterns develop easily from the behavioral potential of ground-living primates, or, in other terms, these species are genetically predisposed for brushing and rolling movements. In this case, potato-washing is new only insofar as the cleaning movements are performed in water. Wheat-washing, instead, contains an element that is definitely not an easily realized part of the primate's behavioral potential; food already collected must be first thrown away before it is eaten. This would come more easily if primates were used to hoarding food and thus to abandoning it temporarily, or to sharing it, or at least to carrying it away before eating it. Wheat-washing behavior may thus depend on a higher degree of behavioral maturity and therefore be acquired later in life than potato-washing.

Whether or not these explanations are correct for the particular case is not my concern here; what I wish to exemplify is the type of the explanation: that the possibility of a behavioral innovation depends in part on the genetically determined range of potential modifications, and that different behavioral modifications are related to different stages of individual maturation in which they are realized most easily. Kawai himself rightly refrains from attempting an explanation.

We have seen that newly acquired behavior is most readily transmitted among animals with a close social affinity. The pathways of habit propagation follow, as it were, a preestablished network of affinities within the group and reveal a structure of subgroups with frequent positive interaction. In the Koshima group, habit propagation was greatly influenced by kinship. Entire "lineages" consisting of a mother and her descendants tended to acquire or reject a new behavior as a unit. Between 1951 and 1960, for example, the sons and daughters of the female Eba acquired an average of 3.6 of the various new behaviors invented by the group in this period whereas Nami and her descendants acquired only 1.6 new habits per individual. The children tend to be as receptive as their mother, but it is as yet unknown how much of their similarity stems from their common genes and how much is due to their learning from the same mother.

Among the most interesting aspects of the Koshima events are the secondary effects of the new traditions. The changes in feeding behavior reverberated into superficially remote parts of the socioecological system. The habit of washing primarily facilitated the rapid ingestion of food, but beyond this it opened the way to a hitherto irrelevant part of the habitat, the sea. The youngsters of the new generations took up bathing as part of their playful and exploratory activities. Splashing became a preferred pastime in hot weather. The juveniles learned to swim; some of them began to dive and brought up seaweed from the bottom; at least one of them left Koshima and swam to a neighboring island. The sea thus became a potential food source, and it was no longer an absolute barrier to would-be migrators or to socially hard-pressed refugees from the island group. One habit had prepared the way for expansive changes in the group's ecology and social structure. The stable system has now entered a phase of changes which perhaps will trigger still more changes, until the possibilities of the habitat and their behavioral limitations interlock in a new stability. New selective pressures could begin to affect the gene pool and induce further changes, such as extensive foraging in the sea.

The Koshima macaques may be so limited in their behavioral potential that a new stability will soon be reached. But it can be imagined that a primate species of quite another kind might never reach stability again: Changes in its habitat-oriented behavior might breed even more changes that would finally increase exponentially into a runaway development. This, it seems, is happening to our own species.

Monkey see, monkey do*

X films 'turn on' chimps

CHESSINGTON, England (UPI)—The Chessington zoo has come up with a new way of increasing its chimpanzee population—show some mildly blue chimp sex films.

And if that doesn't work, a spokesman said, the zoo may show the chimps some of the hard core stuff.

Zoo officials said Monday that they showed chimpanzees at the zoo a British Broadcasting Corp (BBC) television documentary showing other chimps kissing and cuddling.

Most of the Chessington chimps loved it and copied every move, a zoo spokesman said. Especially an 8-year-old female named Cressida who the spokesman said was "turned on."

"We hope to hear the patter of tiny chimpanzee feet here soon, and all thanks to the film," said spokesman Andy Bowen.

"We tried it in three cages in the ape house," he said. "The orangutans were only interested in the projector. The gorillas became aggressive but Cressida was just overcome with passion."

Cressida particularly swooned over the chimp male star of the film.

"He's the equivalent of Rudolph Valentino for her," Bowen said. "There was a male chimp in the cage with Cressida, but so far he has not reacted.

"We are planning some replays of the film in the next two weeks, Bowen said. "Then we hope to show more explicit sex films to them."

[A8667]

* Ventura County (Calif.) Star-Free Press.

May 29, 1973. Permission to Reprint from—United Press International.

The Cross-Cultural Survey † *

T HE plan rests, at bottom, on the conviction that all human cultures, despite their diversity, have fundamentally a great deal in common, and that these common aspects are susceptible to scientific analysis. Its theoretical orientation may be expressed in a series of seven basic assumptions. These are not claimed to be original, since many of them are shared by all social scientists, and all of them by many.

1. *Culture Is Learned.* Culture is not instinctive, or innate, or transmitted biologically, but is composed of habits, i. e., learned tendencies to react, acquired by each individual through his own life experience after birth. This assumption, of course, is shared by all anthropologists outside of the totalitarian states, but it has a corollary which is not always so clearly recognized. If culture is learned, it must obey the laws of learning, which the psychologists have by now worked out in considerable detail. The principles of learning are known to be essentially the same, not only for all mankind but also for most mammalian species. Hence, we should expect all cultures, being learned, to reveal certain uniformities reflecting this universal common factor.

2. *Culture Is Inculcated.* All animals are capable of learning, but man alone seems able, in any considerable measure, to pass on his acquired habits to his offspring. We can housebreak a dog, teach him tricks, and implant in him other germs of culture, but he will not transmit them to his puppies. They will receive only the biological inheritance of their species, to which they in turn will add habits on the basis of their own experience. The factor of language presumably accounts for man's preëminence in this respect. At any rate, many of the habits learned by human beings are transmitted from parent to child over successive generations, and, through repeated inculcation, acquire that persistency over time, that relative independence of individual bearers, which justifies classifying them collectively as "culture." This assumption, too, is generally accepted by anthropologists, but again there is an underestimated corollary. If culture is inculcated, then all cultures should show certain common effects

† By George Peter Murdock, Yale University.

* Reprinted by permission of The American Sociological Association and the author.

of the inculcation process. Inculcation involves not only the imparting of techniques and knowledge but also the disciplining of the child's animal impulses to adjust him to social life. That there are regularities in behavior reflecting the ways in which these impulses are thwarted and redirected during the formative years of life, seems clear from the evidence of psychoanalysis, e. g., the apparent universality of intrafamily incest taboos.

3. *Culture Is Social.* Habits of the cultural order are not only inculcated and thus transmitted over time; they are also social, that is, shared by human beings living in organized aggregates or societies and kept relatively uniform by social pressure. They are, in short, group habits. The habits which the members of a social group share with one another constitute the culture of that group. This assumption is accepted by most anthropologists, but not by all. Lowie, for example, insists that "a culture is invariably an artificial unit segregated for purposes of expediency. . . There is only one natural unit for the ethnologist—the culture of all humanity at all periods and in all places . . . ." The author finds it quite impossible to accept this statement. To him, the collective or shared habits of a social group—no matter whether it be a family, a village, a class, or a tribe—constitute, not "an artificial unit" but a natural unit—a culture or subculture. To deny this is, in his opinion, to repudiate the most substantial contribution which sociology has made to anthropology. If culture is social, then the fate of a culture depends on the fate of the society which bears it, and all cultures which have survived to be studied should reveal certain similarities because they have all had to provide for societal survival. Among these cultural universals, we can probably list such things as sentiments of group cohesion, mechanisms of social control, organization for defense against hostile neighbors, and provision for the perpetuation of the population.

4. *Culture Is Ideational.* To a considerable extent, the group habits of which culture consists are conceptualized (or verbalized) as ideal norms or patterns of behavior. There are, of course, exceptions; grammatical rules, for example, though they represent collective linguistic habits and are thus cultural, are only in small part consciously formulated. Nevertheless, as every field ethnographer knows, most people show in marked degree an awareness of their own cultural norms, an ability to differentiate them from purely individual habits, and a facility in con-

ceptualizing and reporting them in detail, including the circumstances where each is considered appropriate and the sanctions to be expected for nonconformity. Within limits, therefore, it is useful to conceive of culture as ideational, and of an element of culture as a traditionally accepted idea,[5] held by the members of a group or subgroup, that a particular kind of behavior (overt, verbal, or implicit) should conform to an established precedent. These ideal norms should not be confused with actual behavior. In any particular instance, an individual behaves in response to the state of his organism (his drives) at the moment, and to his perception of the total situation in which he finds himself. In so doing, he naturally tends to follow his established habits, including his culture, but either his impulses or the nature of the circumstances may lead him to deviate therefrom to a greater or lesser degree. Behavior, therefore, does not automatically follow culture, which is only one of its determinants. There are norms of behavior, of course, as well as of culture, but, unlike the latter, they can be established only by statistical means. Confusion often arises between anthropologists and sociologists on this point. The former, until recently, have been primarily preoccupied with ideal norms or patterns, whereas sociologists, belonging to the same society as both their subjects and their audience, assume general familiarity with the culture and commonly report only the statistical norms of actual behavior. A typical community study like *Middletown* and an ethnographic monograph, though often compared, are thus in reality poles apart. To the extent that culture is ideational, we may conclude, all cultures should reveal certain similarities, flowing from the universal laws governing the symbolic mental processes, e. g., the worldwide parallels in the principles of magic.

5. *Culture Is Gratifying.* Culture always, and necessarily, satisfies basic biological needs and secondary needs derived there-

[5] From the point of view of behavioristic psychology, of course, an idea is merely a habit of a special sort, a tendency to react with implicit linguistic or symbolic behavior rather than with overt muscular responses. The underlying mechanisms, e. g., of learning, are similar if not identical. Fundamentally, therefore, our fourth assumption should be subsumed under our first—that culture is learned—as a special case thereof. In view of the importance of symbolic, especially linguistic, behavior in man, however, it has seemed advisable to segregate the ideational point for separate exposition.

from. Its elements are tested habitual techniques for gratifying human impulses in man's interaction with the external world of nature and fellow man.[6] This assumption is an inescapable conclusion from modern stimulus-response psychology. Culture consists of habits, and psychology has demonstrated that habits persist only so long as they bring satisfaction. Gratification reinforces habits, strengthens and perpetuates them, while lack of gratification inevitably results in their extinction or disappearance. Elements of culture, therefore, can continue to exist only when they yield to the individuals of a society a margin of satisfaction, a favorable balance of pleasure over pain.[7] Malinowski has been insisting on this point for years, but the majority of anthropologists have either rejected the assumption or have paid it but inadequate lip service. To them, the fact that culture persists has seemed to raise no problem; it has been blithely taken for granted. Phychologists, however, have seen the problem, and have given it a definitive answer, which anthropologists can ignore at their peril. If culture is gratifying, widespread similarities should exist in all cultures, owing to the fact that basic human impulses, which are universally the same, demand similar forms of satisfaction. The "universal culture pattern" propounded by Wissler [8] would seem to rest on this foundation.

6. *Culture Is Adaptive.* Culture changes; and the process of change appears to be an adaptive one, comparable to evolution in the organic realm but of a different order.[9] Cultures tend, through periods of time, to become adjusted to the geographic environment, as the anthropogeographers have shown, although environmental influences are no longer conceived as determinative of cultural development. Cultures also adapt, through borrowing and organization, to the social environment of neighbor-

---

[6] The only exceptions are partial and temporary ones, with respect to elements of culture in the process of dying out or being supplanted.

[7] Culture is gratifying, of course, not in an absolute but in a relative sense. To a slave, for example, the submission and drudgery demanded by his status are not actually pleasant; relative, however, to the painful alternative of punishment or death for rebellious behavior, observance of the cultural requirements of his status is gratifying or "reinforcing." Agricultural labor, again, may not be enjoyable in itself, but it is gratifying because it brings rewards, e. g., in food.

[8] C. Wissler, Man and Culture, 73–79, New York, 1923.

[9] See A. G. Keller, Societal Evolution, New York, 1915.

ing peoples. Finally, cultures unquestionably tend to become adjusted to the biological and psychological demands of the human organism. As life conditions change, traditional forms cease to provide a margin of satisfaction and are eliminated; new needs arise or are perceived, and new cultural adjustments are made to them. The assumption that culture is adaptive by no means commits one to an idea of progress, or to a theory of evolutionary stages of development, or to a rigid determinism of any sort. On the contrary, one can agree with Opler,[10] who has pointed out on the basis of his Apache material, that different cultural forms may represent adjustments to like problems, and similar cultural forms to different problems. It is probable, nevertheless, that a certain proportion of the parallels in different cultures represent independent adjustments to comparable conditions.

The conception of cultural change as an adaptive process seems to many anthropologists inconsistent with, and contradictory to, the conception of cultural change as an historical process. To the author, there seems nothing inconsistent or antagonistic in the two positions—the "functional" and the "historical," as they are commonly labeled. On the contrary, he believes that both are correct, that they supplement one another, and that the best anthropological work emerges when the two are used in conjunction. Culture history is a succession of unique events, in which later events are conditioned by earlier ones. From the point of view of culture, the events which affect later ones in the same historical sequence are often, if not usually, accidental, since they have their origin outside the continuum of culture. They include natural events, like floods and droughts; biological events, like epidemics and deaths; and psychological events, like emotional outbursts and inventive intuitions. Such changes alter a society's life conditions. They create new needs and render old cultural forms unsatisfactory, stimulating trial and error behavior and cultural innovations. Perhaps the most significant events, however, are historical contacts with peoples of differing cultures, for men tend first to ransack the cultural resources of their neighbors for solutions to their problems of living, and rely only secondarily upon their own inventive ingenuity. Full recognition of the historical character of culture, and especially of the role

[10] M. E. Opler, "Apache Data Concerning the Relation of Kinship Terminology to Social Classification," Amer. Anthropol., n.s. XXXIX (1937), 207–208.

of diffusion, is thus a prime prerequisite if a search for cross-cultural generalizations is to have any prospect of success. It is necessary to insist, however, that historical events, like geographic factors, exert only a conditioning rather than a determining influence on the course of culture. Man adjusts to them, and draws selectively upon them to solve his problems and satisfy his needs.

7. *Culture Is Integrative.* As one product of the adaptive process, the elements of a given culture tend to form a consistent and integrated whole. We use the word "tend" advisedly, for we do not accept the position of certain extreme functionalists that cultures actually are integrated systems, with their several parts in perfect equilibrium. We adhere, rather, to the position of Sumner [11] that the folkways are "subject to a strain of consistency with each other," but that actual integration is never achieved for the obvious reason that historical events are constantly exerting a disturbing influence. Integration takes time—there is always what Ogburn [12] has called a "cultural lag"—and long before one process has been completed, many others have been initiated. In our own culture, for example, the changes wrought in habits of work, recreation, sex, and religion through the introduction of the automobile are probably still incomplete. If culture is integrative, then correspondences or correlations between similar traits should repeatedly occur in unrelated cultures. Lowie,[13] for example, has pointed out a number of such correlations.

If the seven fundamental assumptions outlined above, or even any considerable proportion of them, are valid, then it must necessarily follow that human cultures in general, despite their historical diversity, will exhibit certain regularities or recurrences which are susceptible to scientific analysis, and which, under such analysis, should yield a body of scientific generalizations. A primary objective of the Cross-Cultural Survey is to formulate and test generalizations of this sort.

[11] W. G. Sumner, Folkways, 5–6, Boston, 1906.

[12] W. F. Ogburn, Social Change, 200, New York, 1922.

[13] R. H. Lowie, Primitive Society, New York, 1920.

III. Communicating with each Other

Many of the ways in which we learn and transmit culture depend on the use of language. The first article in this section by Edward T. Hall and William Foote Whyte recognizes this fact but suggests that there are other, less obvious ways, in which humans communicate with each other. The next article by Leo Rosten about the torments of translation suggests some of the problems encountered when we try to shift from one language to another. In the final article in this section, Bertha Desiderio shows that language has other functions in addition to the obvious one of communication. She not only illustrates the richness of the Navajo language but shows that the pride she has in the Navajo language is part of the pride she has in being a Navajo.

Intercultural Communication: A Guide to Men of Action [†] [*]

How can anthropological knowledge help the man of action in dealing with people of another culture? We shall seek to answer that question by examining the process of intercultural communication.

Anthropologists have long claimed that a knowledge of culture is valuable to the administrator. More and more people in business and government are willing to take this claim seriously, but they ask that we put culture to them in terms they can understand and act upon.

[†] Dr. Edward T. Hall is with the Governmental Affairs Institute in Washington, D. C.

Dr. William Foote Whyte is in the New York State School of Industrial and Labor Relations, Cornell University, Ithaca, N. Y.

[*] "Reproduced by permission of Society for Applied Anthropology from Human Organization" Vol. 19, # 1 1960 and of Edward T. Hall.

When the layman thinks of culture, he is likely to think in terms of 1) the way people dress, 2) the beliefs they hold, and 3) the customs they practice—with an accent upon the esoteric. Without undertaking any comprehensive definition, we can concede that all three are aspects of culture, and yet point out that they do not get us very far, either theoretically or practically.

Dress is misleading, if we assume that differences in dress indicate differences in belief and behavior. If that were the case, then we should expect to find people dressed like ourselves to be thinking and acting like ourselves. While there are still peoples wearing "colorful" apparel quite different from ours, we find in many industrializing societies that the people with whom we deal dress much as we do—and yet think and act quite differently.

Knowledge of beliefs may leave us up in the air because the connections between beliefs and behavior are seldom obvious. In the case of religious beliefs, we may know, for example, that the Mohammedan must pray to Allah a certain number of times a day and that therefore the working day must provide for praying time. This is important, to be sure, but the point is so obvious that it is unlikely to be overlooked by anyone. The administrator must also grasp the less dramatic aspects of everyday behavior, and here a knowledge of beliefs is a very imperfect guide.

Customs provide more guidance, providing we do not limit ourselves to the esoteric and also search for the pattern of behavior into which a given custom fits. The anthropologist, in dealing with customary behavior, is not content with identifying individual items. To him, these items are not miscellaneous. They have meaning only as they are fitted together into a pattern.

But even assuming that the pattern can be communicated to the administrator, there is still something important lacking. The pattern shows how the people act—when among themselves. The administrator is not directly concerned with that situation. Whatever background information he has, he needs to interpret to himself how the people act *in relation to himself*. He is dealing with a cross-cultural situation. The link between the two cultures is provided by acts of communication between the administrator, representing one culture, and people representing another. If communication is effective, then understanding grows with collaborative action. If communication is faulty, then no book knowledge of culture can assure effective action.

This is not to devalue the knowledge of culture that can be provided by the anthropologist. It is only to suggest that the point of implementation of the knowledge must be in the communication process. Let us therefore examine the process of intercultural communication. By so doing we can accomplish two things: A) Broaden knowledge of ourselves by revealing some of our own unconscious communicative acts. B) Clear away heretofore almost insurmountable obstacles to understanding in the cross-cultural process. We also learn that communication, as it is used here, goes far beyond words and includes many other acts upon which judgments are based of what is transpiring and from which we draw conclusions as to what has occurred in the past.

Culture affects communication in various ways. It determines the time and timing of interpersonal events, the places where it is appropriate to discuss particular topics, the physical distance separating one speaker from another, the tone of voice that is appropriate to the subject matter. Culture, in this sense, delineates the amount and type of physical contact, if any, which convention permits or demands, and the intensity of emotion which goes with it. Culture includes the relationship of *what is said to what is meant*—as when "no" means "maybe" and "tomorrow" means "never." Culture, too, determines whether a given matter—say, a business contract—should be initially discussed between two persons or hacked out in a day-long conference which includes four or five senior officials from each side, with perhaps an assist from the little man who brings in the coffee.

These are important matters which the businessman who hopes to trade abroad ignores at his peril. They are also elusive, for every man takes his own culture for granted. Even a well-informed national of another country is hard put to explain why, in his own land, the custom is thus-and-so rather than so-and-thus; as hard put, indeed, as you would probably be if asked what is the "rule" which governs the precise time in a relationship that you begin using another man's first name. One "just knows." In other words, you do not know and cannot explain satisfactorily because you learn this sort of thing unconsciously in your upbringing, in your culture, and you take such knowledge for granted. Yet the impact of culture on communication can be observed and the lessons taught.

Since the most obvious form of communication is by language, we will first consider words, meanings, voice tones, emotions, and physical contact; then take up, in turn, the cultural impact of time, place, and social class relations on business situations in various lands. Finally, we will suggest what the individual administrator may do to increase his effectiveness abroad, and what students of culture may do to advance this application of anthropology.

Beyond Language

Americans are often accused of not being very good at language, or at least not very much interested in learning foreign languages. There is little evidence that any people are inherently "better" at languages than any other, given the opportunity and incentive to learn. The West and Central European who has since childhood been in daily contact with two or three languages learns to speak them all, and frequently to read and write them as well. Under similar conditions, American children do the same. Indeed, a not uncommon sight on the backroads of Western Europe is a mute, red-faced American military family lost on a Sunday drive while the youngest child, barely able to lisp his own English, leans from the window to interpret the directions of some gnarled farmer whose dialect is largely unintelligible to most of his own countrymen.

We should not underestimate the damage our lack of language facility as a nation has done to our relations all over the world. Obviously, if you cannot speak a man's language, you are terribly handicapped in communicating with him.

But languages can be learned and yet most, if not all, of the disabling errors described in this article could still be made. Vocabulary, grammar, even verbal facility are not enough. Unless a man understands the subtle cues that are implicit in language, tone, gestures and expression, he will not only consistently misinterpret what is said to him, but he may offend irretrievably without knowing how or why.

Do They Mean What They Say?

Can't you believe what a man says? We all recognize that the basic honesty of the speaker is involved. What we often fail to recognize, however, is that the question involves cultural influences that have nothing to do with the honesty or dependability of the individual.

In the United States we put a premium on direct expression. The "good" American is supposed to say what he means and to mean what he says. If, on important matters, we discover that someone spoke deviously or evasively, we would be inclined to regard him thereafter as unreliable if not out-and-out dishonest.

In some other cultures, the words and their meanings do not have such a direct connection. People may be more concerned with the emotional context of the situation than with the meaning of particular words. This leads them to give an agreeable and pleasant answer to a question when a literal, factual answer might be unpleasant or embarrassing.

This situation is not unknown in our culture, of course. How many times have you muttered your delighted appreciation for a boring evening? We term this simple politeness and understand each other perfectly.

On the other hand, analogous "polite" behavior on a matter of factory production would be incomprehensible. An American businessman would be most unlikely to question another businessman's word if he were technically qualified and said that his plant could produce 1000 gross of widgets a month. We are "taught" that it is none of our business to inquire too deeply into the details of his production system. This would be prying and might be considered an attempt to steal his operational plans.

Yet this cultural pattern has trapped many an American into believing that when a Japanese manufacturer answered a direct question with the reply that he could produce 1000 gross of widgets, he meant what he said. If the American had been escorted through the factory and saw quite clearly that its capacity was, at the most, perhaps 500 gross of widgets per month, he would be likely to say to himself:

Well, this fellow probably has a brother-in-law who has a factory who can make up the difference. He isn't telling the whole story because he's afraid I might try to make a better deal with the brother-in-law. Besides, what business is it of mine, so long as he meets the schedule?

The cables begin to burn after the American returns home and only 500 gross of widgets arrive each month.

What the American did not know was that in Japanese culture one avoids the direct question unless the questioner is absolutely certain that the answer will not embarrass the Japanese business-man in any way whatsoever. In Japan for one to admit being unable to perform a given operation or measure up to a given standard means a bitter loss of face. Given a foreigner who is so stupid, ignorant, or insensitive as to ask an embarrassing question, the Japanese is likely to choose what appears to him the lesser of two evils.

Americans caught in this cross-cultural communications trap are apt to feel doubly deceived because the Japanese manufac-turer may well be an established and respected member of the business community.

Excitable People?

Man communicates not by words alone. His tone of voice, his facial expressions, his gestures all contribute to the infinitely varied calculus of meaning. But the confusion of tongues is more than matched by the confusion of gesture and other culture cues. One man's nod is another man's negative. Each culture has its own rich array of meaningful signs, symbols, gestures, emotional connotations, historical references, traditional re-sponses and—equally significant—pointed silences. These have been built up over the millennia as (who can say?) snarls, growls, and love murmurs gathered meaning and dignity with long use, to end up perhaps as the worn coinage of trite expression.

Consider the Anglo-Saxon tradition of preserving one's calm. The American is taught by his culture to suppress his feelings. He is conditioned to regard emotion as generally bad (except in weak women who can't help themselves) and a stern self-control as good. The more important a matter, the more solemn and outwardly dispassionate he is likely to be. A cool head, granite visage, dispassionate logic—it is no accident that the Western story hero consistently displays these characteristics.

In the Middle East it is otherwise. From childhood, the Arab is permitted, even encouraged, to express his feelings without inhibition. Grown men can weep, shout, gesture expressively and violently, jump up and down—and be admired as sincere.

The modulated, controlled Anglo-Saxon is likely to be regarded with suspicion—he must be hiding something, practicing to deceive.

The exuberant and emotional Arab is likely to disturb the Anglo-Saxon, cause him to writhe inwardly with embarrassment —for isn't this childish behavior? And aren't things getting rather out of hand?

Then, again, there is the matter of how loudly one should talk.

In the Arab world, in discussions among equals, the men attain a decibel level that would be considered aggressive, objectionable, and obnoxious in the United States. Loudness connotes strength and sincerity among Arabs; a soft tone implies weakness, deviousness. This is so "right" in the Arab culture that several Arabs have told us they discounted anything heard over the "Voice of America" because the signal was so weak!

Personal status modulates voice tone, however, even in Arab society. The Saudi Arab shows respect to his superior—to a sheik, say—by lowering his voice and mumbling. The affluent American may also be addressed in this fashion, making almost impossible an already difficult situation. Since in the American culture one unconsciously "asks" another to raise his voice by raising one's own, the American speaks louder. This lowers the Arab's tone more and increases the mumble. This triggers a shouting response in the American—which cues the Arab into a frightened "I'm not being respectful enough" tone well below audibility.

They are not likely to part with much respect for each other.

To Touch or Not to Touch?

How much physical contact should appropriately accompany social or business conversation?

In the United States we discourage physical contact, particularly between adult males. The most common physical contact is the handshake and, compared to Europeans, we use it sparingly.

· The handshake is the most detached and impersonal form of greeting or farewell in Latin America. Somewhat more friendly is the left hand placed on another man's shoulder during a handshake. Definitely more intimate and warm is the *"doble abrazo"* in which two men embrace by placing their arms around each other's shoulders.

These are not difficult conventions to live with, particularly since the North American can easily permit the Latin American to take the initiative in any form of contact more intimate than the handshake. Far more difficult for the North American to learn to live with comfortably are the less stylized forms of physical contact such as the hand on one's arm during conversation. To the North American this is edging toward what in his culture is an uncomfortable something—possibly sexual—which inhibits his own communication.

Yet there are cultures which restrict physical contact far more than we do. An American at a cocktail party in Java tripped over the invisible cultural ropes which mark the boundaries of acceptable behavior. He was seeking to develop a business relationship with a prominent Javanese and seemed to be doing very well. Yet, when the cocktail party ended, so apparently did a promising beginning. For the North American spent nearly six months trying to arrange a second meeting. He finally learned, through pitying intermediaries, that at the cocktail party he had momentarily placed his arm on the shoulder of the Javanese— and in the presence of other people. Humiliating! Almost unpardonable in traditional Javanese etiquette.

In this particular case, the unwitting breach was mended by a graceful apology. It is worth noting, however, that a truly cordial business relationship never did develop.

The Five Dimensions of Time

If we peel away a few layers of cultural clothing, we begin to reach almost totally unconscious reactions. Our ideas of time, for example, are deeply instilled in us when we are children. If they are contradicted by another's behavior, we react with anger, not knowing exactly why. For the businessman, five important temporal concepts are: appointment time, discussion time, acquaintance time, visiting time, and time schedules.

Anyone who has travelled abroad or dealt at all extensively with non-Americans learns that punctuality is variously interpreted. It is one thing to recognize this with the mind; to adjust to a different kind of *appointment time* is quite another.

In Latin America, you should expect to spend hours waiting in outer offices. If you bring your American interpretation of what constitutes punctuality to a Latin-American office, you will fray your temper and elevate your blood pressure. For a forty-five-minute wait is not unusual—no more unusual than a five-minute wait would be in the United States. No insult is intended, no arbitrary pecking order is being established. If, in the United States, you would not be outraged by a five-minute wait, you should not be outraged by the Latin-American's forty-five-minute delay in seeing you. The time pie is differently cut, that's all.

Further, the Latin American doesn't usually schedule individual appointments to the exclusion of other appointments. The informal clock of his upbringing ticks more slowly and he rather enjoys seeing several people on different matters at the same time. The three-ring circus atmosphere which results, if interpreted in the American's scale of time and propriety, seems to signal him to go away, to tell him that he is not being properly treated, to indicate that his dignity is under attack. Not so. The clock on the wall may look the same but it tells a different sort of time.

The cultural error may be compounded by a further miscalculation. In the United States, a consistently tardy man is likely to be considered undependable, and by our cultural clock this is a reasonable conclusion. For you to judge a Latin American by your scale of time values is to risk a major error.

Suppose you have waited forty-five minutes and there is a man in his office, by some miracle alone in the room with you. Do you now get down to business and stop "wasting time"?

If you are not forewarned by experience or a friendly advisor, you may try to do this. And it would usually be a mistake. For, in the American culture, *discussion* is a means to an end: the deal. You try to make your point quickly, efficiently, neatly. If your purpose is to arrange some major affairs, your instinct is probably to settle the major issues first, leave the details for later, possibly for the technical people to work out.

For the Latin American, the discussion is a part of the spice of life. Just as he tends not to be overly concerned about reserving you your specific segment of time, he tends not as rigidly to separate business from non-business. He runs it all together and wants to make something of a social event out of what you, in your culture, regard as strictly business.

The Latin American is not alone in this. The Greek business-man, partly for the same and partly for different reasons, does not lean toward the "hit-and-run" school of business behavior, either. The Greek businessman adds to the social element, how-ever, a feeling about what length of discussion time constitutes good faith. In America, we show good faith by ignoring the de-tails. "Let's agree on the main points. The details will take care of themselves."

Not so the Greek. He signifies good will and good faith by what may seem to you an interminable discussion which includes every conceivable detail. Otherwise, you see, he cannot help but feel that the other man might be trying to pull the wool over his eyes. Our habit, in what we feel to be our relaxed and friend-ly way, of postponing details until later smacks the Greek between the eyes as a maneuver to flank him. Even if you can somehow convince him that this is not the case, the meeting must still go on a certain indefinite—but, by our standards, long—time or he will feel disquieted.

The American desire to get down to business and on with other things works to our disadvantage in other parts of the world, too; and not only in business. The head of a large, successful Japanese firm commented: "You Americans have a terrible weakness. We Japanese know about it and exploit it every chance we get. You are impatient. We have learned that if we just make you wait long enough, you'll agree to anything."

Whether this is literally true or not, the Japanese executive singled out a trait of American culture which most of us share and which, one may assume from the newspapers, the Russians have not overlooked, either.

By *acquaintance time* we mean how long you must know a man before you are willing to do business with him.

In the United States, if we know that a salesman represents a well-known, reputable company, and if we need his product, he may walk away from the first meeting with an order in his pocket. A few minutes conversation to decide matters of price, delivery, payment, model of product—nothing more is involved. In Central America, local custom does not permit a salesman to land in town, call on the customer and walk away with an order, no matter how badly your prospect wants and needs your product. It is traditional there that you must see your man at least three times before you can discuss the nature of your business.

Does this mean that the South American businessman does not recognize the merits of one product over another? Of course it doesn't. It is just that the weight of tradition presses him to do business within a circle of friends. If a product he needs is not available within his circle, he does not go outside it so much as he enlarges the circle itself to include a new friend who can supply the want. Apart from his cultural need to "feel right" about a new relationship, there is the logic of his business system. One of the realities of his life is that it is dangerous to enter into business with someone over whom you have no more than formal, legal "control." In the past decades, his legal system has not always been as firm as ours and he has learned through experience that he needs the sanctions implicit in the informal system of friendship.

Visiting time involves the question of who sets the time for a visit. George Coelho, a social psychologist from India, gives an illustrative case. A U. S. businessman received this invitation from an Indian businessman: "Won't you and your family come and see us? Come anytime." Several weeks later, the Indian repeated the invitation in the same words. Each time the American replied that he would certainly like to drop in—but he never did. The reason is obvious in terms of our culture. Here "come any time" is just an expression of friendliness. You are not really expected to show up unless your host proposes a specific time. In India, on the contrary, the words are meant literally— that the host is putting himself at the disposal of his guest and really expects him to come. It is the essence of politeness to leave it to the guest to set a time at his convenience. If the guest never comes, the Indian naturally assumes that he does not want to come. Such a misunderstanding can lead to a serious rift between men who are trying to do business with each other.

Time schedules present Americans with another problem in many parts of the world. Without schedules, deadlines, priorities, and timetables, we tend to feel that our country could not run at all. Not only are they essential to getting work done, but they also play an important role in the informal communication process. Deadlines indicate priorities and priorities signal the relative importance of people and the processes they control.

These are all so much a part of our lives that a day hardly passes without some reference to them. "I have to be there by 6:30." "If I don't have these plans out by 5:00 they'll be useless." "I told J. B. I'd be finished by noon tomorrow and now he tells me to drop everything and get hot on the McDermott account. What do I do now?"

In our system, there are severe penalties for not completing work on time and important rewards for holding to schedules. One's integrity and reputation are at stake.

You can imagine the fundamental conflicts that arise when we attempt to do business with people who are just as strongly oriented away from time schedules as we are toward them.

The Middle Eastern peoples are a case in point. Not only is our idea of time schedules no part of Arab life but the mere mention of a deadline to an Arab is like waving a red flag in front of a bull. In his culture, your emphasis on a deadline has the emotional effect on him that his backing you into a corner and threatening you with a club would have on you.

One effect of this conflict of unconscious habit patterns is that hundreds of American-owned radio sets are lying on the shelves of Arab radio repair shops, untouched. The Americans made the serious cross-cultural error of asking to have the repair completed by a certain time.

How do you cope with this? How does the Arab get another Arab to do anything? Every culture has its own ways of bringing pressure to get results. The usual Arab way is one which Americans avoid as "bad manners." It is needling.

An Arab businessman whose car broke down explained it this way:

> First, I go to the garage and tell the mechanic what is wrong with my car. I wouldn't want to give him the idea that I didn't know. After that, I leave the car and walk around the block. When I come back to the garage, I ask him if he has started to work yet. On my way home from lunch I stop in and ask him how things are going. When I go back to the office I stop by again. In the evening, I return and peer over his shoulder for a while. If I didn't keep this up, he'd be off working on someone else's car.

If you haven't been needled by an Arab, you just haven't been needled.

A Place for Everything

We say that there is a time and place for everything, but compared to other countries and cultures we give very little emphasis to place distinctions. Business is almost a universal value with us; it can be discussed almost anywhere, except perhaps in church. One can even talk business on the church steps going to and from the service. Politics is only slightly more restricted in the places appropriate for its discussion.

In other parts of the world, there are decided place restrictions on the discussion of business and politics. The American who is not conscious of the unwritten laws will offend if he abides by his own rather than by the local rules.

In India, you should not talk business when visiting a man's home. If you do, you prejudice your chances of ever working out a satisfactory business relationship.

In Latin America, although university students take an active interest in politics, tradition decrees that a politician should avoid political subjects when speaking on university grounds. A Latin American politician commented to anthropologist Allan Holmberg that neither he nor his fellow politicians would have dared attempt a political speech on the grounds of the University of San Marcos in Peru—as did Vice-President Nixon.

To complicate matters further, the student body of San Marcos, anticipating the visit, had voted that Mr. Nixon would not be welcome. The University Rector had issued no invitation, presumably because he expected what did, in fact, happen.

As a final touch, Mr. Nixon's interpreter was a man in full military uniform. In Latin American countries, some of which had recently overthrown military dictators, the symbolism of the military uniform could hardly contribute to a cordial atmosphere. Latin Americans need no reminder that the United States is a great military power.

Mr. Nixon's efforts were planned in the best traditions of our own culture: he hoped to improve relations through a direct, frank, and face-to-face discussion with students—the future leaders of their country. Unfortunately, this approach did not fit in at all with the culture of the host country. Of course, elements hostile to the United States did their best to capitalize upon this cross-cultural misunderstanding. However, even Latin Americans friendly to us, while admiring the Vice President's courage, found themselves acutely embarrassed by the behavior of their people and ours in the ensuing difficulties.

Being Comfortable in Space

Like time and place, differing ideas of space hide traps for the uninformed. Without realizing it, almost any person raised in the United States is likely to give an unintended snub to a Latin American simply in the way we handle space relationships, particularly during conversations.

In North America, the "proper" distance to stand when talking to another adult male you do not know well is about two feet, at least in a formal business conversation. (Naturally at a cocktail party, the distance shrinks, but anything under eight to ten inches is likely to provoke an apology or an attempt to back up.)

To a Latin American, with his cultural traditions and habits, a distance of two feet seems to him approximately what five feet would to us. To him, we seem distant and cold. To us, he gives an impression of pushiness.

As soon as a Latin American moves close enough for him to feel comfortable, we feel uncomfortable and edge back. We once observed a conversation between a Latin and a North American which began at one end of a forty-foot hall. At intervals we noticed them again, finally at the other end of the hall. This rather amusing displacement had been accomplished by an almost continual series of small backward steps on the part of the American, trying unconsciously to reach a comfortable talking distance, and an equal closing of the gap by the Latin American as he attempted to reach his accustomed conversation space.

Americans in their offices in Latin America tend to keep their native acquaintances at our distance—not the Latin American's distance—by taking up a position behind a desk or typewriter. The barricade approach to communication is practiced even by old hands in Latin America who are completely unaware of its cultural significance. They know only that they are comfortable without realizing that the distance and equipment unconsciously make the Latin American uncomfortable.

How Class Channels Communication

We would be mistaken to regard the communication patterns which we observe around the world as no more than a miscellaneous collection of customs. The communication pattern of a given society is part of its total culture pattern and can only be understood in that context.

We cannot undertake here to relate many examples of communication behavior to the underlying culture of the country. For the businessman, it might be useful to mention the difficulties in the relationship between social levels and the problem of information feedback from lower to higher levels in industrial organizations abroad.

There is in Latin America a pattern of human relations and union-management relations quite different from that with which we are familiar in the United States. Everett Hagen of MIT has noted the heavier emphasis upon line authority and the lesser development of staff organizations in Latin-American plants when compared with North America counterparts. To a much greater extent than in the United States, the government becomes involved in the handling of all kinds of labor problems.

These differences seem to be clearly related to the culture and social organization of Latin America. We find there that society has been much more rigidly stratified than it has with us. As a corollary, we find a greater emphasis upon authority in family and the community.

This emphasis upon status and class distinction makes it very difficult for people of different status levels to express themselves freely and frankly in discussion and argument. In the past, the pattern has been for the man of lower status to express deference to his superior in any face-to-face contact. This is so even when everyone knows that the subordinate dislikes the superior. The culture of Latin America places a great premium upon keeping personal relations harmonious on the surface.

In the United States, we feel that it is not only desirable but natural to speak up to your superior, to tell the boss exactly what you think, even when you disagree with him. Of course, we do not always do this, but we think that we should, and we feel guilty if we fail to speak our minds frankly. When workers in our factories first get elected to local union office, they may

find themselves quite self-conscious about speaking up to the
boss and arguing grievances. Many of them, however, quickly
learn to do it and enjoy the experience. American culture emphasizes the thrashing-out of differences in face-to-face contacts. It de-emphasizes the importance of status. As a result,
we have built institutions for handling industrial disputes on the
basis of the local situation, and we rely on direct discussion by
the parties immediately involved.

In Latin America, where it is exceedingly difficult for people
to express their differences face-to-face and where status differences and authority are much more strongly emphasized than
here, the workers tend to look to a third party—the government
—to take care of their problems. Though the workers have
great difficulty in thrashing out their problems with management, they find no difficulty in telling government representatives their problems. And it is to their government that they
look for an authority to settle their grievances with management.

Status and class also decide whether business will be done on an
individual or a group basis.

In the United States, we are growing more and more accustomed to working as members of large organizations. Despite this, we still assume that there is no need to send a delega-
tion to do a job that one capable man might well handle.

In some other parts of the world, the individual cannot expect
to gain the respect necessary to accomplish this purpose, no
matter how capable he is, unless he brings along an appropriate
number of associates.

In the United States, we would rarely think it necessary or
proper to call on a customer in a group. He might well be an-
tagonized by the hard sell. In Japan—as an example—the importance of the occasion and of the man is measured by whom he
takes along.

This practice goes far down in the business and government
hierarchies. Even a university professor is likely to bring one
or two retainers along on academic business. Otherwise people
might think that he was a nobody and that his affairs were of
little moment.

Even when a group is involved in the U.S., the head man is
the spokesman and sets the tone. This is not always the case

in Japan. Two young Japanese once requested an older American widely respected in Tokyo to accompany them so that they could "stand on his face." He was not expected to enter into the negotiation; his function was simply to be present as an indication that their intentions were serious.

Adjustment Goes Both Ways

One need not have devoted his life to a study of various cultures to see that none of them is static. All are constantly changing and one element of change is the very fact that U.S. enterprise enters a foreign field. This is inevitable and may be constructive if we know how to utilize our knowledge. The problem is for us to be aware of our impact and to learn how to induce changes skillfully.

Rather than try to answer the general question of how two cultures interact, we will consider the key problem of personnel selection and development in two particular intercultural situations, both in Latin cultures.

One U.S. company had totally different experiences with "Smith" and "Jones" in the handling of its labor relations. The local union leaders were bitterly hostile to Smith, whereas they could not praise Jones enough. These were puzzling reactions to higher management. Smith seemed a fair-minded and understanding man; it was difficult to fathom how anyone could be bitter against him. At the same time, Jones did not appear to be currying favor by his generosity in giving away the firm's assets. To management, he seemed to be just as firm a negotiator as Smith.

The explanation was found in the two men's communication characteristics. When the union leaders came in to negotiate with Smith, he would let them state their case fully and freely—without interruption, but also without comment. When they had finished, he would say, "I'm sorry. We can't do it." He would follow this blunt statement with a brief and entirely cogent explanation of his reasons for refusal. If the union leaders persisted in their arguments, Smith would paraphrase his first statement calmly and succinctly. In either case, the discussion was over in a few minutes. The union leaders would storm out of Smith's office complaining bitterly about the cold and heartless man with whom they had to deal.

Jones handled the situation differently. His final conclusion was the same as Smith's—but he would state it only after two or three hours of discussion. Furthermore, Jones participated actively in these discussions, questioning the union leaders for more information, relating the case in question to previous cases, philosophizing about labor relations and human rights and exchanging stories about work experience. When the discussion came to an end, the union leaders would leave the office, commenting on how warmhearted and understanding he was, and how confident they were that he would help them when it was possible for him to do so. They actually seemed more satisfied with a negative decision from Jones than they did with a hard-won concession from Smith.

This was clearly a case where the personality of Jones happened to match certain discernible requirements of the Latin American culture. It was happenstance in this case that Jones worked out and Smith did not, for by American standards both were top-flight men. Since a talent for the kind of negotiation that the Latin American considers graceful and acceptable can hardly be developed in a grown man (or perhaps even in a young one), the basic problem is one of personnel selection in terms of the culture where the candidate is to work.

The second case is more complicated because it involves much deeper intercultural adjustments. The management of the parent U.S. company concerned had learned—as have the directors of most large firms with good-sized installations overseas—that one cannot afford to have all of the top and middle-management positions manned by North Americans. It is necessary to advance nationals up the overseas-management ladder as rapidly as their abilities permit. So the nationals have to learn not only the technical aspects of their jobs but also how to function at higher levels in the organization.

Latin culture emphasizes authority in the home, church, and community. Within the organization this produces a built-in hesitancy about speaking up to one's superiors. The initiative, the acceptance of responsibility which we value in our organizations had to be stimulated. How could it be done?

We observed one management man who had done a remarkable job of building up these very qualities in his general foremen and foremen. To begin with, he stimulated informal contacts between himself and these men through social events to which the men and their wives came. He saw to it that his senior North American assistants and their wives were also present. Knowing the language, he mixed freely with all. At the plant, he circulated about, dropped in not to inspect or check up, but to joke and to break down the great barrier that existed in the local traditions between authority and the subordinates.

Next, he developed a pattern of three-level meetings. At the top, he himself, the superintendents, and the general foremen. At the middle level, the superintendents, general foremen, and foremen. Then the general foremen, foremen, and workers.

At the top level meeting, the American management chief set the pattern of encouraging his subordinates to challenge his own ideas, to come up with original thoughts. When his superintendents (also North Americans) disagreed with him, he made it clear that they were to state their objections fully. At first, the general foreman looked surprised and uneasy. They noted, however, that the senior men who argued with the boss were encouraged and praised. Timorously, with great hesitation, they began to add their own suggestions. As time went on, they more and more accepted the new convention and pitched in without inhibition.

The idea of challenging the boss with constructive new ideas gradually filtered down to the second and third level meetings. It took a lot of time and gentle handling, but out of this approach grew an extraordinary morale. The native general foremen and foremen developed new pride in themselves, accepted new responsibilities, even reached out for more. They began to work to improve their capacities and to look forward to moving up in the hierarchy.

Conformity or Adjustment?

To work with people, must we be just like them? Obviously not. If we try to conform completely, the Arab, the Latin American, the Italian, whoever he might be, finds our behavior confusing and insincere. He suspects our motive. We are expected to be different. But we are also expected to respect and accept the other people as they are. And we may, without doing violence to our own personalities, learn to communicate with them by observing the unwritten patterns they are accustomed to.

Alger—Cult.Anthropology WC—5

To be aware that there are pitfalls in cross-cultural dealings is the first big step forward. And to accept the fact that our convictions are in no respect more eternally "right" than someone else's is another constructive step.

Beyond these:

1. We can learn to control our so-called frankness in a culture which puts a high value on maintaining pleasant surface relations.

2. We can avoid expressing quick decisions when their utterance without a long period of polite preparation would show disrespect.

3. We can be on the lookout for the conversation patterns of nationals of whatever country we are in and accustom ourselves to closer quarters than we are used to. (This is uncomfortable at first but understanding the reason why it is important helps greatly.)

4. Where the situation demands it, we can learn to express our emotions more freely—most people find this rather exhilarating.

5. We can try to distinguish between the organizational practices which are really necessary to effectiveness and those that we employ from habit because they happen to be effective in the United States.

Research for Organizational Effectiveness

We have outlined a point of view the individual can seek to apply in order to increase his own effectiveness. Valuable as that may be, we must recognize the limitations of an individual approach. Since each family transported overseas represents an investment of between $25,000 and $100,000 per year to the organization, the losses involved in poor selection or inadequate training can be enormous.

While no ready-made answers are now available, research can serve the organization both in *selection* and *training* of personnel.

It would be a mistake to assume that the ideal training program would fit just any administrator effectively into any given culture. We must assume that some personalities will fit more readily than others. By the time man reaches adulthood, his personality is rather solidly formed, and basic changes are difficult if not impossible to induce. It is therefore important to work to improve the selection process so that men with little chance of fitting into a foreign culture will not be sent where they are bound to fail.

Our Latin-American case of Smith and Jones is relevant here. One who had observed Smith in his native setting should have been able to predict that he would not be effective in handling labor relations in Latin America. However, that statement is based upon the hindsight observation that there was a very obvious lack of fit between Smith's personality and the cultural requirements of his job. It remains for research men to devise schemes of observation and testing which will enable personnel men to base their selections upon criteria of personality *and* culture.

To what extent can training improve the effectiveness of individuals in intercultural communication? Training of men in overseas operations is going on all the time. So far as we know, little of it currently deals with the considerations outlined in this article. Until organizations are prepared to develop training along these lines—and support research on the effects of such training—we shall not know to what extent intercultural communications can be improved through training.

We do not mean to give the impression that behavioral scientists already have the knowledge needed regarding intercultural communication. What we have presented here is only a demonstration of the importance of the topic. We have not presented a systematic analysis of the problems of communication from culture A to culture B. We have just said in effect: "These are some of the things that are important. Watch out for them."

What more is needed? In the first place, the problem calls for a new emphasis in anthropological research. In the past, anthropologists have been primarily concerned with the *internal* pattern of a given culture. In giving attention to intercultural problems, they have examined the impact of one culture upon another. Very little attention has been given to the actual communication process between representatives of different cultures.

Much could be learned, for example, if we observed North Americans in interaction with people of another culture. We would want also to be able to interview both parties to the interaction to study how A was interpreting B and how B was interpreting A. In this way we might discover points of friction

and miscommunication whose existence we now do not even suspect. Such studies, furthermore, would provide systematic
knowledge much more useful than the fragments provided in this
article.

The Torments of Translation † *

Dismantling the Tower of Babel

Each language spoken by man (there are over 2,800) is honey-
combed with uniqueness. Human languages are as different as
peas in a pod (if you examined them under a microscope). What
human tongues have in common is only purpose: the use of words
to try to describe, understand, and communicate the measure-
less sensations of existence, the swarm of impressions on the
self, the marvelous symbolic productions of the human mind, the
infinite fantasies of the imagination, the divine and the wretched
parameters of the human condition.

A language is a *Weltanschauung*. Even languages very close in
origin, history, and structure develop surprising differences. The
English "conscience" is not the same as the French *conscience*
(which means consciousness or conscientiousness). German had
no word for "bully" until the twentieth century (a mordant comment on Teutonic values) and can only render the Englishman's
idea of "fair play" as *"fair" Spielen*. If this be true of tongues
so close to each other in birth, so laden with cognates, so cross-
fertilized by usage and literature, how much more does it intrude
when one tries to translate Yiddish or Hebrew into any of them?

Translation is not simply a matter of dexterity in transferring
synonyms. Translation does not contend with words, but with
meanings. To translate is to decode: to transpose one mode of
thinking, feeling, fearing, appraising into the word-patterns of
another. No language can be separated from its historical skele-
ton, its psychological skin, or its sociological garments. Languages are acculturated verbalizations of experience and thought.

† By Leo Rosten.

* Harper's Magazine July 1972, pp.
72–73 reprinted by permission of the
author.

Christian missionaries in the Orient, for instance, were sorely perplexed because Chinese has neither a word for "word" nor a word for, or an idea of, "sin." (The closest is *tsui*, which means "crime"). And in Africa or Polynesia, the Christian messengers of the Lord found bewildering difficulty in trying to communicate the idea of God—i. e., one supreme deity—to people mystified by such an impoverished theology. In language, which is a system of "culturally ordained categories," each of us "builds the house of his consciousness." [1]

When an English or American speaker in the United Nations says, "I assume," interpreters render it in French as "I deduce" and in Russian as "I consider."

It is hard for us truly to believe that each culture teaches its people what to say about what that culture has taught them to think, feel, see, or even hear. The pioneering studies of Edward Sapir (whom I was fortunate enough to know) and Benjamin Lee Whorf have forced us to consider the surprising degree to which our sensations, our thoughts, even our actions are influenced by the particular system of sounds and symbols we inherit. We all assume that we are experiencing the real world; "but in many cases we are free only to experience the possibilities and limitations of grammar." [2]

For instance: do you think dogs go "woof-woof," "bow-wow," or "arf-arf"? In English prose, they bark that way. But in German, dogs go "wau-wau"; in Chinese, "wang-wang"; in Vietnamese, "gau-gau"; and in Japanese, "wan-wan." In Yiddish, dogs go "how-how," and there is a saying: "The dog who barks 'ho-ho' is not dangerous, but the one who growls 'how-how' is." (I cannot help wondering how a Laplander or Litvak would translate "going to the dogs.")

In German, frogs are said to croak "quak-quak," which would confuse an American duck. Scottish roosters would surely be flabbergasted to learn that French roosters go "cocorico" (at least in French novels). As for Arabian donkeys, which Arabian writers tell us go "ham-ham," I quail to think of what they would think if they learned that, in Rumanian, it is dogs who go "ham-ham."

[1] John L. Mish, The World of Translation (New York: The PEN Conference, 1970), pp. 241–7.

[2] Walter Nash, Our Experience of Language (London: Battsford, 1971), p. 18.

Any sensible American will tell you that scissors go "snip-snip," "snip-snap," or "snap-snap." But to a Greek, believe it or not, scissors go "kritz-kritz." And to a Chinese, scissors hiss "su-su." As for Spaniards, Italians, and Portuguese, their scissors retain as marked a national identity as any other, being written respectively as "ri-ri," "kri-kri," and "terre-terre." [3]

All this may disturb your comfortable assumption that in onomatopoeia, at least, there is universal agreement; that everyone, whether Choctaw or Irish or Cypriot, produces the same oral renditions of and for the same heard sounds; that different languages must employ the same vocalizations for objectively uniform acoustics.

But the notion that onomatopoeia crosses the frontiers of language rests on the misconception that verbal allusions accurately mirror "real" sounds: they do not; they record and reflect those sounds our culture has instructed us to hear, or predisposed us *not* to hear. A German child is taught to hear the buzzing of a bee not as "bzz-bzz" (which English bees do, apparently in order to validate our word "buzzing") but as "sum-sum." If you will repeat "sum-sum" for a while, you may come to prefer it to "bzz-bzz"—or you may, in the interest of world peace, henceforth describe all bees as going "bzz-bzz sum-sum."

Do you think that in every society men grow so angry they "see red?" Well, "our classification of the spectrum into . . . red, orange, yellow, green, blue and violet is culturally arbitrary, and persons in other cultures divide the spectrum quite differently. Perception itself is an aspect of human *behavior*." [4]

Optical recordings often express learned ways of seeing and inferring. I once wrote: "We see things as *we* are, not as they are." Professor E. H. Gombrich tells us that ancient artists drew eyelashes on the lower lids of horses' eyes (the drawings *they* had seen and studied showed eyelashes on horses' lower lids); but lower eyelashes do not happen to exist on real, undrawn horses. As Degas once blurted: "Drawing is not what one sees, but what others must be made to see."

[3] Helmut Braem, "Languages Are Comparable Yet Unique," The World of Translation, pp. 121–34.

[4] M. Segall, D. Campbell, M. J. Herskovits, The Influence of Culture on Visual Perception (Indianapolis: Bobbs-Merrill, 1966), pp. 37, 213.

Have I wandered? Only to illustrate, I hope, how complicated simple things become if we examine them with care. The mere change of sound, in translating, can alter the sensual glow and hum of the original. I commend to you Bernard Berenson's appraisal of critics: they break a watch into its parts, to hear how it ticks. Changing one word's *position* can alter meaning drastically: "What is harder than getting a pregnant elephant in a Volkswagen? Getting an elephant pregnant in a Volkswagen."

The most tormenting aspect of translation is this: what is idiomatic in one tongue is idiotic in another. Think for a moment of what happens if a translator of English does not realize that "tell it to Sweeney" is a rebuff, not a request; that "a Northern Spy" may have been an undercover agent for Ulysses S. Grant —or is only a variety of apple; that Ockham never used his razor for shaving, any more than Cleopatra used her needle for sewing; that "jack-in-the-pulpit" does not mean the preacher's name is Jack; that "behind the eight ball" is gibberish in nine-tenths of the world; and that when athletes engage in a "rhubarb" they do not sit down to consume a legume.

It gives me the greatest pleasure to inform you that Russian physicists believe that the first nuclear atomic pile in history was constructed in a pumpkin field—that being their natural translation of "squash court," the site in the concrete bowels of the stadium (Stagg Field) of the University of Chicago.

As for poetry, I can do no better than give you Chaim Bialik's despairing dictum: "Reading poetry in translation is like kissing a woman through a veil."

I cannot help feeling that where a translator, however fine a scholar, is not a writer, translation starts under a deadly handicap. For if a writer is anything, he is one who is more sensitive than others to words, who loves their texture, their nuances, their conceptual echoes and ideational overtones. An empathy for language—which is to say, a refined and heightened sensitivity to words—is simply a *sine qua non* (how do you say that in English?) for translators. The man who cannot echo the *beat* of a word, much less a sentence, or who is insensitive to simile and metaphor, or who does not savor parallel construction, or who is word-blind and cadence-deaf, is bound to butcher his task. A seventeenth-century man of letters, John Denham bristled:

> *Such is our pride, our folly and our fate*
> *That only those who cannot write, translate.*

The Bill of Rights composed by the 1971 International Conference on Literary Translation reads:

> *The translator's chief obligation is to create the work in a new language with the appropriate music and the utmost response to the silences of the original.*[5]

As an admirer of the manifesto, I wish that its writers had said "another," not "a new," language: translators are surely not obliged to invent a tongue from scratch.

"A good translation," said Benedetto Croce, "is a work of art."

My Language: Navajo Dirty Word? † *

F OR a Navajo child to be "literate" in the Navajo language he needs to know about 5,000 words, compared to the 2,000 words of English an Anglo child needs to know.

Like most Indian languages Navajo is highly complex, subtle and expressive. There are 325 phonetic sounds in Navajo, writes Navajo scholar Herbert Blatchford, but only eighty phonetic sounds in English. However, a child who spoke Navajo used to be considered "illiterate." Until recently Indian students were forbidden to speak their native languages in school. (My Language: Is Navajo a Dirty Word?" Bertha Desiderio, *The Word-Passer,* Vol. I, No. 3, March-April, 1969, p. 7) Now, texts and curriculum in Navajo, Cherokee, and Dakota are being developed. Bilingual and bicultural education have rediscovered the riches of native languages.

I came into this world as a Navajo child. As I grew up I learned to speak a language. This language I came to treasure, to feel at ease when I spoke it, and it brought me an identification as a true proud Navajo. I spoke this language before I heard another language called English. My parents taught me how to pronounce the Navajo words right and taught me what they meant. I treasured the language as I went through my early

---

5 The World of Translation, p. 8.

† By Bertha Desiderio.

* By permission of the editor. The Indian Historian, Vol. 6, No. 2. (Spring 1973): p. 43.

youth, even though I was learning a new language that I would need as I got through life, but still, I never wanted to lose my own language.

When I conversed with this language that I treasured I was proud because it was mine and it was given to me by my ancestors. I was never ashamed to speak Navajo in front of a group of Navajo students. The language that I was proud of has been changed into a "twisted" language. These days it seems like I can't say anything in Navajo without getting embarrassed. When I do talk in Navajo, my words are changed into dirty thoughts by people who do not realize that our language is supposed to be a value for us. Instead, they take our language as trash.

I wonder how students who twist their language into dirty thoughts feel about their culture going down the drain. Again I wonder if it ever bothers them not to take their culture into consideration. As an individual, I dread to see my culture fade out just because some of us students don't care to use our language as it is supposed to be used.

Are you really proud to be a Navajo? Then talk as if you took pride in your language.

*

IV. Those Other People

In many parts of the world there are people who are discriminated against because they belong to a particular category of people. Such discrimination may be based on race, caste, religion or a number of other criteria. The articles in this section will consider certain types of discrimination and will show how such discrimination is reinforced in some cultures.

The first article in this section by S. L. Washburn carefully defines the term "race". The next two articles, "Creeping Jensenism" and "On the Continuing Revival of Scientific Racism," are directed against the "scientific racism" of such people as Arthur Jensen and William Schockley. The opponents of "scientific racism" maintain that Jensen and Schockley are using poor scientific method in their attempts to prove that certain races are innately inferior. Richard J. Ossenberg's article investigates the differences in bar behavior between members of different social classes in an urban setting. The selection by George De Vos and Hiroshi Wagatsuma might be used profitably to draw parallels between the Japanese beliefs about the Eta and some current racist beliefs about certain racial or minority groups in the United States. The concluding selection, a newspaper clipping, illustrates the tenacious hold a caste system can have on a people even when they are faced with death.

The Study of Race † *

. . . . **D**ISCUSSION of the races of man seems to generate endless emotion and confusion. I am under no illusion that this paper can do much to dispel the confusion; it may add to the emotion. The latest information available supports the traditional findings of anthropologists and other social scientists—

† By S. L. Washburn.

* "Reproduced by permission of the American Anthropological Associa-tion from the American Anthropologist" Vol. 65, No. 3, 1963 and the author.

that there is no scientific basis of any kind for racial discrimination. I think that the way this conclusion has been reached needs to be restated. The continuation of antiquated biological notions in anthropology and the oversimplification of facts weakens the anthropological position. We must realize that great changes have taken place in the study of race over the last 20 years and it is up to us to bring our profession into the forefront of the newer understandings, so that our statements will be authoritative and useful.

This paper will be concerned with three topics—the modern concept of race, the interpretation of racial differences, and the social significances of race. . . .

The races of man are the result of human evolution, of the evolution of our species. The races are open parts of the species, and the species is a closed system. If we look, then, upon long-term human evolution, our first problem must be the species and the things which have caused the evolution of all mankind, not the races, which are the results of local forces and which are minor in terms of the evolution of the whole species. . . .

The evolution of races is due, according to modern genetics, to mutation, selection, migration, and genetic drift. It is easy to shift from this statement of genetic theory to complications of hemoglobin, blood groups or other technical information. But the point I want to stress is that the primary implication of genetics for anthropology is that it affirms the relation of culture and biology in a far firmer and more important way than ever in our history before. Selection is for reproductive success, and in man reproductive success is primarily determined by the social system and by culture. Effective behavior is the question, not something else.

Drift depends on the size of population, and population size, again, is dependent upon culture, not upon genetic factors as such. Obviously, migration depends on clothes, transportation, economy, and warfare and is reflected in the archeological record. Even mutation rates are now affected by technology.

Genetic theory forces the consideration of culture as the major factor in the evolution of man. It thus reaffirms the fundamental belief of anthropologists that we must study man both as a biological and as a social organism. This is no longer a question of something that might be desirable; it must be done if genetic theory is correct.

We have, then, on the one hand the history of genetic systems, and on the other hand the history of cultural systems, and, finally, the interrelation between these two. There is no evolution in the traditional anthropological sense. What Boas referred to as evolution was orthogenesis—which receives no support from modern genetic theory. What the geneticist sees as evolution is far closer to what Boas called history than to what he called evolution, and some anthropologists are still fighting a nineteenth-century battle in their presentation of evolution. We have, then, the history of cultural systems, which you may call history; and the history of genetic systems, which you may call evolution if you want to, but if you use this word word remember that it means selection, migration, drift—it is real history that you are talking about and not some mystic force which constrains mankind to evolve according to some orthogenetic principle.

There is, then, no possibility of studying human raciation, the process of race formation, without studying human culture. Archeology is as important in the study of the origin of races as is genetics; all we can do is reconstruct as best we can the long-term past, and this is going to be very difficult. .   .   .

Genetics shows us that typology must be completely removed from our thinking if we are to progress. For example, let us take the case of the Bushmen. The Bushmen have been described as the result of a mixture between Negro and Mongoloid. Such a statement could only be put in the literature without any possible consideration of migration routes, of numbers of people, of cultures, of any way that such a mixing could actually take place. The fact is that the Bushmen had a substantial record in South Africa and in East Africa and there is no evidence that they ever were anywhere else except in these areas. In other words, they are a race which belongs exactly where they are.

If we are concerned with history let us consider, on the one hand, the ancestors of these Bushmen 15,000 years ago and the area available to them, to their way of life, and, on the other hand, the ancestors of Europeans at the same time in the area available to them, with their way of life. We will find that the area available to the Bushmen was at least twice that available to the Europeans. The Bushmen were living in a land of optimum game; the Europeans were living close to an ice sheet. There were perhaps from three to five times as many Bushmen ancestors as there were European ancestors only 15,000 years ago.

If one were to name a major race, or a primary race, the Bushmen have a far better claim in terms of the archeological record than the Europeans. During the time of glacial advance more than half of the Old World available to man for life was in Africa. The numbers and distributions that we think of as normal and the races whose last results we see today are relics of an earlier and far different time in human history.

There are no three primary races, no three major groups. The idea of three primary races stems from nineteenth-century typology; it is totally misleading to put the black-skinned people of the world together—to put the Australian in the same grouping with the inhabitants of Africa. And there are certainly at least three independent origins of the small, dark people, the Pygmies, and probably more than that. There is no single Pygmy race. . . .

The concept of race is fundamentally changed if we actually look for selection, migration, and study people as they are (who they are, where they are, how many they are) ; and the majority of anthropological textbooks need substantial revision along these lines.

Since races are open systems which are intergrading, the number of races will depend on the purpose of the classification. This is, I think, a tremendously important point. It is significant that as I was reviewing classifications in preparing this lecture, I found that almost none of them mentioned any purpose for which people were being classified. Race isn't very important biologically. If we are classifying races in order to understand human history, there aren't many human races, and there is very substantial agreement as to what they are. There are from six to nine races, and this difference in number is very largely a matter of definition. These races occupied the major separate geographical areas in the Old World.

If one has no purpose for classification, the number of races can be multiplied almost indefinitely, and it seems to me that the eratically varying number of races is a source of confusion to student, to layman, and to specialist. I think we should require people who propose a classification of races to state in the first place why they wish to divide the human species and to give in detail the important reasons for subdividing our whole species. If important reasons for such classification are given, I think you will find that the number of races is always exceedingly small.

If we consider these six or nine geographical races and the factors which produced them, I think the first thing we want to stress is migration. . . .

Migration has always been important in human history and there is no such thing as human populations which are completely separated from other human populations. And migration necessarily brings in new genes, necessarily reduces the differences between the races. For raciation to take place, then, there must be other factors operating which create difference. Under certain circumstances, in very small populations, differences may be created by genetic drift, or because the founders are for chance reasons very different from other members of the species.

However, the primary factor in the creation of racial differences in the long term is selection. This means that the origin of races must depend on adaptation and that the differences between the races which we see must in times past have been adaptive. I stress the question of time here, because it is perfectly logical to maintain that in time past a shovel-shaped incisor, for example, was more efficient than an incisor of other forms and that selection would have been for this, and at the same time to assert that today this dental difference is of absolutely no social importance. It is important to make this point because people generally take the view that something is always adaptive or never adaptive, and this is a fundamental oversimplification of the facts.

Adaptation is always within a given situation. There is no such thing as a gene which has a particular adaptive value; it has this value only under set circumstances. For example, the sickle-cell gene, if Alison and others are right, protects against malaria. This is adaptive if there is malaria, but if there is not malaria it is not adaptive. The adaptive value of the gene, then, is dependent on the state of medicine and has no absolute value. The same is true of the other characteristics associated with race. . . .

I turn now to a brief statement on the influence of culture upon race. Beginning with agriculture and continuing at an ever-increasing rate, human customs have been interposed between the organism and the environment. The increase of our species from perhaps as few as five million before agriculture to three billion today is the result of new technology, not of biological evolution. The conditions under which the races evolved are mainly gone, and there are new causes of mutation, new kinds of selection, and vast migration. Today the numbers and distribution of the peoples of the world are due primarily to culture. Some people think the new conditions are so different that it is better no longer to use the word race or the word evolution, but I personally think this confuses more than it clarifies.

All this does not mean that evolution has stopped, because the new conditions will change gene frequencies, but the conditions which produced the old races are gone. In this crowded world of civilization and science, the claim has been made repeatedly that one or another of the races is superior to the others. Obviously, this argument cannot be based on the past; because something was useful in times past and was selected for under conditions which are now gone, does not mean that it will be useful in the present or in the future.

The essential point at issue is whether the abilities of large populations are so different that their capacity to participate in modern technical culture is affected. Remember in the first place that no race has evolved to fit the selective pressures of the modern world. Technical civilization is new and the races are old. Remember also that all the species of *Homo* have been adapting to the human way of life for many thousands of years. Tools even antedate our genus, and our human biological adaptation is the result of culture. Man and his capacity for culture have evolved together, as Dr. Dobzhansky has pointed out. All men are adapted to learn language—any language; to perform skillful tasks—a fabulous variety of tasks; to cooperate; to enjoy art; to practice religion, philosophy, and science.

Our species only survives in culture, and, in a profound sense, we are the product of the new selection pressures that came with culture.

Infinitely more is known about the language and culture of all the groups of mankind than is known about the biology of racial differences. We know that the members of every racial group have learned a vast variety of languages and ways of life.

The interaction of genes and custom over the millenia has produced a species whose populations can learn to live in an amazing variety of complex cultural ways.

Racism is based on a profound misunderstanding of culture, of learning, and of the biology of the human species. The study of cultures should give a profound respect for the biology of man's capacity to learn. Much of the earlier discussion of racial inferiority centered on the discussion of intelligence; or, to put the matter more accurately, usually on that small part of biological intelligence which is measured by the IQ. In the earlier days of intelligence testing, there was a widespread belief that the tests revealed something which was genetically fixed within a rather narrow range. The whole climate of opinion that fostered this point of view has changed. At that time animals were regarded as primarily instinctive in their behavior, and the genes were supposed to exert their effects in an almost mechanical way, regardless of the environment. All this intellectual climate has changed. Learning has proved to be far more important in the behavior of many animal species, and the action of the complexes of genes is now known to be affected by the environment, as is, to a great degree, the performance that results from them. For example, Harlow has shown that monkeys learn to learn. Monkeys become test wise. They become skillful in the solution of tests—so monkeys in Dr. Harlow's laboratories are spoken of as naive or as experienced in the use of tests. To suppose that humans cannot learn to take tests is to suppose that humans are rather less intelligent than monkeys. .   .   .

We can generalize this point. All kinds of human performance —whether social, athletic, intellectual—are built on genetic and environmental elements. The level of all kinds of performance can be increased by improving the environmental situation so that every genetic constitution may be developed to its full capacity. Any kind of social discrimination against groups of people, whether these are races, castes, or classes, reduces the achievements of our species, of mankind.

The cost of discrimination is reflected in length of life. The Founding Fathers were wise to join life, liberty, and the pursuit of happiness, because these are intimately linked in the social and cultural system. Just as the restriction of social and economic opportunity reduces intelligence so it reduces length of life.

In 1900 the life expectancy of White males in the United States was 48 years, and in that same year the expectancy of a Negro male was 32 years; that is a difference of 50 per cent, or 16 years. By 1940 the difference had been reduced to ten years, and by 1958 to six. As the life expectancy of the Whites increased from 48 to 62 to 67 years, that of the Negroes increased from 32 to 52 to 61 years. They died of the same causes, but they died at different rates.

Discrimination, by denying equal social opportunity to the Negro, made his progress lag approximately 20 years behind that of the White. Somebody said to me, "Well, 61, 67, that's only six years." But it depends on whose six years it is. There are about 19 million people in this country sociologically classified as Negroes. If they die according to the death rate given above, approximately 100 million years of life will be lost owing to discrimination.

In 1958 the death rate for Negroes in the first year of life was 52 per thousand and for Whites 26. Thousands of Negro infants died unnecessarily. The social conscience is an extraordinary thing. A lynching stirs the whole community to action, yet only a single life is lost. Discrimination, through denying education, medical care, and economic progress, kills at a far higher rate. A ghetto of hatred kills more surely than a concentration camp, because it kills by accepted custom, and it kills every day in the year.

A few years ago in South Africa, the expectation of life for a Black man was 40 years, but it was 60 at the same time for a White man. At that same time a White woman could expect 25 more years of life than a Black woman. Among the Blacks the women lived no longer than the men. People speak of the greater longevity of women, but this is only because of modern medicine. High birth rates, high infant mortality, high maternal mortality —these are the hallmarks of the history of mankind.

Of course there are biological differences between male and female, but whether a woman is allowed to vote, or the rate that she must die in childbirth, these are a matter of medical knowledge and of custom. Biological difference only expresses itself through the social system.

Who may live longer in the future—Whites or Negroes? There's no way of telling. Who may live longer in the future—

males or females? There is no way of telling. These things are dependent on the progress in medical science and on the degree to which this progress is made available to all races and to both sexes.

When environment is important, the only way genetic difference may be determined is by equalizing the environment. If you believe in mankind, then you will want mankind to live on in an enriched environment. No one can tell what may be the ultimate length of life, but we do know that many people could live much longer if given a chance.

Whether we consider intelligence, or length of life, or happiness the genetic potential of a population is only realized in a social system. It is that system which gives life or death to its members, and in so doing changes the gene frequencies. We know of no society which has begun to realize the genetic potential of its members. We are the primitives living by antiquated customs in the midst of scientific progress. Races are products of the past. They are relics of times and conditions which have long ceased to exist.

Racism is equally a relic supported by no phase of modern science. We may not know how to interpret the form of the Mongoloid face, or why Rho is of high incidence in Africa, but we do know the benefits of education and of economic progress. We know the price of discrimination is death, frustration, and hatred. We know that the roots of happiness lie in the biology of the whole species and that the potential of the species can only be realized in a culture, in a social system. It is knowledge and the social system which give life or take it away, and in so doing change the gene frequencies and continue the million-year-old interaction of culture and biology. Human biology finds its realization in a culturally determined way of life, and the infinite variety of genetic combinations can only express themselves efficiently in a free and open society.

On Creeping Jensenism † *

Concern about the meaning of the physical differences between human populations dates back to before the dawn of written history, but it did not really become a major issue until the Renaissance, when the revolution in ocean-going transportation brought large numbers of diverse people physically face to face. The superior technology of the Europeans enabled them to coerce and exploit the peoples encountered, many of whom were forcibly uprooted and relocated as slaves. While one could argue that this was one of the most extraordinary examples of barbarism in the annals of "civilization," it was justified at the time, not so much on the basis of race, but because the people being enslaved were "heathens." Actually the "Christianity" of the unprincipled and largely illiterate slaving crews was often a convenient fiction, and the real reasons why the slave trade continued were greed and the force of firearms.

The phenomenon of the Christianized (and even literate) slave removed the initial rationale, but, needless to say, the institution persisted. Economics and the established social order in the American South assured its perpetuation while the Calvinistic fatalism of the North tended to maintain the status quo with little question. For example, in 1706 that godly Puritan, Cotton Mather, heartily supported the Christianization of "the Negro" on the one hand, while arguing on the other that baptism does not entitle a slave to liberty (Osofsky 1967:389). Although Quakers publicly and repeatedly extended Christian principles to the extreme of condemning slavery from the latter third of the seventeenth century on, this did not become a matter of general concern until the winds of "enlightenment" ushered in the Age of Reason, complete with elegant statements on the nature of man and human rights, and culminating in the American Revolution. Backlash followed the excesses of the revolutions in

† By C. Loring Brace & Frank B. Livingstone, Department of Anthropology University of Michigan.

* Reproduced by permission of the American Anthropological Association from Race and Intelligence.

Edited by C. L. Brace, G. R. Gamble and J. T. Bond, Anthropological Studies No. 8. American Anthropological Association (pp. 64–71) and the authors.

Santa Domingo and France, and it was more than half a century before the momentum of the Enlightenment was regained and slavery was finally abolished—in name, at least. (For excellent and detailed historical treatment, see Jordan 1968 and Stanton 1960.)

The intellectual legacy from late eighteenth century idealism, however, is apparent in the continuing debate concerning the meaning of human physical differences. Clouding this debate has been another legacy of considerably less exalted origins. This legacy survives in the wretched social and environmental surroundings that continue to characterize the living conditions of Negroes in the United States. Quite recently there has been an explicit recognition of this situation—witness the belated extension (in 1954 and 1969) of eighteenth century Constitutional guarantees to Americans of African ancestry—but, at the same time, there has also been a continuation of the attempts to justify bloc differences in human treatment that began when slavery was already an accomplished fact.

Enforced inferior status—slavery—was initially justified by the heathen state of African peoples. All the other attributes of Negroes were automatically stigmatized and, although the justification changed through time, their association with inferiority has remained a continuing item of faith. Black skin color was regarded as the result of the curse placed on Ham and all his descendants. Negroes then were identified with the Biblical Canaanites, their servitude was considered justified by Noah's curse, and their attributes were regarded as visible evidence of the Lord's displeasure. With the rise of a rational world view in the latter part of the eighteenth century, this became an increasingly unsatisfactory explanation to thoughtful men. Separate creations—separate and unequal—were suggested, although this was offensive to the faithful who preferred something which remained compatible with the Biblical original pair. The result was a pre-Darwinian development of a form of evolution by means of a crudely conceived kind of natural selection (Smith 1965). Inevitably, however, vested interests of a social and political nature clouded all efforts at objectivity, as they continue to do. The record of published attempts to justify existing social inequalities on the basis of innate or biological differences extends unbroken from the Renaissance era of exploration and subsequent colonization (Jordan 1968) through the nineteenth century (Barzun 1965, Stocking 1968) to the present day. The association with events that maximize human misery (epitomized in the American Civil War and World War II for instance) is so clear that each new attempt to justify differential treatment of large numbers of human beings, often prejudged en masse, should be examined with the greatest of care.

We offer this cautionary preamble because yet another such attempt has been made, this time couched in the language of modern science, published in circumstances which tend to enhance its prestige, and given widespread if uncritical publicity. The presentation we refer to is Jensen's (1969a) monograph-length article in the *Harvard Educational Review*. Pointing up the obvious seriousness of its implications is the fact that the very next issue of the *Review* (Vol. 39, Spring 1969) contained responses from more than a half-dozen scholars. Many of the points raised are well-taken, but, in the haste of immediate reaction, documentation was incomplete, important aspects were missed entirely, and organization suffered.[1] Adding further to this unfortunate confusion is the treatment it has been given in the popular press. The discussion in the prestigious *New York Times Magazine* (Edson 1969), attempting journalistic impartiality, presents the various arguments and rebuttals as though they were all of equal probability. The result has been the widespread circulation of conclusions which are possibly pernicious, and certainly premature, to a readership which, though highly literate, is largely unable to make a reliable independent evaluation.

Seen in perspective, "jensenism, n. the theory that IQ is largely determined by the genes" (Edson 1969), is the extreme if logical outcome of the preoccupation which the field of behavior genetics has had with the "defeat" of the environmentalist heritage of Watsonian behaviorism (Hirsch 1967b:118–119).

---

[1] Since the preparation of this manuscript (for the November 1969 Annual Meeting of the American Anthropological Association), another paper by Jensen has appeared (1969b) in conjunction with more thoroughly documented critiques in the summer issue of the Harvard Educational Review. Some of the points we raise are discussed in greater detail than in our presentation, but since other important ones are not even mentioned we have decided to let our paper stand substantially as originally written

The extreme of the environmentalist position is best expressed in Watson's (1924:82) famous dictum:

> Give me a dozen healthy infants . . . and I'll guarantee to take any one at random and train him to become any type of specialist I might select—doctor, lawyer, artist, merchant-chief and, yes, even beggar-man and thief, regardless of his . . . abilities . . . and race of his ancestors.

Fulminations against this position by committed racists, who anathemize it as "equalitarian doctrine," are well known (Putnam 1961). Objections to extreme environmentalism have also been repeatedly offered by students of behavior genetics, one of whom, Hirsch, has variously characterized it as a "counterfactual assumption" (1961:480), a "counterfactual dogma" (1963), and a "counterfactual . . . postulate" (1967a), based on "fallacious reasoning" and "excessively anti-intellectual" (1967b). Both these positions, the racist and the behavior geneticist, represent reactions to the emotionally based humanitarianism in much of recent social science.

Leaving the racists out of it for the moment, it is evident that the advances in behavior genetics and ethology must be considered of prime importance among the recent major developments in biological, psychological, and anthropological science. This has led to the organization of many symposia and fostered the production of a series of popular books such as those by Lorenz (1966), Ardrey (1966), Morris (1968, 1969), and Tiger (1969). Questions being asked include "Why are men aggressive?" "Does man have a pair bond?" and "Is there such a thing as male bonding?" The interest in basic human biology is apparent, and much of this new questioning is concerned with supposed "species-specific" characteristics of man, although there is a tendency to postulate a genetic cause for human behavioral differences—Lorenz's (1966:236) discussion of Ute aggression, for example. Given these recent trends, it seems inevitable that attention would be focused on intelligence differences and that genetic causation should be stressed.

In the general picture, caution should be urged on two accounts, and Jensen's work illustrates what can happen when neither problem is adequately considered. First the distinction between individual and population performance should be clearly perceived; and, second, if genetic differences are to be the object of concern, thorough control of the environmental component of observed variation should be achieved.

Considering the first issue, one of the roots of the problem is the inability of Western science—and biological science in particular—to recognize and differentiate between individual and populational phenomena. Certainly birth rates, death rates, or intelligence levels are the result of individual performances, but their variability among human populations is not primarily due to individual genetic differences, however much these may be involved. Many of the recent discussions of incest, inbreeding, and sexual behavior demonstrate the same inability to differentiate populational and individual phenomena (Roberts 1967; Livingstone 1969). Ironically, Hirsch, one of the people most responsible for the trend of research which Jensen has carried to something of an extreme, has apparently sensed the fact that the approach he has promoted is being carried too far and has recently articulated a brief critique which could be applied to Jensen's work (Hirsch 1968:42):

> What is the relative importance of genetic endowment and of environmental milieu in the development of the intelligence of *an* individual? The answers given to that question . . . have nothing to do with *an* individual, nor are they based on the study of development. The answers have been based on the test performance of a cross-section of a *population* of individuals at a single time in their lives.

In his critical comment, Kagan (1969) in fact notes that Jensen makes no effort to resolve this issue.

Turning to the environmental component in observed behavior, we see that again Jensen has made little effort to grapple with the problem. Admittedly, the thrust of recent work in behavior genetics has been to discount the environmental contribution, but, again, Hirsch, who has been a major part of this thrust, has recently provided a warning against excesses in this direction. While he refers to the heredity-environment question as "a pseudo-question to which there is no answer" (1968:42), he goes on to warn that:

> it should also be noted that one cannot infer from a high heritability value that the influence of environment is small

or unimportant, *as so many people try to do* [1968:43, italics Hirsch's].

To illustrate the unwarranted extreme of what Medawar (1961:60) has called "geneticism," Hirsch refers to the controversial pronouncements of William B. Shockley, Nobel laureate in physics.   (For excerpts of Shockley's speech, see Birch 1968:49, and for a responsible rebuttal, see Crow, Neel, and Stern 1967). Mention of Shockley in this regard is particularly important since Jensen was apparently much impressed by Shockley when he was visiting Stanford in 1966–67.   The result was what has been called his "most unfortunate speech" illustrating "the dangers of inappropriate use of both the concept of heritability and that of race by the biometrically unsophisticated" (Hirsch 1967a: 434).   Jensen's speech, in turn, provided the background for the article which is the focus of our concern here.

The first half of Jensen's article is a comprehensive review of quantitative genetics.   He concludes this review with the statement (1969a:65) that:

> the question of whether heritability estimates can contribute anything to our understanding of the relative importance of genetic and environmental factors in accounting for average phenotypic differences between racial groups (or any other socially defined group) is too complex to be considered here.

Since heritability estimates are specific to the populations studied—at the time studied—and since they vary considerably with environmental circumstances, Jensen, as quoted, correctly expresses the problem and should have stopped there. He does not stop, however, and proceeds under the assumption that there is a definite intelligence heritability of .8. Not only is this the highest found, but it is based on twin data, which are most unlikely to differentiate the environmental component.[2] This estimate he then generalizes to all humanity.

Despite his statement that the matter is "too complex," his further discussion of racial differences apparently implies that the preceding review of quantitative genetics supports his view.

[2] For an elegant demonstration of the inappropriateness of Jensen's use of twin data, see the critique by Light and Smith (1969).   Fehr (1969) also shows the inaccuracy of Jensen's use of twin data to arrive at his assumed heritability level.

It does not.   Furthermore, we fail to see how, after pointing out that environment can change IQ by as much as 70 points, he can make the statement that "in short it is doubtful that there is any significant environmental effect on IQ."

For purposes of comparison, let us take the case of stature. As a "trait," it is sufficiently complex to warrant the expression of doubts concerning simplistic treatment, although it is somewhat less of a "typological reification" (Hirsch 1968:44) than intelligence.   Treating them for the moment as though they were comparable traits, it is evident that both are under polygenic control.   Proceeding with this in mind, Kagan (1969), in his initial reaction to Jensen's article, cites the difference in stature between rural and urban populations in Latin America to show the effect of environment on an inherited trait.   Hunt (1969), on his part, makes casual mention of stature in colonial Jamestown, Plymouth, and during the American Revolution, noting the radical changes that have taken place since that time.[3]

Other examples are well known and documented, but perhaps the changes in Sweden and the Low Countries in the past 100 years constitute a better example (Chamla 1964).   Stature certainly has a major genetic component.   Estimates concerning its heritability vary widely, although they average about .5, comparable to the average for IQ despite what Jensen claims.   For example, Kagan and Moss (1959) have found an average correlation of .43 between parents and offspring for IQ, and an average correlation of .36 for stature.   In the past 100 years, or about four generations, very little genetic change could have occurred, particularly when one considers the lack of evidence for strong selection.   However, in that time, the stature of the average adult male in many European countries has changed 4–5 in., or almost two standard deviations.   Since populational differences in IQ are at most about one standard deviation, we do not see why anyone would maintain that the same amount of nongenetic change could not occur where IQ is concerned—particularly when the trend of IQ increase is not only known but, in some cases, even greater than the trend for increase in stature.

The principal reason for the observed increase in stature appears to be a change in nutrition, particularly an increase in the

---

[3] Jensen (1969b) offers a rebuttal to the somewhat anecdotal accounts of Kagan and Hunt but, again, uses a single debatable account to generalize for all mankind.

amount of protein in the diet. A similar increase in stature is occurring in Japan (Kimura 1967), and there is a strong correlation between stature and protein intake (Takahashi 1966). Recently evidence has been accumulating to suggest that mental development can be markedly influenced by nutritional inadequacy—particularly where protein-calorie malnutrition occurs during the period in development when the brain is growing most rapidly (Cravioto, DeLicardie, and Birch 1966; Davison and Dobbing 1966; Eichenwald and Fry 1969).

Brain weight, amount of brain protein, and RNA increase linearly during the first year of human life—all being directly proportional to the increase in head circumference. The amount of brain DNA is regarded as a good indication of cell number and, although it largely ceases to increase at six months, it too maintains a direct relation to head circumference during the first year of life (Winick and Rosso 1969). With this in mind, it is of grim interest to note that in cases of severe malnutrition, head circumferences have been recorded that were two standard deviations below the mean for normal children of the same age. Brain weight and protein were reduced proportionately, while DNA content was reduced at least as much and in some cases more (Winick and Rosso 1969:776). In one instance, rehabilitation was tried on malnourished children and behavioral recovery was measured by the Gesell method. Children who were under six months of age on admission retained their deficit, leading to the conclusion (Cravioto and Robles 1965:463) that "there is a high possibility that at least the children severely malnourished during the first six months of their lives might retain a permanent mental deficit." In another instance, recovery of head circumference following early malnutrition lagged way behind other aspects of growth recovery (Graham 1968, esp. Fig. 3).

The studies cited above deal principally with the consequences of malnutrition in Latin America, but the record from Africa is equally clear: small fetal and neonatal brain sizes among the starving people of Biafra (Gans 1969), decreased cranial circumference and reduced brain weight among the malnourished of Uganda (Brown 1965, 1966), reduced cranial circumference and lower intelligence test scores in the Cape Coloured of South Africa. In the latter case, the reduction in circumference and test score was in comparison with a control population, also of

Cape Coloured, but one which was not suffering from severe malnutrition. The differences were statistically significant $(P = <.01)$ but, interestingly enough, there was no significant difference between the parents of the two groups (Stoch and Smythe 1963, 1968).

One could argue that the works we have mentioned deal principally with extremes of malnutrition, and in fact, Jensen does so, claiming that there is little extreme malnutrition in the United States. Yet with substantially more than half of the American black population living at or below the poverty level as defined by the US Department of Health, Education, and Welfare, with the shocking deprivation recently and belatedly brought to the attention of the US Congress (Javits 1969; Hollings and Jablow 1970), and with the obstacles to survival facing the American poor so graphically depicted by Coles (1969), it would be most surprising if malnutrition did *not* contribute something to the lowering of intelligence test scores in American Negroes—all other things being equal, which, of course, is not the case.

Before leaving strictly biological matters, we should note that deprivation need not be extreme for its consequences to show. Admittedly, these data are derived from studies on experimental animals rather than on human beings, but this can hardly justify ignoring their implications. Inadequate nutrition delays development of the myelin nerve sheaths in rats, and the deficit is not completely made up. The importance of this particular study is to be seen in the fact that the deprivation was that of the lower end of the "normal" range and did *not* constitute "starvation" (Dobbing 1964:508). Demonstration of the reduction in cell number of other brain tissues following early deprivation is equally clear (Dickerson 1968:335; Dobbing 1968:195). Not surprisingly, the behavioral consequences are also apparent (Eichenwald and Fry 1969:646):

> Protein deprivation in early life not only causes   .   .   .
> behavioral changes but also reduces the capacity of the
> experimental animal to learn at a later age. Furthermore,
> rats born of and suckled by malnourished mothers are simi-
> larly deficient in their learning capacity.

So far we have stressed the role of nutrition—particularly protein-calorie malnutrition—in the stunting of mental development.   Vitamin deficiency, illness susceptibility, and chronic ill-health all contribute to a malnutrition-disease syndrome (see Scrimshaw and Gordon 1968) which, given nothing else, should certainly lower performance levels on intelligence tests.   These factors alone can go a long way towards accounting for the differences in the tested intelligence of the world's populations, but they constitute only a part of the nongenetic background of testable mental performance.   However, strictly experiential factors can have an even more pronounced effect on intelligence test performance and may completely mask the nutritional and genetic factors.

Obviously there are many problems associated with estimating the heritability of behavioral traits.   Data on IQ tests derived from family studies do indicate a genetic component, although this may in fact be somewhat less than the heritability for physical traits.   The heritable component is extremely difficult to separate from the nonheritable component in assessing the results of most tests of complex behavior, and it is apparent that Jensen really does not make the effort to do so.   The cumulative interaction of particular types of experience with facets of biological maturation produces an elaboration that is extremely difficult to assess in terms of what percentage of which part is represented in the end-product.   This is what Hirsch meant when he referred to the nature-nurture problem as a "pseudo-question to which there is no answer," but if Jensen expects to demonstrate the credibility of his conclusions, it is a question to the solution of which he must direct research efforts more carefully planned and better controlled than any that have yet been undertaken or even proposed.[4]

Studies on the heritability of behavioral traits in *Drosophila* are frequently cited to bolster estimates on behavorial heritability in man, but, even ignoring the enormous phylogenetic gap, recent research has shown the heritability of the oft-mentioned geotactic and phototactic responses to be quite low.   Richmond (1969), for example, found the heritability of both to be less than .2 in all cases and not significantly different from .0 in one instance. Dobzhansky and Spassky (1969) found realized heritabilities for these traits to be below .1.

---

[4] This criticism of Jensen's approach has been eloquently and forcefully made by Stinchcombe (1969) and Deutsch (1969).

We should like to make it quite clear that we do not deny the existence of a genetic component that contributes to differences in performance on IQ tests—*within* a single population, where conditions of early experience and education are relatively similar. The differences, however, are less important than implied by Jensen.[5] For example, he has noted that there are significant correlations between the IQ scores of adopted children and their real parents, while correlations with their foster parents tend to be nonsignificant. However, he does not mention the fact that adopted children consistently display a substantially higher IQ than their biological parents. Skodak and Skeels (1949) found that the average IQ of the real mothers was 86 while that of their children adopted into other families was 106—well over a whole standard deviation higher. Surely this indicates that, with an improved socioeconomic background, one can accomplish in one generation a change that is greater than any difference between racial or religious groups in the United States. The overwhelming component of this difference is certainly environmental.

In their review of behavior genetics, Spuhler and Lindzey (1967) come to much the same conclusion with regard to racial differences in IQ. While citing many cases of behavioral differences among humans which have a known genetic basis, they show that there is a very significant relationship between IQ and educational expenditure. They conclude (1967:405): that "we do not *know* whether there are significant differences between races in the kinds and frequencies of polygenes controlling general intellectual ability." In our turn, we do not see how anyone would disagree with this statement, but would go further. We suggest that it is possible to explain all the measured differ-

[5] The interaction of heredity and environment in the development of a trait has been brought into focus by Stinchcombe (1969), but an even more important point is made by Gregg and Sanday in their contribution to this present volume. They note that heritability figures for given traits will vary in inverse proportion to the similarity of the environments of the populations being considered. This illustrates the generalization offered some time ago by Lerner (1958:63, italics his): "The heritability of a given trait may differ from one population to another, or vary in the same population at different times . . . *strictly speaking, any intra-genera-tion estimate of heritability is valid only for the particular generation of the specific population from which the data used in arriving at it derive.*" As Hirsch (1969:138) has phrased it, "Heredity is a property of populations and not of traits."

ences among major groups of men primarily by environmental factors, while noting, on the other hand, that it is not possible to provide genetic explanations which are evolutionarily plausible for most of these differences.

Within a given population there certainly is a spectrum of the inherited component of "intelligence," and there may be some association between this and certain demanding occupations, but from the perspective of biological evolution, the time depth of the professions in question is so shallow that little change in the genetic structure of the population can have occurred. Furthermore, Jensen's reaffirmation of the time-honored assumption that there are average differences in innate intelligence between social classes is also without demonstrable foundation and is very probably incorrect. At the top end of the social scale in America, the initial establishment of position may have had some relationship to ability, although demonstrable unprincipled ruthlessness was at least as important (Lundberg 1968). Once established, position is retained with little relation to the continuing presence of ability in the families in question and reproductive behavior is notoriously unrelated to the *intellectual* attributes of the partners chosen.

At the bottom of the social hierarchy there is one outstanding factor that makes suspect any claims concerning inherited ability. This factor is poverty. It is not unexpected that "in most settings there is a positive association between poor nutrition and poor social conditions" (Richardson 1968:355). And if this itself does not assure retardation in the development of mental ability, an atmosphere of social impoverishment certainly does. Inculcation into the ways of "the culture of poverty" (Lewis 1966) does not train people to perform well on IQ tests. Nor has ability or its lack had much to do with recruitment into the ranks of the extremely poor. Mere possession of a black skin was sufficient until quite recently and, with the addition of certain geographic provisos, still is.

One of Jensen's basic assumptions is made explicit in the comment printed with his approval in *The New York Times Magazine* (Sept. 21, 1969, p. 14). In this he clearly regards "intelligence as the ability to adapt to civilization," adding that "races differ in this ability according to the civilizations in which they live." Building on this, he further assumes that "the Stanford-Binet IQ test measures the ability to adapt to Western civilization," an ability in which he claims American Negroes to be inferior to "Orientals," with the clear implication that, as a blanket category, they are far less well-endowed than American whites. For an educated man to hold such beliefs is regrettable, but for a presumed "scientist" to be allowed to publish them in a popular journal without informed editorial supervision is an example of the unfortunate failure of intellectual responsibility.

First of all, "Western civilization," if this is indeed a valid category in this context, is largely a product of the Industrial Revolution and has a maximum time depth of little more than two centuries. Even if natural selection had been operating at maximum efficiency during this time, it would have been hard put to change a polygenic trait as much as a full standard deviation for an entire population. In terms of actual reproductive performance, there is little reason to believe that the intellectually highly endowed were in fact favored to such an extent. If it is fair to make such sweeping judgments, we can make a case for the fact that most of the labor roles which were created by and ensured the success of the Industrial Revolution—and, hence, Western civilization—required relatively little learning and no creative decision-making on the part of their occupants. This, of course, is why child labor was practical until it was outlawed. In terms of the kind of folk knowledge and unwritten tradition necessary for survival, it is perhaps fair to claim that the average European (i. e., peasant) of the sixteenth century lived a life that had more elements of similarity with that of the average West African than it did with that of the descendants of either one in the Europe or America of the twentieth century.

Obviously in saying this we are making a value judgment that cannot be proven one way or the other, but, nevertheless, it would appear to square with the data of both anthropology and history rather better than Jensen's suggestion that races differ in intelligence "according to the civilizations in which they live." Considering the fact that, with a few numerically unimportant exceptions, all human populations now live under conditions characterized by cultural adaptations—"civilizations" in Jensen's terms—that are radically different from those of their lineal predecessors only a few thousand years ago (and often much less), it is reasonable to conclude that *no* races are really adapted to the "civilizations in which they live."

The time is not so long past when instructing Negroes in the mechanics of reading and writing was contrary to law in parts of the American South. Educational opportunities remain drastically substandard, and there is scarcely a rudimentary form of the tradition in child-rearing, so characteristic of the middle and upper-middle classes, which promotes literacy as the key to worldly success. When used to compare groups with different cultural backgrounds, the Stanford-Binet IQ test is less a comparative measure of ability than an index of enculturation into the ways of the American middle class. Since Negroes have been systematically (see the account in Woodward 1966) denied entrance to the middle-class world, it is not surprising that their learned behavior is measurably different from that on which the IQ test is based. Certainly before the results of IQ tests can be taken as indicating inherited differences in ability, some cognizance should be taken of the effect of tester expectation on performance (Rosenthal 1966), or motivation in its various aspects (Katz 1967), and of the results of nonverbal tests where conceptual styles of the groups being studied are markedly different (Cohen 1969).

Finally, Jensen's assertion that intelligence or brain differences must exist among the "races" of man is an argument by analogy which ends up assuming what he presumably was trying to demonstrate. As he notes, separate breeding isolates will very likely show differences on some genetic characteristics which will be due to the various evolutionary forces. In most cases, these differences, if at all considerable, will coincide with differences in selective forces to which the populations are subject. To conclude from this perfectly reasonable genetic statement, as Jensen does, that it is "practically axiomatic" that two populations will be different in *any* characteristic having high heritability (1969a:80) and, ergo, that the races of man differ in their genetic capacities for intelligence or in the genetic properties of their brains is simply a non sequitur. Certainly it is contrary to all we have learned from evolutionary biology. All human populations have 10 fingers, 10 toes, 2 eyes, and 32 teeth per individual. These all have high heritability and some variability within human isolates, but are constant between isolates. This is primarily due to the operation of natural selection, a factor which Jensen deemphasizes.

Behavior or brain function is obviously under the control of many loci, and, equally obviously, it is subject to the influence

Alger—Cult.Anthropology WC—7

of natural selection. If differences exist at these loci among human populations, these differences would be correlated with differences in the forces of selection. These in turn would be reflected in the cultural and behavioral attributes designed to counteract them. Within any continent there are as many differences in cultural and behavioral adaptation as there are between continents.

However, implicit and even explicit in much of behavior genetics is the assumption that cultural differences are caused by genetic differences. The anthropological findings that cultural differences represent responses to varying environmentally imposed selective forces are simply ignored. Selective force distributions do not neatly coincide as a rule. Some may covary in some areas, some may show crosscutting distributions, and others may vary completely at random with respect to each other. Given this situation, we have elsewhere suggested that, in order to make sense out of human biological variation, the typological gestalt of the race concept be abandoned and human adaptation be studied trait by trait in the contexts where the relevant selective forces have been at work (Livingstone 1962, 1964; Brace 1964a, b). We cannot resist adding the comment that this approach, if taken seriously, can completely defuse the potentially explosive situation which Jensen has created.

Jensen (1969a:89) cites the Harlows (Harlow and Harlow 1962) to the effect that if the average IQ were lower and thus fewer geniuses were produced, then there would be fewer people to make inventions and discoveries and thus cultural evolution would have been slower. We suggest that, just as mutation rate does not control the speed of biological evolutionary change, neither does the frequency of the occurrence of genius have anything to do with the rate of cultural evolution. We can even offer a converse suggestion and raise the suspicion that levels of cultural complexity are inversely related to IQ. Survival takes less innate wit for the socially and economically privileged than it does for those to whom culture does not offer ready-made solutions for most of life's problems. It is possible that the average level of intelligence is highest among populations where culture is least complex. Post-Pleistocene food preparation techniques, including, especially, pots in which boiling was easy and common, have rendered the human dentition of far less importance to survival than before. The sharp reductions in the Post-

Pleistocene human face are concentrated in the dentition and have proceeded farthest in just those people whose forbears have been longest associated with "high civilization" (Brabant and Twiesselmann 1964:55). It is not possible that supraregional political and economic organization increased the survival chances of any given individual without regard for his inherited ability? Why then should we not expect an average lowering of basic intelligence to accumulate under such circumstances? We offer this solely as an hypothesis for possible testing. Jensen, on the other hand, feels that failure to test the hypothesis that Negroes are intellectually inferior for genetic reasons may constitute "our society's greatest injustice to Negro Americans" (1969c:6). Unless there is a latent racist bias to the kind of research Jensen feels is urgent,[6] it is difficult to see why the testing of the hypothesis we have outlined above is not considered at least of equal importance with the testing of its converse, and yet the possibility is not even mentioned, let alone seriously entertained. Ironically, the possible consequences of our failure to take this issue seriously will be enormous for *all* Americans, but particularly for non-Negro Americans, i. e., "whites."

Knowledge of both cultural and biological dimensions is required for a full understanding of the human condition. The stress on "geneticism" (to use Medawar's word again) should be tempered by an insistence that the environmental component be thoroughly controlled. Certainly as much effort and sophistication should be devoted to this task as to comparative performance assessments. Jensen's work is conspicuously lacking in this regard. As such, it is the logical antithesis to the old environmentalist thesis. Perhaps the synthesis will contain the reasonable parts of each.

Finally, in the words of Jensen (1969:78), "If a society completely believed and practiced the ideal of treating every person as an individual, it would be hard to see why there should be any

---

[6] The regretful comment made by a collaborator and admirer of Jensen's experimental research is worth quoting here: "I believe the impact of Jensen's article was destructive; that it has had negative implications for the struggle against racism and for the improvement of the educational system. The conclusions he draws are, I believe, unwarranted by the existing data and reflect a consistent bias towards a racist hypothesis" (Deutsch 1969:525).

problems about 'race' per se." Unfortunately Jensen ignores this ideal in practice and, in the absence of adequate control, insists on treating a substantial portion of the American population as though a stereotype were sufficient and as though the individual could be ignored. In effect this guarantees that there *will* continue to be problems about race per se and that Jensen and his like will only intensify them.

References Cited

Ardrey, R.
   1966   The Territorial Imperative. New York: Delta.

Bajema, C. J.
   1963   Estimation of the Direction and Intensity of Natural Selection in Relation to Human Intelligence by Means of the Intrinsic Rate of Natural Increase. Eugenics Quarterly 10:175–187.

Barzun, Jacques
   1965   Race: A Study in Superstition. New York: Harper Torchbooks.

Birch, Herbert G.
   1968   Boldness and Judgment in Behavior Genetics. In Science and the Concept of Race. M. Mead, T. Dobzhansky, E. Tobach, and R. Light, eds. New York: Columbia University Press.

Brabant, H., and F. Twiesselmann
   1964   Observations sur l'Evolution de la Denture permanente humain en Europe Occidentale. Bulletin du Groupement International pour la Recherche scientifique en Stomatologie 7:11–84.

Brace, C. L.
   1964a   The Concept or Race. Current Anthropology 5:313–320.
   1964b   A Non-Racial Approach Toward the Understanding of Human Diversity. In The Concept of Race. M. F. A. Montagu, ed. New York: Free Press.

Brown, Roy E.
   1965   Decreased Brain Weight in Malnutrition and Its Implications. East Africa Medical Journal 42:584–595.
   1966   Organ Weight in Malnutrition with Special Reference to Brain Weight. Developmental Medicine and Child Neurology 8:512–522.

Chamla, M–C.
   1964   L'accroisement de la Stature en France de 1800 à 1960; Comparison avec les pays d'Europe occidentale. Bulletins

et Mémoires de la Société d'Anthropologie de Paris, Série 11, 6:201–278.

Cohen, Rosalie A.
1969 Conceptual Styles, Culture Conflict, and Nonverbal Tests of Intelligence. American Anthropologist 71:828–856.

Coles, Robert
1969 Still Hungry in America. Cleveland: North American Library.

Cravioto, J., E. R. DeLicardie, and H. G. Birch
1966 Nutrition, Growth and Neuro-Integrative Development: An Experimental and Ecologic Study. Pediatrics 38:319–372.

Cravioto, J., and B. Robles
1965 Evolution of Adaptive and Motor Behavior During Rehabilitation from Kwashiorkor. American Journal of Orthopsychiatry 35:449–464.

Crow, James F., James V. Neel, and Curt Stern
1967 Racial Studies: Academy States Position on Call for New Research. Science 158:892–893.

Davison, A. N., and J. Dobbing
1968 Myelination as a Vulnerable Period in Brain Development. British Medical Bulletin 22:40–44.

Dickerson, J. W. T.
1968 The Relation of the Timing and Severity of Undernutrition to Its Effect on the Chemical Structure of the Central Nervous System. In Calorie Deficiencies and Protein Deficiencies. R. A. McCance and E. M. Widdowson, eds. London: J. A. Churchill.

Dobbing, J.
1964 The Influence of Nutrition on the Development and Myelination of the Brain. Proceedings of the Royal Society of London, Series B, Biological Sciences 159:503–509.
1968 Effects of Experimental Undernutrition on Development of the Nervous System. In Malnutrition, Learning and Behavior. N. S. Scrimshaw and J. E. Gordon, eds. Cambridge: MIT Press.

Dobzhansky, T., and B. Spassky
1969 Artificial and Natural Selection for Two Behavioral Traits in Drosophila pseudoobscura. Proceedings of the National Academy of Sciences 62:75–80.

Edson, Lee
1969 jensenism, n. the theory that IQ is largely determined by the genes. The New York Times Magazine, August 31, pp. 10–11, 40–41, 43–47.

Eichenwald, Heinz F., and Peggy Crooke Fry
1969 Nutrition and Learning. Science 163:644–648.

Gans, Bruno
1969 A Biafran Relief Mission. The Lancet 1969–I:660–665.

Graham, G. G.
1968 The Later Growth of Malnourished Infants: Effects of Age, Severity and Subsequent Diet. In Calorie Deficiencies and Protein Deficiencies. R. A. McCance and E. M. Widdowson, eds. London: J. A. Churchill.

Hirsch, Jerry
1961 Genetics of Mental Disease Symposium, 1960: Discussion: The Role of Assumptions in the Analysis and Interpretation of Data. American Journal of Orthopsychiatry 31:474–480.
1963 Behavior Genetics and Individuality Understood: Behaviorism's Counterfactual Dogma Blinded the Behavioral Sciences to the Significance of Meiosis. Science 142:1436–1442.
1967a ed. Behavior Genetic Analysis. New York: McGraw-Hill.
1967b Behavior-Genetic, or "Experimental," Analysis: The Challenge of Science Versus the Lure of Technology. American Psychologist 22:118–130.
1968 Behavior-Genetic Analysis and the Study of Man. In Science and the Concept of Race. M. Mead, T. Dobzhansky, E. Tobach, and R. Light, eds. New York: Columbia University Press.

Hollings, Ernest F., as told by Paul Jablow
1970 We Must Wipe out Hunger in America. Good Housekeeping, January, pp. 68–69, 144–146.

Hunt, J. McV.
1969 Has Compensatory Education Failed? Has It Been Attempted? Harvard Educational Review 39:278–300.

Javits, Jacob
1969 Hunger in America. Playboy, December, p. 147.

Jensen, Arthur R.
1969a How Much Can We Boost IQ and Scholastic Achievement? Harvard Educational Review 39:1–123.
1969c Arthur Jensen Replies. Psychology Today 3:4, 6.

Jordan, Winthrop D.
1968 White over Black: American Attitudes Toward the Negro, 1550–1812, Chapel Hill: University of North Carolina Press.

Kagan, Jerome S.
    1969   Inadequate Evidence and Illogical Conclusions.   Harvard
    Educational Review 39:274–277.

Kagan, J. S., and H. A. Moss
    1959   Parental Correlates of Child's IQ and Height: A Cross-
    Validation of the Berkeley Growth Study Results.   Child De-
    velopment 30:325–332.

Katz, Irwin
    1967   Some Motivational Determinants of Racial Differences in
    Intellectual Achievement.   International Journal of Psy-
    chology 2:1–12.

Kimura, K.
    1967   A Consideration of the Secular Trend in Japanese for
    Height and Weight by a Graphic Method, American Jour-
    nal of Physical Anthropology 27:89–94.

Lewis, Oscar
    1966   The Culture of Poverty.   Scientific American 215:19–25.

Livingstone, Frank B.
    1962   On the Nonexistence of Human Races.   Current Anthro-
    pology 3:279–281.

    1964   On the Nonexistence of Human Races.   In the Concept
    of Race.   Ashley Montagu, ed. New York: Free Press of
    Glencoe.

    1969   Genetics, Ecology and the Origins of Incest and Exogamy.
    Current Anthropology 10:45–61.

Lorenz, Konrad
    1966   On Aggression.   New York: Bantam.

Lundberg, Ferdinand
    1968   The Rich and the Super-Rich: A Study in the Power of
    Money Today.   New York: Lyle Stuart.

Medawar, P. B.
    1961   The Future of Man.   New York: Mentor.

Morris, Desmond
    1968   The Naked Ape.   New York: McGraw-Hill.
    1969   The Human Zoo.   New York: McGraw-Hill.

Osofsky, Gilbert
    1967   The Burden of Race: A Documentary History of Negro-
    White Relations in America.   New York: Harper and Row.

Putnam, Carleton
    1961   Race and Reason: A Yankee View.   Washington: Public
    Affairs Press.

Richardson, Stephen A.
    1968   The Influence of Social-Environmental and Nutritional
           Factors on Mental Ability.   In Malnutrition, Learning and
           Behavior.   N. S. Scrimshaw and J. E. Gordon, eds. Cam-
           bridge: MIT Press.

Richmond, R. C.
    1969   Heritability of Phototactic and Geotactic Responses in
           Drosophila pseudoobscura.   American Naturalist 103:315–
           316.

Roberts, D. F.
    1967   Incest, Inbreeding and Mental Abilities.   British Medical
           Journal 4:336–337.

Rosenthal, Robert
    1966   Experimenter Effects in Behavioral Research.   New York:
           Appleton-Century-Crofts.

Scrimshaw, Nevin S., and John E. Gordon (eds.)
    1968   Malnutrition, Learning and Behavior.   Cambridge: MIT
           Press.

Skodak, M., and H. M. Skeels
    1949   A Final Follow-up Study of One Hundred Adopted Chil-
           dren.   Journal of Genetic Psychology 75:85–125.

Smith, Samuel Stanhope
    1965   An Essay on the Causes of Variety of Complexion and
           Figure in the Human Species (reprint of the 1810 version).
           Winthrop D. Jordan, ed. Cambridge: The Belknap Press.

Spuhler, J. N., and G. Lindzey
    1967   Racial Differences in Behavior.   In Behavior-Genetic
           Analysis.   Jerry Hirsch, ed. New York: McGraw-Hill.

Stanton, William
    1960   The Leopard's Spots: Scientific Attitudes Toward Race
           in America, 1815–59.   Chicago: University of Chicago
           Press.

Stoch, Mavis B., and P. M. Smythe
    1963   Does Undernutrition During Infancy Inhibit Brain
           Growth and Subsequent Intellectual Development?   Ar-
           chives of Diseases of Childhood 38:546–552.
    1968   Undernutrition During Infancy, and Subsequent Brain
           Growth and Intellectual Development.   In Malnutrition,
           Learning and Behavior.   N. S. Scrimshaw and J. E. Gordon,
           eds. Cambridge: MIT Press.

Stocking, George W., Jr.
    1968   Race, Culture and Evolution: Essays in the History of
           Anthropology.   New York: Free Press.

Takahashi, E.
   1966   Growth and Environmental Factors in Japan.   Human Biology 38:112–130.

Tiger, Lionel
   1969   Men in Groups.   New York: Random House.

Watson, J. B.
   1924   Behaviorism.   New York: W. W. Norton.

Winick, Myron, and Pedro Rosso
   1969   Head Circumference and Cellular Growth of the Brain in Normal and Marasmic Children.   The Journal of Pediatrics 74:774–778.

Woodward, C. Vann
   1966   The Strange Career of Jim Crow.   New York: Galaxy Book.

Supplementary References

Deutsch, Martin
   1969   Happenings on the Way Back to the Forum: Social Science, IQ and Race Differences Revisited.   Harvard Educational Review 39:523–557.

Fehr, F. S.
   1969   Critique of Hereditarian Accounts of "Intelligence" and Contrary Findings: A Reply to Jensen.   Harvard Educational Review 39:571–580.

Harlow, H. F., and M. K. Harlow.
   1962   The Mind of Man.   In Yearbook of Science and Technology, pp. 31–39.

Hirsch, Jerry
   1969   Biosocial Hybrid Vigor Sought, Babel Discovered.   Review of Genetics: Second of a Series on Biology and Behavior, edited by David C. Glass.   Contemporary Psychology 14:138–139.

Jensen, Arthur R.
   1969b   Reducing the Heredity-Environment Uncertainty: A Reply.   Harvard Educational Review 39:449–483.

Lerner, I. Michael
   1958   The Genetic Basis of Selection.   New York: John Wiley.

Light, Richard J., and Paul V. Smith.
     1969　Social Allocation Models of Intelligence: A Methodologi-
          cal Inquiry.　Harvard Educational Review 39:484–510.
Stinchcombe, Arthur L.
     1969　Environment: The Cumulation of Effects Is Yet to be
          Understood.　Harvard Educational Review 39:511–522.

On The Continuing Revival of Scientific Racism † *

T HE publication of an article entitled "I.Q." by Richard Herrnstein of Harvard in the September 1971 issue of *The Atlantic
Monthly* demonstrates that despite extensive scientific refutation
the doctrines of jensenism are still with us, 2 years after the
American Anthropological Association took a public stand
against them.　(For one such refutation, see Brace and others,
Race and Intelligence, American Anthropological Association,
1971).

Two years ago, Arthur Jensen summarized his conclusion as
follows:

> There are intelligence genes, which are found in populations
> in different proportions, somewhat like the distributions of
> blood types.　The number of intelligence genes seems to be
> lower, overall, in the black population than in the white
> [*New York Times,* Aug 31, 1969].

More recently, William Shockley, a Stanford University electrical
engineering professor, echoed Jensen's views in his address to
the American Psychological Association.　Shockley said, in part,
that:

> Nature has color-coded groups of individuals so that statis-
> tically reliable predictions of their adaptability to intellec-
> tually rewarding and effective lives can easily be made and

† By James C. Faris, Anthony S.
Kroch and Peter Newcomer, University of Connecticut.

* Reproduced by permission of the
American Anthropological Association
from AAA Newsletter, Vol. 13, No. 2,
1972, and the authors.

profitably used by the pragmatic man in the street [*Boston Sunday Globe,* Sept 1971].

He also proposed as a "thinking exercise" that the government consider paying people with low IQ's to submit to sterilization.

Richard Herrnstein takes the psychological theories of Jensen and turns them into a social philosophy for mass dissemination by the popular press. He sees our society as one in which the condition of oppressed groups is coming ever more to depend on genetically determined low intelligence:

> Against this background, the main significance of intelligence testing is what it says about a society built around human inequalities. The message is so clear that it can be made in the form of a syllogism:
>
> 1. If differences in mental abilities are inherited, and
> 2. If success requires those abilities, and
> 3. If earnings and prestige depend on success,
> 4. Then social standing (which reflects earnings and prestige) will be based to some extent on inherited differences among people [*Atlantic Monthly,* Sept 1971, pp 58, 63].

The syllogism implies that in times to come, the tendency to be unemployed may run in the genes of a family about as certainly as bad teeth do now [Ibid, p 63].

The gradient of occupations is, then, a natural measure of value and scarcity. And beneath this gradient is a scale of inborn ability which is what gives the syllogism its unique potency [Ibid, p 64].

Herrnstein relegates three groups to the bottom of the social pyramid as genetically inferior; namely, workers, women and racial minorities:

> As far as IQ alone is concerned, virtually anyone can be, for example, a welder, but half of mankind (the half below IQ 100) is not eligible for auditing, even if the brightest welder may equal the brightest auditor in IQ [Ibid, p 51].
>
> Highly bright boys were easier to locate than highly bright girls. And the disparity increased slightly with age, suggesting that whatever the IQ is, boys maintain it better than girls [Ibid, p 51].

In Aldous Huxley's *Brave New World* it was malevolent or misguided science that created the "alphas," "gammas," and the other distinct types of people. But nature itself is more likely to do the job or something similar, as the less well-known but far more prescient book by Michael Young, *The Rise of the Meritocracy,* has depicted. Young's social science-fiction tale of the antimeritocratic upheavals of the early twenty-first century is the perfect setting for his timely neologism, the word "meritocracy." The troubles he anticipated and that the syllogism explains, like Edward Banfield, whose book *The Unheavenly City* describes the increasingly chronic lower class in America's central cities. While Sunday supplements and popular magazines crank out horror stories about genetic engineering (often with anxious but self-serving testimonials from geneticists), our society may be sorting itself willy-nilly into inherited castes [Ibid, p 63].

Herrnstein, Jensen and Shockley rely on their academic positions to get wide, uncritical dissemination of their views. The more the press spreads their ideas, the easier it becomes for reactionary forces in society to justify as inevitable oppression and repression. Alvin Poussaint, a Black doctor at Harvard Medical School, made this point clearly in a recent newspaper article. He said:

> Richard Herrnstein, professor of psychology at Harvard, may or may not be a racist. Perhaps it doesn't matter. Whether he intended it or not, he has become an enemy of black people and his pronouncements are a threat to the survival of every black person in America [*Boston Globe,* Dec 3, 1971].

> The effect of his theories is to play down the significance of socio-economic and racist factors that are the main causes of the present oppressed condition of blacks and others in this country. With the unwitting psychological support of Jensen and Herrnstein, the guards at Attica will find it easier to pull the trigger on rebellious black prisoners [Ibid].

The editors of *The Atlantic Monthly* also understand the import of Herrnstein's article. They conclude their introduction to the article (p 44) with the following:

> *The Atlantic* believes that it is not only *possible* but *necessary* to have public discussion of important, albeit painful,

social issues. The subject of intelligence is such an issue—important because social legislation must come to terms with actual human potentialities, painful because the actualities are sometimes not what we vainly hope.

Dr. Poussaint's assessment of the dangerousness of Herrnstein's theories is not overdrawn. For example, the *Indiana Teacher,* a magazine read by most teachers in that state, devoted a full page of its fall 1971 issue to a favorable report of Herrnstein's conclusions. How much easier Herrnstein's article makes it for school authorities and racist teachers to blame the failures of the schools on the children.

The work of Herrnstein and his colleagues cannot be viewed simply as erroneous scholarship. Their views have political consequences and intentions. Jensen opposes compensatory education, Shockley argues for eugenics and Herrnstein opposes egalitarian social movements. Ignoring the weight of scientific evidence, they reinforce racial and class prejudices. These comments of Marvin Harris apply directly to their views:

> Many raciological studies employing the major geographic races as basic taxonomic units reinforce popular but genetically false stereotypes about pure races and racial essences. Failure to distinguish between the scientific sense of geographic race and the popular, demagogic sense may reasonably be construed by concerned citizens as a political act [*Culture, Man, and Nature,* p 96].

Intelligent and educated men like Herrnstein and Jensen are badly needed by the beneficiaries of racist and anti-working class ideology in modern American society. Through the publications which spread them, their theories "educate" the public to accept unemployment and the oppression of minorities. Billions of dollars in additional profits have accrued to the industrial elite through the maintenance of a pool of unemployed workers (disproportionately Black and Latin in composition) to keep down the wages of the employed through the provision of inferior services to Black and White working-class communities, and through the use of racist and male supremacist ideology to justify paying Black and women workers less than White males for the same work.

On the basis of the above discussion, we urge support for and passage of the Resolution Against Theories of Race, Sex and Class

Inferiority, which by vote of the AAA Council meeting, November, 1971, will be submitted to the membership for a mail ballot in the coming weeks.

Social Class and Bar Behavior During an Urban Festival † *

VERY little seems to be known about who actually participates in "community" festivals. Social scientists as well as laymen apparently assume that people generally, regardless of status in the community, more or less participate in and benefit from such festivals. In discussing crowds in general, for example, Davis states: "The individuals who constitute any particular crowd . . . are together by accident. . . . Having no organization and being ephemeral, the crowd does not select its participants. . . . Necessarily, the members . . . are drawn *from all walks of life* and are present in the situation only because, in pursuing their private ends, they have to make use of common conveniences . . . " (italics added).[1] And in their view of "conventional crowds" (including institutionalized festivals), Killian and Turner state that these ". . . function in facilitating the resolution of cultural conflict,"[2] thereby implying that community solidarity is temporarily restored.

It must be obvious from daily observations, however, that such views, while democratic, are anything but accurate. Every community has its distinctive geographical and social boundary lines between rich and poor and between majority and minority ethnic

† Richard J. Ossenberg is an Associate Professor of Sociology at the University of Calgary, Calgary, Alberta, Canada. He wishes to acknowledge the generous assistance of Geoffrey Caldwell, a graduate student in Sociology at The University of Calgary, in preparing this paper.

* "Reproduced by permission of Society for Applied Anthropology from Human Organization, Vol. 28, No. 1, 1969." and the author.

[1] Kingsley Davis, Human Society, The MacMillan Company, New York, 1949, p. 350.

[2] Ralph H. Turner and Lewis Killian, Collective Behavior, Prentice-Hall, Englewood Cliffs, New Jersey, 1957, p. 155.

groups. Certainly these lines are not absolute; but there is bound to be disproportionate representation of the various status groups in the crowds that gather for different community activities, whether for nocturnal recreation or Saturday shopping or something else. The "red-light district" thus attracts a rather different clientele than more exclusive entertainment areas, and "hock-shops" and second-hand stores are not frequented by the same persons who patronize exclusive specialty and department stores.

Certain social groups also are known to be more likely than others to participate in relatively uncontrolled forms of collective behavior such as lynchings, race riots, and political separatist movements.[3] On the other hand, it is argued that community festivals (such as the Calgary Stampede discussed here) function specifically to enhance community solidarity through generalized participation in tension-release behavior.[4] An historical example was the "King-of-Fools" festival of the Middle Ages which was subsidized by the aristocracy who actively participated in the fun and games, but which featured a temporary inversion of the class structure. The annual Japanese village festivals also appear to have the same purpose and consist of extremely unorthodox behavior as well as inversion of the class structure and other releases from everyday constrictions.[5] Similar ceremonies in urbanized societies have not received, to my knowledge, as much attention from social scientists. As a result, we lack adequate studies of the Oktober-Fest of Germany, the Mardi Gras of New Orleans, the Winter Carnival of Quebec, and the Calgary Stampede of Alberta, not to mention thousands of other

3 See, for example, Durward Pruden, "A Sociological Study of a Texas Lynching," Studies in Sociology, Vol. 1, No. i, 1963, pp. 3–9; Howard Odum, Folk, Region and Society: Selected Papers of Howard W. Odum (Catherine Jocher, et al., editors and arrangers), The University of North Carolina Press, Chapel Hill, 1964, pp. 37–38; E. V. Essien-Udom, Black Nationalism, University of Chicago Press, Chicago, 1962; and R. J. Ossenberg, "The Conquest Revisited: Another Look at Canadian Dualism," The Canadian Review of Sociology and Anthropology, Vol. 4, No. 4, Nov., 1967, pp. 201–218.

4 Turner and Killian, op. cit., pp. 153–154.

5 William Caudill, "Observations on the Cultural Context of Japanese Psychiatry," in Marvin K. Opler (ed.), Culture and Mental Health, The Macmillan Company, New York, 1959, pp. 218–219.

community festivals in the United States, Canada, and Western Europe.

Both the paucity of analyzed cases and the implicit acceptance by many sociologists and anthropologists of a functionalist view of the integrating effect of community ritual suggested the present study of selective participation. It is based on observations made during a systematic "pub-crawl" on two evenings of the week-long Stampede which is held every July in Calgary, Alberta, the fastest-growing city of Canada. The study was prompted by curiosity about the role of social stratification in encouraging or discouraging participation in this type of collective behavior, which would be designated by Davis as a "planned expressive group" and by Turner and Killian as a "conventional crowd." [6] From a theoretical point of view, it was assumed that variations in the social class structure of communities largely determine differentiated participation in planned community festivals. In *Gemeinschaft* communities where "mechanical solidarity" within a small and homogeneous population prevails, generalized participation in festival occasions is probably usual. In urban *Gesellechaft* communities, however, social class structure seems too complex to expect the same general response.

In Canada and the United States we have considerable evidence pertaining to the "life-styles" of the different socio-economic classes. In general, for example, it can be said that middle-class attitudes abound with inhibitions and taboos against aggressive and deviant behavior, while people in lower socio-economic class positions are more concerned with immediate gratifications that sometimes explode into temporary violence. On the other hand, members of the middle class are more sensitive to legal and other restrictive norms and consequently may be more responsive to the relaxation of social controls represented by the relatively lax enforcement of those norms during community festivals like the Stampede.

It is therefore hypothesized that participation in the Calgary Stampede (as measured by bar behavior) will be high among middle-class people and low among lower-class people. More specifically, patrons of middle-class drinking establishments during the Calgary Stampede will exhibit more festival-related ag-

6 Davis, op. cit., p. 355; Turner and
Killian, op. cit., p. 153.

gressive/expressive behavior than patrons of lower-class drinking establishments.

Background and Methods

The annual Calgary Stampede features a rodeo and related "cowboy" themes as central attractions.   There is also the usual carnival midway (larger than most), and street dancing is common.   In addition, there is a general relaxation of formal social controls, with fewer arrests than usual of ambitious tipplers, "car-cowboys," women of ill repute, and the like.

The Stampede is actively promoted in local and national mass media and has become reasonably well known throughout most of North America.   As a result, it attracts a generous influx of tourists from the western United States.   Since its founding in 1912, it has undergone the usual transition from agricultural fair and exhibition to urban commercial carnival which has accompanied the rapid growth of cities.   The population of Calgary has increased from about 20,000 in 1912 to around 350,000 in 1966.   Symbolic of this transition was the new "salute to petroleum" theme in 1966, which brought a large and expensive petroleum exhibit to the Stampede grounds.   The Western Cowboy and farm themes are still present, but they are somewhat obscured by the many diverse features of the contemporary festival.   In 1966, attendance exceeded 600,000, establishing a record.

In order to study one important aspect of the festival behavior, nine beer parlors and cocktail lounges [7]—representing a cross-section of social-class-related drinking establishments in Calgary—were visited on two separate evenings during Stampede Week.   The research team consisted of the author and a graduate student.   I had gained some knowledge previously of the social class characteristics and behavioral patterns of customers usually found in these establishments through periodic visits in the year prior to the Stampede festival.   During this year I had casually observed behavior in all of these bars in the process of searching for a "shorthand" method of discovering social class structure in Calgary.   That is, as other researchers have suggested, bars are an effective informal index of the social struc-

[7] Distinctions are made in Calgary between "beer parlor" which may only serve beer, and "licensed lounge" which may serve any alcoholic beverage, including beer.   In general, beer parlors tend to serve a lower-class clientele while licensed lounges tend to attract the middle-class.

ture in which they exist.[8]   In this connection, each of the drinking establishments was visited on at least three different occasions, including both weekdays and Saturdays.

The establishments selected for study are located in the central business district, as well as the surrounding fringe area, or "Zone-in-transition," which contains the cheaper hotels and entertainment areas found in most medium-to-large cities in North America.   This fringe area, which includes Calgary's priority urban renewal project, is populated by economically-deprived people. Unlike many older industrial cities, Calgary's ecological pattern also includes deprived areas in what would normally be "affluent" sectors of other cities.   Thus, in areas equidistant from the city center can be found *nouveau riche* suburbs as well as deprived and ramshackle neighborhoods.   The two types are of course separated, and the annexation by the city of Calgary of formerly rural and presently deprived communities largely accounts for this ecological anomaly.

The bars that were visited were chosen both because of my knowledge of their usual social composition and activities and because of their proximity to the Stampede Grounds, thus assuring a maximum sample of celebrants.   The sample was then divided into "class" groups as follows: two upper-class; three middle-class; and four lower-class.   The definition of the social class identity of the bars is admittedly subjective and informal but, I believe, valid.

The upper-class establishments are usually patronized by the elite oil and ranching group as well as the *nouveau riche* and the occasional white-collar couple celebrating an anniversary. The middle-class bars are patronized by clerical workers, small businessmen, and generally middle-range employees of the larger local firms, with occasional laborers drifting in.   The lower-class bars are the clearest in definition.   They are patronized by service personnel, laborers, winos and deprived Indians as well as by members of newly-arrived immigrant groups.   The class distribution of bars in the sample was "biased" toward the lower-

[8] See, for example, John Dollard, "Drinking Mores of the Social Classes," in Alcohol Studies and Society, Yale University, Center of Alcohol Studies, 1954, esp. p. 96; and Marshall B. Clinard, Sociology of Deviant Behavior Today, Holt, Rinehart and Winston, Inc., New York, 1963, pp. 331–332.

status groups. Calgary has a higher proportion of white-collar and professional workers than most cities and if the choice of bars had been based on this consideration, only two or three lower-class bars would have been included. My knowledge of composition and activities of the lower-class bars, however, was greater than that of the middle and upper-class bars and the choice was made accordingly.

Being rather conservative with respect to confirming our hypothesis, we selected two evenings in which cross-class interaction could reasonably be expected to be maximized: namely, the first night of Stampede week, and the night before the final day of festivities. We reasoned that these evenings, unlike the "in-between" nights, would reveal the most frantic collective search for gratifications and, if only accidentally, result in cross-class contacts. The anticipation of festivities is so great in Calgary during the few days prior to the Stampede that the first "green light" day witnesses the greatest crowds, both at the rodeo grounds and in the bars. The last day is perceived as the "last chance;" it was assumed that celebrants would then attempt to "let loose" one last time.

We chose drinking establishments rather than other sites of festival activity for the following reasons:

1. We felt that participant observation would be more easily facilitated in bars than "on the streets" or at the Stampede Rodeo grounds;

2. It was reasonable to assume that inhibitions concerning cross-class interaction are more easily dissolved with the aid of alcoholic beverages;

3. We theorized that excessive drinking represents a form of deviant behavior which becomes "normal" and even goal-directed during many community festivals; and

4. We enjoy beer.

Within the bars, we concentrated on:

1. The apparent social class composition of patrons;

2. The wearing of costumes suitable to the "Western cowboy theme" of the Calgary Stampede;

3. The noise level (including the spontaneity and intent of expressive vocalization) ; and

4. Physical and social interaction, including evidences of aggression and general themes of conversation.

Findings

Lower-class establishments.   In three of the four beer parlors visited, activities could be described as "business as usual."   Beer parlors in general are lower-class, and the patrons appeared to be the same as those who frequent these establishments throughout the year.   Most of the customers were dressed in their normal work clothes or service-trade uniforms.   If anything, there were fewer patrons than usual.

Beer parlors normally abound in service personnel, laborers, marginal drifters, and members of economically-depressed minority groups, most of whom live within walking distance.   Conversations generally consist of work problems, family problems, sex exploits, cars, dialogue with self (the drifters), and general backslapping and spontaneous camaraderie.   Sex distinctions are maintained by segregating the men's parlor from "ladies and escorts," and fights between patrons erupt about once an hour.   Police patrols outside of these bars are conspicuous at most times of the year.

During the evenings of observation only about one out of ten of the tipplers wore Western cowboy costume, and most of those who did were completely ignored by other patrons.   The noise level was lower than usual.   There were virtually no "yippies" or "yahoos" or other shouts of the sort commonly associated with rodeos.   Social interaction was quite normal, and there were fewer than the usual number of fights between patrons.   None of the conversation overheard dealt even remotely with the Calgary Stampede.   Two patrons whom we questioned specifically about the Stampede indicated that they "couldn't care less," and that the Stampede was " a big fraud."   One of these, a loner wearing the service-personnel uniform of a local firm, suggested that if he had his way, he would abolish the Stampede because it interfered with his usual drinking activities by "draining" the number of friends he usually found at the bar.   When questioned specifically about this, he responded that during Stampede, "they just stay home."   The other patron, a travelling resident of a neighboring province, exclaimed that all he wanted was peace and quiet and he just wished he "had all the money that is spent on the phony Stampede."

The most interesting pattern was the maintenance of sex segregation. In Calgary, as in some other Canadian cities, beer parlors are divided by license into rooms for "men" and for "ladies and escorts." During the Stampede the legal ban against an "open" drinking establishment was lifted. However, patrons of three of the four lower-class establishments sampled continued their usual segregated drinking. In fact, several of us were specifically barred from entering the "ladies and escorts' " sections of these bars; and we observed that at least eight of every ten males were in the "men's section, leaving a more than usual surplus of females in the "ladies and escorts' " section.

The only evidence of unusual behavior was the greater than usual number of "streetwalker" prostitutes in all four of the beer parlors. During a usual evening about one in ten females in those pubs is a prostitute, whereas one in five appeared to be a prostitute during the evenings under study. We concluded that these girls were present for two reasons: (1) some may have anticipated that there would be more "tricks" in the lower-class pubs on the assumption that "slumming" parties would gravitate toward lower-class areas; and (2) some may have been excluded from middle-class establishments by bouncers hired for the occasion, or may have been discouraged by the general confusion of such places at Stampede time.

In the fourth beer parlor, patterns of behavior deviated more from the usual daily routine. About half of the customers were in the Stampede "spirit." This included appropriate costumes, spontaneous "yippees" and "yahoos," physical interstimulation (e.g., backslapping), cross-sex interaction in the form of indiscriminate necking, and conversations characterized by expressive pleasure-seeking themes such as "sex in the office," "I'll get that bastard [boss]," "let's really rip tonight," "how's about a gang-bang," and the like. The other half of the customers behaved like the patrons of the other three lower-class establishments, but there was very little evidence of any cross-class interaction between them and patrons of different status backgrounds. Apparently the fourth beer parlor differed from the others because of its proximity to the central "high-class" entertainment core of Calgary and to the Rodeo Grounds. Accidental "drifting" seemed to account for the disruption of normal business. Certainly, this conclusion is reasonable in the light of the following observations of middle-class drinking places.

Middle-Class Establishments. Two of the three middle-class drinking establishments were cocktail lounges and the other was a beer parlor in a relatively plush hotel. Since the legal requirements for a lounge generally distinguish the "haves" from the "have nots" in Canada, it is not surprising that the majority of customers at Stampede time were apparently middle-class. Nevertheless, the middle-class constituted a higher percentage than usual at these places. Many of the patrons were frequent and accepted visitors. But some were out-of-towners whose class identification depended on affluent costuming and the spontaneity with which they related to and were accepted by the "regulars." Absent was the usual smattering of blue-collar workers who tend to drift into these bars and are tolerated so long as they "behave themselves."

At least ninety percent of the patrons in these establishments wore cowboy and Western costumes. It is interesting to note that we were consistently ridiculed for not being dressed in similar costumes (hopefully, this will increase our research sophistication in the future although we still may not be able to afford cowboy outfits). The noise level in these middle-class establishments was almost intolerable. There were dozens of spontaneous "yippees" and "yahoos' competing with each other; and verbal and physical stimulation such as males clapping each other on shoulders and couples necking indiscriminately was virtually universal. From the conversations we overheard, we gathered that the collective search for sensate gratifications was extensive. Most of the customers were obviously well along the continuum from sobriety to inebriation. The majority of the table groupings seemed to consist of people who worked in the same office, with executive types freely interacting with secretaries and sundry female assistants. In spite of this clustering, however, there was considerable table-hopping; and tourists were quickly assimilated by locals who seemed ebullient about showing them a good time. For example, a rather lost looking "out-of-towner" who wandered into one of the bars wearing expensive cowboy garb was invited by one of the local celebrants to "come join us pardner." He was immediately introduced to a newly-acquired "harem" of girls sitting at the table. In another case, a jubilant couple from a neighboring province invited themselves to a table and were immediately accepted as friends. In this latter case, all of the celebrants, including the visitors, whipped off to a party together. Even in the one middle-class beer parlor there was absolutely no sex segregation, and customers took full advantage of the temporary freedom of cross-sex interaction in contrast to the more highly segregated patterns observed in the lower-class establishments.

The prostitutes at the middle-class bars were of the more sophisticated call-girl type. Streetwalkers and lower-class revellers generally were barred from entering these establishments by guards and bouncers stationed at all entrances. The few streetwalkers who wandered in seemed confused by the chaos and shortly departed without seriously attempting to solicit "tricks." We concluded that even during community festivals middle-class people tend to be endogamous in their deviant behavior.

Upper Middle-Class Establishments. The two cocktail lounges visited are located in two of Calgary's most plush and reputable hotels. We had not formulated hypotheses about expected behavior patterns of patrons in these lounges but did expect that emotional expressive release encouraged during Stampede week would not so directly affect relatively elite members of the community. Actually, the two cocktail lounges throughout the year cater to both upper-middle-class customers and upper-class customers who for various reasons are not drinking in their private clubs. Our expectation was based on the premise that upper-class people, similar in some ways to members of the lower class in terms of assured status and spontaneity, manage to minimize inhibitions against deviant behavior in everyday life, and consequently generally engage more in tension-release behavior.

Our speculation was largely confirmed. Although there was a higher proportion of costumed patrons than in the lower-class beer parlors (about 25 per cent), there was very little noise or celebration. Again, it was generally a picture of "business as usual." The costumed customers who were attempting to stimulate behavior more in keeping with the festival soon became discouraged by the lack of spontaneous emotional contagion and wandered out to seek more gratifying places. We overheard one member of such a group exclaim (with disappointment and disgust), "Let's blow this joint—it's like a graveyard." He was a member of a group of three, all of whom were elaborately costumed and obviously disappointed by the lack of conviviality. He specifically pointed to me as I was jotting down notes and exclaimed, "Jesus, he's working at a time like this!"

Conclusion

Observations of behavior in drinking establishments during the Calgary Stampede confirmed our initial hypothesis. Middle-class customers were obviously engaging in more spontaneous expressive behavior than either lower- or upper-class patrons. The Stampede week therefore seems more "functional" for people who tend to be inhibited in their daily lives and look forward to the "green light" of tolerated deviance during a community festival.

We cannot of course conclude that our findings suggest similar selective factors relating to participation in all community festivals. As we suggested earlier, the appeal of a festival probably depends on variations in the nature of social class structure of various communities. More specifically, festival participation may depend on the rigidity of the class structure and the extent to which ventilation of frustrations is inhibited and punished through formal social control. For example, we would expect that members of a lower social class group or a minority group who are systematically exploited and punished for deviant behavior, would participate in "legitimate" community festivals to a much greater extent than found in the present study. We suggest that such situations might include the separate Negro parade and festivities during the Mardi Gras of New Orleans and the widespread "peasant" participation in Rio de Janeiro's "Carnival."

The findings suggest that community festivals held in cities such as Calgary reflect social class structure but do not "function" to reinforce social solidarity of members of different social class status groups. The Calgary Stampede, according to our observations, is a middle-class "binge," suggesting that even socially-approved deviant behavior is endogamous. In a sense, the Calgary Stampede does serve to partially invert social class structure by allowing middle-class celebrants to indulge in the spontaneous and aggressive behavior permitted to members of the lower class throughout the year. Members of the lower class, if our sample is any indication, view the contrived Stampede as frivolous and phony and apparently attempt to avoid being contaminated by the festivities.

The Outcastes in Japan † *

THE history of the outcaste in Japan, like that of low social classes generally, is poorly documented. The available descriptions were written primarily by an elite minority centered around the capital and the major towns; they do not faithfully record the culture of the countryside majority.

Since outcastes are ideologically outside normal society, they have either been systematically ignored or information concerning them has been distorted. During the Tokugawa period (1603–1868 A.D.) outcastes were often not listed in census tabulations, and when they were, they were often listed separately from "people." Some maps were made without outcaste settlements drawn in, and distances indicated or maps were even foreshortened to exclude these communities. After their emancipation in 1871, the outcastes were officially defined as commoners and then largely ignored for official purposes. It has been government policy to contend that there are no outcastes and hence no outcaste problem apart from that of general social welfare. Thus the outcastes, who in fact were maintained as outcastes, and who expanded in population and number of communities in the past century, are not distinguishable in most population data. It is only in the last fifty years, with the introduction of a scientific tradition, that Japanese outcaste culture has begun to receive full exploration and description.

Even the most recent interpretations of the history of outcaste culture are of questionable validity because they are so heavily biased by an interpretation of history in terms of a political variant of the Marxian dialectics of class struggle. Researchers in the Buraku Mondai Kenkyūjo (Buraku Problems Research Institute) have spent considerable time in refuting popularly held racial, religious, and occupational theories about the origin and social maintenance of the outcastes, only to substitute a some-

† Selected from: (pp. 10–15) Chapter I "A history of the Outcaste: Untouchability in Japan" by John Price.

From Japan's Invisible Race: Caste in Culture and Personality: Edited by George De Vos and Hiroshi Wagatasuma. Revised Edition 1972, University of California Press-Berkeley.

* Originally published by the University of California Press; reprinted by permission of The Regents of the University of California.

what dogmatic political theory. Even the claim that there are today three million outcastes seems to be advanced by the Buraku Mondai Kenkyūjo more for political purposes than for scholarly accuracy. Nevertheless, the abundant documentation this Institute is now producing will be invaluable to future researchers.

For over a thousand years it has been popularly held that certain low caste peoples are physically inferior to "ordinary" Japanese. Originally, this inferiority was attributed to the practice of defiling trades and the association with blood and death. By long association with supernatural or ritual impurities the very nature of a man was believed to change. This adverse change not only carried over to a man's descendants but was in a sense communicable. The simple presence of an outcaste or "untouchable" was slightly defiling. Today, with the germ theory of disease and a genetic basis for heredity, it is difficult to understand the nature of supernatural defilement.

In the past century, more "modern" rationalizations were added to the previous beliefs in supernatural defilement. In the Tokugawa period the outcastes were usually identifiable, at least within their local areas, by their residential communities, occupations, kinship ties, and often by such additional features as forms of dress, a patch of leather sewn on their kimono, hair tied together by straw, barefootedness, or deferential behavior. The dogma of ritually defiling trades was still a strong undercurrent, but local variations required additional explanations: whole outcaste communities had not practiced the defiling trades for centuries. Belief in outcaste physical deviance came to involve such things as meat in the diet, particular diseases, extreme inbreeding, and inherited abnormalities.

One of the most prevalent theories in the last century for the supposed physical inferiority of outcastes is that they are derived from an inferior race or an animal-like ethnic group.[6] Ideas of outcaste affinity to animals are seen in the old folklore. "One rib-bone is lacking"; "they have one dog's bone in them"; "they have distorted sexual organs"; "they have defective excretory systems"; and "they being animals, dirt does not stick to their feet when they walk barefooted."

[6] We commonly find terms that associate outcastes with animals; *yotsu* ("four," i. e., less than five, a perfect number, or four legs, implying animals) is used metaphorically whereas *ningai* ("outside of the human") is unequivocal in meaning.

At least four theories have used the evidence of similar names to postulate the origin of the Eta. One theory held that a Philippine Negrito people, also called Eta, are ancestral to the Japanese Eta. Another theory is that the Eta are descended from a Hindu tribe called Weda. Oe Taku over forty years ago postulated that the Eta were descendants of a lost tribe of Hebrews, on the following similarity of names: Hora, a village near Nara, has the tomb of an ancient culture hero, Emperor Jimmu, who was cared for by the local Eta; Hafurai, a people who were supposedly made subjects by Emperor Jimmu; Heburai, the Japanese pronunciation of Hebrew, and presumably with the term Hora, is a variant derivative from Hafurai.

In 1923 Kikuchi San-ya presented the hypothesis that the Eta were closely related to the Orochon branch of the Tungus who live today in Sakhalin. The Orochon call themselves *etta,* and he infers that in Japan the name was modified to Eta and given a new derogatory meaning in the Chinese characters used. Kikuchi claimed that the Eta were distinct from the Japanese in that they have reddish and non-Mongolian eyes, prominent cheek bones, dolichocephalic heads, and short necks and stature. There is no sound evidence for any of the racial theories based only on the chance similarity of names.

A more popular racial view is that the Eta are descended from Koreans who came as early war captives or who were immigrants who practiced tanning and furriery. Often they are held to be descended from captives taken in a battle during the regency of the Empress Jingū (201–269 A.D.), but even the battle is not fully substantiated. Some slight credence could be given to a modified Korean descent theory for three reasons. First, over two thousand years ago southern Korea and western Japan were occupied by essentially the same race and culture. Distinctive variations of East Asian culture and the Mongoloid race have since emerged in Korea and Japan, but these differences today cannot be validly projected back much over 1,500 years. Second, Koreans did immigrate to Japan in the early historic periods as skilled tradesmen, although most of them were accorded high status, immunities, and privileges, and thus would not enter the lower classes. Third, with modern discrimination in housing, employment, and marriage in Japan against the Koreans, a few Koreans have married outcastes, moved into outcaste communities, and thus in social fact have become pariahs. However, the majority of Koreans who immigrated to Japan formed their own enclaves within the cities, and seem to have emerged as one of the new low class segments of Japanese society rather than a separate caste.

Taken as a whole, the outcastes are not descendant from Koreans, but are Japanese. In fact, the earliest outcaste communities are in the Kinki district, the very heartland of historic Japanese culture, rather than in the extreme west where we would expect to find more "Korean genes," or the extreme north, where more "Ainu genes" are present. The outcastes form a race only in the sense of an "invisible race," a race visible only to the eyes of members of a certain cultural tradition.

Outcaste status and attitudes about untouchability developed within medieval Japanese culture because of a complex set of economic, social, political, and ideological conditions. And once established, outcaste status has had great staying power. The formal rational explanations and protests on the parts of members of the majority society, or by the outcastes themselves, have had little effect on hastening change in outcaste history. The official emancipation proclamation and later liberation movements are comprehensible as products of Japan's modern social revolution in general, but they have not resulted in any rapid shift in deeply rooted emotional attitudes toward outcaste individuals.

The outcastes in Japan today do not form any highly distinct, corporate, and separate subculture diffused throughout Japan. Rather, by residing in widely scattered communities, they reflect the regional and local variations of culture throughout the country. While the segregated character of their communities helps to foster and perpetuate some attributes of a separate subculture, the scattered character of the communities tends to weaken cross-community similarities.

Some of the diverse origins and past social positions are reflected in the variety of local and often colloquial names for outcastes. Most of these stress occupations,[10] but some indicate

10 *Hagi* (skinner), *kawata* (leather worker), *onbō* (cremator, funeral worker), *banta* (watchman for the bodies of criminals after execution), *shuku* (tomb watcher), *chasen* (tea whisk maker), *kojiki* (beggar), *doetta* (damn *etta*), and *kaito* (within the fence, i. e., a servant employed in a large establishment).

such things as the animal nature of outcastes, their inferior residential sites, their leaders, or are simply modern euphemisms.[11]

In the history of Japan there are thousands of somewhat distinct social groups that can be described as either classes, castes, guilds, or occupationally specialized communities. The outcastes constitute only a minor segment within this variety of segmented social groups, historically less than one percent of the total population, although rising in certain provinces at times to nearly five percent of the provincial population. Comprising about two percent of the total population today, they probably are a larger portion than ever before. During the past century the outcaste population increased seven times faster than Japanese society generally. This great increase was caused by "recruiting" from outside, by the redefinition of the outcaste segment, and by improved diet and health practices in the society as a whole. But since the proportion of outcastes in the total population is still low, and since the outcastes live primarily in segregated communities confined mainly to western Japan, only a small percentage of the Japanese have any firsthand acquaintance with them.

The first fairly well-documented origins of caste in Japan can be traced to the development of occupational specializations in the ninth and tenth centuries. The geographical region of outcaste development was that of the Imperial capital, built in imitation of the capital of the Tang dynasty in China, where economic diversity and the vertical ranking of a social hierarchy were at their greatest. Japanese culture, under the influence of Buddhism brought in from China, depended on plant rather than animal foods and abhorred the ritual impurity of blood and death. Cattle were raised for plowing and other agricultural work rather than for their meat or milk. The growing popularity of Buddhism, with its strictures against taking life, helped to produce an outcaste segment in the society composed of those communities specializing in such occupations as slaughtering and processing of animal products. But Buddhism alone was not a sufficient cause for outcastism; it was only one of several forces. In fact,

---

11 *Yaban* (savage), *yotsu* (four, i. e., four legs), *ningai* (outside the human), *kawara mono* (river bank dweller), *yama no mono* (hill dweller), *danzaemon* (the name of an outcaste leader in nineteenth century Edo and a title after his death), *chōri* (police hand), *shin-heimin* (new common people), *ichibu kokumin* (minority people).

we find that some occupations were defined as outcaste that were only remotely connected with taking life, such as hawk tending for the elite (hawks were used in sport hunting) and burial-tomb tending.

Although outcaste groups appeared far beyond the capital region, the outcastes were invariably occupational specialists who operated within and for a small-scale local economy. They emerged as one functional segment of relatively closed corporate communities where economic interdependence and the inheritance of occupation and social position helped reinforce the endogamy required of a caste separate from normal society. Traditional occupational roles became spheres of monopoly as the outcastes formed guilds in the face of the economic competition and the increasingly severe discrimination of the fifteenth through nineteenth centuries. Concurrent with the growth of competition was the breakup of closed corporate communities, the growth of a national transport and trade network, and the ideological crystallization of class structure. In the Tokugawa period (1603–1868 A.D.) legally sanctioned caste and untouchability reached their height in Japan.

The social and economic functions that supported the existence of outcastes have largely disappeared in Japan's phenomenal post-Tokugawa modernization, and the hierarchical trends of Japanese traditional social organization and ideology were seriously weakened by this economic growth. Modern egalitarian ideologies, more in keeping with a socially mobile industrial society, have swept Japan. Since the outcastes have no distinctive physical traits and today possess few distinctive cultural traits, they can "pass" into the normal society once they are outside their home areas. Still, outcastism is disappearing at a seemingly slow pace. History describes the process; social science attempts to explain it.

6   Part I—Sat., July 7, 1973   Los Angeles Times ★

INDIA CASTE SYSTEM OBSERVED—AND 78 DIE*

NEW DELHI—The Indian caste system cost 78 lives when passengers on a stranded bus refused to haul themselves to safety along the same rope.

The Hindustan Times newspaper reported Friday a bus carrying 86 persons was trapped by floodwaters Monday 100 miles southwest of Delhi.

Karim Khan waded out to the bus with a rope which he had tied to a truck. He asked the passengers to haul themselves to safety.

But the passengers, who belonged to two different high-caste communities, refused to share the same rope and stayed in the bus, which was swept away.

[A8666]

* REUTERS

*

V. Our Daily Bread

Like all living organisms man must have an adequate nutrition in order to live. Man gets his food by hunting other animals, gathering vegetable and other foodstuffs, by domesticating animals or plants, and by acquiring money or some other medium of exchange and thereby acquiring food from others. The articles in this section will illustrate some of the many possible ways in which men gain their daily bread.

Robert L. Carneiro, in his article on the hunting practices of the Amahuaca, shows that hunting can still be important to a people who have practiced horticulture for centuries and that successful hunting can rely on supernatural beliefs as well as a knowledge of animals and weapons. The article on the slash-and-burn technique by W. M. S. Russell describes a technique that has both historical and contemporary importance for agriculturalists in many parts of the world. The article on the Turkmen Nomads by William Irons concerns problems that are common to many pastoral people in the world today as their lands are being taken away from them and they are often forced into adopting an unwanted new life style. The final article in this section by Stanley M. Garn and Walter D. Block suggests that man cannot live on man alone.

Hunting and Hunting Magic Among the Amahuaca of the Peruvian Montaña [1] † *

T HE Amahuaca Indians inhabit the heavily forested region between the Ucayali and upper Juruá and Purús rivers in Eastern Peru. At its greatest extent their territory encompassed perhaps 20,000 square miles (see map in Carneiro 1962:29), but today it has diminished to about a quarter of that size. The population of the Amahuaca, estimated at 6,000 to 9,000 around 1900 (von Hassel 1905:31), is today no more than about 500. Population density, formerly something like one person per two or three square miles, had diminished at the time of field work in 1960–61 to roughly one person for every eight or ten square miles.

Amahuaca settlements are small. About fifteen persons, occupying three or four houses, form the average community. Settlements are located on or near small streams, usually several hours' walking distance apart. Each community is completely autonomous economically as well as politically. Indeed, the same might almost be said of each nuclear or extended family within a community. There are no headmen or shamans, no kin groups larger than the extended family, and very little ceremonialism. All told, Amahuaca social organization is exceedingly simple.

Feuding among Amahuaca communities is very common, and sometimes they fight with their traditional enemies, the Yaminahua. The result is that an Amahuaca settlement is often on the alert against the possibility of attack.

Subsistence is divided almost equally between hunting and horticulture. To be more precise, I would say that about 50 per cent of the food consumed by the Amahuaca is derived from horti-

---

[1] Some of the data incorporated into this paper were very kindly provided by Mr. Robert L. Russell of the Summer Institute of Linguistics, who has worked among the Amahuaca for a number of years. However, Mr. Russell is in no way responsible for any errors of fact that may appear here.

† By Robert L. Carneiro, American Museum of Natural History.

* Ethnology, Vol. 1X #4: pp. 331–341 (October 1970.) Reproduced by permission of the editor of Ethnology.

culture and 40 per cent from hunting, with the rest coming from fishing and gathering. Although hunting is thus not quite half of subsistence, it nevertheless plays a very important role in determining the small size of Amahuaca local groups, their location, and the frequency with which they are moved, which is about once every year or two.

The habitat of the Amahuaca is an unbroken expanse of tropical rainforest. There are no grasslands anywhere, and even abandoned garden plots revert directly to secondary forest without passing through an intermediate grass stage. The terrain consists of a series of rugged hills and ridges, often rising 200 or 300 feet above the adjacent streams. The heart of the Amahuaca territory is the height of land between the Ucayali and Juruá and Purús river systems. Here the headwater tributaries are born, and as they flow out of this area, are still narrow and shallow. The fish in these streams are small enough in size and few enough in number to make fishing an almost negligible part of subsistence. The primary source of animal protein is hunting, and the forests of the region are well stocked with game.

Meat is an important part of the Amahuaca diet, and no meal is considered really complete without it. A man who is a good provider sees to it that his household never lacks for meat.

Every man is a hunter, and every good hunter enjoys the chase. Such a man may go hunting even when there is still meat at home. Those not so skilled go less often, but because meat is commonly shared among all families in a community no one is without it for long.

The game found in the surrounding forests is abundant and varied. No single species predominates. Being generalized hunters, the Amahuaca seek out and kill most species of mammals in the area. These include monkeys of several kinds, deer, tapir, peccaries (both collared and white-lipped), agoutis, pacas, capybaras, anteaters, armadillos, sloths, porcupines, coatis, and squirrels. Most species of large game birds are hunted, including curassows and partridges. Caimans, lizards, and turtles are also taken.

The only class of animals not eaten by the Amahuaca are carnivores, including jaguars, pumas, ocelots, jaguarundis, tayras, otters, and various types of wolves or wild dogs. A few noncarnivorous animals are also avoided as food, principally giant armadillos, silky anteaters, raccoons, rabbits, opossums, bats, and mice. Other animals not eaten include snakes, vultures and eagles, and a number of smaller birds.

According to Robert L. Russell of the Summer Institute of Linguistics, who has lived in close contact with the Amahuaca for a number of years, the order of importance of game animals in terms of the weight of meat derived from them is as follows: (1) tapir, (2) howler monkey, (3) spider monkey, (4) deer, (5) collared peccary, (6) paca, (7) cebus monkey, (8) paujil (wattled curassow), (9) guan, (10) pucacunga (bare-faced curassow), and (11) agouti. As far as taste is concerned, the two kinds of game most favored by the Amahuaca are tapir and spider monkey. Despite such dietary preferences, however, it is difficult to predict what a day's hunt will bring. For example, on one occasion two brothers living in adjacent houses shot two tapirs in three days but went several weeks before killing another one.

The hunting technology of the Amahuaca is very simple. The bow and arrow constitutes their principal weapon, and almost their only one. Spears and blowguns are lacking, as are snares, nooses, pitfalls, deadfalls, and any kind of hunting traps or nets. Except on rare occasions when a number of men may co-operate in attacking a passing herd of white-lipped peccaries, there is no collective hunting.

The bow and arrow is the inseparable companion of every Amahuaca man. Not only is it the means of obtaining much of his food, but it is also his principal weapon of attack or defense in a frequently hostile environment. Rarely does a man so much as leave his house without taking his bow and arrows with him. And in the hands of an Amahuaca, trained from childhood in its use, the bow and arrow becomes a very effective weapon.

The stave of an Amahuaca bow is made from the wood of the *pihuayo* or peach palm (*Guilielma speciosa*). This is the strongest and most resilient of the palms in the region, and probably equal or superior to any bow wood available in Amazonia.[2] The average length of Amahuaca bows is between 6 and 6½ feet, but occasionally they are up to a foot longer.

[2] In the ethnographic literature for the Montaña one often finds the statement that bows are made of "chonta" palm. This term is a rather indefinite one. It is sometimes applied to *Guilielma speciosa*, but also to palms of the genus *Bactris*, and, by popular writers, to almost any palm.

The bowstring is made from the inner bark fibers of the *setico* tree (*Cecropia leucocoma*), twined by the hunter on his thigh.[3] In total length a bowstring may be 15 feet or more, the extra length being wrapped around the upper limb of the bow to use as a spare in case the bowstring should break. The Amahuaca always keep their bows strung, ready to use. The resiliency of *pihuayo* wood is such that it loses little of its "cast" even when kept under continuous tension for a long time.

Some men wrap a thin strip of smooth, flattish bark from a vine around the bowstave in order to protect the bow hand from the fine slivers which, with repeated flexing, sometimes separate from the bow.

Arrows are somewhat over 5 feet in length. The shaft of the arrow is made from the long straight flower stem of the cane *Gynerium saggitatum*.[4] Into the soft pithy center of this cane is driven a foreshaft of hard wood, usually *pihuayo*. The most common type of point attached to this foreshaft is made from bamboo. It is lanceolate in shape and some 12 to 15 inches long. As these arrow points are dulled or broken in use, they are re-sharpened, and an old point may have been trimmed down until it is no longer than 5 or 6 inches. While designed especially for use against large game, such as tapir, deer, and peccaries, bamboo points are commonly used against game of any size.

Bamboo, which has a thin siliceous layer on the outside, takes a fine cutting edge and a very sharp point. Thus an arrow with such a point has great penetrating power.[5] Sometimes, however, the sides of a bamboo point are not left smooth, but are notched

[3] *Cecropia* bast fiber, which is very strong, appears to be the favorite material for the manufacture of bowstrings among Amazonian tribes generally.

[4] This type of cane grows wild in the low marshy areas bordering the Urubamba River, but not in the hilly regions where the Amahuaca live. However, the Amahuaca plant *Gynerium* in their gardens, or in special plots, especially for the arrow cane. When the cane flowers, the long straight flower stems are removed and stored in barkcloth cylinders suspended from the roof of the house until needed.

[5] Even when propelled by only the force of gravity an arrow can penetrate deeply. One Amahuaca was said to have been killed when his own arrow, falling out of a tree as he attempted to retrieve it, pierced his neck and entered his chest cavity. Two other men whom I knew each bore a couple of scars on their bodies where they had been wounded by their own arrows in the same manner.

to make it more difficult for an animal to shake itself free of the arrow.

A less common type of arrow point consists of a somewhat longer *pihuayo* wood foreshaft, self-barbed, and sharpened to a point. A sliver of monkey bone, sharpened at each end, may sometimes be attached at an angle to the tip of the foreshaft. Arrows of these two types are designed for use against smaller game—monkeys, birds, rodents, etc. Blunt-headed wooden arrow points are occasionally made for shooting birds. Their advantage is that they do less damage to the bird's plumage, and are not so likely to stick in the trees.

The Amahuaca do not poison their arrows. They do, however, apply a thin layer of an orange-colored resin—apparently a form of copal—to their bamboo points. Although the Amahuaca believe that this resin will cause a wounded animal to die faster, it seems in fact to be more of an irritant than an actual poison.

Arrow feathers are attached only at their ends,[6] and are applied with a slight spiral so that the arrow rotates in flight, thus increasing its stability.

A hunter draws his bow to a point well behind his ear, and at full draw the average bow pulls 60 to 75 pounds. This relatively heavy bow weight, combined with a sharp, tapering bamboo blade, can send an arrow entirely through an animal.

Hunting is a year-round activity. During the dry season, when a man spends a good deal of time clearing and planting his garden plot, he hunts less frequently, but during the rainy season, when no such chores occupy his time, he goes hunting about every second or third day. Some men prefer to hunt alone, but two men, especially brothers or a father and son, may often hunt together. Generally, though, no more than three men comprise a hunting party, since more than this are said to frighten the game. Rarely, a man may go into the forest with his wife, spending the day hunting while she collects fruits, nuts, or other forest products.

---

[6] This is the so-called "bridge feathering," typical of the tribes of the Ucayali basin. Some Amahuaca had arrows showing "Peruvian cemented feathering," in which the feathers are secured in place by being wrapped along their entire length with cotton thread, and then cemented with beeswax. The Amahuaca appear to have learned this type of feathering from the Yaminahua to the east.

Hunters leave early in the morning, often before six o'clock, to take full advantage of the daylight hours. If he sees little game, a man may spend the entire day looking, returning home around dusk. Even if successful, a hunter may stay out a good part of the day, killing as much game as he can before returning. Some men go hunting without breakfast and take no food with them, feeling that the added incentive of hunger will help them make an early kill. Others, however, take a little food with them in a small carrying basket, or perhaps wrapped in a leaf.

Sometimes a man may set out to hunt a particular kind of game, especially tapir or spider monkey, because these are the animals whose flesh is most prized. Tapirs may also be hunted for their fat, which is mixed with achiote (*Bixa orellana*) for body painting during feasts. Similarly, a man may hunt agoutis or pacas expressly for their chisel-like incisors. In such instances, the hunter heads toward an area of the forest where he has reason to think these animals are most likely to be found. When hoping to kill a tapir, for example, an Amahuaca often heads for the Curiuja River, an area where there is less hunting and therefore more game of every sort. On a relatively long trip like this a hunter may spend the night in the forest and return home the next day. He does not encumber himself by taking along his hammock, but, when night overtakes him, makes himself a sleeping mat out of palm leaves and erects a simple shelter.

The Amahuaca do not have defined territories, and a man may hunt in any area of the forest, even if it is close to another settlement, without asking permission and without being considered guilty of trespass. Because Amahuaca communities are so small, so widely scattered, and so frequently moved, there is little reason for them to demarcate a territory precisely, or to try to keep others from hunting in it.

When a hunter sets out, he usually avoids an area recently hunted by someone else, since the game there may have been shot or driven away. A network of hunting trails fans out from each settlement, and hunters follow these trails, at least at first. Often the hunter makes a circuit, leaving by one trail and returning by another, thus seeing more of the forest and increasing his chances of finding game.

After following a trail or a stream bed for awhile, a hunter may then cut across to another trail or stream. He is always on the alert, listening for animals, watching for movements of the undergrowth or of branches which may reveal their presence. If he hears the cry or the movement of an animal, he hurries toward it, yet moving carefully and taking advantage of the natural cover in order to conceal his presence. Whenever possible, he stays downwind of the animal.

Disguises are never worn in hunting, but a man may occasionally make some attempt at camouflage by sprinkling or smearing himself with the juice of the huito fruit (*Genipa americana*). When exposed to the air for an hour or two, the juice of this fruit turns black, and the mottled pattern formed on his body renders him less conspicuous. To cover up his scent a hunter often rubs aromatic leaves, such as vanilla, over his body, or places these leaves under his belt.

Although an Amahuaca is a good marksman with bow and arrow, what makes him an outstanding hunter is not so much his archery as his skill in tracking game and in working in close enough for a good shot. Every significant detail of the life habits of game animals is part of an Amahuaca hunter's knowledge. He knows the sound of their cries, what food they eat, and what their excrement looks like. He can detect the presence of peccaries or howler monkeys by their sharp scent, and can identify spider monkeys by the characteristic noise they make while eating fruit in the trees. From the tooth marks on a fruit he can tell what animal has been feeding on it, and approximately when it left.

If a hunter comes upon the trail of an animal, and it is fresh enough, he will follow it. The freshness of a set of tracks is gauged not only by how wet it is but also by the amount of dust and debris that has accumulated on it. On soft ground a man can tell not only what animal's tracks he is seeing, but also how large it was, how fast it was moving, and how long ago it went by.

The tracks of virtually every game animal are readily distinguished. During one hunting trip on which I accompanied two hunters I had pointed out to me the tracks of an armadillo, a raccoon, a deer, an agouti, a collared peccary, a paca, a giant armadillo, an otter, a tapir, a caiman, and an oriole.

If animal tracks are old, or if the ground is hard and the tracks are not readily visible, a hunter may still be able to detect the recent presence of game. He scans the forest floor for bits of fruit or fresh excrement, and studies the displacement of leaves and twigs. From the amount of exudation on a broken twig, for example, a hunter can judge how long ago an animal passed by.

When a hunter hears an animal, he attempts to fix its location more precisely by imitating its cry and trying to get it to respond.[7] Monkeys may reply by chattering, and a tapir by giving its shrill whistle. A deer may paw the ground. In any case, the animal's response enables the hunter to ascertain its position more exactly and thus to approach closer. The hunter may even succeed in drawing a curious animal close to him. For example, should a hunter chance upon some young, such as a fawn or a baby peccary, he will seize it, knowing that its plaintive cry is likely to bring the mother within arrow range.

The whole purpose of tracking and mimicry is to allow the hunter to approach as near as possible before shooting. Long distance shots are avoided, not only because marksmanship decreases with distance, but also because the intervening foliage can easily deflect an arrow. Generally, a hunter tries to close to within 40 feet or less before shooting. When he finally looses an arrow, he aims for a vital spot if he can, often just behind the rib cage. A bamboo point has such a long cutting edge that it may sever many blood vessels and cause considerable bleeding. If wounded by a well-placed arrow, an animal may be unable to travel far before collapsing. Barbed arrows do less cutting, but, lodging in the animal more securely, they help slow it down by rubbing or catching against the brush as it attempts to flee.

If two or three men are hunting together, they generally separate when they hear an animal and attempt to close in on it from opposite sides. The first one to shoot an arrow at the animal may be allowed to finish it off. But if it appears likely that the animal is about to escape, his companions shoot too.

As mentioned earlier, the only occasion when a number of men co-operate in hunting is when a herd of white-lipped peccaries is detected near the settlement. Unlike collared peccaries, which travel singly or in pairs, white-lipped peccaries travel in herds of up to 100. A group of hunters may be able to kill as

[7] Once, when I asked a man to demonstrate the art of imitating animal cries, he proceeded to imitate no fewer than 35 different animals, one after another.

many as ten peccaries before the rest take flight. A lone hunter coming upon a herd of feeding peccaries from the downwind side, approaches them stealthily and attempts to kill one or two before the others discover his presence. Once alerted, the peccaries either flee or charge. Because of their sharp tusks and their compact ranks, their charge is dangerous, and a hunter caught in their path can save himself only by climbing a tree.

The Amahuaca have dogs, and these are an important asset in hunting.[8] By catching the scent of animals and following their spoor, dogs enable the hunter to locate more game than he could by himself. Dogs are also very helpful in locating animals living in burrows or hollow tree trunks. Besides finding game, dogs also help in killing it by bringing it to bay, or by so annoying an animal that it stops to bite or snarl at his pursuers, thus allowing the hunter to catch up with it.

The Amahuaca erect hunting blinds at places where animals come to drink, or where the ripe fruit of a tree are falling, or some other place which game is likely to frequent. Blinds are sometimes also built near garden plots if agoutis or deer or other predators have been eating the crops. They are made by inserting the butt ends of four or more palm leaves into the ground, and drawing together and tying the upper ends. Here and there the leaflets are separated to provide peepholes. A blind is about 5 feet in diameter and tall enough to allow a man to stand inside.

Sometimes a man builds a blind in the trees to hunt monkeys, such as red howlers, which frequent the higher branches and are not easily seen from the ground. Or a hunter may simply climb a tree to a vantage point above a passing troop of monkeys and shoot down on them. In this way he may manage to shoot two or three monkeys before the rest realize what is happening. Tree climbing is usually done by means of a climbing ring made by coiling a length of thin vine. The ring thus formed is placed around the insteps, and permits the climber to brace his feet against opposite sides of a small tree, as he reaches up to take a firm handhold. Once he has his new hold, he then pulls his feet up behind him.

---

[8] The dog may well be post-Columbian among the Amahuaca, as it seems to be among most Amazonian tribes. There is little direct evidence for this, but the Amahuaca do call the dog *indo*, the same term they use for jaguar.

A few other hunting techniques used by the Amahuaca may be mentioned. In hunting tapirs, use is sometimes made of a palm-wood sword up to four feet long with sharp edges tapering to a fine point. A cornered tapir is stabbed with such a sword.

Clubbing is the usual way to kill an armadillo, since its carapace is hard enough to ward off an arrow. Clubs may also be used against white-lipped peccaries, caimans, and agoutis.

Burrowing animals like armadillos or agoutis may be lured out of their holes with cries, or smoked out with dry palm leaves which have been ignited. If this fails, one end of the burrow may be stopped up and the animal dug out.

To bring back the game he has killed a hunter accommodates it in a palm leaf basket which he braids on the spot and carries on his back by means of a tumpline. Smaller game, like monkeys, is brought back whole, but larger game may be cut up for easier carrying. The two feet on each side of a deer may be tied together, the hunter's arms inserted through the loops thus formed, and the animal carried home like a knapsack.

Tapirs, which may weigh as much as 500 or 600 pounds, are naturally too large to bring back in one trip. A hunter will cut up a tapir, remove the viscera and other internal organs, and carry these and as much of the meat as he can back to the house. The parts of the animal left behind to be retrieved the next day must be carefully protected from scavengers. Leaves are usually placed over them, weighted down with sticks, and then covered with dirt. This prevents jaguars and other carnivores from catching the scent.[9]

That evening, when he is back at the settlement, or early next morning, the hunter hoots in a conventional way to inform the rest of the men that he has shot a tapir and is going to retrieve it. This is an invitation to others to come along, and those who accompany him are allowed to keep the portions of the carcass they bring back. When the men go out to retrieve a tapir, their womenfolk spend a good part of the day gathering firewood and making a babracot on which to roast the meat.

A lone hunter, returning from the forest, may appear at his house sad-eyed and empty-handed, as if he had had no luck. But

[9] If an animal is killed early in the hunt its carcass may be placed in a stream to retard spoilage until the hunter is ready to return and retrieve it.

this is often a deception, and a carrying basket full of meat may at that moment be sitting by the trail just outside the clearing. When the hunter finally tells his wife about it, she goes to fetch it. It is considered impolite to ask a hunter who has just returned from the forest what success he has had, for if he has caught nothing, he is embarrassed, and the Amahuaca never embarrass one another.

Large game, even if brought back by the hunter unaided, is often shared with other families. Smaller game, however, is consumed by the hunter's family alone. A tapir may provide meat enough for a week, even if shared. To preserve it that long the meat is roasted over a slow fire until thoroughly dry.

There are no rules for the distribution of game. No specific portion of the animal is reserved for the hunter or for particular kinsmen.

HUNTING MAGIC

It has often been observed that supernaturalism tends to surround those activities which are either uncertain or hazardous or both, while, conversely, little or no supernaturalism accompanies those spheres of life where security and predictability prevail.[10] The Amahuaca certainly bear out this generalization. Almost no supernaturalism is connected with horticulture, which yields very abundantly and reliably. On the other hand, hunting, whose outcome is never certain, and often involves an element of personal danger, is attended by considerable supernaturalism.

Not all aspects of Amahuaca hunting are, however, permeated with magical practices. For example, propitiation of the spirits of game animals, so prominent a feature in hunting among North American Indians, does not occur among the Amahuaca. Only a few game animals are thought to have spirits, and these are never propitiated, either before or after the animals are killed.[11]

[10] ". . . supernaturalism varies inversely with the extent and effectiveness of naturalistic control. In activities where man has little actual control, or where chance and circumstances play a prominent part . . . recourse to supernaturalism is great. In activities where man's control is extensive and effective . . . re-sort to supernaturalism will tend to be meager and perhaps only perfunctory" (White 1959:272). See also Linton (1936:429–431), Malinowski (1954:-30–31), and Oberg (1940:151).

[11] For an account of Amahuaca spirit beliefs see Carneiro (1964).

Nor is any attempt made to secure the assistance of animal spirits in hunting.

The Amahuaca do not have totem animals, and do not prohibit the killing of any animal, whether it is eaten or not. It is true that certain animals—especially carnivorous ones—are not eaten, but the failure to eat such animals appears to derive from a general repugnance to their eating habits rather than from an explicit religious prohibition.[12] Vultures, for example, are considered unfit to eat "because they eat rotten things."

Also absent from Amahuaca hunting magic are rituals designed to make animals increase in numbers. The depletion of game in an area is recognized as being the result of overhunting, and the only remedy sought is the purely rational one of moving the settlement to another part of the forest.

Amahuaca supernaturalism, as it relates to hunting, can best be summarized by saying that it is positive rather than negative. There is little or nothing that a hunter must not do to have success in hunting, but there are many things he can and does do. Positive kinds of hunting magic vary considerably. Some of it acts on the hunter himself, or on his weapons, helping him to find game sooner, to see more of it, or to make his arrow fly truer. Other hunting magic acts on the game, making animals "tamer" so they can be seen and shot more readily. Some of these practices may now be examined.

Smearing blood from an animal on the bowstring or bowstave is thought to make the bow more effective against other animals of that species. This is done especially with a new bow, or with blood from the first animal of that species killed with the bow. Arrows as well as bows may be magically treated. A man may run the further end of his arrow through the body of an animal several times, smearing it with blood and thus making it shoot straighter.[13] Some hunters say that the blood of certain animals

[12] A number of Amazonian tribes do not eat deer because they believe it to be the ultimate repository of human souls. The Amahuaca have no such belief.

[13] One Amahuaca, on the island of Chumichinía in the Ucayali River, told me that if a man had sexual relations before going hunting his arrow would miss its mark. This belief, however, seems to have been derived from the neighboring Conibo or Campa, and is absent among the Amahuaca on the upper Inuya. There, a man may have sexual relations with his wife even while he is out hunting with her in the forest. More-

—a small lizard, for example—is particularly effective in this respect.

The blood of an animal may also be applied to the hunter's own body. It is common for a boy who is beginning to hunt to have the blood of a tapir rubbed over his body so he will turn out to be a successful hunter. Some informants reported that the blood of the tapir, peccary, agouti and spider monkey was occasionally drunk for better luck in hunting these animals.[14]

Plants of various sorts also figure in hunting magic. Certain kinds of leaves are often wrapped around the bowstave or tucked under a hunter's belt for luck. Herbal infusions are also employed. Most common among these is *kumba ra'o* (called *chiricsanago* in Peruvian jungle Spanish), which appears to come from a species of *Rauwolfia*. The roots of the plant are scraped into water, which is then heated almost to boiling. After drinking this potion a man becomes dizzy and his body feels cold, "as if it had rained on you," one informant said. After taking it, one's aim improves and game animals become "tame," allowing themselves to be easily killed. Various kinds of *kumba ra'o* are specific for particular species of animal.

Another class of plants used in hunting magic are called *sako* in Amahuaca and *piripiri* in jungle Spanish. Most of these appear to be sedges of the genus *Cyperus*. The leaves are crushed in water and smeared on the arms and wrists. Or the infusion may be boiled and applied to the body. As with *kumba ra'o*, there are *piripiri* plants specific to various game animals. *Piripiri* is said to enable a man to see a lot of game.

Still another type of hunting magic involves drinking the excrement of the boa constrictor. Picking at certain scales on the tail markings of the boa is also thought to be magically effective. In addition, an infusion made by boiling hawk's talons may be smeared on the hands and wrists of a boy or young man to make him a better hunter. The talons themselves may be scraped

over, the behavior of women who remain at home while their husbands are out hunting is in no way restricted.

[14] The Amahuaca sometimes drink human blood, too, but not as part of hunting magic. It is usually done by the close female relative of a man who has been wounded by an animal or an arrow. The blood may be drunk directly from the wound, or collected in a small bowl and drunk from this. The practice is considered therapeutic for the injured man.

along the back of the hands until blood is drawn, "so that no spider monkey will escape."

Strips of inner bark from a tree with a very caustic sap are occasionally tied around a boy's wrists or forearms, burning a ring around the arm which remains as a permanent scar. This is done so that, again, "no animal will escape." During one hunting trip I observed a man crush the leaves of a certain plant in his upraised hands and allow the caustic juice to trickle down the inside of his arms to the biceps. This, he said, would bring him luck in hunting spider monkeys.

Stronger forms of magic are sometimes resorted to, especially if a hunter has had several unsuccessful hunting trips in succession. He may cut a wasps' nest from a tree and stand holding it, allowing himself to be stung by the wasps. If the pain becomes unbearable, he runs through the forest, still carrying the nest, so that fewer wasps will sting him. For the next two or three days he may be very ill and badly swollen from the effect of the stings, but he is sure to emerge from the ordeal a better hunter.[15]

But the strongest hunting magic of all is for a man to inoculate himself with the very toxic secretion of a small frog which the Amahuaca call *kambó*.[16] This secretion is scraped off the back of the frog with a stick. Then, taking a live brand, a man burns himself in several places on the arms or chest, and rubs this secretion into the burns. Within a short time he becomes violently ill, suffering uncontrollable vomiting and diarrhea. For the next three days, while under the influence of the toxin, he has vivid hallucinations which are regarded as supernatural experiences.[17] When he finally recovers, he is convinced that his hunting is bound to improve.

[15] I have also seen a hunter allow himself to be stung by ants he encountered on the trail in the forest, for the same purpose.

[16] I was not able to identify this frog, but it may be related to the *kokoi* frog, *Phyllobates bicolor* (or *Dendrobates tinctorius*) of Colombia, whose secretion is used by the Chocó Indians to poison their blowgun darts (Wassén 1935:99–100; 1955–56:78–81). *Kokoi* poison has recently been discovered to be the most toxic natural substance known (Anonymous 1965:-112).

[17] The Amahuaca also drink *ayahuasca* (*Banisteriopsis caapi*) to induce spirit visions, but do not do so to assist them in hunting.

Even dogs are treated magically. To enable a dog to find land turtles, an infusion from a certain *piripiri* plant may be given to it to drink or put into its nose or eyes. The owner of a dog which is no longer hunting well attempts to sharpen its scent by putting tapir dung, pepper juice, or a paste of ants' nest up the dog's nostrils. A poor hunting dog may even have its tail docked, to see if this will help.

Summary

Although the Amahuaca have practiced horticulture for centuries, they continue to rely heavily on hunting in their subsistence. The dense forest in which they live provides game in variety and abundance. Highly skilled in the use of the bow and arrow and in tracking and stalking animals, the Amahuaca are very proficient hunters. But not content with their physical skill alone, they attempt to improve their hunting by magical means. The effect of this magic, as the hunter sees it, is, on the one hand, to enhance his own ability and, on the other, to increase the susceptibility of the game.

Bibliography

Anonymous. 1965. Lethal Kokoi Venom Related to Hormones. MD 9:112.

Carneiro, R. L. 1962. The Amahuaca Indians of Eastern Peru. Explorers Journal 40:iv, 26–37.

———— 1964. The Amahuaca and the Spirit World. Ethnology 3:6–11.

Hassel, Jorge M. von. 1905. Las tribus salvajes de la región amazónica del Perú. Boletín de la Sociedad Geográfica de Lima 17:27–73.

Linton, R. 1936. The Study of Man. New York.

Malinowski, B. 1954. Magic, Science and Religion and Other Essays. Garden City, N. Y.

Oberg, K. 1940. The Social Economy of the Tlingit Indians. Ph.D. dissertation, University of Chicago.

Wassén, S. H. 1935. Notes on Southern Groups of Chocó Indians in Colombia. Etnologiska Studier 1:35–182.

———— 1955–56. On Dendrobates-Frog-Poison Material Among Emperá (Chocó)-Speaking Indians in Western Caldas, Colombia. Etnografiska Museet Arstryck, pp. 73–94.

White, L. A. 1959. The Evolution of Culture. New York.

The Slash-and-Burn Technique † *

Swidden Farming Follows a Rotation Pattern in Which Woodlands Supply Ashes That Enrich the Soil Ahead of Food Crops; It is Still Practiced by Millions of Agriculturists in Regions on Both Sides of the Equator

F ROM the layers of plant pollen found buried in Danish and Irish bogs we know the kinds of vegetation that grew there during successive periods of time. An examination of the deposits also tells the story of a simple farming method that reached Europe about 5000 B.C., and that still persists in various parts of the world.

Before the Europeans could begin raising crops, something had to be done about the great forests. They did it by slashing and burning the trees. Evidence of the burning shows in the pollen record as a layer of oak charcoal. On the cleared plot the ancient agriculturists then grew wheat and barley for anywhere from ten to twenty-five years, until the declining yield showed that the soil was exhausted. Whereupon they moved on to open up a new area in similar fashion, leaving the old clearing to become overgrown by brush, and then trees. Years later, others might again clear the same plot by the slash-and-burn method, thus beginning a new cycle.

This kind of shifting cultivation was a natural one for simple farmers in their first encounter with tree-covered land. A similarly mobile type of agriculture appeared nearly 7,000 years later when the first European corn-growing pioneers plunged into the temperate-zone forests of North America. Eventually, of course, the growth of settlements and increase of population made it necessary to clear the forest permanently for the continuous use of the same patches of land. In Europe the requirements of this settled type of agriculture were gradually met by an increasingly elaborate balance of mixed farming, with crop rotations and animal manure serving to keep the soil fertile. In

† By W. M. S. Russell.

* Reprinted from Natural History Magazine, March, 1968. Copyright ⓒ The American Museum of Natural History, 1968.

North America's forest belt, such permanent settlement developed much faster, and not without disastrous impoverishment of
some of the land. At any rate, on both continents today a choice
is made: The old temperate-zone woodlands are either conserv-
ed, for their timber-growing potential or for recreation, or else
they are permanently cleared, for a settled agriculture equipped
with all the resources of modern technology.

Only in the cold far north of Europe did temporary clearing
linger on to any marked extent. One reason was that the oak
forests there gave way to damp spruce and pine woods growing
on poor, sandy soils. The trees were cut, the litter was burned
to make a thick layer of mineral-rich ash, the ground was hoed
(in later periods, plowed) between the tree stumps, and oats or
rye (which tolerate the cold) were grown for a while; then the
farmers moved elsewhere, leaving the deserted plot to birch and
alder, and at last to the returning pines. This was the same
method that had been used in the oak forests. It lasted into the
late nineteenth century in northern Russia, until 1918 in northern
Sweden, and persists today in parts of Finland.

For the Finns, the farm in the clearing must long have been
a familiar sight; in their ancient national epic, *Kalevala,* the
voice of the old hero Väinämöinen is said to stumble like the hoe
among the pine roots. But certainly by A.D. 1781, and probably
much earlier, some Finns had transformed the old, casually shifting cultivation into a regular rotation of forest farming. In the
first year, they felled the trees. In the second, they burned
them. For the next four to six years they grew crops among
the stumps. For twenty to thirty years after that they allowed
the clearing to revert to forest, then they returned to the same
plot and same cycle. Such systematic rotation appeared in Sweden, too, probably brought by Finnish immigrants.

But this way of farming eventually declined, along with the
older, casual procedure, as the demand for northern timber increased among peoples farther south and as modern methods
made settled agriculture more productive even in the north.

Although forest farming is dying in temperate lands, it remains much alive in the rain forests and savanna woodlands
that exist on either side of the Equator, covering vast areas in
Central and South America, Africa, Asia, and the islands of the

Pacific. Such farming is not a curiosity for anthropologists, a quaint survival among a few backward tribes; it is the way of life for a substantial fraction of the human race. Figures for 1957 estimate that farming on temporary clearings was practiced by over 200 million people (nearly 1 in 12 of the world population), on 14 million square miles (about 30 per cent of the world's cultivable land).

A few isolated tribes with rather simple cultures, for instance in the Amazon Basin and on the uplands of Burma and Thailand, practice the haphazard shifting cultivation of the pioneers. But most forest farmers long ago adopted systematic land use. The area under crops shifts its position, but any given plot is regularly rotated between cropping and fallow. In the fallow period the forest returns, hence this system is sometimes called forest fallow rotation.

Systematic slash-and-burn agriculture has evolved independently in all tropic regions. The farming system and the cleared plot are usually known by the same name, but this varies with locality, so the same practice is called by many names. From Central and South America we have milpa, coamile, ichali, conuco, roça; from Africa, masole, chitemene, tavy; and from the Far East, chena, djum, bewar, dippa, erka, jara, kumari, podu, prenda, dahi, parka, taungya, tamrai rây, hwajon, djuma, humah, tagal, ladang, kaingin. English-speaking scientists have coined several additional terms, including slash-and-burn, fire agriculture, and forest fallow rotation; they now generally call the typical plots in all these places swiddens (from an old English country word for burned clearings), and the system is swidden farming.

The basic practice is similar all over the tropics. A swidden site is carefully selected. Trees are either felled, usually leaving the stumps, or completely stripped of their branches; creepers and underbrush are slashed away; and the resulting litter, or slash, is spread over the swidden. This is done in the dry season, so the debris soon dries out. It is then set on fire (sometimes with precautions to prevent the fire spreading). This leaves the swidden covered with a layer of ash, ready for planting crops in time to take advantage of the coming rains.

In Europe, and even more so in North America, a farm field conveys the idea of rows and rows of crop plants all of the same kind. By contrast, a swidden is generally like a North American vegetable garden run wild, covered with all sorts of crop plants that will be harvested at different times. In a typical Central American swidden, for instance, squash vines spread over the ground surface, cornstalks rise into the air, beans climb up the cornstalks. The most sophisticated swidden farmers known are the Hanunóo on Mindoro Island in the Philippines, who are impressive botanists. About 1,200 plant species are known in their region, but the Hanunóo themselves distinguish 1,600 different kinds—evidently their classification goes down to plant varieties. Of this number, they actually breed more than 400 kinds in their swiddens. Various other species reproduce themselves. To protect these when the swidden is burned, the farmers wrap them in green plant material.

Generally, among such peoples the swidden is cultivated intensively for a year or so, then gradually less intensively, and finally abandoned. For instance, in Ondo Province, Nigeria, one practice is to clear the swidden in February and burn soon after. Yams and corn are planted with the first rains, together with pumpkins, melons, and calabashes. When the farmers harvest the first corn, in June, they plant beans, manioc, okra, and cocoyams. In September-October they harvest the yams; in October-November they harvest a second crop of corn, which was planted in August. A third corn crop may be planted in the next rainy season, and the farmers may return for a year or two thereafter to dig the manioc and cocoyams, but they generally do not immediately plant this plot again. Fruit trees are often included among swidden crops, and their fruit may be harvested for several years after the swidden is abandoned. Meanwhile, through regeneration from stumps (which are left three feet high in Nigeria for this purpose) and by growth of seeds from the surrounding bush, the swidden gradually reverts to forest. It will not be cleared again for some time. In the interval, other swidden sites are cleared and go through the same cycle.

The periods under intensive cropping and under fallow vary in different places, but when the system is working effectively the cropping period is always relatively short, and the fallow period relatively long, as seen in the chart below.

REGION	YEARS UNDER INTENSIVE CROPPING	YEARS UNDER FALLOW
Philippines (Hanunóo)	2–4	8–10
New Guinea	1	15–20
Ceylon	1–3	8–20
Sierra Leone	2	12–15
Ghana	1–3	10–15
Nigeria (rain forest)	1–2	8–14
Nigeria (savanna woodland)	4	Up to 30

The method of selecting new swidden sites has been studied in detail among the Hanunoo. These people choose sites where the composition of the fallow vegetation has reached the stage ready for slash-and-burn. This may be from eight to ten years after the previous cropping period. The expert Hanunóo do not work with map and calendar. They are guided by botanical criteria that are flexible and highly relevant for their purpose. This method allows for local differences (between soils for instance) and ensures that the fallow period has lasted long enough.

In some parts of the tropics, specially modified forms of swidden farming are practiced, such as the system characteristic of Zambia but found in many other woodland areas of East Africa. In this chitemene system, the farmers slash and burn not only the trees and underbrush of the swidden; they add branches brought in from the surrounding woods. In Sudan, several tribes omit burning the swidden, and instead take advantage of the fact that termites quickly reduce the woody litter to powder. Also in this region are the Dinka, who practice a kind of termite-chitemene system—they collect wood from some distance and pile it in the swidden for the termites.

Not all swidden farmers are people with extremely simple cultures. The Hanunóo, for instance, can write, so they post notices warning neighbors to avoid walking into a clearing that has been slashed but not yet burned. However, the actual farming method is basic to the way of life of all these peoples. It is also encumbered with considerable ritual. To early European observers, the whole procedure seemed senseless, primitive, and a gross waste of land.

Yet there is often method, even in the rituals. The Hanunóo drive a hollow bamboo stick into the ground at a possible swidden site. If the soil does not rise high enough inside the stick, they discard the site and clear elsewhere. Although they regard this as a purely magical test, it can be a crude agronomic way of appraising the soil's structural readiness for tillage. And on many points, these and other swidden farmers can often give excellent scientific reasons for their practices.

Many Europeans must have had the experience that Bishop Mackenzie described to fellow missionary and explorer Dr. David Livingstone in the mid-nineteenth century. "When telling the people in England what were my objects in going out to Africa," said the Bishop, "I stated that, among other things, I meant to teach these people agriculture; but I now see that they know far more about it than I do."

Furthermore, the swidden system is extraordinarily suitable for the tropical environment. Considerable experimental work in Africa, for example, indicates how the system conserves soil fertility. To begin with, the heavy rains keep many tropical forest and woodland soils poor in nitrogen, phosphorus, and other mineral elements that plants need. Nitrogen is normally present in soils either in an insoluble form unusable to plants, in organic matter, or in soluble forms (chiefly nitrates) that plants can take up. Every year, in the tropical rainy season, much of the nitrogen in organic matter is converted by soil bacteria into nitrate. Some of this is used by the plants, but much, being soluble in the rain water, is washed out of the topsoil. This means the stock of available nitrogen is steadily diminished. Phosphorus and other mineral nutrients are also leached down beyond reach of the plant roots.

This leaching problem often also affects the damp, sandy pine-woods of northern Europe, and the benefits of forest fallow have been experimentally demonstrated in Finland as well as in Africa. When leached soils are continuously cropped without manuring, the available nutrient elements are soon used up; crop yields fall and eventually fail. This had begun to happen by 1933, for instance, in parts of Zambia where continuous cash crops of corn had replaced the chitemene system.

Forest fallow restores fertility in at least two ways. First, it constantly returns plant material to the soil as litter (leaves, dead branches, and so forth); then soil bacteria, stimulated by the tropical warmth, quickly convert the litter to organic matter, where the nitrogen content is safe from leaching. Thus the reserves of soil nitrogen gradually increase. Secondly, deep tree roots bring back phosphorus and other mineral nutrients that were leached down to lower depths, and concentrate them at the soil surface or in plant growth—"living fallow." If the fallow is allowed to remain long enough, the topsoil is much enriched in organic matter and mineral nutrients by the next time the plot is cleared.

Early European visitors supposed that burning the slash must be harmful. But agronomists have shown the reverse to be true. The phosphorus and other minerals stored in growing trees are all deposited in the ash, which makes an excellent fertilizer (especially when the forest outside the swidden is also exploited, as in the chitemene system). Although nitrogen in the growing trees is lost to the atmosphere when they are burned, very little of the new store of organic matter in the soil is destroyed by the fire. Experiments in Malawi, Sierra Leone, and Zambia have shown that the burning is in itself beneficial, for burning slash on the swidden gives a higher crop yield than burning it elsewhere and bringing the ash to the swidden. Experiments in Brazil suggest that burning affects soil bacteria (by killing some and stimulating others) in just the right way to improve the soil nitrogen cycle. It is because of this that the crops on a swidden grow and yield well for a few years—until the rebuilt stores of nutrients are exhausted.

Swidden farming can offer other benefits in the tropics. A frequent problem, for example, is actual destruction of the soil by erosion resulting from heavy tropical rains. Where soil is unprotected by fallow, the raindrops may break up part of the surface, and batter the rest to form a waterproof cap. Then the rain water, instead of soaking into the soil, runs down slopes. This runoff may finally tear away the soil in sheets or gouge it into deep gullies.

On steep slopes, one elaborate answer to this problem is building terraces to check the force of the runoff and allow time for water and silt to accumulate on the terrace steps where the crops

are grown.   Terrace building is laborious, however, and not usually done on a plot used for only a few years at a time.

The swidden system is easier and has many built-in safeguards
against soil erosion.   When choosing a site for clearing, the Hanunóo carefully avoid uneven ground and unstable soils vulnerable to erosion;   for this they use their elaborate classification
of soils, which agrees well with results of scientific soil analysis.
Then, during the critical period when the newly cleared swidden
is exposed to the danger of wind erosion, the drying slash is
spread over every square foot of soil as a dead cover, or mulch.
(Hanunóo teen-agers who find this chore a nuisance are lec-
tured by their elders about soil erosion.)   Creeping, erect, and
climbing plants protect the soil during cropping.   Afterward
the new covering of forest fallow takes over: the foliage and
litter break the rain's force, so that it sinks gradually into the
soil.

But there is another tropical hazard—the rank growth of
weeds, including grasses.   Within a year or two after it is cleared, the swidden may become choked by these light-loving plants.
Indeed, this often is why the swidden is abandoned so soon.   If
the forest fallow is able to regenerate, the shade of the trees
will eventually suppress the weeds.   A way to aid this process
is to leave tree stumps and protect some trees during the fire,
so they can provide shade for the tree seeds coming from outside the clearing.   The stumps serve another purpose: new
growth often sprouts directly from them.

By this method the swidden farmers give the forest a chance
to return and compete successfully with the weeds.   But if
cropping goes on too long, the soil may become too poor for
trees to get started, and grass weeds may get too much of a grip.
The balance now tips in favor of grass against trees, and the plot
becomes grassland.

In parts of Africa, swidden farming has become adapted for
grassland fallow.   But in tropical rotations the grasses are less
satisfactory than trees.   Their roots are too shallow to reach
mineral nutrients leached into the lower soil.   Furthermore, the
grass supplies little litter for making organic matter.   Grass
fallow rotation generally supports only low-yielding, small-grain-
ed cereals like the millets, and only on the least-leached soils.
Finally, tough, tall grasses like *Imperata cylindrica,* called cogon

in the Far East, are liable to take over, turning the plot into a cogonal—an intractable sod that cannot be farmed (at least by ancient methods).

Proper swidden techniques, on the other hand, are admirably adapted to the tropical environment. But they accomplish their purpose only when the ratio of fallow period to cropping period remains high. This requires a great deal of land for each family. For example, if the cropping period is two years and the fallow period is eighteen years, then only 10 per cent of the land is under crops at one time. Hence the system will only support a very low population density—generally about 130 people per square mile, according to an estimate made in Java and widely accepted for the tropics as a whole. The system worked, therefore, during the thousands of years when tropical populations were kept low by parasites and infectious diseases.

But in the twentieth century, modern medicine caused a dramatic increase in populations all over the tropics. Inevitably, a greater proportion of the land was used to meet the need for more food. Also inevitably, the cropping period grew longer and the fallow period shorter. By 1964, for instance, the forest fallow period in parts of Sierra Leone had shortened drastically. It had lasted from twelve to fifteen years; it became three or four years. By 1955, it had shortened in Iboland (Nigeria, rain forest zone) from between eight and fourteen years to three or four years. On parts of the Jos Plateau (Nigeria, savanna woodland zone), a sequence of four years under crops and up to thirty years of woodland fallow became four to six years under crops and one to two years under grass fallow—the woodlands had disappeared.

With this changing ratio of cropping to woodland fallow, the fallow often ceased to fulfill its functions, and eventually was unable to regenerate at all. Crop yields steadily declined as the fallow period shortened. In Benue Province (Nigeria), this deterioration was already noticeable by 1927. Today, over large areas of land, forest has been replaced by cogon grass and has become useless for food production; such cogonals cover 18 per cent of all land in the Philippines. Over other large areas, especially in Africa, India, and Burma, soil has been altogether lost by erosion.

Thus, throughout the tropics, the swidden system is tending to break down under the weight of rising populations. This, of course, is only one aspect of the growing population crisis throughout the world. Between 1958 and 1964, world agricultural production was spectacularly increased by prodigies of technological effort; but production per head remained constant because of the swelling population. Even assuming that the population problem will be solved, however, the swidden method faces reappraisal.

One answer may be to replace it with new farming methods. Although many swidden families have settled homes (however much they shift their plots in the surrounding forest), their way of life is difficult to integrate with that of modern civilization. And it will certainly be desirable to make vast areas of land more productive, capable of contributing more to mushrooming urban societies. To this end, intensive efforts are being made to find better forms of tropical farming. But even with all the resources of modern technology, the task is difficult and the problem far from solved (a tribute to the limited but real achievements of swidden farming, which were made without any of these resources).

In the drier parts of tropical regions, continuous cropping may well prove possible on a large scale. Experiments in savanna areas of Africa have shown that continuous cropping with compost, animal manure, or chemical fertilizers is far more productive than rotation with the grass fallows to which many such areas have been reduced. In surviving savanna woodlands, too, such methods may be better than swidden farming, although it is likely that the chemical fertilizers would have to include more nutrients than the conventional nitrogen, phosphorus, and potassium, which generally suffice for soils of temperate zone lands. The development of mixed farming (providing abundant animal manure) is perhaps the most hopeful solution. This would require introducing improved breeds of animals and (in Africa) eliminating the tsetse flies, harbingers of human and animal disease.

But in the heart of the rain forest there can be another answer. Much research is now directed toward developing a modernized swidden system. It would rely on a fallow made by deliberate planting of selected trees (or sometimes creeping plants), which will either restore soil fertility better and faster than natural fallows, or make possible a new combination of farming with forestry. So far, the attempts have shown little improvement over natural fallow, but research continues. It may well be that, in some such modernized form, man's oldest way of forest farming will continue to prove its worth.

The Turkmen Nomads † *

U NTIL a century ago, Turkmen nomads migrated seasonally over the Central Asian steppe in search of pasture, their mobility preserved by their independence from neighboring sedentary governments. Today they have lost their independence, but in remote areas many still cling to their nomadic way of life.

The Turkmen inhabit a region divided between three countries—Afghanistan, Iran, and the Soviet Union—and their population is a million and a half. Although they have all been brought under the control of these countries, conquest and settlement were accomplished piecemeal, affecting some areas sooner and more drastically than others. Among those who have remained nomadic, tradition is largely intact, and when I began my study of the Turkmen in the winter of 1965, I decided to concentrate on this group.

The devotion of these people to a migratory way of life can be understood only in historic perspective. The Turkmen are by tradition a pastoral people, and for them nomadism is a way of using sparse and seasonably variable pasture for livestock production. But it was, in the past, something more: a means of resisting firm government control. Such resistance was a consciously maintained tradition among the Turkmen, and nomadism was the chief means to this end.

Their eagerness to resist the power of sedentary states grew out of an understanding of what government control meant to settled people. In the harsh social environment of the traditional Middle East and Central Asia, settled people were frequently exploited through the imposition of heavy taxes and rents.

† By William Irons.

* Reprinted from Natural History Magazine, November, 1968. Copyright

© The American Museum of Natural History, 1968.

The turkmen not only avoided such exploitation, but by raiding
and collecting tribute from their sedentary neighbors, they went
a step further and put themselves in the position of the exploiter.
A century ago they were notorious as brigands and especially as
slave raiders. Slaving activities were conducted primarily in
northeastern Persia (now Iran): Turkman raiding parties am-
bushed caravans or attacked villages, retreating quickly with
their captives to their own territory.

The portion of the Central Asian steppe inhabited by the Turkmen stretches east from the Caspian Sea to the Amu Darya, a
large river that empties into the Aral Sea. The central part of
this area is the Kara Kum, or "black sand," a vast, largely unin-
habited and uninhabitable desert. The majority of the Turkmen
are concentrated in two somewhat more fertile regions bordering
the Kara Kum. One area consists of the banks of the Amu
Darya; the other is a long strip of plains and low mountains,
lying south of the Kara Kum and separating it from the Iranian
Plateau. My study was carried out in a section of the latter
area—in the Gorgan Plain of northern Iran.

All nomadic Turkmen are divided into residential groups
known as *obas*, and my research was focused on a single *oba*
consisting of sixty-one households. This group migrates within
the Gokcha Hills, a patch of low hills that protrudes into the
Gorgan Plain. An *oba* is associated with a definite territory,
and all of its members share common rights over that territory,
including the right to use the pastures and any natural source of
water there. All have the right to dig wells, but once such wells
have been dug they become the private property of the persons
who expended their labor in digging them. Similarly, all may
plow up virgin land for cultivation, but once someone plows a
section it becomes his private property.

Throughout the year these nomads live in yurts, a Central
Asian tent, which consists of a hemispherical wooden frame covered with felt. They make their living primarily by raising
sheep and goats, and their pattern of migration is largely determined by the needs of their animals and by variations in pasture
and water supply. The climate of the Gorgan Plain is characterized by definite wet and dry seasons. The wet season begins
in the winter, and during this season the Gokcha Hills and surrounding steppe are covered with a short, but relatively thick,

crop of grass giving the appearance of a vast, freshly mowed lawn. Winter temperatures are mild, rarely dipping below the freezing point. The rainwater, as well as occasional melted snow, collects in scattered depressions to form pools from which water is taken for household needs. During this season, the nomads camp where water and suitable pasture can be found. Ample pasture is usually available close to their dry-season location, so that most of their migrations are quite short. In this respect, they differ considerably from many of the pastoral peoples in and around the Iranian Plateau who make long seasonal moves ranging over vastly differing ecological zones.

Among the Turkmen, the seasonal migrations of camps differ from the movements of livestock. The nomad camps of the Gokcha Hills alternately collect at wells and disperse over the surrounding territory, while the livestock move between the Gokcha Hills and the Gorgan River, thirty miles to the south, thus covering a larger area. This means that the Turkmen camp near their herds only during a portion of the year.

The reason for this lies in the needs of their livestock. During the latter part of the winter, the lambing season begins and the Turkmen must be near their herds to assist in cases of difficult birth and to care for the lambs, which are kept inside the yurts at night to protect them from the cold. Because the lambs are too weak to travel far, they must be pastured near the camp. Even after the young animals are weaned, the adult females must be milked daily, and for this reason, the nomads still keep the livestock near their camp.

With the onset of summer, the dry season begins, and the green pastures of spring are gradually transformed to a barren brown. The rainwater pools disappear, and now the nomads must camp near their wells. When the pastures become sparse and desiccated, the animals stop giving milk, and it is no longer necessary to keep them nearby. They are then sent south to the banks of the Gorgan River, where they graze the stubble of harvested fields. The younger men of each household accompany their family's livestock and live separately from the rest of the household, with only a small lean-to-like tent for shelter.

This division of labor is possible because herding, as well as other forms of economic production, is organized by extended families, consisting of an older man and his wife, his married

sons with their wives and children, and his unmarried sons and
daughters. Each family produces only a part of what it con-
sumes: milk and milk products, meat, felts and carpets for their
yurts, and a small amount of grain. In hope of a late spring
harvest, wheat and barley are planted during the winter in valley
bottoms or other depressions where water tends to collect. This
is a gamble, however, since often the crop does not develop, but
when a crop can be harvested, the yield is generally sufficient to
make up for the losses of grain put down as seed in bad years.

The rest of their needs must be purchased. Cash income
comes from the sale of wool, felts, carpets, and animals for meat.
The basic item in their diet is bread, and they purchase the bulk
of the wheat from which the bread is made. Rice, tea, and sugar
must all be bought. Clothing, cloth, metal tools, and nowadays,
a handpowered sewing machine and a transistor radio, are other
items that a typical nomadic Turkmen family buys. About once
a month, two or three men from each *oba* travel to the nearest
city to purchase supplies and to sell their products: animals,
wool, and carpets. Thus, the pastoral economy of the Turkmen
is market-oriented, even though production is organized along
family lines.

The organization of the extended family reflects a strong emphasis on descent in the male line, which runs through all Turkmen social institutions. When a man's daughters marry they go
to live with their husbands' families, whereas his sons bring their
wives into his household, where they assume the dual role of
wife and daughter-in-law. A man's grandchildren in the male
line grow up in his household, and he commonly refers to them
as his "sons" and "daughters." When, with the passing of generations, his grandsons become old men and the heads of extended families of their own, they will camp together and co-operation between them will be extensive. If any one of them is offended by an outsider, the group will band together to seek redress. Small patrilineages of this sort provide the model in
terms of which the larger political units of Turkmen society are
organized.

The older men, who make the important decisions, know their
genealogies well. Each of them can, on the basis of his genealogy, identify a group of people who share with him a common
ancestor in the male line four generations back, and a slightly

larger group of people descended from a common ancestor five generations back, and so on, until he has identified himself with descent groups including thousands of families. Ultimately all Turkmen believe they are united by their genealogies as the desecendants of a single man, Oghuz Khan. Although the remoter generations of these genealogies are vague and legendary in character, this is of no practical importance since the Turkmen take them seriously as a basis for arranging their social obligations.

Traditionally, the primary function of these descent groups was defense of the individual's rights through violence, or the threat of violence. Defending one's patrilineal kinsmen when their rights were violated was a basic duty in Turkmen social life. This was extremely important, because the absence of state control and of tribal offices with sufficient authority to enforce law and order meant that the strength of a Turkmen's patrilineage was the only guarantee of his rights.

When someone violated a Turkmen's rights by robbing him, injuring him, or killing him, his patrilineal kinsmen were obligated to seek redress by whatever means was necessary, even including violence. In cases of murder, for example, either the murderer or one of his lineage-mates was killed in revenge. Who sought redress for the victim and who defended the culprit were matters determined by genealogy and by the gravity of the affair. Small problems could be handled by the imediate families of the victim and the culprit. As matters increased in seriousness, a wider and wider circle of people who shared common patrilineal descent was called upon for assistance.

Those who were, on the basis of their genealogy, close to neither party also had a prescribed role. It was their obligation to attempt to bring about a peaceful settlement and, if possible, to prevent bloodshed. If the offense was slight, they merely advocated peaceful discussion and suggested compromise. In cases of murder, the neutral party aided the culprit by hiding him from the victim's kinsmen and by helping to arrange his escape to some distant place of refuge. Protecting those who came seeking refuge was part of the obligation of neutral parties to prevent bloodshed. The Iranian government has been attempting to eliminate this traditional system of self-help and to enforce law and order itself; in remoter areas, however, it has not always been successful.

The composition of Turkmen *obas*, like many other aspects of Turkmen social structure, reflects the importance of patrilineal descent. Most of the men of any *oba* are closely related in the male line; in addition, there are usually a number of unrelated families who have come to the *oba* fleeing feuds in their home territory. While these refugees reside there, the *oba* will protect their rights of person and property against outsiders.

The men of an *oba* traditionally selected a headman, who took charge of all dealings with the outside world. Today, in theory, he is appointed by the government, but in practice the local officials usually allow the men of the *oba* to indicate the man they want as their headman. The headman has no authority, but merely acts as a spokesman for the *oba* as a whole. Any important decision must be based on consensus; it must be preceded by discussion by all the men of the *oba*. Usually a headman is selected for his intelligence and integrity and for his ability to speak Persian, the language of the government officials with whom he must deal.

Ordinarily a group of fifteen to thirty *obas*, which belong to the same descent group and occupy contiguous tracts of land, form what the Turkmen call an *il*, a word best translated as tribe. In the days of intertribal warfare, the *obas* of such a tribe were usually on peaceful terms with one another. Tribes that adjoined were usually hostile, and there was much raiding between them.

One of the functions of the Turkmen tribe that has not survived government control is the practice of protecting neighboring sedentary villages. These villages were especially vulnerable to the raids of the Turkmen, and to gain a measure of security and protection each village paid tribute to the Turkmen tribe nearest it. In return, the tribe agreed not to raid the village, and to prevent raids by other Turkmen tribes. They also agreed to compensate the village for losses if they were unsuccessful in preventing raids by other tribes. In effect, the exchange of protection for tribute was a peaceful substitute for raiding.

The Turkmen were able to resist government control, to raid, and to collect tribute because their nomadic way of life made them an effective military force. They were good horsemen and were well supplied with horses. Raids, both of sedentary villages and of other nomads, were frequent events and provided the

Turkmen with excellent military conditioning. When clashes with the Persian military forces occurred, normally hostile tribes would unite to turn out a large body of cavalry. This seasoned cavalry could usually hold its ground against the Persian forces, but even when met by superior strength, the Turkmen did not surrender. Instead, they would retreat into the desert north of the Gorgan River, taking their families and livestock with them.

Thus, mobility preserved the power and independence of the Turkmen; this was why they consistently avoided anything that would compromise it. Much of the territory they inhabited was naturally fertile and was crossed by numerous streams. The construction of irrigation works and the practice of intensive agriculture could have made this land more productive. Permanent houses at their dry-season locations could have increased their comfort. The Turkmen, however, would not accept such trends away from nomadic life. They concentrated instead on livestock production, on raiding, and on the collection of tribute.

During the last century, the political independence of the Turkmen has gradually been whittled away. Advances in military technology have shifted the balance of power between the nomadic tribes and settled society and have led to the conquest of the nomads by sedentary powers. Most of the Turkmen were conquered by the Russians during the latter half of the nineteenth century. Those on Iranian soil were subdued and brought under firm control in 1925.

The objective of conquering governments has been to encourage a transition to a more sedentary and peaceful way of life. Such a transition, however, could rarely be accomplished at once. The nomads viewed settlement as a consolidation of governmental authority over them, and were not eager to take up sedentary life. For this reason, in the thirties the Iranian government began a policy of forced settlement not only of the Turkmen but of all of the Iranian tribes. The nomads I studied had been forced to build permanent houses at their dry-season locations in 1936. For five years, under the watchful eyes of government authorities, they lived in these houses during the dry season and migrated with their yurts only during the wet season. This form of semisedentary life developed naturally out of their pattern of pasturing sheep away from their dry-season camps. That it caused no economic difficulties is revealing. The nomads had maintained a completely mobile existence for political rather than for economic reasons, and a transition to a semisedentary existence could be made without economic difficulty.

In 1941, Russia occupied northern Iran because it was fearful of Iranian co-operation with the Germans, and the process of settlement was reversed. The Iranians had been interested in modernization, but the Russians were interested only in sufficient order to keep their supply lines to their Western allies open. Many of the Turkmen who had resented forced settlement reverted to nomadism. The people with whom I recently lived destroyed the houses they had been forced to build and returned to living year-round in yurts. Security deteriorated, and banditry became rife in the remoter and more arid regions, such as the Gokcha Hills.

After the Second World War, the authority of the Iranian government was restored in the Gorgan Plain and efforts to modernize the Turkmen were renewed. The government had come to understand the limited value of the type of force measures used in the thirties. Its objective was not to reduce the Turkmen to the traditional position of exploited peasantry, but rather to integrate them into a society that was on the way to becoming a modern nation. This meant the terms would have to be satisfactory to the Turkmen themselves. In line with this policy, persuasion was used rather than force. Great progress was made in the fertile and populous region south of the Gorgan River.

In the Gokcha Hills, things changed more slowly. By 1960, the government had eliminated banditry, clearing the way for further progress. The Turkmen of this region, however, have remained nomadic to the present. Nevertheless, there are indications that they too will eventually be caught up in the trend of modernization.

The Gokcha Hills Turkmen are beginning to realize that their nomadic way of life has no place in the future. In 1967, when I left the *oba* that I had studied, their headman had begun to discuss the need of a school for their children. He is an intelligent man, aware that his own children will have new opportunities if they become literate. He is convinced, however, that they cannot persuade a government school teacher to live in a community that consists only of yurts. He has been telling the men of his *oba* that they need a school, and that in order to have one they will have to build houses as they did in 1936.

The headman will find that winning the men of his *oba* to this view is a difficult task. Eventually, however, they will build houses and a school, and ultimately they will be drawn into the mainstream of Iranian national life.

The Limited Nutritional Value of Cannibalism † *

IN the many discussions on cannibalism, attention has been given to human flesh as a source of quality protein, but without the necessary quantification. A few calculations are therefore in order.

A 50 kg man might yield 30 kg edible muscle mass if well and skillfully butchered, and 30 kg edible muscle would yield about 4.5 kg (4500 gm) protein, or 4.0 kg protein assuming 90% digestibility.

Assuming quality protein requirements as 1 gm per kilogram of body weight, this would provide one-day's protein requirements for approximately 60 60-kilogram adults. One man, in other words, serves 60, skimpily.

Reducing the man-a-day ration to a more realistic man a week, this would barely amount to 9 gm quality protein per day, which might still be viewed as a useful protein *supplement* in a one-cereal culture experiencing protein malnutrition.

Less than one man per week for a group of 60 would not appear to be nutritionally worthwhile, even as a protein supplement to a cereal or tuber diet with limiting amino acids.

Considering its cost, then, the nutritional value of cannibalism may therefore be viewed as questionable, unless a group is in a position to consume its own number in a year. While human flesh may serve as an emergency source of both protein and calories, it is doubtful that regular people-eating ever had much nutritional meaning.

† By Stanley M. Garn & Walter D. Block. Center for Human Growth and Development and School of Public Health University of Michigan.

* Reproduced by permission of the American Anthropological Association from the American Anthropologist 72:106, 1970.

*

VI. From Womb to Tomb

Men, like other animals, are conceived, spend some time in prenatal life, are born, pass through various stages of life, and finally die. Although all men participate in these events the specific details of each event and the ideas that each person holds about the event may be conditioned by the beliefs of his particular culture. The first article in this section by H. Arlo Nimmo about the Bajau, a boat-dwelling people of the southern Philippines, shows us how just one of the many cultures in the world views the human universals of sex and reproduction. Suzanne Keller's article on the future of the family questions many commonly held assumptions about the family and suggests a number of factors that may cause changes in the institution of the family. The next article about marriage among the Guajiro, a pastoral people in northern Columbia and northwestern Venezuela, is noteworthy because the author, Lawrence C. Watson, has written an article on sex and marriage from the woman's viewpoint. This article should be contrasted to the first article in this section on the Bajau in which the author, H. Arlo Nimmo, admits that he was only able to present the male views on sexual behavior in most cases. The next short selection—"The Wife takes a Wife"—illustrates only one of the large number of possible forms of marriage. The article by Ben J. Wallace about spouse exchange among the Pagan Gaddang makes it quite clear that this form of marriage among the Pagan Gaddang is more like a short-term marriage than it is like the "wife-swapping" that is reputed to take place in our society. The web of contractual relationships involved are also noteworthy. The concluding article in this section concerns death and how this event is dealt with in one particular culture. This article also illustrates the blending of aboriginal religion and Christianity that is found in many areas of Latin America.

Bajau Sex and Reproduction † [1] *

THIS paper is a description of Bajau beliefs and practices regarding sexual intercourse, reproduction, and childbirth. The data were collected incidentally to a field investigation of social change among the boat-dwelling Bajau of the southern Philippines, and therefore are not intended to be complete or final. However, since so few ethnographic accounts of the boat-dwelling Bajau are available, it seems wise to publish anthropologically collected data on these people—especially in light of the fact that the traditional culture of the Bajau is rapidly changing as they are currently abandoning their nomadic boat-dwelling habits to become sedentary house-dwellers.[2]

† By H. Arlo Nimmo, California State College at Los Angeles.

[1] This paper is based on two years of field research in Sulu Province, Philippines, sponsored by the East-West Center, Honolulu; the National Science Foundation, Washington, D. C.; the Wenner-Gren Foundation for Anthropological Research, New York; and the Carnegie Corporation of New York. The author gratefully acknowledges the support of these foundations.

* Ethnology.   July   1970:251–262. Reproduced by permission of the editor of Ethnology.

[2] Any paper which proposes to deal with the sexual behavior of a society can rarely be complete for several reasons. In most societies, sex is a delicate subject, the intimacies of which are not normally openly discussed—especially with a note-taking outsider. Consequently, the data of the researcher are biased by the fact that he has obtained them from individuals who are willing to talk about such matters and who may consequently be atypical of their group. Second, the lone investigator must be content to receive a one-sided view of sexual attitudes and behavior. If he is a man, he will come to understand sex as understood by the men of the society and will learn very little about female attitudes except as these are perceived by men. If the investigator is a female, she will have comparable problems with male informants. Third, one must often be content to learn about what people say they do rather than what they actually do. Much anthropological data may be verified through observation to test whether the subject actually does what he says he does. However, since most sexual behavior occurs in extreme privacy, observation is normally excluded. Participant observation may yield additional insights, but these again are one-sided. A final problem may be that of finding a time and place where sex may be discussed with persons who are willing to talk about it. In most societies, certain aspects of sex are not mentioned before members of the opposite sex, certain kinsmen, or children. The intimacy of living, characteristic of most communities studied by anthro-

The Bajau are traditionally known as a nomadic, boat-dwelling people who inhabit the Sulu Islands of the southern Philippines. The Sulu Bajau are only one of several boat-dwelling groups scattered throughout Southeast Asia; others have been reported in parts of the Celebes, southern Malaya, and the Mergui Islands of Burma. Although the historical relationship of these different groups is still unknown, little doubt exists concerning the close relationship of the several groups of Bajau within the Sulu Islands; these groups all speak a single language, share many common cultural features, and were until recent times predominantly boat-dwellers. Today, most of the Sulu Bajau have abandoned their boats as living quarters for land- or reef-based dwellings. The most confirmed boat-dwellers are found in the Tawi-Tawi Islands of Sulu, where they number some 1600 individuals, while the most confirmed house-dwellers live in the Sibutu Islands, especially in Sitangkai, and comprise a population of about 2400. Wherever the Bajau are found, they represent a small minority of the total population. For example, they constitute only 3.1 per cent of the population of the Tawi-Tawi Islands, and in Sibutu they form about 23 per cent of the total Sibutu Islands' population. Within Sulu, the Bajau have always been viewed as an outcaste group by the land-dwelling Muslims,

pologists, sometimes makes it difficult to find the proper privacy for the discussion of sexual matters.

The foregoing is simply a warning to the reader that this discussion of Bajau sexual behavior does not pretend to be complete. Most of the informants were males, although a few females offered views on some of the less intimate aspects of the subject. The fifteen male informants included unmarried, married, divorced, and widowed men, while the three women informants were all married and volunteered their information in the presence of their husbands.

Because of the nature of the subject, the information on childbirth was easier to obtain. The data are based almost entirely upon five interviews with females. These were all mothers, and three of them were renowned as midwives. Most of the women enjoyed discussing the subject, and the three midwives all took pride in displaying their professional knowledge. Perhaps a female anthropologist could have obtained additional insights, but I do not feel that my sex was any great hindrance to my questions on childbirth. To verify some of the data, I was able to observe three births among the Tawi-Tawi Bajau.

Most of the data were collected among the boat-dwelling Bajau of the Tawi-Tawi Islands; a smaller proportion came from interviews conducted among the house-dwelling Bajau of Sitangkai in the Sibutu Islands. Differing views between the two groups have been noted.

but in recent years as many of these sea folk have abandoned boat-dwelling and embraced Islam, they have become incorporated into the Islamic community of Sulu. Those of Tawi-Tawi, however, are still predominantly boat-dwelling subsistence fishermen who continue to follow their traditional life styles (Nimmo 1968).

Although extremely mobile, the Tawi-Tawi Bajau limit their movements to a fairly well-defined sea area, about 250 square miles, southeast of the large island of Tawi-Tawi. Within this area are located the five main Bajau moorages, or villages, and the two small cemetery islands where the sea people bury their dead. These seas are characterized by extensive coral reefs as well as numerous small islands which are farmed by the land-dwelling Muslim peoples upon whom most Bajau are dependent for the vegetable portion of their diet.

The Bajau houseboat typically houses a single nuclear family. Although this family does a great deal of traveling among the various houseboat moorages, it always identifies one moorage as its home; or, if the husband and wife are from two different moorages, the family divides its allegiances and time between these two moorages. Frequently, the nuclear family fishes and travels with married siblings of either the husband or wife to form the second important social unit in Bajau society, the sibling alliance unit. This unit reveals great structural variation and is very ephemeral since houseboats regularly join and leave the unit. Its primary function is that of mutual aid for fishing, ceremonies, and any other activities which require group effort. Each moorage consists of several of these sibling alliance units to comprise a group of cognatically related persons, or a localized kindred, with an older man acting as headman. At the larger moorages, several such localized kindreds may be found, and the headman of the kindred which first began mooring there serves as headman for the entire village. No formal political organization exists beyond the village level to unite the several moorages, but because of the many kin ties and frequent movements among them, the moorages constitute a single, albeit dispersed, Tawi-Tawi community (Nimmo 1969).

Sexual Behavior

Although the intimacies of one's sexual behavior are never discussed openly among the Bajau, sex is not a hushed topic of conversation. Nor does it loom large in the conversations of the Bajau. To the Bajau, the sexual urge and need is almost as natural as any of the other bodily functions, and is nothing to become overly concerned about, an attitude obviously related to the fact that sexual gratification is always available. Premarital sexual relationships are common and expected; consequently, when the Bajau youth begins to feel the stirrings of his sexuality, he need only find a willing partner, which is rarely a problem, to satisfy his urges.[3] Upon marriage, of course, his spouse more conveniently satisfies his sexual desires.

Bajau discuss sexual matters quite frankly in the presence of members of the opposite sex, regardless of age or marital status. Once I heard two women speak with some detail, in the presence of their children and a neighboring man, about the adulterous amours of a village man. On another occasion, two women and a man, affines to one another, discussed rather clinically the probable size of my penis and the possible nature of my sex life. Bajau also joke freely about sex in mixed company and among children. Once, when I was discussing the nature of the Bajau bride-price with a group of adults and children, one of the men told me jokingly that the bride-price was actually paid for the bride's vagina since that was the greatest asset a bride has to offer her husband. The household laughed heartily at the joke, after which we continued our discussion. On another interview occasion with several women, the nature of twins entered the discussion. One of the older women jokingly asked me if I knew how to make twins, and, if so, she wanted me to make some for her. All laughed without embarrassment and thought it a good joke.

Bajau sometimes use euphemisms to refer to sexual matters— not in order to disguise the topic, but rather for the humerous misunderstandings which often result. Once two Bajau girls asked my assistant the price of mangoes in the nearby port town. He told them that they were selling for about ten centavos a bunch. The girls expressed disbelief at the price and said they were much more expensive among the Bajau—at least a peso, and often more than two pesos. My assistant was surprised at the inordinately high price and asked why. They responded that

---

[3] This is less true among the most acculturated Bajau of Sitangkai who are adopting their Islamic neighbors' value of premarital chastity for females.

Bajau mangoes were bigger, sweeter, and lasted longer. The girls then began giggling and my assistant finally realized that they were actually referring to the sexual favors of Bajau girls and not to mangoes. Sometimes a man's penis is referred to as his sail or mast, and reference to either of these structures may lead to a joking conversation filled with sexual metaphors. A young man who is known to be having a rather active sex life is said to be out "laying his eggs." These examples serve to illustrate the freedom with which sex is discussed as well as the lack of embarrassment associated with the topic. However, I do not wish to convey that sex is a constant topic of conversation, for such is certainly not the case.

Although it is a voiced ideal among the Bajau that young people should wait until marriage before engaging in sexual intercourse, it is well known that very few Bajau youth reach marriage without having had sexual experiences. In reality, it is expected that young people will engage in such behavior, which is for the most part condoned by Bajau society. Children early become aware of the nature of the human genitals. They wear no clothes until the age of eight or ten, and commonly explore one another's genitals during these early years. Parents do not become upset with such behavior unless the child displays undue curiosity, when he may be scolded, or more likely teased, until his attention is diverted to something else. Women normally expose their breasts after the birth of their first child, but always wear a sarong to cover their genitals. On the other hand, the loose nature of men's clothing often exposes their genitals—not to mention their common practice of diving in the nude for certain types of fishing. Consequently, the Bajau child matures with little notion of mystery surrounding the human genitalia.

Bajau youth make themselves attractive to members of the opposite sex through the use of numerous beauty aids. Young girls rarely wash their hair, but frequently comb coconut oil into it, the smell of which has a strong feminine association in the Bajau olfactory. Commercially made face powders are sometimes rubbed on the female face to lighten the complexion, or may be caked on heavily in traditional Sulu style so that the face appears masked in white powder. Lipstick is widely used by young girls, and sometimes a really made-up lass may place a spot of it on either cheek. Girls also use fingernail polish and perfumes whenever these are available. To complete her costume, the properly attired young Bajau girl wears jewelry which may include various combinations of earrings, rings, bracelets, necklaces, and brooches. Boys always use heavily scented wax on their hair, and also occasionally use face powder to lighten their complexions. They often let the little fingernail or the thumbnail grow extra long, and may even apply fingernail polish. Those who have whiskers sometimes cultivate mustaches, but such hirsute displays are not widespread owing to the sparsity of facial hair among the Bajau. Both sexes, of course, enjoy dressing in their finest clothes.

A well-filled body is considered beautiful by both sexes; a wiry, muscular body is not considered particularly attractive, nor is an overweight body. Black, oiled hair is preferred over the reddish, sun-bleached shades characteristic of most Bajau. Certain female movements are sexually arousing to the Bajau male. Especially erotic are the slow, languid hip and arm movements of the traditional dances as well as the walking sway of slender female hips.

Love magic, though known in Sulu, is not widely used among the Bajau. Most Bajau men claim to have heard of such magic, but I encountered none who admitted using it. One man, however, claimed that the following formula never fails: If a man gathers sand upon which a girl has stepped, wraps it in a white cloth, and ties it in his boat, the young girl will develop an itching on the soles of her feet which will not stop until she enters the boat, at which time she is very vulnerable to seduction. The informant claimed that a non-Bajau had told him the formula, but he denied ever having tried it himself. Amulets can be worn by females to protect themselves from the love magic of males, but I met only one girl who wore an amulet for this specific purpose—a string necklace which had been made by her grandfather. Since finding a sexual partner is not difficult for the Bajau, it is not surprising to find that love magic is poorly developed among them.

The amours of most Bajau youth take place in the early hours of the evening, shortly after sunset. The unmarried teenagers of the village usually congregate on the nearby beach or exposed reef during the hours of dusk for games and conversation. During this time, romances begin and rendezvous are planned. After dark young people commonly congregate in one of the larger houseboats to play music and sing songs. Here, too, affairs may

begin.   Many Bajau youth make new contacts during ceremonies.
At certain phases of the moon, which complement fishing cycles
and insure that many Bajau houseboats are in the nearby waters,
Bajau ceremonies of healing, circumcision, and marriage are held.
Boats from all the nearby waters come to attend the festivities,
and the size of the host village is consequently greatly expanded.
The early part of the evening celebration is attended by all the
community and consists primarily of music and dancing, but as
the evening wears on the adults and children retire to the houseboats and leave the rest of the night to the unmarried teenagers,
who continue to play music, sing, and size up prospective mates.
Quite often a young couple infatuated with one another may call
upon a third person, boy or girl, to act as go-between in arranging a rendezvous between them.   Girls are often as forward as
boys in initiating such a meeting.   A boy is expected to give the
girl a small gift for her sexual favors, and this practice continues
as long as the girl is amenable to the boy's propositions.

According to Bajau tradition, if a boy and girl are caught in
sex relations the boy may be fined or forced to marry the girl.
The boy is always assumed responsible for the act, while the girl
is never fined even though she may have initiated the rendezvous.
If the couple and their families are agreeable to a marriage between the two, this course is usually taken; otherwise, the fine
is paid by the boy and is divided between the headman who medi-
ates the settlement with the girl's parents.   Fines vary but are
usually no more than twenty pesos, a sizable amount for the
Bajau.   However, there is often much bickering, and the fine
may never be paid.   If a young girl becomes pregnant, she is married immediately.   If she has been having sexual relationships
regularly with a particular boy, he is the one who marries her;
but if she is not sure of the paternity of her child, she picks the
most desirable possibility and points the accusing finger at him.
Consequently, illegitimate births are almost unknown.   Although
it is common knowledge that most girls engage in sexual intercourse before their marriage, it is nonetheless considered improper for a girl to be too free with her sexual favors.   A girl with
such a reputation is unable to command a high bride-price and
may have to settle for a less desirable mate.   This is supported
by the belief that if a girl has sexual relationships with many
different men, her fertility is diminished.   Since children are
highly desired by the Bajau, such a girl is unattractive as a prospective wife.

Unmarried couples have sexual intercourse at any convenient private place, e. g., a vacated houseboat or a lonely part of the beach or reef. For the married couple, the sex act always takes place in their houseboat, after the other members of the household are asleep. This is essential for privacy since the houseboats are small and single-roomed. The regularity with which married persons have sex relations varies: young newlyweds are said to indulge every night, or perhaps several times during a single night, for the first few weeks of marriage, but as the marriage wears on the frequency drops and eventually ceases in old age.

Bajau engage in very little sexual foreplay, and this is usually initiated by the man. He may embrace his mate, fondle her breasts, or manipulate her clitoris. Apparently only among some of the acculturated youth is kissing occasionally practiced; adults express repulsion at the notion of mouth-to-mouth contact. Inquiries regarding any type of oral sexuality were also met with repulsion and with expressions of disbelief that such behavior is practiced by anyone. After arousing his wife, the husband crawls into the sarong which she uses for sleeping. The most common position is the normal one, i. e., the woman lays on her back with spread legs to receive the man, but if there is danger of detection the couple may perform the act on their sides facing one another. If a man's penis is large or if he is entering a virgin, he sometimes finds it necessary to use a lubricant; most commonly his own saliva serves the purpose, but many men claim the white of an egg is even more effective. This apparently has been learned from the land people, however, since the Bajau rarely have eggs to use for any purpose. The sexual act is very brief, partly because of the crowded nature of most households; one must take advantage of the moment before a sleeping household member awakens to ruin the opportunity. The Bajau claim that males reach climax more easily than the females, but most females nonetheless have an orgasm during intercourse, since the male who allows himself to reach climax before his mate is an undesirable lover.

Most Bajau do not recognize any times when sexual intercourse is universally tabued. If one is willing to put up with the uncleanliness of menstruation, sex is legitimate even at that time. A pregnant woman receives her husband throughout her pregnancy until it is uncomfortable for her to do so. In fact, it is

widely believed that frequent intercourse during pregnancy tends
to strengthen the fetus. On the other hand, caul births are believed to result from sexual intercourse during the last month of
pregnancy, and it is consequently considered best to refrain from
sexual intercourse during the final stages of pregnancy.

Bajau identify and name the external reproductive organs, but
they have little detailed knowledge of the internal organs. *Puki*
is a generic term used for the female genitalia, while the vagina
is called *ke puki*, "hole of the puki." The clitoris is called *sellit*,
and the fluid emitted when it is stimulated is called *angomohe*.
The only internal female organ identified by the Bajau is the
womb, which is called *patulian onde-onde*, "sleeping place of the
infant." The female ejaculation is called *boheh puki*, "water of
the puki." The generic term for the male genitalia is *botok*,
which, when used specifically, means penis. The glans penis is
called *kok botok*, "head of the penis," whereas the prepuce is
kulit botok, "skin of the penis." *Buyun* is the scrotum, and the
testicles within are called *big'gih buyun*, "seeds of the scrotum."
The external urethral orifice of the penis is called *boah botok*,
"mouth of the penis," and the sperm is referred to as *boheh botok*,
"water of the penis." The expression for a male orgasm is *angon-
tah boheh botok*, which means literally "to vomit the water of the
penis." Pubic hair is called *bu botok* for men or *bu puki* for wom-
men, "hair of the penis" or "hair of the vagina." The Bajau
claim ignorance of the physiological functioning of the sexual
organs.

It is widely believed throughout Sulu that sexual intercourse
is more enjoyable to both the man and the woman if the man is
circumcised. This is occasionally voiced also among the Bajau,
but it is not a widespread belief, doubtlessly because the Bajau
do not practice true circumcision. The Tausug and some land-
dwelling Samal of Sulu practice true circumcision, that is, an
operation which removes the entire foreskin of the penis. This
is quite unlike the operation which is practiced by the Bajau and
certain land-dwelling Samal groups. At the appropriate age,
usually around thirteen or fourteen, the circumcision ceremony
is held for the Bajau boy. Much celebration surrounds the event,
but the operation itself is very simple. The older man who performs the operation simply stretches the foreskin over the glans
penis and makes a small nick in the foreskin with a knife or piece
of split bamboo. Ashes are then rubbed into the wound, the fore-

skin is pushed back to expose the glans, around which a white cloth is tied. Sometimes if the foreskin is too tight, it must be slit in order to push it back beyond the glans. In most cases, the foreskin is apparently tight enough and short enough so that it remains beyond the glans to give the appearance of true circumcision. Occasionally, the foreskin nevertheless does return to cover the glans, but there is no subsequent operation to remedy this. The Bajau do not presently practice any female genital operation, although some informants claim that a type of clitoridectomy was performed in the past. I could, however, learn nothing of the operation. Apparently such a female operation was also formerly performed by the land people, and is rumored to be still practiced by some of the more traditional inland Tausug.

Adultery occurs among the Bajau but it is difficult to determine its frequency since it is, of course, always clandestine. Adultery is a ground for divorce if the offended spouse cares to push the issue, but more often it causes merely an initial flurry of emotions, and perhaps a brief separation of husband and wife, followed by an eventual reconciliation. A man guilty of adultery must pay a fine, which is divided between the headman and the offended husband. A woman is never fined for her role in an adulterous affair. Only three cases of adultery came to my attention during my sixteen months of research among the Tawi-Tawi boat-dwellers. The cases never emerged as issues for the headman, but everyone in the villages knew of them. All three of the offended spouses were aware of the adulterous affairs of their mates, but for various reasons were content to not interfere; one was an old woman married to a much younger man, another was a somewhat feeble-minded man, and the third was a man married to a young girl with such a long history of extramarital affairs that he apparently no longer took an active concern in her intrigues.

The Bajau claim that masturbation is rarely practiced among them, and such would seemingly be the case since sexual partners are normally available to satisfy any sexual urges that may arise.

Certain herbs found in the Sulu forests may allegedly be mixed into a concoction and drunk by a female to prevent conception. However, I found no informants who could identify the actual herbs, or who had ever used the potion. Bajau also claim that certain herbs can be consumed to bring about miscarriage, but again none professed ever to have used them. The infant mortality rate is so high among the boat-dwellers that no woman would willingly try to prevent conception or destroy her unborn child. Even if she has many children, more are desired since it is likely that some will die before reaching adulthood. For these reasons, the thought of infanticide arouses horror in the Tawi-Tawi Bajau.

CHILDBIRTH

Children are greatly valued by the Bajau, and the young wife who becomes pregnant shortly after her marriage is considered fortunate. Children are desired for very practical reasons, namely, to provide assistance to their parents during their childhood and later to care for their aged parents. So highly valued are children that barrenness is a ground for divorce. The blame for barrenness, however, rests upon neither the husband nor the wife, but rather is usually attributed to fate—an explanation which the Bajau call upon to explain most events they do not understand. Village gossipers occasionally blame a woman's barrenness on some personal misbehavior in her past or that of her husband, but most often the afflicted persons are not considered responsible for their misfortune. Such childless couples sometimes adopt children from kinsmen who have more than they can support, or they may simply go through life childless and depend upon nephews or nieces to care for them in their old age. It is unimaginable to a Bajau that a woman should want to prevent pregnancy. Even if she has many children, other kinsmen are always available to adopt her child. Thus, as noted, contraceptives are unknown.

The Bajau have little understanding of the actual physiological process of pregnancy. They are well aware that conception is dependent upon sexual intercourse, but as to the relation of the two there is little certainty. The most common explanation is that when the semen enters the vaginal tract it brings about a cessation in the menstrual flow which coagulates to form the fetus. The semen must be thick and milky in color to bring about conception; if it is clear and watery, conception will not occur. Most informants claim that sheer chance brings about conception at some times and not at others. There appears to be no knowledge of fertile periods in the menstrual cycle.

Although the Bajau are aware that conception involves the participation of both male and female, it is an unstated assumption that the male has a greater role in conception and the development of the fetus than the female. Several childless women, or women with only one or two children, told me they could not become pregnant because their husbands' semen was not strong enough to penetrate them. Further substantiation of the more important role of the male is the belief that a man should have frequent intercourse with his wife during her pregnancy lest the infant be born very weak or with parts of his limbs missing. The prevailing tabu against patrilateral parallel cousin marriage is also enlightening. Such marriages are believed to be incestuous because cousins in this relationship are considered as closely related as siblings. However, matrilateral parallel cousins and all other cousins are free to marry. The implication seems to be that children created by the semen of brothers are sibling-like, whereas children born of two sisters are less closely related because females are more passive in conception and merely provide a receptacle for the development of the fetus which is implanted by the male. If asked, the Bajau deny that one parent is more important than the other, but the above beliefs attribute a greater significance to the male role.

After a woman becomes pregnant, little change occurs in her daily routine until the final stages, when it may be necessary for her to refrain from some of her more strenuous activities. She observes few if any dietary restrictions; the only one mentioned to me was abstinence from sweets, which are believed to harden the fetus and make delivery difficult. But even this belief is not widespread. Pregnant women experience food cravings, and the Bajau husband occasionally seeks scarce foods to satisfy his wife's cravings. An infant who slobbers a great deal while nursing is believed to do so because his mother's food cravings were not satisfied. A pregnant woman should refrain from ridiculing a person suffering from a physical or mental deformity lest her child suffer the same affliction. Various other superstitions surround pregnancy, e. g., a woman should bathe immediately if she observes clouds passing over a full moon. For the most part, however, pregnancy is not surrounded by many tabus. A woman continues to have regular sexual intercourse with her husband; in fact, as noted, frequent intercourse is believed essential for the proper development of the fetus, except during the final month when it may result in a caul birth.

Some Bajau believe that there are ways to determine the sex of the unborn child. If during the moment of the ejaculation which impregnates his mate, a man breaths inward, the child will be a girl. However, if at this moment he breaths outward, the child will be a boy. Several men claimed faith in the explanation, but all denied ever having tested it since most are never certain which ejaculation brings about conception, and, more importantly, few are concerned at that crucial moment with the direction of their breathing. Women believe that a male fetus makes much more prenatal movement than a female. No Bajau, however, claimed any foolproof method for predicting the sex of the unborn child.

Morning sickness appears to be fairly common among Bajau women during the early months of pregnancy. Sometimes a woman suffering from such illness is given an herbal concoction to drink, but most believe that little can be done for the malady since it is considered a natural incident of pregnancy. If a pregnant woman suffers considerable illness or discomfort, certain ceremonies may be conducted to placate the spirits believed to be causing it. Miscarriages are so common that all the women I interviewed had experienced at least two, and most had had so many they could not even remember the exact number. All agreed that miscarriage occurs most commonly during the early months of pregnancy, and is normally caused by overexertion.

The Bajau woman is able to predict with a fair degree of accuracy the time of her delivery by keeping count of the number of months since the cessation of her menstrual flow. Ten lunar months are considered the normal length of pregnancy. When she begins to feel labor pains, the Bajau woman calls upon her female kinsmen to assist her; if they happen to be in the vicinity her mother and sisters are almost always present. Usually some older woman, locally known as a midwife, delivers the child, while a shaman, male or female, is always present to chant and ward off evil spirits to insure the safe birth of the infant. In addition, a host of other people, children and adults are usually present to witness the birth. The pain of childbirth, of course, varies among individual women, but all my informants agreed that childbirth was the most painful experience they had ever undergone. Furthermore, all claimed to approach each of their deliveries with the fear of death, a fear easily understood in light of the high mortality of women during childbirth.

When a Bajau mother is ready to deliver, she is propped on cushions or bundles in the boat. Often a rope is tied to the roof for her to pull in order to help the delivery and ease the birth pains. As labor increases and delivery is imminent, the shaman bends over the woman, chanting prayers to insure easy delivery as well as good health and fortune for the mother and child. The midwife assists the delivery by pushing on the woman's abdomen to help expel the child, and once the head emerges, she extricates the rest of the body. Bajau mothers claim that often their children are born feet first, and several maintained that birth was less painful this way. The Bajau do not cut the vaginal opening in the event of a difficult birth but rather rely exclusively upon magical remedies.

After the infant has been expelled from the womb, the midwife cleans the mucus from its nose and mouth. If the child is not breathing normally at birth, the midwife may give it mouth-to-mouth resuscitation to instill breathing. However, the infant is never slapped in any way to initiate breathing; most Bajau could not imagine such cruel behavior toward an infant. The midwife holds the umbilical cord between two fingers at the child's stomach and squeezes the liquid from the cord, which is then cut about three inches from the stomach with a piece of split bamboo and tied with any available string. The child is then bathed in usually unheated water—fresh water if it is available, otherwise sea water. The afterbirth is normally expelled shortly after delivery, but, if not, magical chants are used, and sometimes the abdomen is massaged to bring about expulsion.

The placenta and afterbirth are variously disposed of. Among the Tawi-Tawi Bajau, they are normally placed in a coconut shell, and buried on the nearby island by the father. However, the Sitangkai Bajau prefer to bury them in the sea beneath the house of birth to guarantee that the child will become a good swimmer. When carrying the afterbirth away for disposal, the father should look to neither the left nor right, but straight ahead, lest his newly born child become cross-eyed. After the stub of the umbilical cord falls off, it is tied to the cradle. When the stub falls from the cradle of a boy child, it is taken to the deep sea and thrown overboard to insure that the child will become a good fisherman; if the child is a girl, the stub is placed in a tree, the leaves of which are used for mat-making, to insure that the girl will become a good mat-maker.

Shortly after the birth, boughs from citrus trees, cut in the forest by the father and his male relatives, are placed on the top and sides of the boat. These are believed to prevent the entrance of certain evil spirits which may cause harm to the newly born child. For the same reason, during the first few weeks after birth, a black spot of charcoal, called *sinagan*, is placed on the forehead of the baby, and various amulets are tried around his neck and arms.

For several days after delivery, the mother is given a rice mush to eat, but she begins immediately to pursue as many of her normal household tasks as she can. During the one or two days following birth, before the mother's milk begins to flow, the child is nursed by the mother's sister or some other close relative. Within the first week of birth, solid foods are given to the child in the form of a rice or cassava gruel, and certain bananas which are believed to have medicinal value.

Stillbirths are not uncommon among the Bajau and are usually attributed to some serious illness of the mother during pregnancy. Infants born dead are simply buried on any nearby island rather than taken to the cemetery islands where all other Bajau are buried. The Bajau have no knowledge of any special care to administer to premature babies except to increase the number of protective amulets on their persons. Caul births are apparently fairly common and, as noted earlier, are attributed to sexual intercourse during the final month of pregnancy, when the caul is believed to be formed from the father's semen. In the event of a caul birth, the sack is simply removed from the infant. One woman told me this was as easy as removing the cellophane from a package of cigarettes. Informants claim that deformed births are very rare, and attributed their occurrence to fate or to misbehavior on the part of the mother. The Bajau consistently denied any knowledge of multiple births beyond twins and were amazed to hear of triplets, quadruplets, and quintuplets. One old woman claimed that only animals had such births in Sulu, not people. No special explanations are offered for the occurrence of twins except fate. When twins are born, it is almost always assumed that one or both of them will die owing to their smaller size and more delicate constitution. Such an assumption is grounded in experience since I learned of only two sets of living adult twins among the Tawi-Tawi Bajau, and of none among the Sitangkai Bajau.

Because it is considered bad luck to name a child too soon, a baby usually does not receive a name until he is several months old. A boy's name generally takes the suffix of his father's name; for instance, the five sons of Masarani are Mastarani, Sugarani, Armisani, Motorhani, and Honorhani. Much less frequently the suffix of a girl's name follows the suffix of her mother's name. The name itself usually identifies the sex of the child. In addition to his given name, a Bajau often has a nickname, which sometimes replaces his original name.

If a Bajau baby survives his first two years of life, his chances of living to maturity are good. However, the infant mortality rate is extremely high, and it is not uncommon to encounter a family with more deceased than living children. In fact, infant mortality is so high that some parents cannot even recall the number of their deceased children. Common causes of infant death include dysentery and various respiratory diseases. It appears, however, that the infant mortality rate has dropped among the house-dwelling Bajau at Sitangkai. Census data and geneologies reveal a considerable reduction in infant mortality within the present generation of house-dwellers as compared to the preceding generations who lived in boats. This drop is due not only to the more healthful nature of house-living, but also to the partial adoption of modern medicine. If the mortality rate continues to decrease, Sitangkai will soon begin to feel the pressures of overpopulation which other parts of the Philippines already experience.

Bibliography

Nimmo, H. A. 1968. Reflections on Bajau History. Philippine Studies 16:32–59.

——— 1969. The Structure of Bajau Society. Unpublished Ph.D. dissertation, University of Hawaii.

Does the Family Have a Future? † *

S OME thirty-five years ago, two venerable students of human behavior engaged in a six session debate on marriage and the family over the B.B.C. Their names were Bronislaw Malinowski and Robert Briffault, the one a world famous anthropologist best known for his studies of the Trobriand Islands, the other a social historian devoted to resurrecting the matriarchies of prehistory. Of the two, paradoxically, it was Briffault, the self-trained historian, who turned out to be the cultural relativist whereas Malinowski, a pioneer in crosscultural research, exhibited the very ethnocentrism his studies were designed to dispel.

Both men noted that the family was in trouble in their day. Both were distressed by this and sought to discover remedies if not solutions. Despite their common concern, however, they were soon embroiled in vivid and vociferous controversy about the nature of the crisis and its cure. (*Marriage: Past and Present,* ed. M. F. Ashley-Montagu, Boston, Porter Sargent, 1956).

Briffault concluded from his reading of the evidence that the family rests on sentiments rooted in culture and social tradition rather than in human nature. Unless one grasps these social and cultural essentials, one cannot hope to understand, much less cure, what ails it. No recourse to natural instinct or to the "dictatorship of tradition or moral coercion" could save the modern family from its destined decline.

Malinowski disagreed. The family, he admitted, might be passing through a grave crisis but the illness was not fatal. Marriage and the family, "the foundation of human society," and a key source of spiritual and material progress, were here to stay, though not without some needed improvements. Among these were the establishment of a single standard of morality, greater legal and economic equality between husband and wife, and greater freedom in parent-child relations.

The disagreement of these two men stemmed, as it so often does, not from different diagnoses but from different definitions

---

† By Suzanne Keller, Professor of Sociology, Princeton University, New Jersey, U.S.A.

* Reproduced by permission of the editor of Journal of Comparative Family Studies.

of the phenomenon. Malinowski defined the family as a legal union of one man and one woman, together with their offspring, bound by reciprocal rights and duties, and cooperating for the sake of economic and moral survival. Briffault defined the family much more broadly as any association involving economic production and sexual procreation. In his sense, the clan was a family.

The two agreed on only one point: parenthood and above all maternity are the pivots in the anatomy of marriage and the family. If these change so must the familial organization that contained them. Thus if one can identify such pivotal changes their difficulties are overcome while ours may be said to be just beginning.

There is good reason to suppose that such changes are now upon us. The malaise of our time reflects not simply a temporary disenchantment with an ancient institution but a profound convulsion of the social order. The family is indeed suffering a seachange.

It is curious to note how much more quickly the popular press, including the so-called women's magazines, have caught on to changing marital, sexual, and parental styles. While many of the experts are still serving up conventional and tradition-bound idols—the hard-working, responsible, breadwinner husband-father, the self-effacing, ministering, wife-mother, the grateful, respecting children—these magazines tempt the contemporary reader with less standard and more challenging fare. Whether in New York or in Athens, the newsstands flaunt their provocative titles—"Is This the Last Marrying Generation?", "Alimony for Ex-Husbands," "Why We Don't Want to Have Children," "Are Husbands Superfluous?"—in nonchalant profusion. These and other assaults on our sexual and moral codes in the shape of the new theater, the new woman, the new youth, and TV soap operas akin to a psychiatrist's case files, persuade us that something seems to be afoot in the whole sphere of marriage and family relations which many had thought immune to change. In point of fact the question is not *whether* the family is changing but how and how much; how important are these changes, how permanent, how salutary? The answers depend largely on the way we ask our questions and define our terms.

The family means many things to many people but in its essence it refers to those socially patterned ideals and practices concerned with biological and cultural survival of the species. When we speak of the family we are using a kind of shorthand, a label for a social invention not very different, in essence, from other social interventions, let us say the Corporation or the University, and no more permanent than these. This label designates a particular set of social practices concerned with procreation and child rearing; with the heterosexual partnerships that make this possible and the parent-child relations that make it enduring. As is true of all collective habits, once established, such practices are exceedingly resistant to change, in part because they evoke strong sentiments and in part because no acceptable alternatives are offered. Since most individuals are unable to step outside of their cultures, they are unable to note the arbitrary and variable nature of their conventions. Accordingly, they ascribe to their folkways and creeds an antiquity, an inevitability, and a universality these do not possess.

The idea that the family is universal is highly misleading despite its popularity. All surviving societies have indeed found ways to stabilize the processes of reproduction and child care else they would not have survived to tell their tale. But since they differ greatly in how they arrange these matters (and since they are willing to engage in Hot and Cold Wars to defend such differences) the generalization does not help us explain the phenomenon but more nearly explains it away.

In truth there are as many forms of the family as there are forms of society, some so different from ours that we consider them unnatural and incomprehensible. There are, for example, societies in which couples do not share a household and do not have sole responsibility for their offspring; others in which our domestic unit of husband and wife is divided into two separate units, a conjugal one of biological parents and a brother-sister unit for economic sustenance. There are societies in which children virtually rear each other and societies in which the wise father does not know his own child. All of these are clearly very different from our twentieth century, industrial-urban conception of the family as a legally united couple, sharing bed and board, jointly responsible for bearing and rearing their children, and formally isolated from their next of kin in all but a sentimental sense. This product of a long and complicated evolutionary development from prehistoric times is no simple replica of the ancient productive and reproductive institutions from which it derives its name and some of its characteristic features. The contemporary family really has little in common with its historic Hebrew, Greek, and Roman ancestors.

The family of these great civilizations of the West was a household community of hundreds, and sometimes thousands, of members ("familia" is the Latin term for household). Only some of the members were related by blood and by far the larger part were servants and slaves, artisans, friends, and distant relations. In its patriarchal form (again culturally variable), this large community was formally held together by the role of eldest male who more nearly resembled the general of an army than a modern husband-father. In its prime, this household community constituted a miniature society, a decentralized version of a social organization that had grown too large and unwieldly for effective management. In this it resembles the giant bureaucracies of our own day, and their proposed decentralization into locally based, locally staffed subsystems, designed to offset the evils of remote control while nevertheless maintaining their connection with it. Far from having been universal, this ancient family type, with its gods and shrines, schools and handicrafts, was not even widely prevalent within its own social borders. Confined to the landed and propertied upper clases, it remained an unattainable ideal for the bulk of common men who made up the society.

The fallacy of universality has done students of human behavior a great disservice. By leading us to seek and hence to find a single pattern, it has blinded us to historical precedents for multiple legitimate family arrangements. As a result we have been rather impoverished in our speculations and proposals about alternative future arrangements in the family sphere.

A second common fallacy asserts that the family is *the* basic institution of society, hereby revealing a misunderstanding of how a society works. For as a social institution, the family is by definition a specialized element which provides society with certain needed services and depends on it for others. This means that you cannot tamper with a society without expecting the family to be affected in some way and vice versa. In the contemporary jargon, we are in the presence of a feedback system. Whatever social changes we anticipate, therefore the family cannot be kept immune from them.

A final fallacy concerns the presumed naturalness of the family in proof of which a motley and ill assorted grab bag of anecdotal evidence from the animal kingdom is adduced. But careful perusal of ethological accounts suggests that animals vary as greatly as we do, their mating and parental groupings including such novelties as the love death, males who bear children, total and guilt-free "promiscuity," and other "abnormal" features. The range of variation is so wide, in fact, that virtually any human arrangement can be justified by recourse to the habits of some animal species.

In sum, if we wish to understand what is happening to the family—to our family—in our own day, we must examine and observe it in the here and now. In so doing it would be well to keep in mind that the family is an abstraction at best, serving as guide and image of what a particular society considers desirable and appropriate in family relations, not what takes place in actual fact. In reality there are always a number of empirical family types at variance with this, though they usually pay lip service to the overarching cultural ideal.

Challenges to the Contemporary Industrial Family

In the United States, as in other industrial societies, the ideal family consists of a legally constituted husband-wife team, their young, dependent children, living in a household of their own, provided for by the husband's earnings as main breadwinner, and emotionally united by the wife's exclusive concentration on the home. Probably no more than one-third of all families at a particular moment in time, and chiefly in the middle and would-be middle classes, actually live up to this image. The remaining majority all lack one or more of the essential attributes— in lacking a natural parent, or in not being economically self-sufficient, or in having made other necessary modifications.

One contrasting form is the extended family in which the couple share household arrangements and expenses with parents, siblings, or other close relatives. The children are then reared by several generations and have a choice of models on which to pattern their behavior. This type, frequent in working class and immigrant milieus, may be as cohesive and effective as the ideal type but it lacks the cultural legitimacy and desirability of the latter.

A third family type, prevalent among the poor of all ethnic and racial backgrounds, is the mother-child family. Contrary to our prejudices this need not be a deviant or distorted family form for it may be the only viable and appropriate one in its particular setting. Its defects may stem more from adverse social judgments than from intrinsic failings. Deficient in cultural resources and status, it may nevertheless provide a humane and spirited setting for its members, particularly if some sense of stability and continuity has been achieved. Less fortunate are the numerous non-families, ex-families, and non-intact families such as the divorced, the widowed, the unmarriagables, and many other fragmented social forms, who have no recognized social place. None of these, however, threaten the existing order since they are seen and see themselves as involuntarily different, imperfect, or unfortunate. As such they do not challenge the ideals of family and marital relations but simply suggest how difficult it is to live up to them. When we talk of family change or decline, however, it is precisely the ideal standards which we have in mind. A challenge to them cannot be met by simple reaffirmations of old truths, disapproval, shock, or ridicule of the challengers, or feigned indifference. Such challenges must be met head on.

Today the family and its social and psychological underpinnings are being fundamentally challenged from at least three sources: (1) from accumulated failures and contradictions in marriage; (2) from pervasive occupational and educational trends including the changing relations between the sexes, the spread of birth control, and the changing nature of work; and (3) from novel developments in biology. Let me briefly examine each.

It is generally agreed that even in its ideal form, the industrial-urban family makes great, some would say excessive, demands on its members. For one thing it rests on the dyadic principle or pair relationship which, as Georg Simmel observed long ago, is inherently tragic and unstable. Whether in chess, tennis, or marriage, two are required to start and continue the game but only one can destroy it. In this instance, moreover, the two are expected to retain their separate identities as male and female and yet be one in flesh and spirit. No wonder that the image of the couple, a major source of fusion and of schism in our society, is highly contradictory according to whether we think of the sexes as locked in love or in combat. Nor do children, the symbols of their union, necessarily unify them. Their own growing pains and cultural demands force them into mutually exclusive socio-sexual identities thereby increasing the intimate polarity. In fact, children arouse parental ambivalence in a number of ways, not the least of which is that they demand all but give back all too little. And yet their upbringing and sustenance, the moral and emotional climate, as well as the accumulation of economic and educational resources needed for survival, all rest on this small, fragile, essential but very limited unit. Held together by sentimental rather than by corporate bonds, the happiness of the partners is a primary goal although no one is very sure what happiness means nor how it may be achieved and sustained.

To these potentials for stress and strain must be added the loss of many erstwhile functions to school, state, and society, and with it something of the glamour and challenge of family commitments. Few today expect the family to be employment agency, welfare state, old age insurance, or school for life. Yet once upon a time, not too long ago at that, it was all that and more. At the same time, however, with fewer resources, some new burdens have been added stemming from rising standards of child health, education, and welfare. This makes parents even more crucially responsible for the potential fate of their children over whom they have increasingly less exclusive control.

Like most social institutions in the throes of change, moreover, the modern family is also beset by numerous internal contradictions engendered by the conflict between traditional patterns of authority and a new egalitarianism between husbands and wives and parents and children. The equality of the spouses, for example, collides with the continuing greater economic responsibilities, hence authority, of the husband. The voluntary harness of love chafes under the constraint of numerous obligations and duties imposed by marriage, and dominance patterns by sex or age clash with new demands for mutuality, reciprocity, equity, and individualism. These, together with some unavoidable disillusionments and disappointments in marriage, set the stage for the influence of broader and less subjective social trends.

One such trend, demographic in nature but bound to have profound social implications, concerns the lengthened life expectancy and the shortened reproductive span for women. Earlier ages at marriage, fewer children per couple and closer spacing of children, means: the girl who marries at twenty will have all her children by age 26, have all her children in school by her early thirties, have the first child leave home for job, schooling, or marriage in her late thirties, and have all her children out of the home by her early forties. This leaves some thirty to forty years to do with as personal pleasure or social need dictate. The contrast with her grandmother is striking: later marriage, and more children spaced farther apart meant all the children in school no earlier than her middle or late thirties and the last to leave home (if he or she ever did) not before her early fifties. At which time grandmother was probably a widow and close to the end of her own lifespan. The empty nest thus not only occurs earlier today but it lasts longer, affecting not this or that unfortunate individual woman but many if not most women. Hence what may in the past have been an individual misfortune has turned into a social emergency of major proportions. More unexpected free time, more time without a socially recognized or appreciated function, more premature retirements surely puts the conventional modern wife, geared to the domestic welfare of husband, home, and children at a singular disadvantage relative to the never married career woman. Destined to outlive her husband, stripped of major domestic responsibilities in her prime years, what is she to do with this windfall of extra hours and years? Surely we must expect and prepare for a major cultural shift in the education and upbringing of female children. If women cannot afford to make motherhood and domestic concerns the sole foci of their identities, they must be encouraged, early in life, to prepare themselves for some occupation or profession not as an adjunct or as a last resort in case of economic need but as an equally legitimate pursuit. The childrearing of girls must increasingly be geared to developing a feminine identity that stresses autonomy, non-dependency, and self-assertion in work and in life.

Some adjunct trends are indirectly stimulating just such a reorientation. When women are compelled, as they often are, to earn their own living or to supplement inadequate family resources necessitated by the high emphasis on personal consumption and the high cost of services increasingly deemed essential as national standards rise, conventional work-dependency patterns are shattered. For, since the male breadwinner is already fully occupied, often with two jobs, or if he cannot or will not work, his wife is forced to step in. Thus there is generated internal family pressure—arising from a concern for family welfare but ultimately not confined to it—for wives to be gainfully employed outside of the home. And fully, three-fourths in the post-childbearing ages already are, albeit under far from ideal conditions. Torn between home and job, between the precepts of early childhood with its promise of permanent security at the side of a strong male and the pressures of a later reality, unaided by a society unaware or indifferent to her problems, the double duty wife must manage as best she can.

That this need not be so is demonstrated by a number of modern societies whose public policies are far better meshed with changing social realities. Surely one of our more neglected institutions—the single family household which, despite all the appliances, remains essentially backward and primitive in its conditions of work—will need some revamping and modernizing. More household appliances, more and more attractive alternatives to the individually run household, more nursery schools, and a total overhaul of work-schedules not now geared to a woman's life and interests cannot be long in coming. While these will help women in all of their multiple tasks they may also of course further challenge the presumed joys of exclusive domesticity.

All in all, it would appear that the social importance of the family relative to other significant social arenas will, as Briffault among others correctly anticipated, decline. Even today when the family still exerts a strong emotional and sentimental hold its social weight is not what it once was. All of us ideally are still born in intact families but not all of us need to establish families to survive. Marriage and children continue to be extolled as supreme social and personal goals but they are no longer —especially for men—indispensable for a meaningful existence. As individual self-sufficiency, fed by economic affluence or economic self-restraint, increases, so does one's exemption from unwanted economic as well as kinship responsibilities. Today the important frontiers seem to lie elsewhere, in science, politics, and outerspace. This must affect the attractions of family life for both men and women. For men, because they will see less and less reason to assume full economic and social responsibilities for four to five human beings in addition to themselves as it becomes more difficult and less necessary to do so. This, together with the continued decline of patriarchal authority and male dominance—even in the illusory forms in which they have managed to hang on—will remove some of the psychic rewards which prompted many men to marry, while the disappearance of lineage as mainstays of the social and class order, will deprive paternity of its social justification. For women, the household may soon prove too small for the scope of their ambitions and power drives. Until recently these were directed first of all to their children, secondarily to their mates. But with the decline of parental control over children a major erstwhile source of challenge and creativity is removed from the family sphere. This must weaken the mother-wife complex, historically sustained by the necessity and exaltation of motherhood and the taboo on illegitimacy.

Above all, the move towards worldwide population and birth control must affect the salience of parenthood for men and women, as a shift of cultural emphasis and individual priorities deflates maternity as woman's chief social purpose and paternity as the prod to male exertions in the world of work. Very soon, I suspect, the cultural presses of the world will slant their messages against the bearing and rearing of children. Maternity, far from being a duty, not even a right, will then become a rare privilege to be granted to a select and qualified few. Perhaps the day is not far off when reproduction will be confined to a fraction of the population, and what was once inescapable necessity may become voluntary, planned, choice. Just as agricultural societies in which everyone had to produce food were once superseded by industrial societies in which a scant six per cent now produce food for all, so one day the few may produce children for the many.

This along with changing attitudes towards sex, abortion, adoption, illegitimacy, the spread of the pill, better knowledge of human behavior, and a growing scepticism that the family is the only proper crucible for child-rearing, creates a powerful recipe for change. World-wide demands for greater and better opportunities for self-development and a growing awareness that these opportunities are inextricably enhanced or curtailed by the family as a prime determinant of life-chances, will play a major role in this change. Equal opportunity, it is now clear, cannot stop at the crib but must start there. "It is idle" commented Dr. Robert S. Morrison, a Cornell biologist, "to talk of a society of equal opportunity as long as that society abandons its newcomers solely to their families for their most impressionable years." (New York Times, October 30, 1966). One of the great, still largely unchallenged, injustices may well be that one cannot choose one's parents.

The trends that I have sketched would affect marriage, male-female, and parent-child relations even if no other developments were on the horizon. But there are. As yet barely discernible and still far from being applicable to human beings, recent breakthroughs in biology—with their promise of a greatly extended life span, novel modes of reproduction, and dramatic possibilities for genetic intervention—cannot be ignored in a discussion devoted to the future of the family.

Revolution in Biology

If the early part of this century belonged to physics and the middle period to exploratory ventures into outer space, the next few decades belong to biology. The prolongation of life to double or triple its current span seems virtually assured, the extension of female fertility into the sixties is more than a distinct possibility, and novel ways of reproducing the human species have moved from science fiction to the laboratory. The question then arises, what will happen when biological reproduction will not only be inadvisable for the sake of collective well being but superseded by new forms and eventually by non-human forms of reproduction?

A number of already existing possibilities may give us a foretaste of what is to come. For example, the separation of conception from gestation means that motherhood can become specialized, permitting some women to conceive and rear many children and others to bear them without having to provide for them. Frozen sperm banks (of known donors) are envisioned from which prospective mothers could choose the fathers of their children on the basis of particularly admired or desired qualities, thereby advancing an age-old dream of selecting a distinguished paternity for their children based on demonstrated rather than potential male achievement. And it would grant men a sort of immortality to sire offspring long after their biological deaths as well as challenge the implicit equation now made between fathers and husbands. Finally, the as yet remote possibility to reproduce the human species without sexual intercourse, by permanently separating sex from procreation, would permit unmarried women (and men) to have children without being married, reduces a prime motive for marriage and may well dethrone—inconceivable as this may seem—the heterosexual couple. All of these pose questions of legal and social policy to plague the most subtle Solon. Who is the father of a child —the progenitor or the provider where these have become legitimately distinct roles? Who is the mother—the woman who conceives the child or the one who carries it to term? Who will decide on sex ratios once sex determination becomes routine? Along with such challenges and redefinitions of human responsibility, some see the fate of heterosexuality itself to lie in the balance. In part of course this rests on one's assumptions about the nature of sexuality and sexual identity.

Anatomy alone has never been sufficient for the classification of human beings into male and female which each society labors to develop and then calls natural. Anatomy is but one— and by no means always a reliable—identifying characteristic. Despite our beliefs, sex identification, even in the strictest physical sense, is by no means clear cut. Various endeavors to find foolproof methods of classification—for example for participation in the Olympics—have been unsuccessful, as at least nine separate and often uncorrelated components of sexual phenotype have been identified. But if we cannot count on absolute physical differentiations between the sexes, we do even less well when it comes to their social and psychological attributes. Several decades of research have shown beyond doubt that most of what we mean by the difference between the sexes is a blend of cultural myth and social necessity, which must be learned, painstakingly and imperfectly, from birth on. Once acquired, sexual identity is not fixed but needs to be reinforced and propped up in a myriad of ways of which we are quite unaware.

In the past this complicated learning process was guided by what we may call the categorical reproductive imperative which proclaimed procreation as an unquestioned social goal and which steered the procreative and sexual capacities and aspirations of men and women toward appropriate channels virtually from birth on. Many other features strengthened these tendencies— symbolism and sentiment, work patterns and friendships, all kinds of subtle and not so subtle rewards and punishments for

being a "real" man, a real woman.   But once the reproductive
imperative is transformed into a reproductive ban what will be
the rationale for the continuance of the exclusive heterosexual
polarity in the future?   If we keep in mind that only two out of
our forty-six chromosomes are sex-carrying, perhaps these two
will disappear as their utility subsides.   Even without such
dramatic changes, already there is speculation that heterosexuality will become but one among several forms of sexuality, these
having previously been suppressed by strong social sanctions
against sexual deviation as well as by their inability to reproduce
themselves in standard fashion.   More than three decades ago,
Olaf Stapleton, one of the most imaginative science fiction writers of the century, postulated the emergence of at least six sub-
sexes out of the familiar ancient polarity.   At about the same
time, Margaret Mead, in the brilliant epilogue to her book on sex
and temperament, (*Sex and Temperament in Three Primitive
Societies*, William Morrow and Co., New York, 1935) suggested
a reorganization and recategorization of human identity not along
but across traditional sex lines so as to produce a better align-
ment between individual capacity and social necessity.   In our
time we have witnessed the emergence of UniSex (the term is
McLuhan's) and predictions which range from the disappearance
of sex to its manifold elaboration.

Some are speculating about a future in which only one of the
current sexes will survive, the other having become superfluous
or obsolescent.   Depending on the taste, temperament—and sex
—of the particular writer, women and men have alternately been
so honored (or cursed).   It is not always easy to tell which aspect of sex—the anatomical, psychological, or cultural—the
writer has in mind but as the following comment suggests, much
more than anatomy is at stake.

"Does the man and woman thing have a future?   The question may not be hypothetical much longer.   Within 10 years
.   .   .   we may be able to choose the sex of our offspring;
and later to reproduce without mating male and female
cells.   This means it will someday be possible to have a
world with only one sex, woman, and thereby avoid the
squabbles, confusions, and headaches that have dogged this
whole business of sex down the centuries.   A manless world
suggests several scientific scenarios.   The most pessimistic
would have society changing not at all, but continuing on

its manly ways of eager acquisition, hot competition, and mindless aggression. In which case, half the women would become "men" and go right on getting ulcers, shouting "charge" and pinning medals on each other." (George B. Leonard, "The Man and Woman Thing," *Look* 12–25–68).

Long before the demise of heterosexuality as a mainstay of the social order, however, we will have to come to terms with changing sexual attitudes and mores ushered in by what has been called the sexual revolution. This liberalization, this rejection of old taboos, half truths, and hypocrisies, also means a crisis of identity as men and women, programmed for more traditional roles, search for the boundaries of their sexual selves in an attempt to establish a territoriality of the soul.

Confusion is hardly, of course, a novel aspect of the human condition. Not knowing where we have come from, why we are here, nor where we are headed it could hardly be otherwise. There have always been dissatisfied men and women rejecting the roles their cultures have assigned them or the responsibilities attached to these. But these are the stuff of poetry and drama, grist for the analyst's couch or the priest's confessional, in other words private torments and agonies kept concealed from an unsympathetic world. It is only when such torments become transmuted into public grievance and so become publicly heard and acknowledged that we can be said to be undergoing profound changes akin to what we are experiencing today.

Returning now to our main question—does the family have a future—it should be apparent that I expect some basic and irreversible changes in the decades ahead and the emergence of some novel forms of human togetherness. Not that the current scene does not already offer some provocative variations on ancient themes, but most of these gain little public attention, still less approval, and so they are unable to alter professed beliefs and standards. Moreover, every culture has its own forms of self-justification and self-righteousness and in our eagerness to affirm the intrinsic superiority of our ways, we neglect to note the magnitude of variations and deviations from the ideals we espouse. What are we to make, for example, of such dubious allegiance to the monogamous ideal as serial marriages or secret adulteries? Or, less morally questionable what of the quasi-organized part-time family arrangements necessitated by extreme occupational and geographic mobility? Consider for a moment the millions of families of salesmen, pilots, seacaptains, soldiers, sailors, and junior executives where the man of the house is not often *in* the house. These absentee husbands-fathers who magically re-enter the family circle just long enough to be appreciated, leaving their wives in charge of the homes they pay for and of the children they sired, are surely no more than part-time mates. If we know little about the adjustments they have had to make or their children's responses, this is because they clearly do not fit in with our somewhat outmoded stereotyped notions of what family relations ought to be. Or consider another home-grown example, the institution of governesses and boarding schools to rear upper-class children. Where is the upper class mother and how does she spend her time between vacations and homecoming weekends. Then there are of course many countries around the world—Israel, Sweden, the Socialist countries, some of the African societies—where all or nearly all women, most of them mothers, work outside of the home as a matter of course. And because these societies are free from guilt and ambivalence about the working mother, they have managed to incorporate these realities more gracefully into their scheme of things, developing a number of useful innovations along the way. Thus even in our own day, adaptions and modifications exist and have not destroyed all notions of family loyalty, responsibility, and commitment.

In fact, people may be more ready for change than official pronouncements and expert opinions assume. The spread of contraceptive information and the acceptance of full birth control has been remarkable. The relaxation of many erstwhile taboos has proceeded at breakneck speed and the use of public forums to discuss such vital but previously forbidden topics as abortion, homosexuality, or illegitimacy is dramatic and startling in a society rooted in Puritanism. A number of studies, moreover, show that the better educated are more open to re-examination and change in all spheres, including the family. Since these groups are on the increase, we may expect greater receptivity to such changes in the future. Even such startling proposed innovations as egg transplants, test-tube babies, and cloning are not rejected out of hand if they would help achieve the family goals most Americans prize. (See "The Second Genesis" by Albert Rosenfeld and the Louis Harris Poll, *Life*, June, 1969, pp. 31–46.)

Public response to a changing moral and social climate is of course hard to predict. In particular, as regards family concerns, the reactions of women, so crucially bound up with motherhood and childrearing in their self-definitions are of especial interest. In this connection one study of more than 15,000 women college students attending four year liberal arts colleges in the United States is relevant for its findings on how such a nationwide sample of young coeds, a group of great future significance, feels about marriage, motherhood and career. (Charles F. Westoff and Raymond H. Potvin, *College Women and Fertility Values*, Princeton University Press, 1967). Selecting only those items on which there was wide consensus and omitting details of interest to the specialist, the general pattern of answers was unmistakable. The large majority of these would-be wives and mothers disapproved of large families (three or more children), did not consider children to be the most important reason for marriage, favored birth control and birth planning, and thought it possible for a woman to pursue family and career simultaneously. They split evenly on the matter of whether a woman's main satisfaction should come from family rather than career, or community activities, and they were virtually united in thinking that mothers with very young children should not work. The latter strongly identifies them as Americans, I think, where nursery schools and other aids to working mothers—including moral support—are not only lacking but still largely disapproved of.

Thus if we dare to speculate further about the future of the family we will be on safe ground with the following anticipations: (1) a trend towards greater, legitimate variety in sexual and marital experience, (2) a decrease in the negative emotions —exclusiveness, possessiveness, fear and jealousy—associated with these; (3) greater room for personal choice in the kind, extent, and duration of intimate relationships, which may greatly improve their quality as people will both give and demand more of them; (4) entirely new forms of communal living arrangements in which several couples will share the tasks of child rearing and economic support as well as the pleasures of relaxation; (5) multi-stage marriages geared to the changing life cycle and the presence or absence of dependent children. Of these proposals, some, such as Margaret Mead's would have the young and the immature of any age test themselves and their capaci-

ties to relate to others in an individual form of marriage which
would last only so long as it fulfilled both partners. In contrast
to this, older, more experienced and more mature couples who
were ready to take on the burdens of parenthood would make a
deeper and longer lasting commitment. Other proposals would
reverse this sequence and have couples assume parental commitments when young and, having discharged their debt to society, be then free to explore more personal, individualistic partnerships. Neither of these seems as yet to be particularly ap-
pealing to the readers who responded to Mead's proposal as set
forth in Redbook Magazine. (Margaret Mead, "Marriage in Two
Steps," *Redbook Magazine*, July 1966; "The Life Cycle and Its
Variation: The Division of Roles," *Daedalus*, Summer, 1967; "A
Continuing Dialogue on Marriage: Why Just Living Together
Won't Work," *Redbook Magazine*, April 1968.)

For the immediate future, it appears that most Americans
opt for and anticipate their participation in durable, intimate,
heterosexual partnerships as anchors and pivots of their adult
lives. They expect these to be freer and more flexible than was
true in the past, however, and less bound to duty and involuntary
personal restrictions. They cannot imagine and do not wish a
life without them.

Speculating for the long range future, we cannot ignore the
potential implications of the emerging cultural taboo on unre-
stricted reproduction and the shift in public concern away from
the family as the central preoccupation of one's life. Hard as it
may seem, perhaps some day we will cease to relate to families
just as we no longer relate ourselves to clans, and instead be bound
up with some new, as yet unnamed, principle of human association. If and when this happens, we may also see a world of Unisex, Multi-sex, or Nonsex. None of this can happen, however, if
we refuse to shed some of our most cherished preconceptions
such that monogamy is superior to other forms of marriage or
that women naturally make the best mothers. Much as we may
be convinced of these now, time may reveal them as yet another
illusion, another example of made-to-order truths.

Ultimately all social change involves moral doubt and moral
reassessment. If we refuse to consider change while there still
is time, time will pass us by. Only by examining and taking stock
of what is can we hope to affect what will be. This is our chance
to invent and thus to humanize the future.

Marriage and Sexual Adjustment in Guajiro Society † * [1]

O N the basis of a previous study dealing with Guajiro sexual socialization (Watson 1972), one would be led to predict that the harsh effects of severe training in this system, by creating "negative sexual fixation," would lay the basis for subsequent problems of sexual adjustment for the woman in the marital relationship. In actual fact, however, the sexual demands with which she must contend when she marries do not produce the anticipated conflict and anxiety, and evidence of positive sexual adaptation exists.

This paper, in addressing itself to this problem, will attempt to (1) delineate some of the principal aspects of female sexual behavior in marriage and (2) account for the apparent discrepancy between the success achieved in marital sexual adjustment and the negative character of prior training in this area. Possible explanations for the unexpected adult behavior will be considered.

Sexual Behavior and Marriage

On the same day that the formal marriage payment is delivered to the bride's kinsmen, and while the hosts and guests engage in festivities at the home of the bride's parents, the bride herself is closeted in a small *rancho* with her mother, awaiting the arrival of her husband-to-be. She lies in a special nuptial hammock which her mother has made especially for this occasion. The hammock is lined with sheets to catch the virginal blood spilled during intercourse, which will offer an eloquent testimony to the purity of the bride's previous sexual conduct. The groom arrives late in the afternoon bringing with him several head of cattle which he delivers to the mother of the bride as "payment" for the time and effort she has spent giving the girl a "proper" educa-

† By Lawrence C. Watson, California State University, San Diego.

* Ethnology April 1973 pp. 153–161. Reproduced by permission of the editor of Ethnology.

[1] The Guajiro are a cattle pastoral group located in the Guajira Peninsula of northern Colombia and northwestern Venezuela. They have strongly developed matrilineages, each with its own internal authority system headed by a *cacique*. The society is stratified along class lines on the basis of wealth in livestock, control over retainers and slaves, and access to political power.

tion. (Later he must pay compensation to his wife's matrilineal kinsmen for spilling her "uterine blood" during the act of defloration, the proof being the bloodstained sheets.) After receiving payment from her son-in-law, the old woman instructs him to enter the *rancho*. She explains that everything is ready and that the girl is waiting for him.

Both male and female informants insisted that the bride does not react to her "first" sexual experience with any apparent reluctance or aversion (cf. Watson 1970:50–51). The bride, in fact, is described as responding compliantly to her husband's demands, although she is nervous and uncertain about the success of the outcome. One 32-year-old woman gave the following personal account which seems to represent the typical reaction:

> I was awfully nervous when he lay down next to me that first time. It embarrassed me to be so close to a man. But when he started rubbing my breasts and vagina and whispering words of love to me, I didn't get angry for I knew it was all very proper. I must admit I was a little shocked when I saw how big his penis was .   .   .   Although it hurt quite a lot when he entered me, it felt rather nice when he began to move inside of me. I knew, though, I shouldn't get too excited, but I kept thinking how much I enjoyed it.

In the initial period of her marriage, a Guajira should be at least minimally responsive to her husband's sexual needs, for she knows that if she does not satisfy him he may look for another woman (not necessarily another wife). She may, however, resist excessive demands, which are viewed as spiritually degrading (e. g., "A man may use a prostitute as a sexual toy but not a respectable woman"). There is also the notion that extravagant sexual gratification, particularly in the beginning of marriage, is injurious to the health of both parties (e. g., "If a man has too much sex he becomes thin and sickly and loses his energy, but a woman who permits too much sex becomes fat and loses her beauty").

At first a married woman does not show too much overt pleasure during the sexual act, and, while willing, she is nevertheless restrained and decorous in her comportment. If she seems too eager and becomes extremely passionate, or if she suggests an unhealthy interest in "deviant" sexual experimentation (e. g., oral-genital or anal sex), it is believed that the husband will become suspicious of her sexual faithfulness. Guajiro reasoning has it that if an "inexperienced" newly married woman acts aggressively and presumptuously in sexual matters, she exhibits *ipso facto* the characteristics of a loose woman who "has been around," i. e., has had previous sexual encounters. As a logical corollary, the Guajiro also assume that such a woman must actually have been leading a life of pleasure all along, gratifying her shameless sexual desires unbeknownst to her parents and husband. The status of her virginity coming into marriage is seriously thrown into doubt by such forward behavior and may lead her husband to take legal action against her family in order to recover that portion of the original bride payment that presupposed her chastity.

One female informant commented that people's real behavior, as she understood it, was strongly conditioned by these prevailing cultural practices:

> Women are really careful when they're first married because their husbands are suspicious and not sure of them yet. I know that I never gave my husband reason to think I was improper. I usually had sex with him when he wanted it, but I did not initiate it myself, nor did I offend him by asking him to put his mouth to my genitals or to copulate with me in a strange position.

After she has been married several years, provided in the meantime she has been able to develop a relationship of understanding and trust with her husband, the Guajiro wife can begin to express some of her own personal needs and idiosyncrasies in the sphere of marital sexual behavior. This was reflected in the fact that many married female informants experienced varying degrees of interest in sex, in accordance with differences they exhibited along such personality dimensions as general energy level, strength of sexual drive, sexual anxiety, and rigidity of defensive functioning. Some found it desirable to have sexual intercourse at least once every day, and this was generally accepted by the husband; others, however, limited themselves to having sex once every week or two weeks.

The typical Guajiro woman, even after years of marriage, continues to reject any deviant form of sexual expression, such as oral or anal intercourse, which could lead to loss of self-esteem or result in rejection by the husband. She does, however, at this stage of her life have the culturally recognized right to seek sexual satisfaction on her own terms as long as it is achieved through culturally acceptable means; and she may, moreover, justifiably complain if her husband, for his part, is unwilling to have sex or is inadequate in his sexual performance. The following are quotations from female informants:

> We Guajiras do not do these things [have oral or anal sex]. If I, for example, were to suck my husband's penis it would show that I had no respect for him and I would be degrading myself as well. It is possible that some men would like engaging in unusual practices, but if they did they would soon begin treating us like common prostitutes because it is well-known that this is the way prostitutes carry on. For money they make their bodies available as playthings to their clients. A person who no longer has a will to control his own body is really no more than a slave. In marriage, it is important, of course, for a man and woman to enjoy each other, but it is far more important for them to respect each other's pride and morality.

> I enjoy having intercourse with my husband every other night. I know sex is important to keep his love, but speaking for myself I find it very pleasurable. When we do it, I try to move against him so that he will come fairly quickly. If it takes him more than ten minutes to come, he becomes irritable because he must work up a sweat. So, if he comes quickly it is good for him because he experiences unalloyed pleasure and it is good for me because he is satisfied. I have no trouble coming quickly if he seems interested and able. When he is drunk and wants it, I become annoyed because he works like a mule for forty minutes and still can't come. I can't become very excited when I know he can't reach his climax. The morning after one of these sessions, when he is clear-headed, I give him a piece of my mind and suggest jokingly that I might seek a better lover if this sort of thing continues. I know I can control his behavior by threatening not to give him sex.

Though no impressively large figures are available on the percentage of adult married women who have orgasms, it is worth mentioning that seven of the eight female informants who gave me detailed information on their sex lives reported regularly experiencing sexual climax during intercourse. This is an impressive statistic, even with the small sample,[2] when one considers some of the repressive aspects of sexual socialization to which most Guajiro women are subjected before their marriage. Since married Guajiro women apparently achieve no less sexual gratification than women in cultures characterized by more "permissive" sexual socialization, and since sexual failure on the woman's part is no less a serious cause of neglect, desertion, and divorce than it is in other cultures (which suggests that adequate sexual performance is indeed expected), we must look for socio-cultural factors in Guajiro society that counteract or mitigate the possible negative effects of early socialization, thus enabling us to explain the presence of positive forces binding and enhancing the adult sexual relationship from the woman's point of view.

Socio-Cultural Factors Enhancing Female Sexual Adaptation in Marriage

It is possible to view the apparent success of the married woman's sexual adjustment as having its basis in a series of culturally defined experiences and encounters that form an important part of her overall psycho-sexual development. This begins early. We note that even the young girl, although she may be required to suppress her sexual feelings to preserve her chastity, has ample exposure to sexual training which attempts to reorient her thinking in such a way that she develops positive expectations about marital sexuality. The following discussion represents an attempt to identify the unfolding chronological sequence of cultural forces to which the female is exposed, and that break down the potentially stultifying effects of severe sexual training by providing her with a more adaptive socialization for future realities.

1. Discrimination Learning in Childhood Sexual Socialization

In an earlier article dealing with premarital sexual socialization (Watson 1972:152), it was pointed out that severe training tended to produce "negative fixation" in the sexual system, although at that time it was also suggested that the actual, specific effect of this would be to "prevent the socialized female from attempting to gratify her sexual desire in prohibited contexts

---

[2] Superficial, nonpersonal data were elicited from more than the eight subjects mentioned, but it was impossible to estimate frequency of orgasm on the basis of the limited information these other informants volunteered.

associated with adverse reinforcement." Even during this early, preadolescent period of training, the girl is taught to discriminate carefully between negative sexual behavior, involving any form of premarital experimentation, especially full intercourse, and positive, socially sanctioned sexual behavior associated exclusively with the marital relationship. In this respect, the Guajiro girl is never told, or encouraged to believe, that sex is bad on general principle, as was the case, for example, with English and American women during the Victorian era with its attendant massive and crippling psychological consequences. Quite the opposite is the case in Guajiro socialization, for it is explicitly made clear to the girl that sex is "bad" only under certain well-defined circumstances, the negative quality of which is not so much inherent in the sexual act itself as in the effects it produces in other people's attitudes because of their cultural conditioning. The girl is made to understand that when she later grows up and marries, it will be proper for her not only to experience sex but also to enjoy it. Thus the girl develops a specific fear related to certain kinds of sexual activity occurring under specified conditions, rather than a generalized fear of sex itself which may be colored by pervasive guilt feelings.

One adult female informant explained how she communicated some of these ideas to her ten-year-old daughter:

> Once Luisa asked me why it was so bad for a girl to have sexual relations with a boy. I told her, "Daughter, I punish you when you flirt with boys or play with yourself because I want to teach you that it is bad to get interested in sex when you are young and forbidden to engage in it. If you are sexually violated you will never find a decent husband and your condition will embarrass your family. You must learn to hold back your desires until your marriage for that's when you may properly enjoy sex. After all, men and women were made to enjoy each other's bodies, but we Guajiro believe this is proper only between husband and wife.

Another woman explained to her daughter:

> If you don't stop playing with yourself you will have trouble. This will set your body afire and cause you to seek out boys, and you will ruin yourself. You should think about work right now. When you marry, that is the time for you to think about sex.

2. The Reorientation of Sexual Attitudes during the Confinement Ceremony at Puberty

The type of discrimination training in the sexual system characteristic of childhood is given subsequent reinforcement when the girl reaches puberty. At this time she is subjected to a period of confinement (*encierro*) ranging from several months to five years or more, depending on her social status.[3]

During her period of confinement, which follows immediately after her first menses, the pubescent girl is isolated in a special, closed-off section of the main dwelling place and is not allowed to see anybody but her older female relatives. Under no circumstances should she look at men or boys or be seen by them. While she is enclosed, she customarily drinks magic herbal potions to enhance her beauty, and she must observe taboos on various foods which are believed to be injurious to her future development. She also takes cold baths several times each day to keep her skin smooth and wrinkle-free, an important element in a woman's physical attractiveness. Above all, however, the *encierro* is crucially important as a socialization device in capping the girl's formal education in social comportment and economic skills and preparing her for her adult responsibilities. She learns at this time the niceties of social etiquette and the finer points of weaving which she is required to practice over and over again, as this is, perhaps, the married woman's most significant economic duty.

One of the most important things she learns during her confinement, and one that has a direct bearing on this paper, is the nature and scope of the sexual duties she must discharge when she marries and how she should best cope with them. She learns, for example, how crucial it is for her to give sexual pleasure to her future husband without degrading or demeaning herself in doing so. She becomes aware that sex can be a force for positively binding the marital relationship and that sex, potentially, can be used by the woman for her own advantage to control the husband's behavior in many respects. Some girls (and this is by no means a universal feature of the *encierro*) may even learn specific sexual techniques for giving a man added pleasure from an older, experienced woman.

[3] Girls from wealthy, politically powerful families are subjected to a period of confinement that may range from three to five years or more.

Where the element of sexual instruction is developed at all, the girl is told what a man is like sexually, what to expect from him sexually in a general way, and what she can do personally to make the sexual relationship work within the conflicting arena of his demands and her own need for sexual gratification with quiet dignity and restraint, as befits a "proper" married woman. If her training during the confinement has been successful, she should be able to start focusing her thoughts on the social and personal meaning of sex, approaching it in such a way as to maximize its benefits to herself and her future husband, while minimizing its dangers.

One 30-year-old informant described the deep effect which the *encierro* had had on her sexual thinking and how it served to redirect her attitudes:

> Until I was confined, I was really scared of sex because I wasn't quite sure of it. I knew that it wasn't all bad, but I didn't know much more than this. During my *encierro*, I learned all about how good it could be if only I were to approach it right. It stirred up a lot of excitement in me and I began to look forward, in a way, to the day I'd be married. The bad things didn't seem to be so important any more, although I was still a little scared about it.

As the above quotation suggests, one of the by-products of sexual training during the *encierro*, apart from the conscious intent of the socializers to remove earlier fears and uncertainties and impart knowledge and confidence, is to increase the girl's interest in her own growing sexuality. This probably could not be accomplished effectively if the girl came into the experience overwhelmed with massive, generalized anxiety about sex. It should be noted, nevertheless, that since a pubescent girl is subjected to physical confinement and strict chaperonage at this time of burgeoning sexual interest, she is effectively deprived of any real opportunity to translate sexual fantasy into behavioral reality, and thus the training, in essence, while it acts as a stimulus to the positive reorganization of sexual feelings, also helps to insure deferral of sexual gratification to a future occasion when it is socially sanctioned.

3.   The Adjustment of Cultural Expectations to Fit the Woman's Sexual Inexperience When She Enters Marriage

When a Guajiro woman marries, her husband normally expects her to submit to full intercourse on the first night and to be prepared for sex at frequent intervals thereafter, even though he may recognize that this will involve some difficulties.

While instruction during confinement has redirected her thinking toward an acceptance of the sexual relationship, the new bride may nevertheless feel inhibited and experience a certain amount of reluctance to plunge enthusiastically into sex, although she may have no moral aversion to it whatsoever. It is at this transitional point, significantly, that the cultural expectation defining shyness and restraint as proper sexual comportment for somebody in her status comes to the young bride's rescue; this, as we view it, enables her to work through a potentially difficult period of sexual adjustment by allowing her initially to express understandable stiffness and uncertainty when she is confronted by the husband's demands, without this being misinterpreted as connoting either a lack of interest or a rejection of sex on her part.

The groom, from his point of view, approaches his wedding night fully expecting his bride to be nervous and insecure; in fact, if it turns out that she is inhibited and even somewhat unresponsive, he proudly takes this as a sign of her innocence and purity. On the other hand, if she were to react too enthusiastically and knowingly he would suspect that she had had gratifying sexual experiences in the past, and this might seriously jeopardize the marriage.

As time goes on, of course, the woman is permitted to become increasingly direct, demanding, and passionate in acting out her sexual role. This represents what is undeniably a culturally based awareness of the reality of the woman's ultimate capacity for sexual gratification and a formal acknowledgment of her right to develop that capacity.

In this connection, one 30-year-old informant described how she "developed" a healthy interest in sex after she overcame an initial period of insecurity:

> My first husband was old and rich. I didn't like his looks and I was embarrassed to have sexual intercourse with him. I was surprised when I discovered that the experience wasn't unpleasant at all, though it hurt a little. Yet I didn't show much feeling. After five or six months I started to open up a little with the old one and began showing him that I en-

joying having him do it to me. By that time I had convinced him that I was a proper young wife.

4. The Recognition that Adequate Sexual Performance is Important in Binding Marriage and Controlling the Husband's Behavior

After a Guajiro woman has passed the initial period of sexual adjustment in marriage and begins to make sexual demands of her own, in which she expresses a need for sexual gratification, it becomes important for her to maintain at least an adequately satisfying relationship on this basis with her husband in order to bind him exclusively to her so that he does not become sexually indifferent or exasperated and seek another, more amenable sexual partner. Given the reality of polygyny in this culture, this represents a constant threat to the woman's security and inspires anxiety, for she knows that if she loses her physical attractiveness, and/or fails to interest her husband sexually, he has the option of taking a younger, more responsive wife who may eventually come to displace her in his affections.

It is clear, too, that this fear is consonant with cultural reality, and is not wholly irrational, for it was noted that polygynous men often took additional wives who looked sexually exciting because the first wife no longer gave satisfaction.[4] As one man explained:

> After the novelty of marriage wears off, a man begins looking for an interesting sexual partner in a wife or lover if his first wife isn't hot enough for him. It is obvious that if she can't give pleasure, he must try to find another. This is what happened to me, only my second wife isn't much more exciting than the first one.

Even if she is sexually indifferent, however, a Guajiro wife normally tries to make herself desirable to her husband (within certain limits of propriety) by developing and refining aspects of her performance which serve to enhance his pleasure, e. g., thrusting her hips, developing greater vaginal control, scratching.

The indication that a high proportion of Guajiro women apparently achieve some measure of success in their sexual relationship points, I feel, not only to their accurate, adaptive assess-

---

[4] This does not necessarily mean, however, that the man will divorce his first wife, for she may continue to serve him importantly in domestic and social matters.

ment of the sexual demands of marriage, but also to their psychological capacity to act on the basis of their assessment once it is formed. The latter may be directly related to the earlier emphasis in the socialization process on instilling a positive anticipation of adult sexuality in the specific context of marriage and the elimination of the potentially disabling effects of any early generalized sexual anxiety.

Relevant to the above discussion is the statement of one Guajiro woman:

> I am very jealous if my husband shows any interest in another woman and I miss him when he is away. When he is at home I make him feel well cared for. I fix him a nice meal to give him strength. Turtle meat is especially good to make him sexually responsive. Later, I ask him if he would like to get in the hammock with me to "get warm." I always do this if he is cold or unenthusiastic. When we lie down together I begin to manipulate his penis and put his hand on my breasts and vagina. I tell him how much I want him. Pretty soon he comes around, if he isn't drunk by that time, and we have intercourse. I'll go on all night with him if I think he wants it because I know that tomorrow he'll be nicer to me.

As it turns out, sex may also become for a woman a long-range strategy for controlling her husband's behavior in certain crucial respects. And in this she is no doubt guided by the cultural belief that a woman has the power, if she chooses to use it, to subjugate her husband by granting and withholding sexual gratification once he has become sexually dependent on her.

To what extent a Guajiro man is genuinely susceptible to this belief is difficult to determine precisely. Married female informants assured me that such thinking is founded in reality and that a man can, in fact, be turned into a whimpering "sexual slave" if the woman has been proficient enough in her sexual performance to create in him a strong dependency bond, without either arousing his suspicion, making him resent her, or causing him to despise her as a lewd and immoral woman.

In practical terms, to follow Guajiro reasoning, a woman who judiciously doles out sex (and presumably affection and nurturance as well) can get her husband to make important concessions in critical areas. Through sexual manipulation, for example, she

can (1) persuade him to cede valuable property to her children
and herself, property that might otherwise go to his sororal nieces
and nephews; (2) dissuade him from taking additional wives or
having mistresses; and (3) influence him to neglect his other
wives for her. With this kind of massive cultural reinforcement,
the enterprising Guajiro woman would seem to have more than
abundant motivation to pursue various aggressive sexual strategies in her search for personal security and self-fulfillment.

SUMMARY

As we have seen, the original but highly specific fear of the
sexual impulse in the young unmarried woman can be, and often
is, transformed into confidence that sex can be used as a tool for
achieving such diverse needs as impulse gratification, emotional
and physical security, and even interpersonal domination.

The total weight of female sexual socialization, in the final
analysis, seems oriented toward insuring the capacity for adult
sexual gratification, but it also provides strategies for meeting
other needs connected with the marital relationship.

The data presented suggest that it may be unwarranted to
assume that Whiting and Child's (1953) formulation that negative
fixation in a general behavioral system, arising from severe
childhood socialization, necessarily creates an irreversible perception of a particular impulse (or impulse complex) that colors
all subsequent adaptations toward that system in adulthood. The
nature of sexual socialization in Guajiro society indicates that
several factors may interfere with attempts to use the concept of
fixation in making predictions about adult sexual behavior. We
note that (1) childhood training in Guajiro society, though severe, may have such a specific focus on the direction of the
impulse or some limited attribute of sexuality (e. g., premarital
sex) as to have no general effect on the total sexual adaptation
that follows; (2) positive socialization pressures, less dramatic in
nature, perhaps, or more covert in expression (e. g., sexual training during confinement), may serve to counteract, or at least
mitigate the effect of other forms of severe socialization that are
applied to the sexual system; and (3) the institution of marriage
may encourage the positive rather than the negative expression
of adult sexual behavior, acting in consonance with the sup-
portive rather than the inhibiting aspects of earlier training.

In conclusion, if the wider spectrum of Guajiro beliefs and practices concerning sex is considered, and the interrelationship of these elements taken into account, it is possible to reconcile certain apparent contradictions between socialization and adult behavior which arise when fixation theory is applied too mechanically to a limited number of factors in a preconceived organization of ethnographic data.

Bibliography

Watson, L. C.   1970.   Self and Ideal in a Guajiro Life History.   Acta Etnologica et Linguistica 21, Series Americana 5.   Vienna.
———— 1972.   Sexual Socialization in Guajiro Society.   Ethnology 11:150–156.
Whiting, J. W. M., and I. Child.   1953.   Child Training and Personality: A Cross-Cultural Survey.   New Haven.

————————

The Wife Takes a Wife *

P ERHAPS the single most frustrating problem confronting the women's liberation movement is how to get their menfolk to take them seriously—specifically, how to get an unreconstructed male chauvinist away from the TV screen or the local pub and into the kitchen, laundry room or nursery.   Time, pressure and cajolery may or may not resolve this quandary in advanced industrial nations.   But now a new study by a distinguished Philadelphia anthropologist shows how the problem is handled among a number of African tribes—and handled quite effectively: the overworked sisters of Africa simply marry another woman.   This creates a legally sanctioned *ménage à trois*, gives wife No. 1 a permanent female helpmeet and leaves Papa free to drink with his pals and talk politics to his heart's content.

The author of the study, Dr. Denise O'Brien of Temple University, and herself the mother of two, has been studying African marriage practices for nearly a year.   She has found the rite of auxiliary female-to-female marriage fairly common among at least twenty tribes, the most prominent of whom are the Ibos of Nigeria and the Simbiti of Tanzania.

Sharing: By tribal standards, there is nothing immoral about the practice: the marriage ceremonies are conducted in strict accordance with tribal law and custom. O'Brien's research shows that there is no question of lesbianism in these unions. On the contrary, many women who take on a wife do so because they are barren and thus denied the enormous status that attaches to parenthood; any children born to the new wife automatically become the legal offspring of that wife and her female husband. Who fathers the children? It may be any male the wife chooses.

O'Brien notes that African women who take on a wife have often achieved considerable economic success on their own, and that the acquisition of a wife is one way of flaunting their wealth. In some cases, of course, particularly when a male husband has died, it becomes an absolute necessity to take on a wife if the bereaved woman is to be economically productive.

As for the chores assigned to the extra wife, they are for the most part the traditional ones of household organizer, baby tender and cook—in short, many of the same duties assigned in earlier times to that now all but extinct Western household functionary, the maid.

Pagan Gaddang Spouse Exchange † * [1]

† By Ben J. Wallace, University of California at Santa Barbara.

* Reproduced by permission of the editor of Ethnology. Vol. viii, #2 (April 1969).

[1] A version of this paper was read at the 66th annual meeting of the American Anthropological Association. It is based on research conducted in the Philippines from October, 1965, to December, 1966. I would like to express my appreciation to the Midwest Universities Consortium for International Activities, Inc., for supporting the field research and to the Wenner-Gren Foundation for support during analysis of the data. For supporting a return trip to the Philippines during the summer of 1968, I wish to acknowledge the Agricultural Development Council, Inc., and the Wenner-Gren Foundation. William W. Elmendorf and Henry P. Lundsgaarde made discerning and helpful comments on this manuscript but are not responsible for my interpretations.

T HE Pagan Gaddang [2] inhabit the eastern slopes of the Cordillera Central of northern Luzon in the Philippine Islands. They number approximately 2,500 (Troyer 1960; Census of the Philippines 1960) and live in small and scattered settlements in this area. The country is hilly and mountainous, covered alternately with pockets of closed and with semi-closed cover forest and stretches of tropical grassland. Most settlements are located in forest areas, generally along small mountain streams. Although doing some collecting of wild flora, hunting, and fishing, the Gaddang are primarily subsistence farmers. By swidden methods they grow their most important crop, dry rice, in the forests where they live (see Wallace, 1967a, 1967b, 1969). The nuclear family is the basic unit of social organization. Each family builds its own house, works its own farm, and is responsible for its own economic welfare.

The purpose of this paper is to describe briefly a Pagan Gaddang social institution, spouse exchange, which has previously not been reported for the Philippines in the literature.[3] The Gaddang recognize spouse exchange as a legitimate form of cohabitation. As will become apparent, the term "wife swapping" is an inappropriate designation for the phenomenon under discussion. The Gaddang exchange union is basically a short-term replica of marriage. There is negotiation, an exchange of items of wealth, a small ceremony, and a special designative terminology for the parties involved and any ensuing offspring. Of the 45 married or widowed adults in the two communities most familiar to the writer, eighteen (40 per cent) were said by informants to have participated in a spouse exchange.[4] Illicit sexual relations are not uncommon, but this type of activity is not recognized by the Gaddang as spouse exchange.

[2] The Pagan Gaddang should not be confused with the so-called Christian Gaddang or the Yogad (see Galang 1935; Kessing 1962; Lambrecht 1959, 1960; Wallace 1967a).

[3] Robert B. Fox (personal communication) reports that he found evidence suggesting some form of spouse exchange among the Ilongot of northern Luzon, Renato Rosaldo, Jr. (personal communication), currently among the Ilongot, has found no indication of this practice.

[4] Only one exchange was in effect while I was in the field during 1965 and 1966. Informants report that spouse exchange was more common in the past.

Spouse Exchange

The possibility of exchanging wives is discussed informally by two men, but both male and female informants insist that spouse exchange (*solyad*) can only occur with mutual consent of all four individuals involved. If the four people agree, the negotiations and formal arrangements are made by the parents of one of the males.

Male *A* asks his parents to approach the parents of male *B* to negotiate the *solyad*. The parents of the females do not enter into the negotiations. The parents of *A* visit the parents of *B*, and after considerable small talk the question of the *solyad* is broached. This, of course, comes as no surprise to *B*'s parents, as their son has already informed them of the forthcoming visit by *A*'s parents. The father of *A* informs the father of *B* that his son desires to *solyad* with their son and daughter-in-law, and if *B*'s family is receptive they take the matter under consideration.

A few days later the parents of *A* return to the home of the parents of *B*, bringing with them a *kiring* (a valuable bead used in marriage), some betel, and wine. This symbolizes the formal beginning of negotiations. This visit, and any succeeding visit if necessary, is termed in Gaddang *maman* ("betel"). During the *maman*, wine is drunk, betel is chewed, and a chicken is ceremonially killed in celebration of the pending *solyad*. The parents of *A* offer one *kiring* to the parents of *B* as a pledge that their son and daughter-in-law will conduct themselves during the *solyad* in the culturally prescribed manner. The parents of *B* may offer to match the one *kiring*, but, more often than not, they suggest that the parents of *A* offer more collateral. Here many variables come into play, depending upon status, wealth, and the desire of the parties involved. For example, if *A*'s wife is sickly his parents will probably have to extend more collateral. Or if *A* has no children, and enters the *solyad* relationship in the hope that his wife will become pregnant, his parents offer more collateral. *B*'s parents may, of course, also be forced to advance more collateral.

If additional negotiation is necessary, the parents of *A* leave, saying that they will come back in a day or so. A few days later they return, and another *maman* is held. At this time they offer a *lufay* (an earring of considerable worth) in addition to the *kiring.* A *lufay* is always offered as the second type of collateral. The most common practice is for three *'maman* to be held, involving the pledging of two *kiring* and one *lufay*, before the negotiations are completed. The collateral is an important feature of the *solyad* because if one person oversteps its culturally defined bounds, his parents' collateral is forfeited to the other party.

Immediately upon termination of the last *maman*, A goes to the house of B, and B to the house of A. How long a *solyad* lasts depends upon situational factors. If the principal parties reside in distant communities, the exchange is apt to last up to a year. During this period A seldoms comes into contact with B or with his own wife. In such cases, A assumes the socio-economic obligations of B with respect to the latter's wife. If the parties involved live in the same area, the logistics of the *solyad* are varied. A and B may go to the other's house once or twice a week for the purpose of spending the night and having sexual intercourse with their female *solyad* partners. Or A may stay at B's house, or B at A's, for a week or more at a time. Informants were clear that A cannot cohabit with B's wife or B with A's wife without first obtaining the other's permission. If the *solyad* couples live in the same or nearby communities the parties maintain their own economic responsibilities but develop new, though temporary, kin obligations.

A spouse exchange is usually terminated after a period of six months to a year. Thereafter A no longer has sexual access to B's wife and returns to his original family of procreation. The items of collateral are returned to their original owners, and the parties are free to begin negotiations for a new *solyad* if they so desire. It is important to note, however, that a *solyad* can be terminated by one party forfeiting the collateral. The principal grounds for the termination of a *solyad* with loss of collateral are:

(1). If one member of the *solyad* enters into negotiations for a new *solyad* without first terminating the current one;

(2). If one member of the *solyad* has sexual intercourse with anyone other than his wife or his *solyad* mate;

(3).   If one member of the *solyad* is found guilty of cruelty to his *solyad* mate.

During a *solyad* the participants assume new but temporary kin ties and obligations.   The term of reference and address between *solyad* mates of opposite sex is *kayam*, rather than the term for spouse, *atawa*.   A refers to the wife of B as *kayamku* ("my borrowed wife"), and B's wife refers to A in the same manner as *kayamku* ("my borrowed husband").

Although neither A and B nor their wives are related, the participants assume affinal kin obligations as though they were married.   Thus the parents of B's wife become *katwangan* ("parents-in-law"), to A, the siblings of B's wife become A's siblings-in-law (*kayung*), and so forth.   In other words, the kin terminology and associated behavioral patterns of the *solyad*, except for the new term *kayam*, replicates the ordinary Pagan Gaddang kinship system.   The participants still retain, however, their original consanguineal and affinal ties; A's wife is still *atawa*, his children are still *anak*, etc.

If a child is born from the cohabitation of A and his *kayam*, or exchange spouse, the child is a *banay'i* of A but an *anak* ("son or daughter") of his *kayam*.   The term *banay'i* designates the circumstance of the birth and is not a specific kinship term; a child born out of wedlock is designated by another term.   B is the socially recognized father of the *banay'i*, the male who assumes full social responsibility for it in matters of education, marriage, and inheritance.   With the termination of the *solyad*, the child remains with his mother and her husband, who is considered the father of the child despite the fact that he may not be the biological father.   Informants say that ideally a *banay'i* has two complete sets of kinsmen, the kin of his biological father (A in this case) and the kin of his mother and her husband; for example, he addresses both his biological and his social father as *ama* ("father").   In actuality, however, with the passing of time and the termination of the *solyad*, the child is primarily a member of his social family of procreation, and his biological father and the latter's relatives assume little responsibility for him.[5]

---

[5] Paternity is obviously difficult to assess under spouse exchange circumstances.

Some of the terminological features of the *solyad* relationship are illustrated in Figure 1.

Figure 1: Some Terminological Features of Solyad

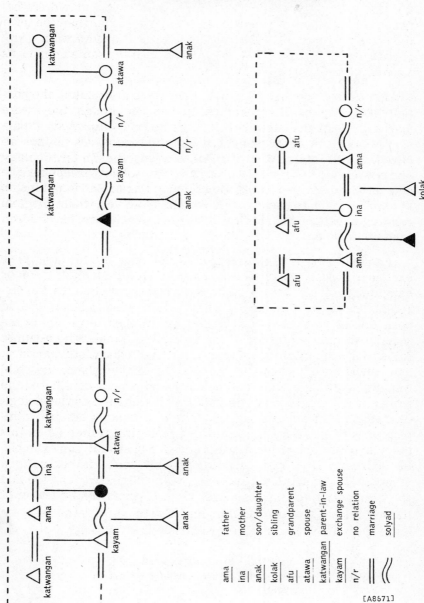

ama	father
ina	mother
anak	son/daughter
kolak	sibling
afu	grandparent
atawa	spouse
katwangan	parent-in-law
kayam	exchange spouse
n/r	no relation
‖	marriage
⟨⟨	solyad

[A8671]

Conclusions

The practice of spouse exchange among the Pagan Gaddang gives rise to numerous questions, many of which it would be pretentious for me to try to answer. Some informants, in addition to noting the obvious function of relieving childlessness, explain the practice of spouse exchange by saying, *tameta a lutu tameta a tantam* ("another cook another flavor") but this is not a full explanation. Other informants say that it comes about because men and women want to demonstrate that they have much *madayaw* ("power"), but again this is only a partial answer. I have no evidence, however, to suggest that these views do not at least in part contribute to the practice of spouse exchange. Granting the folk view as partially explanatory, I would further suggest that part of the answer may be found in Gaddang kinship relations. The *solyad* functions to make nonkinsmen kin, even though of a temporary nature. After termination of the spouse exchange, the ties developed through temporary kinship linger. Through the *solyad*, the potential number of relatives is expanded, creating new economic and social opportunities. Aboriginal Gaddang social organization is illustrative of the way in which a society may adapt to its particular habitat. Swidden cultivation makes it an ecological necessity to disperse the populace over a relatively large territory. Lacking in stable discrete socio-political units, the dispersed settlements are linked together through a formal and informal network of kin and associated obligations. This was particularly important in the past, when head-taking, revenge, and wergild were more common and kinship enhanced safety. The artificial kin ties of the *solyad* system extend social obligations and help preserve group unity despite areal dispersal. A similar argument has been offered by Guemple (1961) for the existence of spouse exchange among certain groups of Eskimo. The Eskimo, not unlike the Pagan Gaddang, move about periodically, appear to be efficiently adapted to their habitat, and seek the advantages afforded by a large circle of kinsmen.

Bibliography

Census of the Philippines. 1960. Manila.

Guemple, D. L. 1961. Inuit Spouse-Exchange. Department of Anthropolgy, University of Chicago (mimeographed).

Keesing, F. M.   1962.   The Ethnohistory of Northern Luzon.   Stanford.

Lambrecht, G.   1959.   The Gaddang of Isabela and Nueva Vizcaya: Survivals of a Primitive Animistic Religion.   Philippine Studies 7:194–218.

——— 1960. Anitu Rites Among the Gaddang.   Philippine Studies 8:584–602.

Troyer, M.   1960.   Gaddang Phonology.   Philippine Journal of Science 88:95–102.

Wallace, B. J.   1967a.   Gaddang Agriculture: The Focus of Cultural and Ecological Change.   Unpublished Ph.D. dissertation, University of Wisconsin.

——— 1967b.   Gaddang Rice Cultivation: A Ligature Between Man and Nature.   Philippine Sociological Review 15:114–122.

——— 1969.   Agricultural Technology of the Pagan Gaddang.   Cultures of the Pacific: Selected Readings, ed. T. G. Harding and B. J. Wallace (forthcoming).   New York.

Death in Chamula † *

"God in the sky, Lord Jesus, Father San Salvador, Father San
    Manuel, Father Savior,
Your own face disappeared, Your own sight disappeared,
How are we going to hide his head, how are we going to hide
    his bones,
We, your children, your younglings,
He is to be buried in the earth, he is to be buried in the mud,
Lord Jesus, Father San Salvador, Father San Manuel,
Let us know more, let us know the prayer, Your words, Your
    speech, Lord Jesus."

*T*he voice of the old man droned on in the damp evening.   He
staggered away from the fresh moist clay of the open grave and
turned to the small group of relatives and neighbors—all male—
who had listened intently to his chant.   A younger man stepped
forward and pulled a bottle of white rum and a stained shot glass
out of his ragged poncho.   Slowly bowing to the reciter, he mut-

† By Patrick Menget.

* Reprinted from Natural History
Magazine, January, 1968. Copyright

© The American Museum of Natural
History, 1968.

*tered a few indistinct words and then extended a full glass of
liquor to the elder, who addressed a ritual toast, in turn, to each
of the men standing by, from the oldest to the youngest. "I
take it" said the old man. "Drink it" answered the younger ones.
After the last exchange the elder gulped down the liquor, spat
on the ground, and made a wry face—as one should to show
that the liquor is nice and strong—then passed the glass to the
next man in line. While the men were ceremoniously and gloomi-
ly emptying the bottle, the women stood silently a short distance
away from the row of graves. A black cluster of weary and sad
faces, huddling their children in the folds of their black shawls,
they stared blankly at their husbands and relatives.*

*It had been a long, painful walk uphill, behind the men who
stumbled on the muddy path under the weight of the casket.
The rain made the children restive and unhappy, but the men
had drunk too much to care. Now the men had finished the last
bottle of liquor. A couple of boys quickly filled up the grave
with earth and trampled it under their feet. They washed their
hands with water from a bucket they had carried uphill to the
graveyard, as did all the men. It would be dark before everyone was back home. The green valley had already turned gray
and misty.*

This burial took place one summer not long ago in the hills of
central Chiapas, Mexico. The rugged moutains of the state of
Chiapas were the last part of southern Mexico to open up to mod-
dern civilization, for not until the 1940's did the Pan-American
highway connect the region of the Isthmus of Tehuantepec to
San Cristobal and even farther to the Guatemalan border. As
you drive along the highway you can see groups of brightly clad
Indians and clusters of thatch-roofed huts among the cornfields.
The region is inhabited by more than 150,000 Maya Indians.
They speak either Tzotzil or Tzeltal, languages closely related
to the ancient Maya of southern Mexico and Guatemala. But
unlike the ancient Maya, who built the palaces and temples and
erected the enigmatic and majestic stelae scattered in the jungle, the Indians of Chiapas do not have a writing system of their
own. They use Spanish for their records and for all communications with the Mexican central government. They live in self-
administered communities, each with its own dialect and customs. Chamula, the largest of those communities, with up-

ward of 40,000 people, is to a great extent the most resistant to Mexican acculturation.

The Chamula are corn farmers, like all the Indians in the state of Chiapas, but their land is not overly fertile and they must supplement their income by working as wage earners on the coffee plantations in the lowlands. This work is seasonal—the coffee growers need extra manpower only for weeding and cleaning the fields and for harvesting. So the Chamula always manage to be back home for the major religious fiestas—Carnival, Holy Week, Saint John's Day (their patron saint), and *Todos Santos* (All Saints' Day).

It is only about seven miles from San Cristobal to Chamula. Both towns have churches, and the people in each place claim to be Catholic. Yet the differences between Catholicism in San Cristobal and what is called Catholicism in Chamula cannot be measured. In Chamula, the Catholic faith has given little more than a few concepts, a place of worship, and idols. Suffice it to say that in Chamula theology Christ is "our Father the sun"; the Virgin is "our Mother the moon." The Chamula will gladly accept baptism from the Catholic priest who vists irregularly, but all the other sacraments are unknown. The people have their own hierarchy of religious officers, replaced every year, that takes care of the arrangements for the fiestas.

The Chamula, it appears, were Christianized in the sixteenth century, fought this influence, and have largely succeeded in retaining their own system of beliefs, while adopting some Spanish terms and generously borrowing images, idols, and other religious paraphernalia. The Dominicans had to abandon evangelizing in the highlands in the early eighteenth century after a particularly bloody insurrection. More recently, the Mexican Revolution and the subsequent agrarian reform of President Cárdenas (1934) have given the Indians more control over their own affairs, and their religious organization has no room for a Catholic priest. In any case, their views of death and the hereafter reveal that their beliefs are heavily aboriginal.

The funeral I described took place in one of the outlying hamlets, Yalichin, about nine miles from Chamula. Neither the ceremony nor the beliefs inherent in it would be very different in any other part of the *municipio* (a self-administered territorial entity roughly equivalent to a county). Even though funeral ceremonies are private rituals and involve no more than a close circle of relatives and a few neighbors, the rules of behavior concerning death and the handling of it are rigid and strictly adhered to. This matter is important not only to insure a safe journey for the soul of the deceased but also for the well-being of the survivors. When someone dies from any cause other than murder or suicide, the body, if not already there, is brought back home. By the time it has been washed and dressed anew, most of the family are already aware of the death and on their way to the house. Since extended families tend to live in clusters of houses, each couple generally in a separate house, the gathering of kin does not take very long. Even a man's daughters, who often reside patrilocally with their husbands' families, will not live beyond the neighboring hamlets. All of the kin will come and stay in the house of the dead until the funeral is over. This may last from one to three full days, according to the resources of the deceased.

The Chamula believe that a man has two souls: one is an animal companion; the other an immortal principle. The animal companion is born and dies in a one-to-one correspondence with its owner and reflects the events of his life. It is, however, most active at night, in the mountains, where it fights for a living, wards off potent animals, and is exposed to many risks. A man will feel the repercussions of this second life, and in his dreams may even be aware of its happenings. But this animal dies when the man dies or vice versa, one death automatically provoking the other. After death the second soul, which has no special shape or appearance but is sometimes thought to be a manlike creature, will go to the underworld, where all souls live for a time equal to the earthly lives of their owners. Then it will be reincarnated in a person of the opposite sex and in a different situation. A myth describes life in the underworld as the inverse of earthly life. When the sun shines over the earth, it is moonlight down below, and at night the sun shines in the underworld. This is why a man has to be buried at sunset; he will accompany the sun on its westward path to the underworld.

A long wake is necessary for the soul to gather the pieces of the self lost during its lifetime, whether around Chamula or in the hot country (lowlands) where most of the Chamula have worked at one time or another. It is not until those bits (hair, nails, and in some cases, lost limbs) have been collected that the soul can undertake the long voyage to the "land of the dead." Additionally, the wake gives the family an opportunity to face together the dangers brought by death, help the deceased in his preparation for the voyage, and reunite the kin after a painful loss.

At the same time that the family is called, the professional musicians are summoned. There are some in every hamlet, and they will play without interruption, during the whole wake, the same monotonous funeral dirge day and night. A guitar, a harp, a two-stringed violin, and sometimes an accordion, will alternate and mix their chords, swaying in repetitious rhythm with the wailing and sobbing of the mourners. Music is a part of most Chamula ceremonies, whether public or private. As essential to a ritual as the smoke of incense and the flames of candles, it pleases the gods and keeps at bay the evil *pukuh* ("bad spirits") who hang around the corpse. Everyone in the village will know from hearing the melody that the house is mourning, and nobody will disturb the bereaved. For the wake the family of the dead buys many bottles of *posh*, the local rum produced by clandestine stills, for there can be no celebration without lots of *posh*. The Chamula seem to have an endless thirst for this cheap liquor, not so much for its taste, but because it is considered an offering to the gods. *Posh* is consumed in large quantities according to a strict etiquette, first by the oldest man, who has to address a toast to each of the men there in descending order of rank and seniority, then by the other men in the same order, finally by the women according to their husbands' positions. Although the order of drinking reaffirms the hierarchical principle, each drinker gets exactly the same amount of *posh*, reflecting a fundamental egalitarianism among the Chamula. Similarly, the property of the deceased will be equally divided among all heirs, male and female. So the drinking etiquette is a metaphor for social hierarchy, and at the same time, for equality among all members of society. The *posh* is always mentioned in prayers to the gods and often referred to as *nichim* ("flower"), a ritual euphemism. The men also pass around a bowl of ground wild tobacco, of which they take a pinch to eat. This powder, *moy,* which is extremely strong and bitter, gives strength and clairvoyance by enabling one to see through the night and to defend oneself against the evil spirits. The same substance, according to the myths, allows powerful shamans to transform themselves into strong animals, such as jaguars.

In the state of dangerous uncertainty brought about by the presence of someone who has ceased to live and is not yet in the land of the dead, men need to be as strong and united as they can, so they drink often "to warm their hearts," swallow lots of tobacco (very intoxicating) "to see better," and take great pains not to quarrel during the wake.

In one corner of the deceased's hut, dimly lit by a candle, the corpse lies, head toward the west. It is surrounded by female relatives, one of them wailing until she becomes tired and is replaced by another. In the smoke-filled hut—the hearth is right in the center on the dirt floor and the smoke escapes from the apex of the thatched roof—men keep milling around, drinking, talking, loudly lamenting. When I was introduced to the brother-in-law of the deceased, he burst out in tears, moaning the loss of his relative. As he poured me a drink, he spilled some of the liquor and suddenly switched from tears to a nervous laughter, in which the other men soon joined. Many men eventually become irritable under the influence of liquor, then crumble on the dirt, and pass out for a few hours. There is no contempt for such drunkenness, and the intoxicated ones will be shaken back to their feet if anyone needs them. As the wake goes on, the corpse is fed regularly with a few drops of *posol* ("corn gruel") placed between his teeth.

Women also prepare the goods that the dead will need on his journey: a set of new clothes, a blanket, little bags of food, a rosary stripped of its metallic parts, a few coins "for refreshment on the way," and a tiny drinking gourd. The food consists of the three staple elements of Chamula diet: tortilla, beans, and *posol*. But the dead are different from the living and the tortilla is completely burned, then ground to a fine black powder. Before putting it in small linen bags, each relative takes a pinch of it to his mouth with his left hand. This represents a communion with the dead, who, contrary to the living, cannot use the right hand for eating. If the deceased is a woman, she takes along three turkey feathers representing needles and a spindle; if a man, he is provided with three miniature sticks in order to fight back the animals on his way. From time to time an older relative will come near the corpse and recite a prayer for the dead that will assist him in gaining admittance to the land of the dead.

In a myth that bears an eerie resemblance to the Greek story of Orpheus, the Chamula tell that upon arriving in hell one has to be ferried across a large river by a black dog. On the other side of the river, a fire burns for which mules—symbolizing punished women—unload firewood. The last element, in spite of its probable Christian inspiration, brings to mind the daily activities of Chamula women who, indeed, collect all the firewood and tend the hearths as strenuously as mules.

The day of the burial proper, the close family of the dead kill all his chickens, which are eaten in equal shares by all present relatives. This reminds one of the ritual use of chicken, the most commonly sacrificed animal, particularly in curing ceremonies. Chickens are symbolically offered to the divinity so that he will admit the dead to the underworld. Upon leaving the house, red pepper is burned in the fire, producing an acrid and unpleasant smoke, the floor is carefully swept, and the door tightly locked. The soul of the dead should not linger around the house, and the smoke of pepper forces it to leave. Even though many relatives sincerely cry at this moment, people agree that they should behave more stoically, for fear that the soul might heed the lamentation and choose to remain in its home.

After this final separation, the procession starts toward the graveyard, located most often on a hilltop "so that the dead may look over the living." The procession stops often, not only to relieve the casket bearers but also to allow women to feed the dead a few drops of *posol*. They will stop more often if the person being buried was old, because then he tires more easily. The walk uphill is a symbol of the journey to the underworld. Once the interment is over and a cross has been erected on top of the fresh grave, the relatives will walk back to the house for a final gathering in order to share the property left by the dead. However, the separation is not completely ultimate. All people who die from natural causes, that is all those who are neither suicides nor the victims of murders, will come back to this world on *Todos Santos*, a time when they are treated with a feast. In each house, the ancestors in the male line will come back and eat the food that has been prepared for them. They will come back to the place where they used to live while the souls of a woman's ancestors will come back to her parents' house, since the Chamula are patrilineal. Those who did not leave anything to their descendants are not expected to return, as if this meeting between the dead and the living were a contractual bond. The Chamula only welcome those of their ancestors who have been beneficial to them. Most of the Chamula who go and work in the lowlands will come back to their parents' houses to join in the celebration of their forefathers. In the house an altar is set, with candles on each side, a sheet of pine needles on the table, a clay incense burner, and bowls of food. The vessels for food are old earthenware used only on this occasion and kept in the family chest the rest of the time. There is meat on the table, cabbage, tamales, *posol*, and salt, all rich and expensive foods. The house cross behind the altar has been decorated with a bow of greenery—pine boughs, branches of laurel, and flowers. Calling the souls of the ancestors, the oldest man in the family starts to sing, accompanying himself on a guitar.

The whole family stands around the altar in clean festive garments. They will wait till the end of the day, then eat what the dead have left. So that the ancestors can recognize the way, the family will have cleaned the grave and decorated it anew with pine boughs and flowers and will have marked the beginning of the path, at the grave, and the end of it, at the house, with pine needles and flower petals. Furthermore, a little stone in front of the house will indicate the entrance.

Meanwhile, at the center of Chamula, the whole body of religious authorities, most dressed in black *chamarras* (ponchos worn only on festive occasions), preceded by the musicians, followed by the civil officials and the ordinary people, will march to the graveyard, next to the old church of San Sebastian. The bells toll, calling for the dead, the music plays the sad melody of *bolomchon* (the "jaguar"). When the procession reaches the graveyard where the tall wooden crosses recently covered with fresh arches of greenery look as vigorous as a spring bush, everyone scatters around the gravesites to tend his dead. On each grave, women set candles, yellow flowers, such as the *flor de difuntos* ("marigold"), or wild orchids and food offerings—perhaps an orange—presented on a little board. Those of the women who have recently lost their husbands kneel at the foot of the graves and moan and cry and complain of their miserable life. One of them, with her baby slung over her shoulder in a black shawl, might squat by the grave and pour a glass of liquor, muttering: "Ay, my lord, here I have come, I am lonely, here is some *posh*, drink one glass as you used to do, my companion" (the man probably died from excessive drinking!).

In the meantime, the *mash*, young boys wearing comic hats of monkey skin, will dance around the graveyard to the music of *bolomchon*. *Todos Santos* is a day when people are both content and sad. Their dead are among them, partake of the food and drink, listen to the music. But everybody knows that they will be gone tomorrow.

Yet, on this day, in front of the old church of San Sebastian, only one half of the graveyard is freshly cleaned and flowered. On the west side, beyond a little separation, the burial mounds do not even have crosses, only marking stones, and these are totally disregarded by the Chamula. No relatives around them, no music for these. Here lie the people who were murdered or who committed suicide. They will never be back, for they do not live in the underworld with the other dead and have quite a special status.

Murder is not infrequent among the Chamula. Among the mestizos of San Cristobal and also among other Indians, they are reputed to be violent, especially under the influence of alcohol. It seems that such a reputation is deserved, for the Chamula have a fairly high rate of murder (36 for 100,000 people per year). Yet compared to the incidence of murder in most large Western cities, Chamula is not a dangerous place. Murders usually occur when members of a family quarrel while drunk. There are some cases of women being murdered by their husbands or of presumed witches being killed. Rarely is someone killed by strangers. When a quarrel arises within a family and turns into violence, the murderer will often simply bury his victim in the backyard. But the news always leaks out, or some relative gets worried and warns the authorities. Besides, the Chamula do not try to escape justice when they have committed murder. Most cases of homicide are quickly solved, as if the murderers were too conscious of their religious plight to flee. They rarely resist arrest and appear resigned to their judicial fate.

When news of a murder is received at the municipal center, the president sends out a commission of *mayoles* (officials acting as policemen), headed by a judge. They march to the place of the killing, looking important with their black staffs of office and

muzzle-loading guns. They force the alleged murderer to disinter
the body. The expedition then walks back to the center, with
the accused carrying the corpse, either wrapped in a mat slung
over his back with a frontal tumpline, or on his back strapped on
a kind of wooden sled. The *mayoles* follow (sometimes covering
their noses with white handkerchiefs) along with possible witnesses. While authorities interrogate the suspects (later they
will be sent to jail in San Cristobal), a doctor is called to perform
the autopsy. The presumed murderer then is expected to dig
a grave and bury the dead, all by himself, with no help. This
always takes place in the western division of the graveyard of
San Sebastian. West, where the sun sets, is the evil direction.
Even if the family of the victim is present, there is no ceremony
whatsoever, no prayer, no grave goods, and no set time for the
interment. The complete absence of ritual contrasts sharply
with the elaborate funerals for those who died normally. The
only common element is that all are buried with heads to the
west.

The Chamula justify their differential treatment of the dead
by saying that in a case of homicide, the murderer assumes all
the sins of his victim, and the latter goes straight to heaven.
This is why in such cases the time of burial is of no importance
since the soul does not have to follow the sun. As for suicide,
the case is mostly hypothetical: the Chamula say that those
people would also go straight up to heaven, but no one I talked
to could recall a single instance of suicide. The Chamula are
not afraid of the souls of such dead, since once they are in heaven,
they are there forever. The murderers have a harsh afterlife
in hell, even though they are buried with a regular funeral and
on the good side of the graveyard (unless, of course, they were
murdered in turn). Murderers never return to earth, neither
on *Todos Santos* nor reincarnated.

Thus the cosmos for the Chamula is a sphere, with the sky in
the upper portion, and heaven on top of it, the earth as a band
in the middle, and the underworld (in Tzotzil, "the sky below")
in the lower half, endowed by some with an outgrowth for the
murderers. The sun travels visibly across the upper sky during
the day, completing its cycle at night when it shines over the
underworld. The over-all picture of the cosmos immediately
brings to mind the concepts of the ancient Maya. For them,
those who had died at war, or women who had died in childbirth,

went to heaven and the others went to hell in the underworld. Yet, we do not understand why people meeting a violent end are not cared for in any way by the Chamula.

In European folklore we can still witness remains of a distinction between the kinds of death. The Church refused to bury murderers, witches, and people who took their own lives. In Russia people who were witches or those who were murdered were buried under public paths, as a sign of contempt. The theme of the castle haunted by one of its former owners who was murdered by his family is a very popular one in Britain. All those people who had not died normally linger on as nuisances and tricksters. At Halloween we are afraid, not of people who died naturally, but of those who died ambiguously. Whereas the "normal" dead are in a definite, well-known (at least in our belief) place forever, the abnormal ones have been denied, for some reason, a permanent haven. They have to be propitiated by men in order to avoid their tricks and malice. The Chamula have an exactly opposite conception: Whereas their "abnormal" dead are in a definite place forever, the normal dead come back periodically and will even come back to earth, eventually. They have to be respected, propitiated, venerated, lest they become harmful.

While the mist spreads around the trees, the old man's wife silently sobs, thinking of the ritual candle she has fixed in his right hand, all wrapped in red ribbons so that they can one day recognize each other and reunite in the underworld. Standing close by, the old reciter mumbles the end of the prayer:

"Where are we going to put him, what place do we have
for him?
He lies there crying, he lies there moaning,
Under the cross, under the crucifix,
His face turned to the other side, he looks toward the
other side.
Our Holy Father, Our sacred Ancestor,
Take him, receive him."

*

VII. The Changing World

The tremendous amount of recent change in the world is too well known to require further documentation here. Many of the problems that have concerned anthropologists in recent years are those created when a traditional culture, in which there has been relatively little change, comes into contact with Western cultures. The articles in this section will illustrate some of these problems.

"Theravada Buddhism: A Vehicle for Technical Change" by Arthur Niehoff shows how a religion, often characterized as being a factor in resistance to change, can in some instances actually be a vehicle for technical change. This article also demonstrates the fact that a religion, in this case Theravada Buddhism, does not have to exist in a vacuum but can be a very important part of everyday life. The article by Davydd J. Greenwood begins by stating that tourism in the twentieth century involves mass movements of people and money but that it has been largely ignored by social scientists. He then goes on to describe how tourism has operated as an agent of change among the Spanish Basque. The final article in this section by Robert A. LeVine illustrates the interplay between economic change and sex roles in areas of Africa.

Theravada Buddhism: A Vehicle for Technical Change † *

BUDDHISM, particularly the southern variant (Theravada), has been consistently singled out by Western specialist-technicians as a resistance factor of primary importance, impeding the introduction of new ideas or techniques into the countries of Southeast Asia. The negative aspects of belief have been stressed al-

† Arthur Niehoff is in the Human Resources Research Office of The George Washington University, Alexandria, Virginia.

* Reproduced by permission of Society for Applied Anthropology from Human Organization, Vol. 23, No. 2, 1964, and the author.

most exclusively. And although these do exist, they are probably no more important than the positive ones. In fact, there is adequate evidence that the attitudes stemming from Buddhist religious beliefs can be usefully employed to introduce change.

Probably most foreign aid technicians in the countries of Laos, Thailand, Cambodia and Burma have taken the attitude that the traditional religion, Theravada Buddhism, produces only negative influence on technical aid projects. This attitude is based on the belief that the religion is tradition-bound and thus resists change. I have heard comments expressed by technicians on many occasions that Buddhism in these countries keeps people satisfied with what they presently have and uninterested in improving their material circumstances. Such technicians often construe their role as that of trying to convince the local people to accept innovations, since it is believed that there is no felt need already existing.

It is widely believed that acceptance of the conditions of life as they exist is a product of Buddhist disinterest in earthly existence. This belief is based on the two doctrinal ideas that this world is unreal and that the worst evil which man has to struggle against is his limitless desire, which in this world is incapable of being satisfied. In order to attain salvation, the individual must therefore disengage himself from the affairs of this world and concentrate on spiritual matters.[1]

Now, although Buddhism may carry the idea of the importance of spirituality to a greater length than some other world religions, it must be agreed that all stress the primary importance of spiritual salvation. Christianity is no exception to this rule, the difference being one of degree only. And certainly the other two major religions of Asia, Islam and Hinduism, emphasize other worldly goals. However, I believe there is enough historical evidence to indicate that none of these religions has prevented their believers from striving for purely worldly goals on a scale as great or greater than that which occurred in Europe before the age of discovery and colonial expansion. Islam, with its doctrine of "kismet" (fate), was still capable of spreading its faith and profoundly influencing the lives of people from the Atlantic to the Pacific Oceans, in a secular as well as religious

[1] Bikkhu U. Thittila, "The Meaning of Buddhism" in Perspectives of Burma, Atlantic Monthly Supplement, New York, 1958, pp. 47–68.

manner. Hindu and Buddhist peoples were capable of establishing impressive colonies throughout Southeast Asia, the most
spectacular of which were Pagan in Burma, Borobadur in Indo-
nesia, and Angkor Wat in Cambodia.[2] Indeed, without the secular aggressiveness of the royalty, Buddhism might never have
spread to the extent it did.[3] It appears that the concepts of the
ascetic or priest have had only a minimal influence on the everyday conduct of secular affairs, whether this influence was Christian, Muslim, Buddhist, or Hindu.

Barriers to Change

The question still remains though,

> Why doesn't the modern Buddhist villager accept the chang-
> es offered by technicians faster than he does?

I believe that in his day-to-day life the peasant is interested in
improving himself, quite as much as a peasant of another religious faith, although perhaps less than a Western industrialized
farmer. The main reason that he is not as enterprising as his
Western counterpart can be explained more logically as being
a result of limited possibilities. The Lao, Thai, Burmese and
Cambodian peasant has been exploited and used by authoritarian
rulers for so long, in conditions where true economic expansion
was next to impossible, that he has developed an attitude of resig-
nation and acceptance. Where this relationship is changing
rapidly, notably in Thailand, the peasant is accepting innovations
of a worldly sort very rapidly also.[4]

The second basic objection of Western innovators toward Buddhism in these countries has been that so much wealth is spent
for religious affairs and such a high percentage of able young
men spend their best years as monks. It is true that a considerable amount of village wealth goes into the support of monks
and their establishments and that many young men do spend
time in service as monks.[5] Furthermore, little can be done about
this in countries where the official religion is Buddhism.

[2] Kenneth P. Landon, Southeast
Asia Crossroads of Religion, University of Chicago Press, Chicago, Ill.,
1948, pp. 61–68.

[3] Edward Conze, Buddhism: Its Essence and Development, Harper, New
York, 1959, p. 72.

[4] John E. De Young, Village Life in
Modern Thailand, University of California Press, Berkeley, 1958, pp. 200–
201.

[5] Manning Nash, "Burmese Buddhism in Everyday Life," American
Anthropologist, LXV, No. 2 (April,

The second objection is less serious, I believe. The attitude toward service as a monk is changing rapidly. Even though every young man is supposed to spend some time in the *sangha* before assuming the duties of a householder, it has been estimated that no more than fifty per cent actually do nowadays in Thailand.[6] The percentage in Laos would probably be smaller. However, the brotherhood still remains one of the most active in the world and probably will remain so for some time. But it is my thesis that rather than condemning this organization, the foreign innovator would do best to utilize it.

Secular leadership in Buddhist villages of Southeast Asia is weak. Ordinarily, there is a headman, either elected by the villagers themselves and then approved by the central government or else appointed directly by the government. Such a person is expected to help in the settlement of minor disputes in the village. The normal procedure in Laos is for the village chief to call a meeting when there is a dispute. The disputants call in the respected older men of the village for support. Evidence is presented, after which the village chief makes a pronouncement. However, the headman has no power of enforcement. If the disputants do not accept his verdict they take the dispute to higher authority, to the chief of district, *Tasseng,* or the chief of county, *Chau Muong.* The *Tasseng* has more authority than the headman and the *Chau Muong* is a government civil servant who in the village situation is quite powerful. The situation in Thailand is roughly the same. The headman called *kamnan* serves only to settle minor disputes. Any criminal actions or land disputes are taken to the district officer, a government civil servant. Previously, it was the villagers themselves who were responsible for maintaining law and order in the village. What this means is that with the rise of national, centralized states the former village patterns of law enforcement and village authority have been replaced by modern police systems and authority based on Western models. The village headman is relatively impotent and there is no other secular authority on the village level who replaces him. Village level leadership is a basic problem in the operation of development projects on a communi-

1963), p. 294 and Frank M. Le Bar and   6 De Young, op. cit., p. 17.
Adrienne   Suddard,   Laos,   HRAF
Press, New Haven, Conn., 1960, pp.
61–68.

ty level, those which can utilize the labor of the peasants to fulfill their own needs without large scale investments. Schools, access roads, small dams, fish ponds, wells, small irrigation facilities, village markets, and drainage systems are some such projects which have been undertaken in this part of the world. In general they fall in the category of "community development."

One of the primary requisites for such projects is that they be done with the willing cooperation and understanding of the villagers themselves. In fact, community development has been considered as serving two purposes—to produce self-help projects on a village level and to assist in the process of building a national consciousness in the villagers. The process is believed to promote some measure of decision-making among the villagers who will then become a functioning part of the local government. One important difficulty that has been found in trying to implement such programs is that the village headman is often incapable of bringing his villagers into such programs and there is usually no one else of the lay community capable of doing it. The constant need in the community development program of Laos was to find capable leadership for such projects. And up until 1961 none was truly found. It is the thesis of this article that an important potential leadership group, that of the Buddhist monks, was ignored. And although the field data are from Laos, it is my belief that roughly the same conditions prevail in the other southern Buddhist countries.

The Role of the Buddhist Brotherhood

The Lao village is normally built around a *wat,* a pagoda compound, which serves as the one center of interest to all villagers. It would be similar to the situation which prevails among Latin American peasants in regard to the Catholic Church or to Muslims in regard to the mosque. The Buddhist monks are the most highly respected men in the village because of their dedication to religious work and also because of their assistance to villagers in religious affairs. They read horoscopes and conduct rituals for blessing the houses, for bringing rain, for counteracting evil spirits, for death rites, and for most of the other supernatural needs of villagers. The villagers support the monks, feeding them daily when they pass with their begging bowls, although also carrying food to the *wat* on special occasion. The

villagers build and maintain the *wat* buildings, both with money
and labor. They gather or make the materials needed for construction or provide the money needed to buy them. The highest act of merit a Buddhist can perform is to assist the local
temple. Besides providing the construction material, the villagers usually provide the labor, which is done under the supervision of the monks. Buddhist temple buildings are almost always the best constructed and maintained in their villages. And
there is no type of communal building in which the villagers are
more interested.

A village self-help program was begun in Laos in 1959 in which
there was very little supervision of projects undertaken. The
program was operated on the basis of the villagers doing the
labor and providing the material they could get, with the United
States aid mission providing the material the villagers did not
have, mainly cement, roofing materials, and metal hardware.
The villagers selected their own projects although these had
to be approved by members of the Lao ministry and their American counterparts. The program worked adequately until it
was interrupted by political events in 1960. Several hundred
village projects were carried out, including the construction of
schools, dispensaries, irrigation canals, roads, markets, bridges,
and dams. However, within six months of the beginning of the
program it became apparent that roughly half the constructions
were Buddhist *wat* buildings. Out of 114 inspected projects in
the three southernmost provinces 61 were *wat* buildings. These
included a type of meeting house, *salahongtham,* which is one
of the buildings found in a *wat* compound but which is used by
villagers generally, and the Buddhist religious school, *hocheck.*

By law the United States government is not allowed to engage
in the construction of religious structures in its aid program
on the assumption that this is not economic development. This
policy is a reflection of the separation of church and state in
American home government. For this and other political reasons it was decided that future self-help projects could not include religious structures. The *hocheck* and the *salahongtham*
could be built with aid funds but not the *pagoda* itself. The important fact that emerges from this data is that, if left alone,
most effort of a communal nature would be for the construction
and maintenance of religious buildings. The most efficient organized cooperative group in the village is the Buddhist brother-

hood.   Not only can they organize their own people toward a given communal task (of a religious nature) but they can draw upon the resources of the community freely and successfully.

This organizational ability of the monks finds many avenues of expression.   Young monks work regular hours, keeping the *wat* clean and actually repairing and constructing the buildings as a part of their discipline.   They have efficient money-making schemes.   When money is needed for religious purposes, the *wat* has recourse to religious fairs, *bouns,* which among other activities involve considerable gambling.   The Lao are very fond of gambling, and attend the games most assiduously.   Their liking for this sport is so great that the government took steps to halt it in 1961.   One of the contributing factors in the government objection to gambling was that the local Chinese got in control of the games and of course made a large profit.   Even gambling at the *wat bouns* was usually in the hands of the Chinese, who paid a percentage to the monks for the right to run the tables. Quite apart from the gambling though, the *wats* collected money or material for new buildings or special purposes by simple solicitation.   Nowhere in the Lao village is there any system comparable to that of the *sangha* for collecting money.

Even if it were agreed that the Buddhist brotherhood is a highly developed organization, the objection of foreign technicians might still remain that it is too tradition-minded to be interested in new ideas.   This attitude is far from certain.   There are, it is true, many practices which indicate an interest in asceticism and other-worldly goals.   Monks do not take food after noon each day, they do not take alcoholic drinks, they isolate themselves from women, they spend most of their creative energy in the learning of Buddhist ritual and Pali, and they wear special clothing to mark their monastic status.   And yet there is much evidence that monks in Laos are quite interested in the changes taking place in the world around them.   Although there are specific prohibitions like that against the taking of alcohol there are many modern practices which the monks have adopted. Smoking cigarettes is almost universal in the brotherhood, carbonated drinks are consumed freely, and the use of modern mechanical implements and gadgets is controlled only by the monks' ability to buy them.   Modern methods of construction are brought into the *wat* as soon as they are practically available. The monks in Laos have adopted galvanized iron roofing widely to cover their temples, on the ground that it is cheaper than tile, and easier to install. Esthetically this has been disastrous to the appearance of the traditional *pagoda* but the monks, like other Lao, have ignored esthetics in favor of ease of installation and cheapness. In neighboring Thailand the use of galvanized roofing for *pagodas* became so widespread that the government made its use illegal.

Also in discussing traditionalism versus modernity it is significant that the desire for learning English is widespread among the monks. The two groups most interested in learning English in Laos were the Chinese merchants and the Lao monks. The Chinese were interested in learning the language primarily for business purposes. The monks wanted to learn it because it was a means of travel, both to the other Theravada Buddhist countries and to the English-speaking Western countries. Educated monks in Thailand, Burma and Ceylon speak English, so a knowledge of English by a Lao monk could mean the difference in getting a Buddhist scholarship. Moreover, many wanted to come to the United States, either as monks or after leaving the order.

A final point of interest concerning the monks is their involvement in politics as an indication of modernity and worldliness. The years 1959–1961 were a period of great political unrest in Laos, most of which time there was leftist guerrilla action. One constantly unknown factor was how much the monks were involved in actual political campaigning. There were incidents in South Laos where monks were caught in direct participation with the leftist party, the Pathet Lao. On one occasion a *wat* in Pakse distributed leaflets for this party in secret and in defiance of the civil authorities. At least one monk was defrocked as a result of this incident. It was also generally believed that the terrorists travelled throughout the country in the garb of monks, staying overnight at the *wats*. How many of these individuals were actual monks and how many were people merely using the costume for disguise was not known.

At the time of a coup d'etat in Vientiane in August, 1960 the monks took direct political action. An army captain, Kong Le, staged a bloodless coup and established a neutralist government which, however, had at the time certain anti-American overtones. He attempted to get mass approval through public harangues and did get a certain part of the population stirred up enough so that they marched on the American compound shouting anti-American slogans.   The processions which I witnessed were made up of a majority of monks, who marched in the forefront, throwing rocks and tearing down signs from the compound fence.   After seeing such a sight it was impossible to accept the stereotype of Buddhist monks as being merely meditative, ascetic, religious scholars.   It will be remembered that the man who assassinated the former prime minister of Ceylon, Bandaranaike, was a Theravada Buddhist monk.

Wells That Mostly Failed

A program of the American aid mission in introducing wells into villages and poor neighborhoods in and around the southern provincial town of Pakse provided some of the best evidence of the utility of involving monks in technical assistance programs. There were three separate programs to introduce wells, all of which ended in failure, although if they had been managed properly at least two of them probably could have been partially successful.   The main difficulty was that the problem of responsibility for maintenance and repair was almost completely ignored.   And it seems from analyzing what happened that the best group to have given this responsibility to would have been the Buddhist brotherhood.   The first project was a group of seven wells dug in the town of Pakse in 1956 by the public works department, although with the advice and financial assistance of the American aid mission.   These were deep wells and fairly expensive to construct.   Most were made by dynamiting through layers of solid rock.   They were placed in various neighborhoods in the town where they could serve large groups of people.   There was a high demand for good water, since most people had to carry it from the Mekong River or buy it from water carriers. However, no one was designated to be responsible for these wells, and they were consequently regarded as government property. By 1958, all were broken.   The American aid advisor of the area repaired them all in that year, but again not bothering about the problem of designating responsibility.   Before he left the country a year later, some were broken again and in 1960 all were out of order.

In 1959 two more well-drilling projects were undertaken in the same area.   One was experimental in nature and did not develop into a useful technique.   It consisted of a method of drilling shallow wells by using hand equipment only, a drilling system which theoretically could be managed by village people themselves. Two wells did produce water for a short time, although both dried up when the water level dropped during the dry season. There was a lot of publicity about this technique, however, and the idea spread that a new easy method was available for bringing in water. For many months afterward there was a procession of Buddhist monks to the local American aid advisor requesting assistance to put wells on their *wat* grounds. Unfortunately, all these people had to be turned away because the system was unreliable. The point is that the Buddhist monks were willing and able to organize parties to drill wells and were the only rural people who took the initiative to do this.

The third project was one in which a contract American well driller came in to drill deep wells with a professional rig. His technique was to consult with the Lao officials to find out what villages needed wells most, then go out with his rig and paid crew and put them in. Technically there was no problem. He put in about fifteen wells, but five of them were at government installations or at the homes of Lao officials. In each of the other ten the villagers were quite happy to get the wells and used them fully as long as they were operating. Within a year, though, at least half of these village wells were not operating. Usually, the breakage was minor and could have been repaired in the local town but the government assumed no responsibility for this. The village people wanted the wells but no individuals assumed direct responsibility for them. Sometimes they made very crude attempts to keep the pumps going. The caste iron handles frequently broke and on one occasion when this happened some village people got together and put a wire on the end of the suction rod, attaching the other end to a pole about four feet long. Two women would put their shoulders under the two ends and do a kind of knee-bend exercise to raise and lower the rod, thus bringing up water.

Not only was there no organization to keep the wells maintained, but there was also no effort to keep the well areas in good condition. The villagers pumped water constantly while the pumps worked, some of them all day and night. They allowed the children to play with the handles and permitted excess water to fall on the ground where it created mudholes for the water buffalo and ducks to puddle in.

There were two exceptions. These were wells which had been put on *wat* grounds. These were not only maintained but improved upon. The grounds around them were kept neat and dry. The *wat* grounds were fenced off so animals could not wander about. Around one of them a concrete base about 20 feet in diameter had been built so excess water would not accumulate. On this same well one of the metal parts of the pump had broken, as it had on so many others. The monks, however, had duplicated this part in very hard wood, which surprisingly enough functioned quite satisfactorily. With these and all other wells located on *wat* grounds, the villagers were quite free to take water but they had to keep the grounds neat and clean, as *wat* grounds are always kept. Incidentally, the Buddhist *wat* is always the cleanest area found in any village, the young monks themselves sweeping it daily and keeping it in order. If village sanitation programs were embarked upon, there could be no better place to start than here.

Help from the Brotherhood

Now, although many principles of introducing innovations into non-Western villages were violated in these programs, two of the most important were neglecting to get the participation of the recipients and neglecting to designate responsibility. No one was ever made responsible for these wells, except in a very perfunctory manner. Where this was done at all, the village headman was considered the leader. But the headman in a Lao village has very limited control and cooperation from the villagers. Two other potential leader types could have been designated— the village schoolteacher or the Buddhist brotherhood. It is difficult to decide which would have been most appropriate because both have the respect of villagers, although for different reasons. The members of the Buddhist *wat* have certain advantages over the teacher. They are a group of men, most of them strong and well nourished, with a pattern of organization which is understood by villagers and which could be applied to innovations which the monks are interested in as much as are the villagers.

An additional motivation for the Buddhist layman to participate in projects backed or controlled by the monks is the positive value placed on ritual merit-making. There is no more laudable or beneficial action by the individual than effort in assisting the brotherhood in its ritual activities. By so doing the lay Buddhist obtains the approbation of his fellow villagers in this life and merit which will influence his destiny in the after-life. Traditionally, the most common types of merit-making activities have been to support the monks physically by providing the necessities of their everyday life and to contribute to the construction and maintenance of the buildings and grounds used for ritual purposes. To build a new *pagoda* is perhaps the highest achievement to which a Buddhist layman can aspire. This, of course, is the reason why the self-help village improvement project described before was converted into a means for building or repairing *pagodas*.

The point is that a high value is placed on sacrifice entailing behavior which could be utilized in conjunction with the efficient organization existing in the priesthood. If the monks supported a project they could expect cooperation from the lay population and could moreover direct these efforts efficiently.

Conclusions

Other uses of the Buddhist brotherhood easily suggest themselves. They could be a focal point of village sanitation programs since they already keep their own establishments quite clean. Village drainage and refuse disposal system could be centered at the *wat*. The monks might be used in school construction programs. Formerly the *wat* school was the only one in the village. When Western-type governments were established, these *wat* schools were by-passed and the present government schools operate quite independently from the *wats*. However, there is no reason why combination schools for both religious training and secular schooling of the village children could not be constructed and maintained. In such a way the villagers could take advantage of the money-raising ability of the monks, as well as organize work parties more easily and efficiently for construction. There is indication that the monks themselves are interested in certain types of secular training, especially in English language training. It might be possible to construct schools that the villagers would use during the day and the monks at night, a time they favor for study anyway. Since American aid expressly forbids building religious structures one could not approve the construction or staffing of *pagodas* but schools, meeting houses, village wells, sanitation programs and other projects which require communal action could be managed with the direct participation of the monks.

The idea of strict separation of church and state is not so valid in countries where the secular ruler is the official protector of the faith.   In the long run the secular government organization will probably become stronger and the need for such groups as the Buddhist monks will be less.   But this will not happen for some time and until efficient secular leadership is provided at the village level it is probably sensible to utilize the already established organizations of the monks.   The attitude of present technicians that monks are a quaint vestige of the past and should only be ignored is a product of the Westerners' cultural biases. New village projects should be undertaken either with the active participation of the monks or at least their approval.

_____

Tourism as an Agent of Change: A Spanish Basque Case † * [1]

O F the various mass phenomena of the twentieth century, tourism has been relatively neglected by the social sciences, despite the enormous movements of people and money which it involves.   The purpose of this paper is to discuss the nature and significance of the changes wrought by tourism on one Iberian town, and thus to make a case for the more concerted investigation of the subject by social scientists.   It analyzes the historical development and socio-economic effects of tourism on the Spanish Basque municipality of Fuenterrabia in the province of Guipúzcoa, with particular emphasis on the effects on agriculture. In Fuenterrabia tourism has given rise to major economic

† By Davydd Greenwood, Cornell University.

* Ethnology (January 1973) pp. 80–91. Reproduced by permission of the Editor of Ethnology.

[1] The field research on which this paper is based was carried out from May, 1968 to September, 1969 supported by Public Health Service Predoctoral Grants 5–F1–MH–29, 027–03 and MH–11, 335–01. This support is gratefully acknowledged as is the guidance and encouragement of L. Keith Brown of the University of Pittsburgh.

growth; it has stimulated the commercialization of agriculture and the creation of service industries, and has ultimately led to the decline of agriculture and the development of a variety of special problems.

Three cautionary remarks are required. First, the field study upon which this paper is based did not focus specifically on tourism, making this analysis a first approximation rather than a definitive synthesis. Second, tourism has developed at the same time as industrialization has taken place in neighboring municipalities, and the effects of these two phenomena are not always easily separated. Third, the effects of tourism on Fuenterrabia's active commercial fishing economy are ignored because I assembled no data on the fishermen while in the field.

THE PHENOMENON OF TOURISM

Tourism is basically a form of recreation expressed either through travel or through a temporary change of residence. It has an appreciable history in the West, as exemplified in the annual movements of patrician Greeks and Romans to summer residences (Sigaux 1966: 9–19). Such annual movements still take place in the Mediterranean world, but, until recently, travel for pleasure and residential change in the summer were restricted to the upper classes. This type of tourism involved a relatively small number of people and was not a major source of economic support for the places they frequented.

The twentieth century has seen an abrupt collapse of the upper-class monopoly over tourism and the rise of an active middle-class involvement in it. Tourism today is a surprisingly large-scale phenomenon, representing one of the largest peacetime movements of people, goods, services, and money in human history. International tourism is the largest single item in foreign trade and is viewed by many countries as a major source of capital for future economic development (Peters 1969: 22).

Europe is the world center of international tourism. According to Peters (1969: 9):

> Over 60 percent of the international tourist expenditure is spent in Europe. . . . In 1967 74 per cent of the tourists crossing international boundaries did so in Europe. Another 16 per cent of crossings were made in North America . . . more than three-quarters of world tourism expen-

ditures and 90 per cent of world tourism movement take place in the two major developed areas of the world.

Tourism is also growing at an extremely rapid rate. Peters (1969: 21) reports:

> Over the 1950–66 period international tourism receipts increased at an average annual rate of 12 per cent, while world exports increased at 7½ per cent annually. International tourist receipts then account for an increasing proportion of the total value of world exports of goods and services. In fact, as a proportion of the total value of world exports they climbed from 3.4 per cent in 1950 to 6.3 per cent in 1965 and 1966.

Comparable figures for tourism within national boundaries, though not readily available, would doubtless show a similar rapid rate of growth.

In Spain, the tourists often appear to outnumber the residents. The Spanish economy, suffering from a sluggish rate of industrial growth, has become highly dependent upon tourist receipts. In 1965, international tourism receipts accounted for 47.7 per cent of Spain's total export receipts and 5.2 per cent of the gross national product (Peters 1969: 23, 29). During 1968, 19,000,000 tourists visited Spain, a startling magnitude when compared with the total national population for that year of about 33,000,000 (Alegre 1969: 9).

As with any specialized industry, tourism has unique characteristics. It requires a mobile clientele, making necessary large investments in transport and communication facilities. Any improvement in transportation, such as availability of cheap automobiles, affects the tourist market. Tourism is also sharply seasonal, creating problems of developing a regional capacity to handle large numbers of people for two months a year without increasing maintenance costs over the total year to the point that the profits are eroded. Where tourists will go is not easily predictable. Inflation, political instability, and the tendency of tourists to shift their attention from country to country make the industry a highly competitive and volatile one.

Tourism, as a service industry, expands employment opportunities in new ways. It provides a ready market for produce, crafts, and services, and often results in the maintenance of monuments and works of art that would otherwise have been destroy-

ed. It thus stimulates economic growth in countries or parts of
countries that have previously been backwaters.

While the need for an integrated social science approach to
this phenomenon is clear, the anthropologist can make an immediate contribution by inquiring about the effects of tourism
on the local communities he studies. At the local level, what
changes does tourism bring about? Are there any characteristic stages in the development of tourism within a local community? How do tourism-related changes interact with changes
brought on by industrialization, population growth, and rural
depopulation in the local context? The following case study
gives a set of provisional answers to these questions.

FUENTERRABIA AS A TOURIST ATTRACTION

Fuenterrabia has all of the ingredients required for success
in the tourist industry. As the tourist leaves France and enters
Spain by the international bridges at Irún or Behobia, he passes
through the main streets of Irún, a city forcibly renovated by the
Civil War. Industrial and without character, it trails off into
a patchwork of small farm plots as the traveler swings north
toward Fuenterrabia. On the right are the meandering Bidasoa
River and the airport, and on the left the north-south spine of
Mount Jaizkibel forms a backdrop for the town. The patchwork
of farm plots ends suddenly at the foot of the high-walled citadel
of Fuenterrabia, the 30-foot walls of which show the effects of
numerous sieges in days when the French and Spanish crowns
were contending for power in the area.

The main road swings around the walled city and continues
north into the fishermen's ward. Here the houses are built in
the Basque style with lime white facades and brightly painted
balconies and eaves. In the center a boulevard with tamarind
trees stretches for blocks between rows of houses, bars, restaurants, and hotels.

Northward, beyond the fishermen's ward lies the beach, enclosed by the penninsula formed by the Jaizkibel on one side
and a man-made sea wall on the other. Along the beachfront
and part way up the face of the Jaizkibel sit the large, elegant
villas of the wealthy summer residents. Only from here can a
clear view of the undulating rural landscape be had, with its
dispersed farms displaying their red tile roofs to the sun.

The walled city itself is entered through an ancient gate, and its dark, narrow cobblestone streets lead between great, old houses that jut out over the street and show off their elaborately carved eaves and lovely wrought iron to the passerby. At the top of the main street stands the church, built into the walls of the city as part of the fortifications. Beyond the church, on the one large plaza, stands the Castle of Charles V. Designed for strength rather than beauty, its pocked walls testify to the many sieges it has witnessed. The fishermen's ward, contrastingly lively and bright, is the hub of all activity and the center of tourist spending.

In the hinterland, the Basque farms stand dispersed, each on its own plot of land. Their large houses contain farm animals, machinery, and fodder on the first floor, with the family living space on the second. Built in a style that reminds the foreigner falsely of the Swiss chalet, many of the farm houses are both large and beautiful, and they are not infrequently 200 to 300 years old.

For the tourist Fuenterrabia offers a walled city, colorful fishermen's ward, a large beach, lovely farms, a mountain to climb, yachting and sailing, golf, fine food, an airport, and proximity to San Sebastián, Bayonne, and Biarritz. Added to these basic attractions, the fine reputation of the Basque chefs and waiters, the mystery of Basque origins, and the reasonable prices of food make the town a most desirable place to spend the summer. Testimony to its attractiveness is the fact that, despite the small size of the town—10,000 inhabitants living on 2,450 hectares of land —an estimated 40,000 tourists spent some time in Fuenterrabia in the summer of 1969.

History of Tourism in Fuenterrabia

Since the beginning of written records (*ca.* 1300), Fuenterrabia has always been the seat of a few noble families, who were the focus of political and economic power. Only since the late nineteenth century, when the Queen Mother, Maria Cristina, popularized the Basque country, have wealthy temporary residents resorted to Fuenterrabia as a summer spot. At that time the Spanish royalty made San Sebastián, some 20 kilometers to the west, their center of activity in the summer, and their presence attracted the nobility and the wealthy from all over Spain to summer in the Basque country, where they often constructed large villas to accommodate themselves.

The archives of Fuenterrabia, in a rapid search, yielded only indirect evidence of the presence of these families for the year 1918. At that time, there were 30 summer residences belonging to outsiders, mostly located along the beachfront interspersed among farms. None of the residences was built inside the walled city, which was in a state of ruin after a series of sieges in the nineteenth century. In relation to the total municipal population of about 4,000, these 30 families formed only a small group. They did not provide an active market for farm produce, although the construction of their houses did employ a few artisans. This group exemplified a style of life that was visible but inaccessible to the local people. As a crude indication, of the eighteen motor vehicles in the municipality at that time seventeen belonged to summer residents and the other was a small public bus. The summer residents did not mix with the local lower classes, and they generally shrouded their lives with an air of conspicuous privacy.

A second phase of tourism began about 1930. The Civil War and World War II, however, postponed the full development of tourism, which did not begin in earnest until about 1949. This phase was characterized by an enormous expansion of mass tourism, coupled with a further proliferation of wealthy summer residents. Masses of middle-class French and Spanish tourists were responsible for this development. Their rising affluence permitted them to imitate life styles previously restricted to the upper classes, and they soon engulfed the whole Cantabrian and Mediterranean coasts of Spain.

The major features of this period were the rapid growth in the number of people involved and the spontaneous, rather than commercially induced, character of the development. Tamames (1968: 336–337, my translation) sketches this chronology for all of Spain:

> Although the growth of foreign tourism in Spain has been especially rapid since 1951, it was already considerable before 1936. In the four-year period 1931–1934 the number of foreigners entering Spain with passports rose to an average of 195,000. . . . The civil war, the second world war, and the political and economic circumstances that fol-

lowed the war opened a long parenthesis in the growth of touristic activities in Spain. Only in 1949 did the number of tourists that visited us surpass that of the prewar period, and the following year there was a substantial increase in their number, which since then has not stopped growing. From a total of 1,263,000 tourists arriving in Spain in 1951, it has risen to 17,800,000 in 1967.

From about 1950, Fuenterrabia experienced an enormous growth in summer tourism of this middle-class type, which has transformed every aspect of life. By 1965 approximately 30,000 tourists visited Fuenterrabia in a summer. Simultaneously the number of elegant summer residences rose to 200. This new variety of tourism provided a huge demand for artisan labor and crafts, food, services, and accommodations. The rhythm of summer invasion and frenzied economic activity was set. Streams of automobiles, bathers strolling in beach clothes, and children with shovels and plastic buckets became part of the summer landscape.

Hardest to delineate is the present phase of development, which can be said to have begun about 1965. This stage is characterized by national touristic planning with an eye to national economic growth and by massive outside intervention by the government and large investors. While the general increase of mass tourism continues in Fuenterrabia as before, the governmental intervention has added new dimensions to the process. Fuenterrabia has been declared a national artistic and historical monument, resulting in much more strict enforcement of building codes designed to retain some of the historic character of the old city. The provincially owned hotel atop Mt. Jaizkibel has been completely renovated, and the local airport has added a new terminal building and a lengthened runway. Access roads to Fuenterrabia from Irún and San Sebastián have been improved or rerouted.

The walls of the city are being reconstructed, and the rubble that filled the streets has been cleared and replaced by new apartments built in traditional style. Under the auspices of the Ministry of Information and Tourism the Castle of Charles V has been totally refurbished and was inaugurated in 1969 by Franco as part of the Ministry's famous chain of *paradores de turismo,* noted for historicity, luxury, and low cost. Also a large corporation has bought a huge tract of farm land and has built a large and exclusive country club. There is a great deal of speculation in land around the club and, indeed, throughout the rural area. Basque boat racing and other sports such as stone-lifting, wood-chopping, and boxing are actively promoted with the aid of national publicity, as are the festivals in honor of Fuenterrabia's patron saint. Though not yet as carnivalesque as some tourist areas, Fuenterrabia's culture and monuments have become centers of promotion, speculation, and manipulation by outside investors. Fuenterrabia is more an enterprise than a town.

THE EFFECTS OF TOURISM

The different phases of tourism's development have affected the municipality in a variety of ways—the rhythm of life, the physical and architectural characteristics of the town, and social life in general.

The effects of aristocratic summer residence on the town during the early part of the century were apparently slight. So few people were involved that the summer residents did not interrupt the normal pattern of life. Nor did they extensively alter the physical and architectural character of the town since they constructed their villas amongst the farms near the beach front. Their consumption needs provided little significant impetus to the production of food and goods. In fact, the only strong evidence of their presence is the repetition of the word *veraneantes* ("summer people") in documents from this period in the municipal archives. They did form a social category apart and had a label of their own.

During the period of the spontaneous growth of mass tourism, major changes began to take place. The rhythm of life in Fuenterrabia was totally altered. Agricultural and fishing rhythms were replaced by the incredible, sleepless frenzy of July and August, followed by ten months of gradual preparation for the reappearance of the tourists. The year became focused around the summer months in a way that had never occurred before. The daily rhythm also changed during the summer, with long lines of tourists moving toward the beach by 10:00 A.M. and returning by 1:30 P.M. Then, after a meal and a peaceful respite, the evening *paseo* began around 5:00 P.M.

Tourism had substantial architectural effects. Funded at first by the municipal budget, the rubble was cleaned out and rebuilding of the city walls begun. Part of the Castle of Charles V was restored for use during festivals and for exhibitions by local artists. Attempts were made to publicize Fuenterrabia's beauty through the circulation of old prints of the town. The fishermen's ward was heavily built up with hotels, bars, restaurants, and stores. The streets were paved, and the tamarind-lined boulevard was established for the evening *paseo*. A long sea wall was built, with governmental aid, to fix the location of the beach, which had previously changed along the river mouth each year. However, no building codes were enforced, and many of the architectural monstrosities that mar the landscape date from this period.

In the rural area, roads were improved and many new villas were built, often after tearing down farmhouses to make room. Many of the remaining houses were renovated by the farmers, and motor vehicles and farm machinery were everywhere in evidence.

Economically, the effects were enormous. All sectors of Fuenterrabia's economy experienced unparalleled economic growth. Craftsmen profited from the construction boom, and the fishermen and farmers made large profits selling to the tourists and to the restaurants that fed them. During the summer all economic activity in the municipality was oriented toward the tourist demand. As a consequence of this commercialization and dependence on tourism, the municipal economy became far more dependent on national and international business cycles than had previously been the case. Balance of payments problems and policies, inflation, and exchange restrictions came to affect the people of Fuenterrabia immediately and directly.

Equally great were the effects on social organization. Social differentiation increased with economic growth. There were both more occupations and wider ranges of wealth within each. Nonoccupational class identification began to develop, so that a prosperous farmer, carpenter, or boat captain all could consider themselves middle-class and engage in similar patterns of consumption.

At the same time older ties of co-operation and mutual aid between families began to lapse because most families had the economic strength to fend for themselves without incurring obligations to neighbors. In addition, families entered into increasingly stiff competition in patterns of consumption, e. g., in house renovation, in the purchase of appliances and machinery, and in sending their children to school beyond the required age.

Municipal activities in construction, both in the rebuilding of the old city and in the control over construction permits, led to a breakdown in the already strained relationships between the local government and the people of Fuenterrabia. Mutual accusations were frequent, and the local people began increasingly to look on the municipal government as an enemy.

Other processes, commonly associated with increasing commercialization were also taking place. Family size decreased, couples married at a younger age, and families became more mobile than before. As life goals shifted, generational conflict increased, and as the value of small family businesses soared, sibling conflict over inheritance errupted violently.

The present period of massive national intervention in tourism has not interrupted the social changes described above but has added new dimensions to the process. Problems have intensified with the passage of time and with the increasingly total commitment to the tourist industry. The promotion of festivals, regattas, the *Parador Carlos V,* and other municipal attractions, for example, has merely augmented the seasonal movements of tourists. On a good day, a regatta will draw an additional 5,000 people into Fuenterrabia.

The national presence also means a much stricter enforcement of building codes and a further strengthening of the municipal government's control over construction. Moreover, the government's massive investments in roads, the airport, and improvement of the railroad system have brought Fuenterrabia within easy reach of more people in a way that could not have been achieved by local initiative alone.

The reconstructed walled city is now a showplace. The walls are nearly complete, and all the rubble has been cleared away. New apartments line the once ruined streets, and the place is alive with young children. The fishermen's ward has seen more construction and a much more careful, though belated, enforcement of building codes. All the bars, restaurants, and hotels are inspected, classified, and controlled by the Ministry of Information and Tourism.

The country club has come to own more than half the land in the largest rural barrio; its management closed out more than fifteen farms in less than a year. This is not a new trend. Between 1920 and 1968 the number of farms declined from 256 to 168, and some informal evidence indicates that the number has dropped to about 120 since then. At the same time the number of villas has risen from 30 to 200. Farming is presently commercial, prosperous, and declining (cf. Greenwood 1970).

The advent of the country club signalizes the local emergence of a non-artistocratic upper-middle class as representatives of the good life, of which cars, money, fine clothes, and gentlemanly recreation are a part. Membership covers a wide range of occupations: store owners, doctors, notaries, lawyers, journalists, owners of construction businesses, artists, writers, and so on. Political power in the municipality is increasingly becoming centered in this group and their ties with outside investors. The battle over plans for the future of the municipality is now being fought between this faction on one side and the farmers and fishermen on the other, with an outcome in favor of the former being in little doubt.

In summary, Fuenterrabia's cultural heritage has become a commodity, a neo-Basque facade packaged and promoted for tourists. As for the Basques themselves, some have identified with the new consumer way of life, whereas the rest appear to be receding into ever more private cultural worlds, leaving only the outward forms of their life for touristic consumption. In the future Fuenterrabia promises to become nearly indistinguishable from all the other tourist towns on the coast of Spain.

A BALANCE SHEET ON THE EFFECTS OF TOURISM

Evaluating the overall effects of any kind of economic development is notoriously difficult, and I do so here only in the interest of further specifying some of the peculiar characteristics of tourism as an agent of change. I shall concentrate attention on the farmers, fishermen, and artisans whose occupations existed before the tourist boom.

The most important characteristic of tourism seems to be that it provides economic growth and does so at an extremely rapid rate. Moreover, it is superimposed on pre-existing economic and social arrangements in a way that industrialization is not, because the beneficiaries do not have to leave their homes and move to the cities in order to participate in it. Tourism comes to the community, and this makes it possible to view the effects of rapid rates of growth on local social relationships that did not necessarily evolve in response to the phenomenon of growth itself.

Economically, tourism has meant a variety of improvements for the people of Fuenterrabia. Since 1950 their standard of living has been climbing steadily. Many now have savings to fall back on in bad times. Homes have been rebuilt and modernized, and every year sees an increase in the profits from tourism.[2]

But this enhanced standard of living has its drawbacks. It is almost completely dependent on national and international economic conditions. Increasing cost of living through inflation in the Spanish economy might drive the tourists, looking for a bargain, to choose Portugal or Yugoslavia instead. Gone is the time that, as during the Civil War and World War II, Fuenterrabia could pull back in on itself and provide largely for its own subsistence. This buffer is gone, and the people are exposed to cycles over which they have no control.

Moreover, a decline in tourism could come about as abruptly as its rise. The Basque country has enjoyed wide popularity in recent years, but there is no guarantee that this will endure. Tourism is an industry in which fashion and vogues, the search for the new and different, plays a major role. If the tourists should decide to move on to Asturias or Galicia, the entire pattern of growth in Fuenterrabia would come to an end. The farmers are aware of this. Springtime is a period of worry and quiet conversation about the probabilities of the tourists' return. Every year there is a genuine doubt, despite the fact that thus far this has always been shortly converted into relief.

One of the unique problems in Fuenterrabia is that, while farm profits are at an all-time high, rural depopulation is increasing at a runaway pace. The profits are not translated into greater production, and the market system of incentives does not seem to operate (see Greenwood 1970).

Within the domestic group, economic growth has brought relative abundance, labor-saving appliances and machinery, increased

---

[2] An extensive analysis of the profitability of tourism in the agricultural economy is presented in Greenwood (1970).

mobility through automobiles, and a general easing of the strains caused by poverty. The celibate siblings, who formerly stayed as subordinates on the farms inherited by their brother or sister, now have sufficient outside work opportunities so that they can gain a modicum of independence and respect within the domestic group.

On the other side, the increasing value of the family enterprises has touched off inheritance battles that often have very destructive consequences. Fuenterrabia's customary law requires that a farm [3] be passed on intact from generation to generation. The parents select one heir and all other children must leave, the daughters with a dowry and the sons with an education or a sum of money to get them started. Any sibling who chooses to stay must not marry and must subordinate himself to the chosen heir.

The Spanish civil code, on the other hand, requires equal inheritance among all children. In the past, families were able to make covert arrangements among the children so that it would appear that the law was followed when in fact it was not. However, now that the value of the inheritance has gone up and the money can be used to start a profitable business, many siblings refuse to accept the parents' designation of the heir and force a division of the property, which often results in a long court fight.

Given the work opportunities in service industries with shorter hours and fewer responsibilities, moreover, parents are now finding it difficult to induce one of their children to commit himself to carrying on the family enterprise, in part because of the danger that their siblings will contest the inheritance. Of 168 farms in 1969, only eight had heirs committed to carrying on the farm into the next generation, and even in these cases the chance of finding a spouse willing to farm is remote. I do not know whether this is a problem for the fishermen and craftsmen.

With increased wealth social relations have also changed. Domestic groups are able to fend for themselves much more completely than before. The use of labor-saving devices and the presence of cash reserves allow them to disengage themselves from ties of mutual dependence and reciprocity. This allows them a much greater degree of privacy than they had had, and this privacy is highly valued.

---

[3] This discussion applies to farming, but it apparently also fits the inheritance of small businesses, though more data are needed in support of this point.

The other side of independence is isolation. Domestic groups are more socially isolated now than at any time in the recent past. Without the mutual aid obligations of the past, they interact only infrequently or on a superficial level. Though a certain amount of competition has always been present, domestic groups often now carry competition in their patterns of consumption to extremes. The purchase of a television set, a new machine, or a car becomes almost a challenge to the neighbors, who follow suit as soon as possible. In the rural area, this kind of competition has led to the acquisition of many more reaping machines and power tillers than are needed for the agricultural operations.

Even more seriously the farmers, fishermen, and small shopkeepers all are threatened by the inroads of outside investors into the local economy. Although this threat is clearly perceived by all, the isolation and competition effectively keep people from banding together to procure legal aid, form co-operatives, or lobby for their cause with outside authorities. In an area where large mutual aid networks and co-operative endeavors, called ties of *vecindad* (neighborhood), were once a commonplace, people easily succumb today as individuals.

From the perspective of the people of Fuenterrabia, the economic changes wrought by tourism have changed the local pattern of social stratification. Upward social mobility through wealth or the education which wealth can purchase is now possible for the children of some of the farmers, fishermen, artisans, and shopkeepers. The middle-class component in Fuenterrabia has expanded, and access to this class is now open to nearly all occupational categories. Moreover, class distinctions have developed within specific occupational categories. There are now middle-class and lower-class farmers, craftsmen, fishermen, and shopkeepers. The development of these social distinctions has weakened the capacity of the several categories to organize and defend themselves against the encroachments of outsiders, who are gaining increasing control over the local economy.

A side effect of the new social mobility is the isolation and abandonment of the aged. In previous generations aging Basques could expect to live with their chosen heir and enjoy a few peaceful years of semi-retirement before death. Now social mobility usually implies residential mobility as well, and there is an increasing tendency for the aged to be left alone or uncared for.

The effects of tourism on ideology deserve brief explanation. It would be possible to view the tourist industry as a vast school for the modernization of a people's values through a massive "demonstration effect." The consumer ideology, the emphasis on leisure, and the attitudes toward work held by tourists might be expected to exert a revolutionizing influence on the small towns of Europe. In Fuenterrabia, however, the rise of the tourist industry does not appear to have been accompanied by a "revolution of rising expectations." The Basques do, in fact, have a consumer mentality, and many of them have abandoned local occupations in favor of urban life and factory jobs, but this seems not to have involved a change in basic ideology. The fundamental Basque values of independence of the individual and the dignity of work have not changed. What has changed is the belief that farming, fishing, artisan labor can satisfy these values. Tourism has played a role in this change by demonstrating the apparent relative advantages of urban occupations in satisfying basic desires for independence, dignity, and abundance, but it is clearly only one of many causative factors not as yet adequately investigated.

Another subject requiring further study is the relationship between the tourists and those who serve them. Wherever tourism occurs, this appears to present a potential source of conflict. Most Basques, though content with the economic rewards, find the tourist trade unpleasant and conflictful. The summer invasion, once it is under way, is resented by all, and September is greeted by manifestations of relief that the tourists are gone. Yet by the end of the winter everyone is worried that the tourists will not return. The entire industry in Fuenterrabia is suffused with anxiety and a general sense of frustration.

The total development of tourism in Fuenterrabia suggests a sequence of phases which raises questions about the contradictions possibly inherent in tourism as an industry and as a source of economic growth. Though a single case cannot establish the growth pattern of an industry, it can suggest questions to be asked of comparable cases.

During stage I, the period of upper-class tourism, there were no appreciable local effects on economic growth. Tourism and the local economy coexisted but were not mutually interdependent. During stage II, that of the mass tourist boom beginning in 1950, the response was largely in terms of local initiative and investment, which yielded substantial economic rewards. Toward the end of this stage and more radically in stage III, the relationship between the development of tourism and the local economy changed. Outside investors and agents of the government intervened, and, while the industry has kept growing, the share of the local inhabitants in its benefits has been declining rapidly. Loss of local control of the industry since 1965 has resulted in the demise of agriculture through rural depopulation and outside competition, a decline in the fishing industry, and even a deterioration of the situation of local artisans through competition with large, outside construction firms. Essentially it appears that the large profits which had attracted outside interest have enabled them, because of their scale and organization, to supplant the local interest.

This raises a fundamental question about tourism. It provides economic growth, but for whom? In this case Spain has profited, but the people of Fuenterrabia are being excluded. The question is whether this pattern is typical, whether tourism always builds on local initiative only to drive the local people out after a certain point in economic development has been reached. If the answer to this question is affirmative, perhaps tourism deserves to rank beside industrialization as a perverse and contradictory agent of change.

Bibliography

Alegre, S. 1969. Spain: Her Economy in Figures. Madrid.

Greenwood, D. J. 1970. Agriculture, Industrialization, and Tourism: The Economics of Modern Basque Farming. Unpublished Ph.D. dissertation, University of Pittsburgh.

Sigaux, G. 1966. History of Tourism. transl. J. White. London.

Tamames, R. 1968. Introducción a la economía española. Madrid.

Sex Roles and Economic Change in Africa † * [1]

CROSS-CULTURAL variations in the relative position of the sexes have long attracted the serious attention of anthropologists. From the nineteenth-century theorists who posited matrilineal and patrilineal stages in cultural evolution,[2] through Mead's (1935) dramatic presentation of sex-role reversals in three New Guinea tribes, to attempts by British anthropologists to show that degree of matrilineality or patrilineality determines beliefs concerning conception (Richards 1950) and marital stability (Gluckman 1950), respectively, there has been an emphasis on the roles of men and women as explanatory variables in the analysis of cultural behavior.

In recent years it has become clear that terms like "matrilineal," "patrilineal," "matriarchal," and "patriarchal" are too general to do justice to the complex variations in sex roles which ethnographers have described. Roles may be differentiated by sex within each of the major institutional aspects of the social system: the family, the economy, the political system, the religious system, etc., and the patterns in one aspect may not be consistent with those of another. To give an example in terms of sex status, it is not difficult to imagine a society in which women play an important part in family decision-making but are discriminated against in the occupational sphere. Furthermore, even within the area of kinship, it appears that the general outlines of a descent system—as given in the terms "matrilineal," "patrilineal," and "bilateral"—are poor indices of sex status or position. Thus there are some patrilineal societies in which

† By Robert A. LeVine, University of Chicago.

* Ethnology Vol. V, #2 (April 1966) pp. 186–193. Reproduced by permission of the editor of Ethnology.

[1] An earlier version of this paper was presented at the American Anthropological Association meetings in San Francisco, November, 1963. The article was written while the author was a recipient of a Research Career Development Award, National Institute of Mental Health, and a fellow of the Foundations' Fund for Research in Psychiatry.

[2] Cf. Murdock (1949: 184–185) for a discussion of the hypothesis of the priority of the matrilineate as put forward by Bachofen and his followers from 1861 onwards.

women have higher relative status than their counterparts in
some matrilineal societies, due to structural factors such as residence and property rights which are more important in status
placement than the method of establishing genealogical connections.   Thus, if one is interested in the psychological or behavioral impact of cross-cultural variations in sex roles, it is
necessary to specify the aspects of sex-role structure which are
to be examined.   In this paper I propose to examine two divergent
patterns of change in the occupational roles of men and women,
and their effects on behavior in husband and wife roles.

There are some conspicuous uniformities throughout the agricultural societies of sub-Saharan Africa in the traditional division
of labor by sex and the husband-wife relationship.   Among most
of these peoples, men clear the bush and do other annual heavy
tasks, while woman have the larger share of routine cultivation.
Women carry the heavy burdens, usually on their heads, while
men occupy their leisure with a variety of prestigeful and important activities: cattle transactions (where there are cattle),
government, and litigation.   Thus women contribute very heavily
to the basic economy, but male activities are much more prestigeful and require less routine physical labor.   In husband-wife relations, the male is ideally dominant.   Polygyny is extremely widespread in these societies, and the plurality of wives often aug-
ments the husband's power in the marital relationship.   His
power is buttressed further in those many groups in which the
wives reside with their husband's kin group rather than their
own.   Within the domestic economy of the polygynous family
each wife, living in her own house, tends to constitute a separate
unit of production, regardless of whether she concentrates on
agriculture or trade.

Thus African women have less prestigeful occupations than
their husbands and are often subordinated to them in the family
in consequence of polygyny, patrilocality, and the ideal of male
dominance; nevertheless, women play essential and semi-auton-
omous roles in the labor force as producers and distributors of
goods.   Furthermore, the typical African woman thinks of herself as a cultivator or trader as well as wife and mother; her
occupational role is part of her self-image.   Since her occupational involvement is so great, it might be expected that changes
in the economy would affect her behavior in family roles.

Within this generalized picture of sex roles in the agricultural societies of Africa there are traditional variations, some of which have been magnified in the course of recent socio-economic change. The contrast of interest here is that between the Bantu agricultural peoples in Kenya and South Africa and certain Nigerian societies. All of these groups of people could be described as "patrilineal" in the usual sense of the term, but differing patterns of economic development have so magnified the traditional differences between them that they provide a striking and instructive instance of contrast in sex roles.

In Kenya and South Africa the agricultural tribes had little occupational specialization or other forms of economic differentiation, and there were no indigenous markets. When European settlement came to both areas, the plantations, industries, cities, and governmental organizations established by the Europeans employed large numbers of Africans. A pattern of labor migration developed, with rural African men leaving home to work far away for a period of years, returning occasionally on vacation, and eventually retiring in their rural homes. Most frequently, though not always, they leave their wives and children behind to continue the agricultural work and maintain the husband's claim to his share in the patrimonial land. The South African government has deliberately fostered this pattern in order to prevent large permanent settlements of Africans in the city, but the similar development in Kenya indicates that it is not simply a function of government regulation. For most of the African migrants in these areas, the rural ties are economically indispensable as well as highly valued in emotional terms; furthermore, the cities do not provide sufficient accommodation for their families. Thus many of the rural areas are depleted of young adult males; it has been estimated, for example, that half of the married women in Basutoland have absent husbands (Sheddick 1953:15). In other South African groups like the Tswana and Pondo, old surveys (Mair 1953:20–27) report 40 to 50 per cent of the adult men under 45 absent from their rural communities; the proportion is likely to be even higher nowadays. A similar though less extreme situation exists in the densely populated areas of central and western Kenya.[3]

---

[3] In North Nyanza District of western Kenya, Wilson (1956) found an average of 45 per cent of adult males absent because of employment. The situation is likely to be the same in the Kikuyu and Kamba areas of central Kenya where labor migration is an old, established pattern.

Labor migration has not resulted in a drastic restructuring of sex-role norms in these rural communities but rather in an accentuation of traditional tendencies. Men were always more mobile and less bound to routine tasks than women, as well as having greater control over property, and this is even more the case under contemporary traditions. Many tasks in which men formerly participated are now relegated exclusively to their wives and children. The men have retained their rights in land and livestock, and they also control the cash income derived from their employment and the sale of cash crops. While the absence of the men unquestionably loosens the control they once had over their wives' activities, the women who remain behind cannot be said to have gained in status relative to men—unlike those South African women who take employment in the cities.

The situation of the rural woman under these conditions can be illustrated from my own data on a Gusii community in western Kenya (LeVine and LeVine 1963). Here the women now do almost all the cultivation—from breaking ground with hoes to harvesting—for most crops, tasks which they once shared with men. In addition they milk the cows, formerly a masculine prerogative, and try to keep an eye on the herding done by preadolescent boys who have replaced young men in this job. The domestic chores of fetching water, gathering firewood, grinding grain, cooking, and child care remain feminine responsibilities, and the married women can look only to their children for assistance.

What is the emotional reaction of the married woman to this burdensome load of responsibilities? From the Gusii evidence, it seems that her children become the ultimate victims of their mother's excessive work burden. In a statistical comparison with mothers from five societies outside Africa, the Gusii mothers were highest on "emotional instability," i. e., "the degree to which mothers shift unpredictably from friendly to hostile moods" *vis-à-vis* their children (Minturn, Lambert, *et al.* 1964). Observation of these mothers indicated that this shifting is related to their work load and fatigue at particular times of day and seasons of the year, which makes them more irritable and hostile with their children than they would otherwise be. The Gusii mothers were also least tolerant, among the six societies, of their children becoming angry when scolded, and most likely to punish a child for this. They were second highest on intensity and frequency of physical punishment. All of this supports the interpretation that these mothers are expressing in their relationship with their children aggression derived from the frustrations of their heavy work load.

Despite their daily frustrations, the indications are that the Gusii women, and other African women who share their situation, find some emotional comfort in their status in society that they might not receive in a more independent role. The traditional supports for their subordination and the rewards accruing to occupation of a clearly defined social position appear to have remained effective. Although this is hard to prove, some evidence concerning the Zulu in South Africa, who have been immensely affected by labor migration, may be relevant. A study by Scotch (1960) of blood pressure among rural and urban Zulu shows numerous relations between social conditions producing stress and the frequency of elevated blood pressures among those affected by the conditions.

One finding of this study is that among rural as well as urban Zulu, the separated and widowed women, who have become family heads involuntarily, have a significantly higher frequency of elevated blood pressure than married women. Scotch (1960: 1007) explains this in terms of the reluctance of Zulu women to assume the role of family head. Another way for a Zulu woman to become emancipated from her traditionally subordinate role is to become a working woman in the city. Although both men and women living in the city have a higher frequency of elevated blood pressure than rural residents, the rural-urban differential is much greater for women. This is explained by the author (Scotch 1960:1003–1006) in terms of the more clearly defined role of women in the rural community. These findings point to the conclusion that the traditionally institutionalized role of the Zulu woman, despite its currently arduous character, still affords her less stress than a more independent role in the family and domestic economy. I would presume that this is equally true among other groups of East and South Africa where similar socio-economic changes have taken place.

Along the Guinea Coast and in the interior of West Africa, in contrast to the eastern Africa groups I have been discussing, a more specialized and differentiated economy existed prior to European contact. From the viewpoint of this discussion, its most important distinctive feature was the existence of indi-

genous markets in which women played a role as market traders.
There was no substantial settlement of Europeans in West Africa. But under European administration, with the establishment of internal peace and the development of overseas trade,
marketing activities increased, offering new opportunities to women as well as men. In some areas, these opportunities augmented the mobility and economic autonomy of women, causing drastic changes in the husband-wife relationship.

A dramatic example of such a change has been presented by
Nadel (1952) for the Nupe of northern Nigeria. In traditional
Nupe society, female trading—especially itinerant, long-distance
trading—was ideally limited to childless women, whose sexual
laxity while away from their husbands was regarded as permissible. In fact it appears that some child-bearing women also
carried on this type of trade even in those days. As economic
activity grew under British rule, an increasing proportion of
mothers became itinerant traders. In the early 1930s Nadel
found that many Nupe women were contributing a larger share
of the family income than their husbands, who were often poor
farmers. Furthermore, to quote Nadel (1952:21):

> Husbands are often heavily in debt to their wives, and the
> latter assume many of the financial responsibilities which
> should rightly belong to the men as father and family head
> such as finding bride-price for sons, paying for the children's
> education, bearing the expenses of family feasts, and the
> like. This reversal of the institutionalized roles is openly
> resented by the men, who are, however, helpless and unable
> to redress the situation.

Nupe men accuse these trading women of sexual promiscuity,
label them as immoral, and talk nostalgically about the "good
old days" when such behavior was unknown. Moreover, all
witchcraft is attributed to women, with the official head of the
women traders believed to be head of the Nupe witches. Men
are never accused of witchcraft, are often seen as its victims, and
have an exclusively male secret society which "by threats and
torture, 'cleanses' villages of witchcraft." Nadel supports his
linkage of the resented economic role of women to the witchcraft
beliefs by pointing out that the neighboring Gwari tribe, who
are closely related to the Nupe and similar in most aspects of
culture, have much less trading activity and do not recognize a
sex distinction in witchcraft attribution.

Another illustration of change in a Nigerian society is report-ed for the Ibo of Afikpo in eastern Nigeria (Ottenberg 1959). Before European contact, the women made pots, traded, and farmed, but the men controlled most of the income, performed the prestige activities of yam farming and slave trading, and limited the mobility of their wives because of the prevalence of warfare. Under the Pax Britiannica, mobility became possible and trading increased. Most importantly, however, a new crop —cassava—was introduced. The men regarded it with disdain, preferring to farm their prestigeful and ritually important yams. The women were allowed to grow cassava between the yam heaps and to keep the profits for themselves. As time went on, this despised crop eliminated the annual famine before the yam harvest and attained a high and stable market value. The Afikpo women became capable of supporting themselves and their children without aid from their husbands, and nowadays they even rent land independently for cassava cultivation. Once a women becomes self-supporting in this way, she can say, in the words of an elderly Afikpo woman, "What is man? I have my own money" (Ottenberg 1959:215). Afikpo husbands have found it increasingly difficult to keep their wives at home in their formerly subordinate position.

We do not have data on the emotional reactions of Afikpo men to the newfound independence of their wives, but there is some relevant evidence from other Ibo groups where the economic advancement of women has gone much farther, particularly in market trading. In the Ibo town of Onitsha, noted for its wealthy and independent women, there is a developing publishing industry, producing pamphlets in English written by men for male readers. Conspicuous among these publications is a literature of masculine protest, with titles such as "Beware of Women," "Why Men Never Trust Women" (a novel), and "The World is Hard," subtitled "Wife Brought Leprosy to Her Husband after Communicating with a Secret Friend." These pamphlets, both fictional and hortatory, portray women as avaricious, scheming, and immoral creatures who poison their husbands for financial gain and betray them at will. The introductions to these works often contain statements like the following from "Beware of Women":

> When you travel to other continents of the world, you will
> see that women of that parts behave better and more lovely

than our mongerish African Women. Our women know nothing than to pretend, to talk lies, to trick and say "give me money" if you don't give them the money your word will be ignored. They don't know how to serve, to obey, to love, to pet, and to talk truth. They are rather licensed liars. Only very few are fair. In order to discipline them this little but effective booklet has been produced.

Men are exhorted in dozens of pamphlets to have as little as possible to do with women in order to protect their health and achieve financial success.

A final illustration from Nigeria comes from the Yoruba people, whose women are perhaps the most independent in Africa.[4] The Yoruba case is particularly interesting because it appears that their traditional sex-role arrangements allowed women a more autonomous economic role and a higher degree of mobility than the other groups we have been discussing although change has proceeded in the same direction. The role of woman as independent market trader is and has long been highly institutionalized. Yoruba men attribute witchcraft to women, but their masculine protest lacks the naive quality of surprise that is reported for the Nupe and the Ibo. Despite the overt signs of deference, wives are expected to be economically independent, quick to divorce their husbands if they find a more advantageous match, and generally difficult to control.

The Yoruba men manifest two tendencies other than simple hostility toward women which may be related to this long-standing pattern of feminine independence. One is a widespread and intense preoccupation with impotence. Many married men report experiencing impotence, others fear it, and it is an extremely common topic of conversation. Medical practitioners are beseiged by impotent men seeking cures.[5] The other tendency is the

---

[4] The author carried out field work among the Yoruba in 1961–62 and 1963 with the support of grants from the National Institute of Mental Health (M–4865), the Ford Foundation Child Development Project of the University of Ibadan Institute of Education, and the University of Chicago.

[5] In the report of their psychiatric study in western Yorubaland, Leigh-

ton et al. state, "The worst thing that can happen to a man, we were told, is not to be potent" (1963:50), and "Men are greatly concerned with potency" (1963:153). Their survey of 170 men in community settings revealed 19 per cent who reported a current potency problem (1963:243). For the 76 men of the same sample who were rated as suffering from clearcut psychological disturbance, the figure was 40 per occurrence of male transvestism in ritual and cultural fantasy. The donning of female clothing and/or hair styles is required of male priests in several cults on ceremonial occasions, and, in addition, there is a male masquerade cult in one part of Yorubaland which requires all its members to dress as females for its annual festival.[6] Outside of ritual, professional male transvestite dancers wearing European dresses tour the villages and provide a popular entertainment. Yoruba folklore contains male pregnancy tales, one of which was made into a popular song, recorded by a famous band, and requested frequently on the disc-jockey shows of the Ibadan and Lagos radio stations during the period of field work.

These fragments of disparate evidence suggest that among the Yoruba the alteration of traditional sex roles has reached the stage where men are not simply resentful of female independence but feel emasculated by it and envy it. Whether the manifestations of envy in transvestism arise from the boy's per-

cent (1963:253). The lack of comparable figures for other groups and of evidence that the potency problems were psychogenic in origin restricts the drawing of definite conclusions from these data; at this point all we can say is that this epidemiological survey appears to confirm independently the present author's impression that impotence is a distinctively serious source of concern for Yoruba men.

[6] See Beier (1958) and Prince (1964). Prince (1964:109–110) states:
Men join the cult because of impotence, because their wives are barren or because of other diseases or misfortunes caused by witchcraft. . . .
During the annual festival, the men masquerade as women, wearing women's clothes and flaunting prominent bullet-like breasts. Some look grossly pregnant. . . .

During my interview with the Gelede elders, two or three old crones several times poked their heads in the window to correct and scold the men. I had never before witnessed such an attitude of officiousness and arrogance on the part of women during my interviews with elders of other cults or with healers. It seemed to be part of the general picture of the cult as dominated by the "mothers," that is, the witches. As one of Beier's informants told him, "Gelede is the secret of women. We the men are merely their slaves. We dance to appease our mothers."

As with impotence, so in the case of transvestism among the Yoruba, the lack of comparable evidence from other groups makes definite conclusions difficult. Ritual transvestism certainly is not limited, in Africa or elsewhere, to societies in which the status of women is equivalent to that of Yoruba women. The conspicuousness of Yoruba transvestite practices to several independent observers, however, suggests that the pattern may be a more pervasive element in their culture than in others.

ception of his mother or the husband's feelings about his wives remains an open question.

CONCLUSIONS

All the societies discussed had a traditional ideal of male domination in the husband-wife relationship. Where, as in the East and South African societies, the pattern of labor migration has allowed continued control by husbands of the larger share of family income while placing an increasing burden of work on the wives, the traditional ideal has not been challenged. Thus, though the overworked women may become irritable and punitive with their children, they do not acquire a sense of deprivation concerning their status in society. Where, as in the Nigerian societies mentioned, economic development has, through the expansion of their traditional marketing role, allowed wives to attain independent and sometimes greater incomes than their husbands, the ideal of male domination in marital relations has been seriously challenged. The men in these societies experience intense relative deprivation which results in their hostility to women, feelings of sexual inadequacy, and envy of women, all of which have cultural expressions. These divergent outcomes are determined by the degree of perceived deviation from the traditional ideal of male domination characteristic of most African societies. The general validity of this analysis remains to be tested in systematic research.

Bibliography

Beier, U. 1958. Gelede Masks, Odu 6:5–23.

Gluckman, M. 1950. Kinship and Marriage among the Lozi of northern Rhodesia and the Zulu of Natal. African Systems of Kinship and Marriage, ed. A. R. Radcliffe-Brown and D. Forde, pp. 166–206. London.

Leighton, A., et al. 1963. Psychiatric Disorder among the Yoruba. Ithaca.

LeVine, R. A., and B. B. LeVine. 1963. Nyansongo: A Gusii Community in Kenya, Six Cultures: Studies of Child Rearing, ed. B. B. Whiting, pp. 15–202. New York.

Mair, L. P. 1953. African Marriage and Social Change. Survey of African Marriage and Family Life, ed. A. Phillips, pp. 20–27. London.

Mead, M. 1935. Sex and Temperament in Three Primitive Societies. New York.

Minturn, L. M., W. W. Lambert, et al. 1964. Mothers of Six Societies. New York.

Murdock, G. P. 1949. Social Structure. New York.

Nadel, S. F. 1952. Witchcraft in Four African Societies: An Essay in Comparison. American Anthropologist 54:18–29.

Ottenberg, P. V. 1959. The Changing Economic Position of Women among the Afikpo Ibo. Continuity and Change in African Cultures, ed. W. R. Bascom and M. J. Herskovits, pp. 205–223. Chicago.

Prince, R. 1964. Indigenous Yoruba Psychiatry. Magic, Faith and Healing: Studies in Primitive Psychiatry Today, ed. A. Kiev, pp. 84–120. New York.

Richards, A. I. Some Types of Family Structure Amongst the Central Bantu. African Systems of Kinship and Marriage, ed. A. R. Radcliffe-Brown and D. Forde, pp. 207–251. London.

Scotch, N. A. 1960. A Preliminary Report on the Relation of Sociocultural Factors to Hypertension among the Zulu. Culture, Society and Health, ed. V. Rubin. Annals of the New York Academy of Sciences 84:xvii, 1000–1009.

Sheddick, V. G. J. 1953. The Southern Sotho. London.

Wilson, G. 1956. Village Surveys: Bunyore, Nyangori, Maragoli, Tiriki, Boholo. Unpublished manuscript.

*

VIII. When You Need
a Doctor

All cultures have varying degrees of medical knowledge, and most cultures have some form of medical system. All of these medical systems have some degree of success. Some of this success depends on accumulated empirical knowledge, but much of this success depends on the fact that many of the illnesses various medical practitioners treat are culture-specific illnesses—that is, they are conditions that are caused by particular strains within that culture. For this reason many such illnesses are often only treatable within the context of their specific system of medical beliefs.

One of the most universally encountered types of medical practitioners in the world is the shaman (often, unfortunately stereotyped as a "witch-doctor") and such a person is described in the first article in this section by George Peter Murdock. Although it is easy to say that shamans are only successful when treating culture-specific illnesses, or others with psychological components, it is also true that shamans are often able to cure organically caused illnesses. The second article in this section by Louis C. Whiton describes how he was cured of such an organic disease—bursitis, in this case. The next article was written by the editor of this reader especially for this volume and discusses various types of Latin American native healers who are part of a medical system known as *curanderismo*. The concluding article in this section describes the unusual medical beliefs of a rather exotic people known as the Nacirema.

Tenino Shamanism † *

T HE Tenino are a Sahaptin-speaking tribe who formerly lived on and near the Columbia River in north central Oregon. They subsisted primarily by fishing, augmented substantially by hunting, gathering, and trade. Their annual round of economic activities and their social organization have been described elsewhere (Murdock 1958).

During field work on the Warmsprings Reservation in the summers of 1934 and 1935, I established a somewhat unusual relationship with one informant, John Quinn, the oldest and most respected shaman of the tribe. When we came to discuss the treatment of illness, I encouraged him to unburden himself of his knowledge by trading him, item by item, comparable information from other primitive societies. It soon came to pass, to my surprise, that he assumed that I, too, was a knowledgeable shaman, and thereafter our discussions, though conducted through an interpreter, took the form of extended "shop talk" between two interested professional specialists. The data on shamanism in this paper derive almost exclusively from his revelations.

Since the second half of the nineteenth century the Tenino have subscribed concurrently to two religious systems. One, a form of the widespread Prophet Dance (see Spier 1935) of the Plateau, fused elements derived from Christianity and from the preachings of historical prophets from a number of neighboring tribes with a substantial core of indigenous beliefs and practices. At the time of observation it was organized as a church, whose communicants included all but a few families of the tribe. It recognized a High God and a fairly elaborate cosmology and cosmogony. Before the world was populated by men, it was inhabited by animals. Later the High God created a number of demiurges of both sexes, each representing an activity appropriate to one sex, e. g., hunting, basketmaking, berry gathering. The demiurges mated in pairs, producing the first human beings, to whom they transmitted their cultural knowledge.

† By George Peter Murdock, University of Pittsburgh.

* Ethnology Vol. IV, No. 2 (April 1965) pp. 165–171. Reproduced by permission of the editor of Ethnology and the author.

With the Prophet Dance were integrated the two major indigenous annual ceremonies—a first-fruits festival in April concerned with salmon and roots, and a subsequent first-fruits ceremony in July centering on venison and berries. It also incorporated the aboriginal eschatology and a conception of sin and a moral order of the universe derived in part from Christianity but largely from the preachings of a series of native Salishan and Sahaptin prophets.

The specifically Christian elements were relatively few in number and oddly assorted. The High God was not named but was referred to by an expression translatable as "Our Father in Heaven." Grace was said before meals, tossing bits of food over the shoulder, and Sunday was observed as a day of rest and religious observances. There was also a conception of a last judgment and the resurrection of the dead, when the bones of the righteous will rise from their graves with a vast clanking noise to be reborn for eternity. There were, however, no traces of a divine Savior, no conception of a Trinity, no rituals resembling Communion or the Mass. These absences would be incredible if the borrowing had occurred through direct contact with Christian missionaries, and Spier (1935) is probably correct in assuming that they were acquired at third or fourth hand through intermediaries of other tribes.

The second religious system—the one with which we shall hereafter be exclusively concerned—centered on the concept of supernatural power derived from animal guardian spirits. It embraced shamanistic therapy, sorcery, magical tricks, and the impersonation of spirits at winter dance ceremonies. This shamanistic religion was essentially amoral, albeit with unmistakable judicial overtones, and it had no church organization. The two systems overlapped only slightly, but were not inherently inconsistent, and most Tenino as late as the 1930s found no more difficulty in subscribing to both than have the Chinese in concurrently accepting Confucianism, Taoism, and Buddhism.

At the age of six or a little older, every child, male or female, was sent out alone at night into the wilderness in search of a guardian spirit, and this procedure was repeated from time to time until the child had accumulated five such spirits as lifelong helpers. For the most part these tutelary beings were animals or birds, but occasionally a plant, an inert object, or a natural phenomenon would reveal itself to the seeker as a supernatural guardian. The child did not go out unprepared. He was instructed by an experienced old man or woman where to go, how to behave (e. g., to keep awake by erecting piles of rocks), and what to expect. Moreover, through attendance at the winter dances he had become familiar with the distinctive cries, movements, and songs of most of the spirits he was likely to encounter.

Nevertheless, one need only project oneself backward to the aboriginal situation to imagine how anxiety-provoking a spirit quest must have been. Alone at night, remote from his family and his village, the child was fully aware of the danger of encountering an actual wolf, bear, cougar, or rattlesnake. With no light except from the moon or stars, his heightened sensory perceptions could easily magnify dim shadows and rustlings in the bush into the imagined form and movements of any animal, and he had to tense himself for any eventuality. When the dimly sensed shapes and sounds appeared to crystallize into a human figure speaking the Tenino language—for it was always thus that a spirit addressed a seeker—the child must have felt immensely relieved, and his imagination could readily structure the actual, presumed, or visionary encounter in terms of cultural expectations.

Upon revealing itself to the child in human form, the spirit uttered its characteristic animal cry, sang its special spirit song, explained the specific power it was conferring and how to evoke it, and finally resumed its animal form and disappeared. The power bestowed could be that of invulnerability in war, prowess in hunting, ability to cure sickness or control the weather, clairvoyance, fire-walking, or a variety of other skills or immunities. A power offered could not be rejected or revealed to others, on penalty of punishment or its loss, but the successful seeker was expected to sing his spirit song and dance his spirit dance at the next winter ceremony. In this manner people became aware of the spirit helpers of their neighbors, but only in a general way of the powers they controlled.

A person became a shaman by discovering after puberty, and hence after the completion of the normal spirit quests, that other spirits were attracted to him. These were the guardians of deceased people, especially of dead shamans, who were conceived to be "hungry" and eager to attach themselves to a new master who would "feed" them. Unlike ordinary people, who were limited to five supernatural helpers, shamans acquired a large number of guardian spirits. John Quinn claimed to control 55 and considered this only slightly more than the average.

The additional spirits accumulated by a shaman were for the most part those of animals. The powers conferred by different animal spirits were sharply differentiated, and were scaled with reference to one another, largely in terms of projections from the innate or traditional characteristics or propensities of the natural animals themselves. Among the strongest animal spirits were the grizzly bear, the rattlesnake, and the eagle. The grizzly bear had ascendancy over most other animal spirits, but not over the rattlesnake, which in turn yielded ascendancy to certain bird spirits, including the eagle. In accordance with the prevailing theory of disease, that of spirit possession, a shaman could employ his spirit helpers either to injure or to cure. He could cause a victim to fall ill or die by projecting one of his spirits into his victim's body, or he could cure a patient thus afflicted by injecting a stronger spirit into the body to eject the intrusive one.

In addition to a variety of spirits which he could use for purposes of therapy or sorcery, a shaman normally had one or more spirits of two special categories. One was a diagnostic spirit—·characteristically a curious animal like a magpie—whom he could inject into the body of a prospective patient to ascertain the identity of the intrusive spirit and thereby learn which of his own spirits he might employ to extract it. The second type was not an animal spirit at all, but a human ghost, e. g., that of a dead baby whom the shaman had attached to himself. Control over such a ghost-spirit enabled the shaman to treat illnesses explained by a rarer secondary theory, that of soul loss. Occasionally, when a person was particularly distraught over the death of a beloved parent, spouse, or child, his soul would leave the body and follow that of the dear one to the after world in the west. The body would then waste away, and a shaman would be called in to effect a cure. When his diagnostic spirit discovered that the cause of the illness was not an instrusive spirit but the absence of the patient's own soul, the shaman summoned his ghost-spirit, dispatched it to the after world to fetch back the lost soul, and restored the latter to the body.

To practice, it was not sufficiently merely to have accumulated the requisite number and variety of spirit helpers. The prospective shaman also had to pass the equivalent of a state medical board examination conducted by the shamans who had already been admitted to practice. These experienced practitioners led the neophyte to the edge of a high "rim rock," where he was required to demonstrate his control over his spirits. Only shamans, it was believed, could see and hear the guardian spirits of other people, and the theory was that they could judge the expertise of the neophyte in controlling his spirits on the test errands on which he was directed to dispatch them.

As scientists, of course, we must assume that there were no spirits for the neophyte to direct or his elders to observe—or rather, perhaps, that they were figments of an hallucinatory imagination. What, then, was the function of the examination? At the very least, the older shamans could determine the genuineness of the neophyte's conviction, regarding his own powers; a faker would scarcely have dared subject himself to the ordeal. Moreover, as became clear in my discussions with John Quinn, the older shamans took advantage of the occasion to review carefully the entire life of the candidate. They had known him, of course, since childhood and were thoroughly familiar with his strengths and defects of character, his honesty and moral fiber, his judgment, the degree of his control over his aggressive impulses, etc. Actually, though not ostensibly, their decision as to whether or not to admit him to practice seems clearly to have rested on their collective estimate of his personal characteristics, of his fitness to be entrusted with the exercise of great power. The personality of John Quinn himself, as well as all that I could learn from him, convinces me that Tenino shamans, far from being dishonest, exploitive, or hysterical individuals, were people of unusual decency, upright character, judgment, and responsibility. Those who proved seriously defective in these respects were eliminated through sorcery.

Once he was accepted by his seniors, the young shaman could begin to practice. For his first five cases, however, he could accept no fees. Thereafter he was generously rewarded with gifts, but he received these only if his cures were effective. Women as well as men could become shamans, and they were not considered inferior in power, but they were appreciably fewer in number. When operating in a professional capacity, shamans commonly wore insignia appropriate to their guardian spirits, e. g., bear claws, eagle feathers, or a rattlesnake's rattles. Shamans sometimes assisted one another, and they acted in concert in the examination of neophytes, but otherwise they lacked any collective organization.

By far the principal function of Tenino shamans was the practice of magical therapy. When a person fell ill and did not respond to lay treatment, his family summoned a shaman, who immediately proceeded to his bedside. In the house were assembled the relatives and friends of the patient, lending him social support and enhancing his faith in the therapeutic procedures and his will to recover. On hand were the necessary accessories, including especially a coiled basket full of water. During the performance the audience sang and beat time on a dry log with short sticks, and the shaman accentuated the drama of the occasion by singing his spirit songs, uttering explosive sounds, making biting motions, and pantomiming the struggle of the spirits.

The necessary first step in the cure was diagnosis. After washing his hands, smoking, blowing on the basket of water, and sprinkling the patient, the shaman summoned his diagnostic spirit and projected it into the patient's body, usually through a tube. After an interval of time for its exploration of the interior of the body, the spirit returned to the mouth of the shaman and informed him of the identity of the intrusive spirit (or alternatively, as we have seen, of the absence of the soul). If the shaman had no guardian spirit with ascendancy over the intrusive one—if, for example, the latter was the grizzly bear and he did not control a rattlesnake spirit—he resigned immediately from the case and recommended another shaman to take over. Otherwise he would have lost his life when his spirit was overcome by the intrusive one in the ensuing struggle.

If, however, the shaman's roster of supernatural helpers included one with ascendancy over the intrusive spirit, he summoned it and meanwhile called upon two strong men to assist him. They stood on either side of him, grasping his arms, while he blew his spirit helper into the patient's body. When the latter encountered the intrusive spirit, a violent conflict ensued between them, during which the patient writhed helplessly. When a moment of calm intervened, the shaman sucked the intrusive spirit into his mouth. Then began a titanic and dramatic struggle—this time between the vanquished spirit and the shaman—in which the shaman's body tensed, was thrown into contortions, and then became inert as he lost consciousness. His two assistants exerted themselves valiantly to keep him erect, for had he fallen he would have lost his life. Ultimately the convulsions subsided, and the shaman spat the intrusive spirit into his cupped hands, thereby initiating a new struggle in which the shaman, with the help of his assistants, with great effort gradually lowered his hands into the basket of water. This finally subdued the spirit.

The shaman then withdrew his hands from the water and exhibited the vanquished spirit to the audience on the palm of his hand. Only the shamans present, of course, could actually see it, but perhaps the reader may be interested in a shaman's description of an extracted spirit. According to John Quinn, such a spirit, regardless of the animal it represented, was approximately the size and shape of a cigarette butt, was grayish in color, and had a colloidal or mucus-like substance. After the viewing, the shaman, with a puff of breath, sent the spirit back to its proper place in nature. He then retrieved and similarly dispatched his own guardian spirit.

John Quinn readily admitted that shamanistic therapy was not invariably successful. Failure was explicable on such grounds as that the shaman had been summoned too late or that no spirit was available with ascendancy over the intrusive one. There is no reason to doubt, however, that genuine cures were often effected, at least in cases of "functional" ailments. Social support, a faith unshaken by skepticism, confidence in the integrity of the shaman, and the dramatic quality of the curing performance must all have contributed to a favorable result, as most modern psychiatrists are prepared to agree.

Next in importance among a shaman's activities was the sponsorship or direction of the winter dances in which guardian spirits were impersonated. Much less frequent, but socially very significant, was the practice of sorcery. This was usually, though not exclusively, directed toward tribal enemies, in times of peace as well as of war. The Tenino community credited John Quinn with having killed three fellow tribesmen by sorcery during his lifetime, and this was corroborated by psychoanalytic colleagues of mine through the analysis of a collection of his dreams which I had gathered.

Special interest attaches to one of these cases, since the death was inadvertently caused, and the deep sense of guilt which John Quinn felt as a result ran like a thread through many of his dreams. A Tenino shaman was expected to keep tight rein over his thoughts as well as his actions. In the case in question, John Quinn had had a momentary hostile thought about another man. Though he himself was scarcely aware of it, it was noticed by one of his guardian spirits, who was present and who immediately dashed out of the house to do what he understood to be his master's bidding by possessing the body of the presumed enemy. As it happened, however, an innocent girl was just then passing the door, and the spirit accidentally collided with her and entered her body instead of that of its intended victim. She sickened and died before John Quinn became aware of her predicament or another shaman could be summoned to cure her.

From the other two cases and other evidence, admittedly inconclusive, I strongly suspect that in-group sorcery served primarily a judicial purpose among the Tenino. Under aboriginal conditions they lacked any political organization transcending the village, and the local headman had functions that were more advisory and hortative than authoritarian. No legal mechanism existed for coping with serious and repeated criminals—murderers, rapists, perennial troublemakers, or the like. I believe that this void was filled by the shamans through the practice of sorcery. It was clear that John Quinn felt that two of his own in-group-sorcery murders were socially justified. It was also clear that a person who engaged in shamanistic practices without permission, or who, as a shaman, used his power unduly for maleficent purposes, laid himself open to sorcery from the respected shamans. If the latter refused to come to his aid when he fell ill, he was helpless, for no one shaman by himself controlled the entire range of therapeutic powers.

It therefore seems highly probable that a Tenino shaman was expected to keep close track of malefactors within the community. When the transgressions of one of the latter exceeded the limits of toleration, in the shaman's opinion and that of his neighbors as he sensed it, he presumably assumed the responsibility, possibly after consultation with his fellow shamans, for dispatching one of his guardian spirits to possess the evil-doer as an act of justified social vengeance. In other words, he acted in an emergency as judge, jury, and executioner combined. The fact that shamans were known to be capable of sorcery, and the presumption that they were prepared to use it for judicial purposes, doubtless operated to reduce the rate of serious crime and thereby to limit sharply the incidence of sorcery within the community.

If the above interpretation is correct, it would account for the high premium placed by the Tenino on personal character, responsibility, and judgment in their shamans. After all, these are the same qualities that we ourselves expect in our judges. Whatever the situation may be in other societies, the shaman's role among the Tenino certainly did not provide a social niche for the accommodation of deviant, abnormal, and neurotic personalities.

The foregoing account includes a number of specific features which the author has not encountered elsewhere in the literature on American Indian shamanism. Among them are the examining board of shamans, the specialized diagostic and human-ghost spirits, and the emphasis placed on judicial qualities in the selection of shamans. To the extent that such facts may be novel and theoretically illuminating, the author hopes that much of the credit will be accorded to the interest and generosity of his respected former friend and "professional colleague," John Quinn.

Bibliography

Murdock, G. P.   1958.   Social Organization of the Tenino.   Miscellanea Paul Rivet 1:229–315.   Mexico.

Spier, L.   1935.   The Prophet Dance of the Northwest and Its Derivatives.   General Series in Anthropology 1:1–74.   Menasha.

Under the Power of the Gran Gadu † *

In a Secluded But Amid the Gloom of the Surinam Rain Forest, Witch Doctor Raineh Practiced an Old Form of Psychotherapy

IN some areas of the world supernatural practitioners known as witch doctors, shamans, or medicine men still treat the ailing. Generally relying on psychological means, rather than on jungle medicines, they occasionally appear to succeed when trained medical men fail.

† By Louis C. Whiton.

* Reprinted from Natural History Magazine, August-September, 1971.

I was cured by such a witch doctor under unusual circumstances. For two years I had suffered from lameness and severe pain in my right leg and hip, originally caused by acute trochanteric bursitis. Over a period of eighteen months, specialists and my own physician had used some of the latest methods of treatment, including three applications of local anesthesia, with no abatement of either the pain or the lameness.

During the previous twelve years, I had made a number of anthropological studies in Surinam, South America (formerly Dutch Guiana), among the jungle people known as Bush Negroes, descendants of six thousand slaves who had escaped from Dutch plantations in the early 1700's. Today some 27,000 of these people live in the remote rain forest. In their isolation they have retained to a marked degree the traditions, religions, and magic practices of their African ancestors.

I had become especially interested in observing the ceremonies, rituals, and evident cures by the tribal witch doctors. Since conventional medical methods had not eliminated my physical discomfort, the possible effectiveness of a jungle treatment intrigued me. I had planned my fifth expedition to Surinam, and by a stroke of good fortune, my personal physician was taking his vacation at the same time. Because of his interest in this unusual type of psychotherapy, he decided to join the expedition.

Among the Bush Negroes, there are so-called witches who practice black magic, inflicting curses on both men and women, generally for a sizable fee. Such malicious practices are considered mortal sins, for they are forbidden by their gods. In contrast to a witch, a witch doctor's professional function is to overcome the effects of black magic, to which are attributed most illnesses and death (a notion not uncommon in Western societies until a few centuries ago).

To insure the maximum chance of success, I sought out the most prominent witch doctor in Paramaribo, a man named Raineh. His forceful personality and his success with the Surinamese had previously impressed me, and many of the city's more educated people employed his talents even though they attended Christian churches and also consulted Western-trained physicians. Furthermore, he qualified for all three classifications of witch doctor: as a *lukuman,* or soothsayer; a *bonoman,* or medicine man capable of "pulling out the witch" from sufferers af-

flicted with a curse; and as a voodoo priest, one of whose functions is to exorcise the evil spirit. In Surinam Raineh is known
as an *obiaman*.

Unlike the conventional concept of a witch doctor, Raineh is
normal in appearance. Thirty-three years old, he is handsome,
tall—six feet three inches—and has an athletic build, a necessity
because he undergoes considerable physical strain and effort
during his treatments. When I previously attended his curing
ceremonies, I noted that his facial expression and personality differed for each of the three types of *obiaman* that he became.
At times I found his expression disturbing. His eyes appeared to
be focused at some point through and beyond me.

Although he came from a tribe in the rain forest, as a child his
mother had taken him to Paramaribo, the capital city of Surinam.
She was a convert to Roman Catholicism, and Raineh had attended the parochial school where he obtained a better education than
most boys. He spoke Dutch perfectly and was fairly fluent in
English, as well as in the Surinam language known as *takki-takki,*
a type of pidgin English-Dutch-African developed by the early
slaves. He told me that at the age of twelve, he had learned in
a vision that he was endowed with power and knowledge from
supernatural sources, and that Gran Gadu, creator of the world,
would enable him to cure and help people. He confided this to his
church confessor, who advised him that as a Holy Christian
Father, his own duty on earth was to accomplish the same good
deeds, and that the Christian God and Gran Gadu were obviously
one and the same deity.

According to Raineh, after several years of study under older
members of the profession, he spent a year in Haiti learning the
rituals of Haitian voodoo and the art of hypnosis. He said that
his snake altar came from Haiti and consisted of snake bones
wrapped in a bundle and attached to a six-foot plank, with a small
bell hanging beneath it. According to the voodoo religion, it is
the snake bones that are possessed by the god. Voodoo differs
materially in the several countries where this form of worship
is followed: in Dahomey, Africa, where it originated; in the
Caribbean Islands; in Surinam; and even in certain quarters of
New Orleans, among others.

Shortly before midnight, my physician, five European and
American friends, and the editor of a Surinamese newspaper ac-

companied me to the rendezvous in the forest about forty miles from Paramaribo. Although I understood the native Surinam language, the editor was to act as an interpreter because he was an expert in the type of ceremony we were about to engage in.

We drove along a trail until we saw a cloth tied to a tree. This was the signal to leave the automobiles. Here we were met by a Bush Negro carrying a torch, who led us slushing through a swamp—the barrier between the comparative civilization of the rough jungle road and the isolated area where the rituals could be practiced in complete seclusion.

The following account of the ceremony is based on the report dictated on tape by my physician during the event and also on the detailed shorthand notes taken by another friend. My own recollection is remarkably clear, in view of the impressionistic events, but more subjective.

The ceremony began at midnight and lasted until 4:30 in the morning. It took place in a large thatched hut called the "hospital," open on the sides except for a partition at one end and lit by a flickering torch of kerosine-soaked hemp. In the center was the magic circle, four feet in diameter and bounded by twelve bottles of various liquors. Within the circle was a low wooden stool for me to sit on, with a burning candle in front of it.

A white chicken, its legs tied together, lay on the ground outside the circle. On either side of the hut were red flags of indigenous Indian gods, considered by the blacks to be exceptionally powerful because they were the gods of the land before the African slaves arrived in the seventeenth century. On one side a voodoo altar rested on a wooden box. The melodramatic effect of the setting was ideally suited to the psychological treatment of a patient.

I was led to the partition in the rear of the hut and told to strip. A loin cloth was draped around me, and a wide white cloth was tied around my forehead. My body was rubbed with *pemba dotee* (clay) that had been mixed with the leaves of the *sangea fu-fu* and various other herbs. When such clay has been blessed with the proper ritual, it is believed to have the power to ward off evil.

To protect me, this clay was also sprinkled on the ground ahead of me as I was led barefooted to the magic circle. Sitting on the low stool, I fixed my eyes on the candle flame in front of me. Raineh commenced to chant, and the words and melody were repeated by ten male and female assistants, who acted as a response chorus. The monotonous rhythms repeated over and over again for many minutes created a hypnotic effect, in all probability an important part of the ritual. To frighten away evil spirits, large, noisy maracas containing snake bones were constantly shaken close to my ears.

Following the chanting and impassioned prayers to the jungle gods, which somewhat resembled activities at a southern revivalist meeting, Raineh filled his mouth with whiskey and sprayed it through his lips seven times on the chicken, with a prayer for each day of the week. Then he poured beer into the cupped hands of all those present and told them to wash their faces with it, while he prayed for their welfare, good health, and happiness— especially with one of the opposite sex.

The ceremony of questioning my soul about my past life then began. I was given a soup plate containing a heavy mound of *pemba dotee* surrounded by liquor to the brim, which I held in my outstretched hand, my elbow resting on my knee. This is the traditional method used by the Bush Negroes when questioning an incorporeal entity, such as a soul. The questions can be answered by a "yes" or "no." The weight of the plate eventually causes the extended hand to become unsteady, with the result that the liquid drips over the brim of the plate in one direction or another. According to an accepted code, the location on the plate where the liquid spills indicates either an affirmative or negative answer.

The interrogation was in *deepy-takki*, a dialect containing many African words, originally developed by the early slaves so that their masters could not understand them. Raineh's assistants appeared impressed, even shocked, by my disclosures. It therefore did not surprise me that after the questioning Raineh prayed to the god Misah to "protect this Child of the Earth, even though he has sinned, so that no harm will come to him."

During this part of the ceremony, my doctor mentions twice on the tape that he feared I would burn the back of my hand because I was holding the plate so near the candle's flame. Having often observed that natives in a state of trance appear to be impervious to high heat, I have since wondered whether I felt no sensation of excessive heat because I was in a similar state to a minor degree.

At the conclusion of this part of the ritual, the voodoo altar was paraded around my head and the flags of the Indian gods were waved over me. To attract the beneficent local gods, Raineh told the audience to clap their hands, and the tempo and intensity were gradually increased until it was presumed that the gods had arrived.

For two hours I had been sitting on the low wooden stool and had barely moved during the entire time. As evidence of the hyperphysical effect of the ceremony, I experienced no physical discomfort despite my crouched position and the lack of any padding.

The "pulling out the witch" ritual now began, and Raineh's personality changed from that of a soothsayer to that of a shaman who transfers the witch temporarily from the patient to himself. I was told to lie on the ground and the altar was placed beside me. Raineh lay down in the opposite direction, with the top of his head touching mine. The extremely heavy mortar in which the clay and the various herbs had been ground was placed on his chest, while one of his assistants stood on his stomach and another on his thighs. Two men vigorously pounded the mortar with large wooden pestles. I later learned that these precautions were meant to safeguard Raineh when the witch left me and entered his body. They believed that the rhythm of the pounding on his chest would keep his heart beating regularly during the ordeal and that the men standing on him would retard abnormal swelling caused by the witch.

After ten minutes Raineh started to groan as if in pain, and I was instructed to stand up. I felt this was to be the moment of truth. Either my long period of discomfort would be over, or the curing ceremony would have failed. Faith was important, and I made every effort to bolster my confidence in Raineh's powers. No doubt, at the moment I was also susceptible to plain old-fashioned superstition. Still, I was suddenly fearful that Raineh would fail.

I arose from the ground, and it was with controlled emotion that I then realized that all sensation of pain or cramp had disappeared. In the ensuing excitement my doctor grasped my hand and to my surprise said, "I was quite sure that it would work!" It was only later that I understood why he had said this.

Three of Raineh's assistants then attempted to lift him off the ground. He appeared to be in a tonic trance, his body rigid. Finally Raineh's assistants forced him to bend slightly at the waist. They supported him as he sat on the ground.

A remarkable transformation then occurred in his facial expression and his personality. I recognized from my previous experiences at such ceremonies that Raineh was now supposedly totally possessed by the witch and was no longer his usual self or in one of his priest roles. Raineh now became irascible and quarrelsome, and to everyone's surprise, he began to speak in English instead of his native *takki-takki*. Angrily he said, "I don't like these people" (the Bush Negroes) and, referring to me, "I don't like Lou," and other unfriendly statements.

Speaking in English, the local newspaper editor demanded that the "witch" tell where he came from and who his "boss" was. This referred to the person who, through the witch presumably had inflicted me with the curse. Raineh fought against answering. Finally, threatened with never being allowed to return to his own country unless he answered the questions, he slowly and reluctantly replied. He said that he came from a nation in Africa, which he named, and that his boss was from the same country. This startled me. I recalled an unfortunate and disagreeable altercation I had had three years before with a young African dignitary from that very nation, whom I had met at an important tribal ceremony in the distant rain forest in Surinam. Since he was a member of a different tribe, Raineh couldn't have had any knowledge of the event, which had occurred almost two hundred miles away. It is known that the African area referred to is famous for its malevolent *ju-ju* men, who inflict black magic if hired to do so. Also, English is spoken fluently in this former colony, and when Raineh had become possessed by the witch he at once spoke in that language rather than in *takki-takki*.

It seemed to be an unusual and amazing coincidence. I am certain, however, that many well-educated people in Paramaribo would have believed, beyond a doubt, that this was the origin of my trouble.

The next step in the curing ritual was to transfer the spirit of the witch from Raineh to the altar of snake bones. I sat on the low stool and Raineh sat on the ground behind me, his shoulders pressed against my lower back. After a short time he began to utter what seemed to be undulating moans of pain, while the chorus continued to chant and shake the noisy maracas. Raineh proceeded to tremble violently, and when this ceased, his face gradually assumed an expression of gentleness and calm. This indicated that he now was assuming the role of a beneficent voodoo priest who inspires peace and order. The doctor and I assumed that it was at this time that the temporary transfer to the altar occurred.

As a voodoo priest, Raineh always walked on his knees, and he proceeded in this manner around the circle of spectators to give them his blessing, wishing them good health and fortune. They looked on the altar in awe as it was paraded around Raineh several times, while the bell tinkled and the chanting continued.

The next step was transferring the witch's spirit from the altar to the body of the chicken. Taking the bird gently in his arms, Raineh began whispering to it earnestly in *takki-takki*. He appeared to be consoling it for its eventual fate. One end of the plank holding the altar was then placed on the top of my head, and the other end on the head of one of the Dutch spectators. I was instructed to move in the direction indicated by nudges from the plank, which according to their beliefs were imparted by the god Dagowi who possessed the bones on the snake altar.

Directed by these nudges (imbalance of the heavy burden is a probable factor), I followed a zig-zag course between the jungle trees and arrived at a small clearing. Two large bowls containing liquids, mainly water, were brought to the area. With joyous singing by the chorus and thanks and praise to the gods for overpowering the evil spirit, Raineh grasped the chicken by its legs, dipped it in the liquid, and splashed it repeatedly over my body while the chicken vigorously flapped its wings and made raucous sounds.

Raineh then lifted the bird by its neck feathers and held it in front of me. He explained that unless it died without his injuring it in any manner, the witch would not be completely exorcised and might return to me. If my pain recurred this could be used as a reasonable excuse. Since the chicken did not appear to be succumbing, Raineh said that all of the evil might not have been "pulled out of me." Consequently he told me to open the chicken's beak and to spit into it, as this might remove the last traces of the witch in me and pass it to the bird. I did as he directed. For a minute or two the bird flapped its wings violently. Then, with a final squawk, and to my astonishment, it went limp and died.

Raineh assured me that the chicken had died because of the evil that had been transferred to it, and that my disability would never return. I had not observed Raineh doing anything of sufficient violence to the bird to kill it, unless unconsciously, or even intentionally, his grip on the feathers near its throat had been sufficiently strong to strangle it.

The ceremony continued with singing, incantations, shaking of the maracas, and prayers of thanks. Herbs and *pemba dotee* were plastered on my wet body to prevent evil from re-entering it, and finally Raineh anointed me with a spray of liquor from his lips. The chicken was placed on the ground and I was instructed to stand on its body. Its neck and legs were severed by rapid blows of a machete, within a fraction of an inch of my bare feet.

The night had been long and eventful, and it was undeniable that my trouble had completely ceased. The important question was whether this sudden relief would last indefinitely. Now, more than two years have gone by, and I can say that I have never suffered even a momentary twinge of pain in my hip or leg. The scientific explanation given to me by members of the medical profession is as interesting and almost as fantastic to a layman as the ceremony itself.

The bursa, or cushion covering the upper end of the thigh bone, or trochanter, had become inflamed, possibly due to calcium deposits, a condition known as bursitis. After even moderate exercise, the leg muscles attached to my hip would go into spasm, followed by severe pain. Thus, the merry-go-round of spasm-pain-spasm continued even though the bursitis may have subsided after treatment. I was told that if this continues for a long period the symptoms may become even worse, since "a cyclic pattern transmitted through the spinal cord to the brain, of self-perpetuating impulses has been created, which results in chronic discomfort." Several injections of an anesthetic into the area were supposed to interrupt the pattern. Such treatment is classic and frequently results in lasting relief, although in my case it was only temporary. Medical men I have spoken to credit the complicated and mesmeric effect of the voodoo ceremony with psychologically breaking this pattern, since the brain is an important link in the cycle.

The doctors considered many factors significant. Raineh's charismatic personality was one. He was a showman and amateur psychiatrist of no mean ability. He had complete confidence in his powers, so much so that he suggested that I pay only half his fee and forward the balance when I was certain that the effects of the black magic would not return.

Undoubtedly the ritual, with its monotonous rhythmic chanting, the intense and continuous din of the maracas close to my ears, and the ecstatic appeal to the gods, was intended to produce a mesmeric influence. In addition, the eerie atmosphere of the jungle hut lit by the flaming torch, the candle on which I fixed my eyes, the tinkling bell attached to the altar, and even the impact of sacrificing the chicken contributed to the effect. I have since asked myself, "Was I hypnotized to any extent during the ritual?" If I was, I did not recognize it at the time.

Christian religious cures frequently succeed when strictly scientific approaches have failed because they are deeply rooted in spiritual faith, which provides a powerful emotional factor. In the instance of this voodoo ceremonial, this factor also played an important part.

I asked Raineh how he personally avoided subsequent attacks by witches for having foiled their evil practices. He assured me that he possessed a powerful *obia,* or fetish, that protected him. Furthermore, Raineh professed to be able to inflict black magic on the witch. He presented me with an *obia,* an object of no material value, and said, "If the witch ever tries to return to you and you again feel pain, hold this in your hand and you will be well again."

Science and the medical profession have attempted to explain the success of treatments such as Raineh's. But some doctors I have talked to about this subject have expressed regret that the great advances in surgical practices and the use of drugs during the last thirty years have obscured the importance of the mind in curing bodily ills. A professor at one medical school told me that much more attention is now being given to psychosomatic factors in treating physical symptoms. There is obviously much to learn about such phenomena.

The Curandero-Supremo

Norman Alger *

CURANDERISMO is a traditional Latin American folk medical system and includes various theories of disease causality, classification and treatment, that often differ significantly from the beliefs of orthodox Western scientific medicine. This system is found, with different regional variations, throughout most areas of the New World where there are Latin American populations, and the geographical range of belief in this system extends from the United States to Chile. (Foster 1953:204)

The general practitioners in this folk medical system are known as *curanderos* if they are males or as *curanderas* if they are female. There are also a number of more specialized practitioners in this system and they include such curers as *parteras rusticas* (native midwives), *hueseros* (bone setters), *sobadoros* (curers who rely primarily on massage) and *yerberos* or *yerbalistas* (herbalists). These curers often command a great deal of respect in their communities and may be given the honorific title of *"Don"* if they are male, or *"Doña"* if they are female.

In the past there has been a great deal of stereotyping of *curanderismo*. Statement such as "_____ there is a general uniformity of views and techniques so that one may generalize about *curanderismo* without much difficulty" (Kiev 1968:30) have led Press (1971) to state that a stereotype of *curanderismo* had developed that is misleading because it often ignores the fact that *curanderismo* actually embraces a great range of different behavior. Press in describing his idea of this stereotype includes these factors as well: the use of confession as a therapeutic device; performance or diagnosis "familiar" to patient; manifest concern for reintegration of the patient into his community; a lengthy diagnostic and/or curative performance; active involvement of the family or friends in the diagnosis and/or cure; no fees; low fees; non-specified fees or fee ritualization; and religious identification of the curer.

To this list might be added the following characteristics: curers are usually part-time practitioners (Madsen 1964:89); the

* The research on which this paper is based was supported by a National Endowment for the Humanities grant.

setting for curing practices usually includes an altar, flowers, vigil lights, and other religious articles (Kiev 1968:31, Madsen 1961:26); medicaments are usually herbal remedies; and ritual cleaning or sweeping of the patient with raw whole eggs or herbs is common (Foster 1953, Madsen 1964:74); and disease and treatments may be classified as "hot" or "cold". (Currier 1966, Foster 1953, Madsen 1955)

This stereotype of the *curandero* is a limiting approach to curers and curer-related phenomena because it tends to associate the curer almost entirely with the treatment of folk disease and ignores the fact that many of them also treat more mundane illnesses. It tends to associate the *curandero* with the peasant milieu and ignores the fact that there are also urban *curanderos*. Perhaps one of the greatest difficulties of working with this stereotype is that it classifies curers on an "either-or" basis— either the curer fits this stereotype or he is classified as a "marginal practitioner." To do this is to exclude consideration of a number of other curers such as *parteras rusticas, hueseros, sobadoros,* and *yerberos.* Such a stereotype also tended to ignore the existence of a number of other medical resources such as licensed M.D.'s, pharmacists, nurses, homeopaths, etc. (Press 1971:741–742)

Early in our period of fieldwork in Oaxaca, Mexico, in 1972, we found that this stereotype was too limiting and that most of the *curanderos* we interviewed treated a great number of illnesses as defined by modern Western scientific medicine in addition to a number of folk illnesses. Furthermore, we found that the practices and beliefs of 2 of the 13 curers we interviewed were so far out of the range of the stereotyped *curandero* that it was necessary for us to categorize them by some other term. We have decided to call them *"curanderos-supremos"* (super-curers). The term *"curandero-supremo"* as used here is meant to designate certain curers who rely less on traditional techniques of *curanderismo* and more on the use of some approximation of modern Western scientific medical techniques and drugs. The two *"curanderos-supremos"* who will be described here can be further characterized by the following:

1. Makes little, or no, use of herbal remedies. Makes the use of modern drugs an important part of his therapy.
2. Treats fewer of the traditional folk diseases and is more likely to treat diseases defined by modern Western medical

beliefs—such conditions as cancer, diabetes, and various heart conditions.

3. Therapy setting is closer to the appearance of the modern physician's office than it is to the treatment setting of the traditional *curandero.*

4. Uses anatomical charts, often on open display, to inform the patient of his condition and perhaps to reinforce his own expertise as a curer to the patient.

5. Some of his patients may have come to him as a last resort when a licensed physician has given him up as incurable.

6. Is liable to use some modern methods, such as urinalysis tapes and hypodermic syringes, in some of his diagnosis and treatment.

7. Has a potential high income from his practice either because he sees a few patients at very high fees, or because he sees a large number of patients at set fees considerably higher than those charged by the more traditional *curanderos* in the area.

8. Is to be distinguished from the licensed physician by his lack of formal medical training and medical license.

9. Is also to be distinguished from the licensed physician because he does not perform surgical operations, and often attempts to dissuade his patients from having such operations.

The first such *"curandero-supremo"* we met in Oaxaca is a man about 60 years of age who lives in a small village in the Valley of Oaxaca and we shall call him Don Humberto. His house is quite modern, well-built, and his relative affluence is reflected by such things as a new refrigerator on his kitchen porch. Don Humberto is a *curandero,* a *huesero,* and by his own admission, a *brujo* (witch). Although he does use some traditional techniques and treat some folk illnesses, his heavy reliance on modern drugs in therapy and the fact that he will treat almost any modern disease, such as cancer and diabetes mellitus qualify him to be considered a *"curandero-supremo".*

Don Humberto claims that most of his knowledge of curing was taught to him many years ago by a man from Northern Oaxaca with whom he studied for five years. He gained more medical knowledge when he worked in a large hospital (probably as an orderly) for almost 20 years. He also has acquired some medical knowledge from a daughter who is a registered nurse in a large city in Mexico. And lastly, he has gotten much of his knowledge of modern drugs from drug salesmen from various pharmaceutical companies.

Don Humberto has a shaded outdoor waiting area for his patients and there were many patients waiting to see him on the four occasions that we visited him. His treatment room is a mixture of the traditional and the modern. There are many religious calendars on the walls and a family altar with statues, flowers, candles and other religious articles. There are also large anatomical charts on the walls and two tables covered with hypodermic syringes, urinalysis equipment, and enormous quantities of drugs. My first impression was that many of these drugs appeared to be drug samples intended for free distribution to physicians. This suspicion was confirmed when Don Humberto stated that most of his drugs were indeed purchased from the sample stocks of various drug salesmen. He also stated that some of the drugs he was using were being used experimentally and had not yet been approved for general use by prescribing physicians. This is a frightening prospect to someone who is familiar with the lengthy procedures and safeguards followed before experimental drugs are released for general use in the United States. Although Don Humberto did not allow a close scrutiny of his drug stock, I did manage to get a precursory look at some of them. I am not familiar with many Mexican trade names, but I was able to see the generic names of many of the drugs he was using. Some of these drugs are intended for the treatment of such varied conditions as congestive heart failure, diabetes mellitus, and various systemic infections including tuberculosis.

Don Humberto does not perform surgical operations. He does not believe that they are ever necessary and discourages his patients from having them. He does, however, practice as a *huesero* and sets broken bones in both human and farm animals. In common with other *hueseros* he also treats hernias with the use of oil massages. He claims to treat many patients each week for hernias because "the local peasants are worked like farm animals and often develop hernias."

Don Humberto also admits to being a *brujo* (witch). He says that at some time in the past he signed a pact with the Devil using his own blood. He justified his being a *brujo* by saying that this enabled him to study the powers of the Devil and thereby treat diseases caused by evil. He stated that the path of his destiny was ordered by God and God destined him to be a curer and learn all kinds of magic to help people. According to Don Humberto, if God did not allow evil to exist, there could be no good because they cannot exist without each other. Besides claiming knowledge of all kinds of magic, he also claims to be able to inflict harm on others through the use of black magic. Understandably, he did not want to elaborate further on that statement.

Don Humberto would not tell us what his fees were for his treatments, but we were told by informants who had gone to him for help that they were very high by local standards. He did admit that his fees were higher than most other curers, but justified this by claiming that he could cure many diseases that physicians were unable to cure. He further claimed that he had a reputation as a healer that was known all over Mexico and that patients even flew down from Mexico City to consult him for treatment. We were not able to prove, or disapprove this statement, but one of our informants said that he did have a good reputation for healing in the Valley of Oaxaca and that this reputation could have spread to other parts of the country of Mexico.

The other *"curandero-supremo"* that we met was a man about 45 years of age who lives in a small village in the Valley of Oaxaca and whom we shall call Don Gaspar. His house is not too much different than the other better homes in his town. However, Don Gaspar is fairly well off because he is the head of a well paying business. The proceeds from this business support a late model station wagon and a great deal of expensive equipment needed in this business. His business occupies much of his time. His services are in demand and he travels all over the Valley of Oaxaca on business trips. Although he does treat some folk illnesses and use some traditional techniques, the bulk of his practice is concerned with the treatment of modern diseases and the use of modern drugs in therapy. He is quite clearly a *"curandero-supremo"* in the terms that we have defined this occupation.

Don Gaspar learned some of his skills from his late mother who was a traditional *curandera* and used herbal drugs. However, Don Gaspar rarely uses herbal drugs, but uses modern drugs that he purchases from pharmacies in Oaxaca City. There was a supply of these drugs on the desk and shelves of his treatment room. As with Don Humberto, he did not allow us to scrutinize these drugs. However, I was able to look at some of them and recognized drugs used to treat such conditions as asthma, congestive heart failure and systemic infections. He also had a number of psychoactive drugs such as mood elevators and tranquilizers. He claims to have learned the use of these drugs from acquaintances who are physicians.

Don Gaspar treats very few patients because he only accepts those patients that a physician has given up as incurable or those who cannot afford the high cost of surgical operations. Like Don Humberto he believes that surgical operations are never necessary and tries to discourage his patients from having them. He frankly admits that many of his patients are desperate and that he is often their last hope. He claims to be able to cure the average patient in 8 to 15 days with the use of modern drugs. He does not compare himself to the licensed physician but simply states that "the physician does his thing and Don Gaspar does his own thing." The modern diseases he treats includes rheumatism, diabetes mellitus, edema, hearing trouble and severe headaches.

The only folk illnesses he treats are *empacho* and *susto*. He says that empacho is caused by food getting stuck in the stomach and he treats it by simply giving a laxative. *Susto* [1] is the most common folk illness in Latin America and is usually believed to be caused by a fright, either natural or supernatural, that causes the patient's soul to leave his body, and then he exhibits many symptoms of depression and alienation. Don Gaspar says that the local physician laughs when people claim to have *susto* [2] but that even the bravest person can get *susto* from a shock. Don Gaspar pointed to one of his anatomical charts to show us how blood supposedly left the head and went to the hands and feet when a patient has *susto*. Don Gaspar uses modern psychoactive drugs to treat *susto* and does not use any of the theatrical techniques used by the more traditional *curanderos* to treat this illness.

[1] See Rubel 1964 and Gillin 1948 for a detailed description of this important illness.

[2] This statement is not quite true. The local physician realizes the importance of *susto* and regrets that he does not have the time to spend on the psychiatric problems of some of his patients. When he encounters such patients, he suggests to them that they see a good *curandero* who is better qualified than he to treat such a condition.

Don Gaspar starts his diagnosis by asking the patient to describe his symptoms and then takes a case history in the manner of the licensed physician. However, he feels that his most important diagnostic technique is to look into the eyes of his patients. He claims to be able to diagnose any condition with this technique and that it never fails him.

Don Gaspar's therapeutic techniques depend almost entirely on the oral administration of modern drugs. Mexican physicians tend to give many drugs by injection, including a vast number of drugs that are completely effective by the oral route. These hypodermic injections are either given by a clerk in the pharmacy where they are purchased or by people who make a part-time occupation out of giving injections. Don Gaspar feels that Mexican physicians give far too many injections of drugs and he feels that drugs should always be given orally instead. He claims that drugs given by injection go into the body too quickly and are stored in the veins where they often reach dangerous levels. He also says that the oral dosage forms are to be preferred because drugs taken orally do not reach the veins. Don Gaspar's knowledge of the fate of drugs in the body is almost diametrically opposed to the body of knowledge gained from modern pharmacological research.

Don Gaspar charges set fees for his services and his fees appear to be quite high considering the average wage in his town. At the time of our fieldwork the minimum wage in his town, for those who could find employment, was 15 pesos ($1.20 U.S. currency) daily. Don Gaspar charges from 250 to 350 pesos for what he considers minor illnesses such as *susto*. For the more serious chronic disease such as diabetes mellitus or heart conditions he charges 3,500 pesos ($280.00 U.S. currency). He justifies these charges by saying that by the time many of his patients reach him, they have already been to a physician who usually suggests an operation and that surgical operations usually cost around 15,000 pesos ($1,200.00 U.S. currency).

One of the reasons that both Don Gaspar and Don Humberto are able to practice as *"curanderos-supremos"* is related to many differences between the drug laws in the United States and those in Mexico.[3] In both the United States and Mexico, it is possible

---

[3] The description of these differences is meant to be purely descriptive and is not intended to be a criticism of the present drug laws in either country.

to purchase many over-the-counter patient medicines such as simple cough syrups, many analgesics, etc. These medications come labeled with dosages, indications for use and contraindications for their use. In the United States there are several other classes of drugs whose distribution is controlled by requiring a prescription from a licensed medical practitioner before they may be purchased. These different classes of drugs include many drugs that have known potential for abuse. However, many of these drugs are restricted to prescription use because the United States Food and Drug Administration has judged that they should not be used for self-medication. The rationale behind this judgment is not only that many of these drugs may have bad potential side effects but that the proper use of some of these drugs assumes a sophisticated knowledge of diagnosis that the average lay person does not have. When the patient purchases one of these restricted drugs on prescription he does not usually receive the original package with printed directions for use, suggested dosage, and contraindications and warnings for use. The drug is usually re-packaged and individual instructions from the physician are put on the label that the pharmacist is required by law to put on the completed prescription. Most of these drugs that are in these prescription only categories in the United States are available without prescription in Mexico. There are some exceptions to this generalization such as recently enacted legislation in Mexico to control the distribution of amphetamine, and amphetamine-like drugs, but generally speaking, these distinctions still hold true. This simply means that in Mexico you can walk into a pharmacy and ask for most drugs by name and the clerk, not even a pharmacist, simply takes it off the shelf and sells it to you on demand. Furthermore, this package often does not contain indications for use, suggested dosage, or contraindications or warnings for use. The label on the package simply instructs you to take the drug how and when the physician directs. This means that once a physician tells you to take a certain drug for a specific illness, you can simply buy the same drug in the pharmacy whenever you, not necessarily the physician, think you have the same condition. It also means that once you have this knowledge, you can pass it on to others who appear to have the same condition. It is these important differences in the drug laws of the United States and Mexico that allows both of these *"curanderos-supremos"* to continue to practice the type of curing they do in Mexico.

Both Don Gaspar and Don Humberto have been able to gain some knowledge of modern drug therapy from other people and have undoubtedly gained further knowledge through their own experiences in dispensing drugs. It is also probable that their curing experiences have given them some abilities to diagnose modern diseases. Both of these factors should assure them that they will have some success in treating illness. Furthermore, with continuing success, they will enhance their reputations in the community.

Although it would be easy to say that their success in curing depends entirely on the use of modern drugs, there are probably less obvious factors at work. And the fact that they represent the best of two worlds is an important factor in their abilities to cure. They both have some knowledge of traditional folk illnesses and cures and this is coupled with some knowledge of modern illnesses and therapeutic methods. Their treatment rooms are good examples of this syncretism as they contain traditional elements such as altars and other religious articles, and some of the paraphernalia of modern medicine such as anatomical charts, diagnostic equipment and modern drugs. Patients who are discouraged by the institutionalized appearance of the physician's treatment room may be more receptive to treatment in the environment of the treatment room of the *"curandero-supremo"*.

Another factor in the ability of these *"curanderos-supremos"* to attract patients may be that their high fees actually attract, rather than repel, many potential patients. This may happen on the principle that "if it is expensive, it must be good." Press (1971:746) makes a similar observation in Bogota, Colombia, where the total costs for the services of the most successful "urban *curanderos*" were also quite high.

What is the future of the *"curandero-supremo"*? Unless more restrictive drug laws are enacted and enforced in Mexico, these curers may be in business for some time to come. However, passing such restrictive drug laws might place an unbearable burden on the already overburdened orthodox medical services of this developing nation. As long as they continue to charge fees for their services that are less than that of the licensed physician, they will probably continue to attract patients who see the value of modern medical practices but cannot afford to pay the fees of the licensed physician.

Bibliography

Currier, Richard L.
  1966—"The Hot-Cold Syndrome and Symbolic Balance in Mexican and Spanish-American Folk Medicine," Ethnology 5:251–263

Foster, George M.
  1953—"Relationships Between Spanish and Spanish-American Folk Medicine," Journal of American Folklore 66:201–217

Gillin, John
  1948—"Magical Fright", Psychiatry, 11:387–400

Kiev, Ari
  1968—Curanderismo (Mexican-American Folk Psychiatry) New York: The Free Press

Madsen, William
  1955—"Hot and Cold in the Universe of San Francisco Tecospa, Valley of Mexico," Journal of American Folklore 68:123–139
  1961— Society and Health in the Lower Rio Grande Valley Austin: The Hegg Foundation for Mental Health, The University of Texas.
  1964— The Mexican-Americans of South Texas New York: Holt, Rinehart and Winston.

Press, Irwin
  1971—"The Urban Curandero" American Anthropologist, 73:741–756

Rubel, Arthur J.
  1964—"The Epidemiology of a Folk Illness: Susto in Hispanic America," Ethnology 3:268–283

Body Ritual among the Nacirema † *

T HE anthropologist has become so familiar with the diversity of ways in which different peoples behave in similar situations that he is not apt to be surprised by even the most exotic customs. In fact, if all of the logically possible combinations of behavior have not been found somewhere in the world, he is apt to suspect that they must be present in some yet undescribed tribe. This point has, in fact, been expressed with respect to clan organization by Murdock (1949: 71). In this light, the magical beliefs and practices of the Nacirema present such unusual aspects that it seems desirable to describe them as an example of the extremes to which human behavior can go.

Professor Linton first brought the ritual of the Nacirema to the attention of anthropologists twenty years ago (1936: 326), but the culture of this people is still very poorly understood. They are a North American group living in the territory between the Canadian Cree, the Yaqui and Tarahumare of Mexico, and the Carib and Arawak of the Antilles. Little is known of their origin, although tradition states that they came from the east. According to Nacirema mythology, their nation was originated by a culture hero, Notgnihsaw, who is otherwise known for two great feats of strength—the throwing of a piece of wampum across the river Pa-To-Mac and the chopping down of a cherry tree in which the Spirit of Truth resided.

Nacirema culture is characterized by a highly developed market economy which has evolved in a rich natural habitat. While much of the people's time is devoted to economic pursuits, a large part of the fruits of these labors and a considerable portion of the day are spent in ritual activity. The focus of this activity is the human body, the appearance and health of which loom as a dominant concern in the ethos of the people. While such a concern is certainly not unusual, its ceremonial aspects and associated philosophy are unique.

The fundamental belief underlying the whole system appears to be that the human body is ugly and that its natural tendency

† By Horace Miner, University of Michigan.

* Reproduced by permission of the American Anthropological Association from the American Anthropologist, Vol. 58, No. 3, 1956, and the author.

is to debility and disease. Incarcerated in such a body, man's only hope is to avert these characteristics through the use of the powerful influences of ritual and ceremony. Every household has one or more shrines devoted to this purpose. The more powerful individuals in the society have several shrines in their houses and, in fact, the opulence of a house is often referred to in terms of the number of such ritual centers it possesses. Most houses are of wattle and daub construction, but the shrine rooms of the more wealthy are walled with stone. Poorer families imitate the rich by applying pottery plaques to their shrine walls.

While each family has at least one such shrine, the rituals associated with it are not family ceremonies but are private and secret. The rites are normally only discussed with children, and then only during the period when they are being initiated into these mysteries. I was able, however, to establish sufficient rapport with the natives to examine these shrines and to have the rituals described to me.

The focal point of the shrine is a box or chest which is built into the wall. In this chest are kept the many charms and magical potions without which no native believes he could live. These preparations are secured from a variety of specialized practitioners. The most powerful of these are the medicine men, whose assistance must be rewarded with substantial gifts. However, the medicine men do not provide the curative potions for their clients, but decide what the ingredients should be and then write them down in an ancient and secret language. This writing is understood only by the medicine men and by the herbalists who, for another gift, provide the required charm.

The charm is not disposed of after it has served its purpose, but is placed in the charm-box of the household shrine. As these magical materials are specific for certain ills, and the real or imagined maladies of the people are many, the charm-box is usually full to overflowing. The magical packets are so numerous that people forget what their purposes were and fear to use them again. While the natives are very vague on this point, we can only assume that the idea in retaining all the old magical materials is that their presence in the charm-box, before which the body rituals are conducted, will in some way protect the worshipper.

Beneath the charm-box is a small font. Each day every member of the family, in succession, enters the shrine room, bows his head before the charm-box, mingles different sorts of holy water in the font, and proceeds with a brief rite of ablution. The holy waters are secured from the Water Temple of the community, where the priests conduct elaborate ceremonies to make the liquid ritually pure.

In the hierarchy of magical practitioners, and below the medicine men in prestige, are specialists whose designation is best translated "holy-mouth-men." The Nacirema have an almost pathological horror of and fascination with the mouth, the condition of which is believed to have a supernatural influence on all social relationships. Were it not for the rituals of the mouth, they believe that their teeth would fall out, their gums bleed, their jaws shrink, their friends desert them, and their lovers reject them. They also believe that a strong relationship exists between oral and moral characteristics. For example, there is a ritual ablution of the mouth for children which is supposed to improve their moral fiber.

The daily body ritual performed by everyone includes a mouth-rite. Despite the fact that these people are so punctilious about care of the mouth, this rite involves a practice which strikes the uninitiated stranger as revolting. It was reported to me that the ritual consists of inserting a small bundle of hog hairs into the mouth, along with certain magical powders, and then moving the bundle in a highly formalized series of gestures.

In addition to the private mouth-rite, the people seek out a holy-mouth-man once or twice a year. These practitioners have an impressive set of paraphernalia, consisting of a variety of augers, awls, probes, and prods. The use of these objects in the exorcism of the evils of the mouth involves almost unbelievable ritual torture of the client. The holy-mouth-man opens the client's mouth and, using the above mentioned tools, enlarges any holes which decay may have created in the teeth. Magical materials are put into these holes. If there are no naturally occurring holes in the teeth, large sections of one or more teeth are gouged out so that the supernatural substance can be applied. In the client's view, the purpose of these ministrations is to arrest decay and to draw friends. The extremely sacred and traditional character of the rite is evident in the fact that the natives return to the holy-mouth-men year after year, despite the fact that their teeth continue to decay.

It is to be hoped that, when a thorough study of the Nacirema is made, there will be careful inquiry into the personality structure of these people. One has but to watch the gleam in the eye of a holy-mouth-man, as he jabs an awl into an exposed nerve, to suspect that a certain amount of sadism is involved. If this can be established, a very interesting pattern emerges, for most of the population shows definite masochistic tendencies. It was to these that Professor Linton referred in discussing a distinctive part of the daily body ritual which is performed only by men. This part of the rite involves scraping and lacerating the surface of the face with a sharp instrument. Special women's rites are performed only four times during each lunar month, but what they lack in frequency is made up in barbarity. As part of this ceremony, women bake their heads in small ovens for about an hour. The theoretically interesting point is that what seems to be a preponderantly masochistic people have developed sadistic specialists.

The medicine men have an imposing temple, or *latipso*, in every community of any size. The more elaborate ceremonies required to treat very sick patients can only be performed at this temple. These ceremonies involve not only the thaumaturge but a permanent group of vestal maidens who move sedately about the temple chambers in distinctive costume and headdress.

The *latipso* ceremonies are so harsh that it is phenomenal that a fair proportion of the really sick natives who enter the temple ever recover. Small children whose indoctrination is still incomplete have been known to resist attempts to take them to the temple because "that is where you go to die." Despite this fact, sick adults are not only willing but eager to undergo the protracted ritual purification, if they can afford to do so. No matter how ill the supplicant or how grave the emergency, the guardians of many temples will not admit a client if he cannot give a rich gift to the custodian. Even after one has gained admission and survived the ceremonies, the guardians will not permit the neophyte to leave until he makes still another gift.

The supplicant entering the temple is first stripped of all his or her clothes. In every-day life the Nacirema avoids exposure of his body and its natural functions. Bathing and excretory acts are performed only in the secrecy of the household shrine, where they are ritualized as part of the body-rites. Psychological shock results from the fact that body secrecy is suddenly lost upon entry into the *latipso*. A man, whose own wife has never seen him in an excretory act, suddenly finds himself naked and assisted by a vestal maiden while he performs his natural functions into a sacred vessel. This sort of ceremonial treatment is necessitated by the fact that the excreta are used by a diviner to ascertain the course and nature of the client's sickness. Female clients, on the other hand, find their naked bodies are subjected to the scrutiny, manipulation and prodding of the medicine men.

Few supplicants in the temple are well enough to do anything but lie on their hard beds. The daily ceremonies, like the rites of the holy-mouth-men, involve discomfort and torture. With ritual precision, the vestals awaken their miserable charges each dawn and roll them about on their beds of pain while performing ablutions, in the formal movements of which the maidens are highly trained. At other times they insert magic wands in the supplicant's mouth or force him to eat substances which are supposed to be healing. From time to time the medicine men come to their clients and jab magically treated needles into their flesh. The fact that these temple ceremonies may not cure, and may even kill the neophyte, in no way decreases the people's faith in the medicine men.

There remains one other kind of practitioner, known as a "listener." This witch-doctor has the power to exorcise the devils that lodge in the heads of people who have been bewitched. The Nacirema believe that parents bewitch their own children. Mothers are particularly suspected of putting a curse on children while teaching them the secret body rituals. The counter-magic of the witch-doctor is unusual in its lack of ritual. The patient simply tells the "listener" all his troubles and fears, beginning with the earliest difficulties he can remember. The memory displayed by the Nacirema in these exorcism sessions is truly remarkable. It is not uncommon for the patient to bemoan the rejection he felt upon being weaned as a babe, and a few individuals even see their troubles going back to the traumatic effects of their own birth.

In conclusion, mention must be made of certain practices which have their base in native esthetics but which depend upon the pervasive aversion to the natural body and its functions. There are ritual fasts to make fat people thin and ceremonial feasts to make thin people fat. Still other rites are used to make women's breasts larger if they are small, and smaller if they are large. General dissatisfaction with breast shape is symbolized in the fact that the ideal form is virtually outside the range of human variation. A few women afflicted with almost inhuman hypermammary development are so idolized that they make a handsome living by simply going from village to village and permitting the natives to stare at them for a fee.

Reference has already been made to the fact that excretory functions are ritualized, routinized, and relegated to secrecy. Natural reproductive functions are similarly distorted. Intercourse is taboo as a topic and scheduled as an act. Efforts are made to avoid pregnancy by the use of magical materials or by limiting intercourse to certain phases of the moon. Conception is actually very infrequent. When pregnant, women dress so as to hide their condition. Parturition takes place in secret, without friends or relatives to assist, and the majority of women do not nurse their infants.

Our review of the ritual life of the Nacirema has certainly shown them to be a magic-ridden people. It is hard to understand how they have managed to exist so long under the burdens which they have imposed upon themselves. But even such exotic customs as these take on real meaning when they are viewed with the insight provided by Malinowski when he wrote (1948: 70):

> Looking from far and above, from our high places of safety in the developed civilization, it is easy to see all the crudity and irrelevance of magic. But without its power and guidance early man could not have mastered his practical difficulties as he has done, nor could man have advanced to the higher stages of civilization.

References Cited

Linton, Ralph
1936 The Study of Man. New York, D. Appleton-Century Co.
Malinowski, Bronislaw
1948 Magic, Science, and Religion. Glencoe, The Free Press.
Murdock, George P.
1949 Social Structure. New York, The Macmillan Co.

*

IX. We Believe....

People in many cultures, including our own, may spend their entire lives within the confines of their own belief systems and never be exposed to the supernatural beliefs of a different culture. The articles in this section were chosen to provide some brief exposure to beliefs that may differ from our own.

The first selection in this section is about the cosmos of the Campa of eastern Peru. The author, Gerald Weiss, is careful to point out that the Campa belief system has given them an adequate explanation of their universe based on their limited information. The next article by June Nash illustrates how different belief systems can be blended into a workable system of supernatural belief. In this case miners in Bolivia combine the mysteries of witchcraft, alcohol, aboriginal religion, and Christianity into a new behavior pattern. The next two brief selections are concerned with a bizarre sect of Christianity—the snake handlers of Southern Appalachia, and show that strange belief systems are not limited to "exotic" peoples. The concluding article in this section, written by Donald Barthelme, is about a man of knowledge among a people known as the Yankees.

The Campa Cosmos † * [1]

IN Campa thought, the universe in its present form came into existence through a series of transformations and, at some time in the future, will be destroyed by the will of Pává. For the Campa there is no such occurrence as the creation of something out

† Selected from—"Campa Cosmology" by Gerald Weiss.

* Reproduced by permission of the editor of Ethnology. Ethnology, April 1972 pp. 169–171.

[1] The author's field work among the Campa was conducted between 1960 and 1964, funded in part by the American Museum of Natural History, National Science Foundation, and Social Science Research Council. The present paper is a summary of a much more extensive report on the subject.

of nothing, but only the transformation of something out of something else. Consequently, in their thinking, the original condition of the universe was not nothingness but somethingness. The general structure of the universe existed to begin with, as the stage on which all the dramas of Campa mythology were to be acted out. When the curtain goes up, the actors are already on stage; the primal Campa, human beings living here on earth but immortal, many with powers exceeding those possessed by mankind today. There were some special features, later to be changed; thus the sky was much closer to the earth, and the earth spoke. Whatever else existed in the universe at that time is indicated only sketchily in the mythology, but it was an impoverished universe lacking many features that would come into existence through transformation only with the passage of time. Campa mythology is largely the history of how, one by one, the primal Campa became irreversibly transformed into the first representatives of various species of animals and plants, as well as astronomical bodies or features of the terrain. In each case the mechanism of change was either the action of a transformer deity or auto-transformation.

The development of the universe, then, has been primarily a process of diversification, with mankind as the primal substance out of which many if not all of the categories of beings and things in the universe arose, the Campa of today being the descendants of those ancestral Campa who escaped being transformed. Mortality came also to be added as a feature of human life and, with the increasing frequency of death, the earth gradually ceased to speak. The widening gap between mortal life and that of the good spirits was punctuated by the moving apart of the sky and the earth. When the present universe is destroyed, the Campa will be destroyed with it and a new world will take its place, with immortal inhabitants. The sky will again be close to the earth, and the earth will speak once more.

And what is the nature of the universe in which the Campa find themselves? It is a world of semblances; for example, what to us is the solid earth is airy sky to the beings inhabiting the strata below us, and what to us is airy sky is solid ground to those who inhabit the strata above. It is a world of relative semblances, where different kinds of beings see the same things differently; thus human eyes can normally see good spirits only in the form of lightning flashes or birds whereas they see themselves in their

true human form, and similarly in the eyes of jaguars human beings look like peccaries to be hunted. It is a world in which there
exist beings with powers out of all proportion to their appearance;
thus, for example, the gods though visualized as human in size
and form, can bring about sensational transformations by simply
expressing their will or with a puff of breath, and have the physical strength to throw up mountains. It is a world operating according to mechanical principles of the sort we would call magical;
thus, as a form of homeopathic magic, both prospective parents
during pregnancy refrain from eating turtle meat, for fear that
this would make their child slow-moving and slow-witted, and, as
a form of contagious magic, a witch supposedly utilizes someone's
food refuse or exuviae to strike him with sickness—these are examples of "action at a distance," the distinguishing characteristic of magic. It is, again, a world of transformations, of beings
and things passing in and out of visibility, in and out of tangibili-
ty. It is, finally, a world which, for the Campa, is one of death,
of debility, of sickness, of tragedy, because as "mere mortals"
they are the weakest of beings and are in constant danger of being
crushed by the greater forces of the universe. Yet, despite their
understanding of their predicament, the Campa laugh, act vigorously, cling to life, and survive.

It would be easy to dismiss the cosmological thinking of the
Campa as false in its assertions of fact, as absurd in its prem-
ises, and as childish in its simplicity. But to do so may be in
error. We must recognize that the Campa, like every other human group, have attempted to make sense out of existence, have
had to do so on the basis of limited information, and have succeeded adequately for their purposes. They may personify forces
that we would view as impersonal, but this permits them to think
concretely instead of vaguely about matters that affect them in-
tensely. What would be the point of telling the Campa that a
diseased game animal is not really a demon, when its flesh is
actually dangerous for human consumption and the central meaning of *kamári* is "deadly"?

With a clarity that can best be obtained from simplicity, the
Campa have incorporated into their cosmology a number of
fundamental moral concepts of the utmost relevance to the human
predicament. They distinguish between good and evil, dividing
the beings of the universe into two great hosts on this basis, and
they revere the good while despising the evil. They recognize

the difference between good and bad actions, wishing that their actions could be only good but knowing that bad actions are all too easy, and their mythology is full of cautionary tales about Campa who were transformed into lesser creatures as punishment for objectionable behavior.   They have intuited the contrast between chastity and lust, cosmologically expressing their admiration for the former and their contempt for the latter by the way in which they describe both the anatomy and the actions of the good spirits and the demons of their universe.   And they have grasped the essential ingredient of human dignity, that of acting properly and with pride in self, rather than corruptly and ignominiously.   The Campa recognize their own imperfections and limitations, and consequently in the ideal cosmos of their imagination they place themselves in an intermediate position between the cosmic forces of good and evil, and far less powerful than either.   In contemplating data such as these, we may well ponder with special irony the earlier view, as Darwin expressed it, "the low morality of savages, as judged by our standard."

Devils, Witches, and Sudden Death † *

In the Hellish Mines of Bolivia, Workers Call upon Strange Companions to Ease Their Terror

T IN miners in the high Andean plateau of Bolivia earn less than a dollar a day when, to use their phrase, they "bury themselves alive in the bowels of the earth."   The mine shafts—as much as two miles long and half a mile deep—penetrate hills that have been exploited for more than 450 years.   The miners descend to the work areas in open hauls; some stand on the roof and cling to the swaying cable as the winch lowers them deep into the mine.

† By June Nash.

* Reprinted from Natural History Magazine, March, 1972. Copyright ©

The American Museum of Natural History, 1972.

Once they reach their working level, there is always the fear of rockslides as they drill the face of the mine, of landslides when they set off the dynamite, of gas when they enter unfrequented areas. And added to their fear of the accidents that have killed or maimed so many of their workmates is their economic insecurity. Like Wall Street brokers they watch international price quotations on tin, because a difference of a few cents can mean layoffs, loss of bonuses, a cut in contract prices—even a change of government.

Working in the narrow chimneys and corridors of the mine, breathing the dust- and silicate-filled air, their bodies numbed by the vibration of the drilling machines and the din of dynamite blasts, the tin miners have found an ally in the devil, or Tio (uncle), as he is affectionately known. Myths relate the devil to his pre-Christian counterpart Huari, the powerful ogre who owns the treasures of the hills. In Oruro, a 13,800-foot-high mining center in the western Andes of Bolivia, all the miners know the legend of Huari, who persuaded the simple farmers of the Uru Uru tribe to leave their work in the fields and enter the caves to find the riches he had in store. The farmers, supported by their ill-gained wealth from the mines, turned from a virtuous life of tilling the soil and praying to the sun god Inti to a life of drinking and midnight revels. The community would have died, the legend relates, if an Inca maiden, Nusta, had not descended from the sky and taught the people to live in harmony and industry.

Despite four centuries of proselyting, Catholic priests have failed to wipe out belief in the legend, but the principal characters have merged with Catholic deities. Nusta is identified with the Virgin of the Mineshaft, and is represented as the vision that appeared miraculously to an unemployed miner.

The miners believe that Huari lives on in the hills where the mines are located, and they venerate him in the form of the devil, or Tio. They believe he controls the rich veins of ore, revealing them only to those who give him offerings. If they offend the Tio or slight him by failing to give him offerings, he will withhold the rich veins or cause an accident.

Miners make images of the Tio and set them up in the main corridors of each mine level, in niches cut into the walls for the workers to rest. The image of the Tio varies in appearance according to the fancy of the miner who makes him, but his body is always shaped from ore. The hands, face, horns, and legs are sculptured with clay from the mine. Bright pieces of metal or burned-out bulbs from the miners' electric torches are stuck in the eye sockets. Teeth are made of glass or crystal sharpened "like nails," and the mouth is open, gluttonous and ready to receive offerings. Sometimes the plaster of Paris masks worn by the devil dancers at Carnival are used for the head. Some Tios wear embroidered vests, flamboyant capes, and miners' boots. The figure of a bull, which helps miners in contract with the devil by digging out the ore with its horns, occasionally accompanies the image, or there may be *chinas*, female temptresses who are the devil's consorts.

The Tio is a figure of power: he has what everyone wants, in excess. Coca remains lie in his greedy mouth. His hands are stretched out, grasping the bottles of alcohol he is offered. His nose is burned black by the cigarettes he smokes down to the nub. If a Tio is knocked out of his niche by an extra charge of dynamite and survives, the miners consider him to be more powerful than others.

Another spirit present in the mines but rarely represented in images is the Awiche, or old woman. Although some miners deny she is the Pachamama, the earth goddess worshiped by farmers, they relate to her in the same way. Many of the miners greet her when they enter the mine, saying, "Good-day, old woman. Don't let anything happen to me today!" They ask her to intercede with the Tio when they feel in danger; when they leave the mine safely, they thank her for their life.

Quite the opposite kind of feminine image, the Viuda, or widow, appears to miners who have been drinking *chicha*, a fermented corn liquor. Miners who have seen the Viuda describe her as a young and beautiful *chola*, or urbanized Indian, who makes men lose their minds—and sometimes their paychecks. She, too, is a consort of the devil and recruits men to make contracts with him, deluding them with promises of wealth.

When I started working in Oruro during the summer of 1969, the men told me about the *ch'alla*, a ceremonial offering of cigarettes, coca, and alcohol to the Tio. One man described it as follows:

"We make the *ch'alla* in the working areas within the mine. My partner and I do it together every Friday, but on the first Friday of the month we do it with the other workers on our level.

We bring in banners, confetti, and paper streamers. First we put a cigarette in the mouth of the Tio and light it. After this we scatter alcohol on the ground for the Pachamama, then give some to the Tio. Next we take out our coca and begin to chew, and we also smoke. We serve liquor from the bottles each of us brings in. We light the Tio's cigarette, saying 'Tio, help us in our work. Don't let any accidents happen.' We do not kneel before him as we would before a saint, because that would be sacrilegious.

"Then everyone begins to get drunk. We begin to talk about our work, about the sacrifices that we make. When this is finished, we wind the streamers around the neck of the Tio. We prepare our *mesas* [tables of offerings that include sugar cakes, llama embryos, colored wool, rice, and candy balls].

"After some time we say, 'Let's go.' Some have to carry out those who are drunk. We go to where we change our clothes, and when we come out we again make the offering of liquor, banners, and we wrap the streamers around each others' necks. From there on, each one does what he pleases."

I thought I would never be able to participate in a *ch'alla* because the mine managers told me the men didn't like to have women inside the mine, let alone join them in their most sacred rites. Finally a friend high in the governmental bureaucracy gave me permission to go into the mine. Once down on the lowest level of San José mine, 340 meters below the ground, I asked my guide if I could stay with one of the work crews rather than tour the galleries as most visitors did. He was relieved to leave me and get back to work. The men let me try their machines so that I could get a sense of what it was like to hold a 160-pound machine vibrating in a yard-wide tunnel, or to use a mechanical shovel in a gallery where the temperature was 100° F.

They told me of some of their frustrations—not getting enough air pumped in to make the machines work at more than 20 percent efficiency and constant breakdowns of machinery, which slowed them up on their contract.

At noon I refused the superintendent's invitation to eat lunch at level O. Each of the men gave me a bit of his soup or some "seconds," solid food consisting of noodles, potatoes, rice, and spicy meat, which their wives prepare and send down in the elevators.

At the end of the shift all the men in the work group gathered at the Tio's niche in the large corridor. It was the first Friday of the month and the gang leader, Lino Pino, pulled out a bottle of fruit juice and liquor, which his wife had prepared, and each of the men brought out his plastic bag with coca. Lino led the men in offering a cigarette to the Tio, lighting it, and then shaking the liquor on the ground and calling for life, "Hallalla! Hallalla!"

We sat on lumps of ore along the rail lines and Lino's helper served us, in order of seating, from a little tin cup. I was not given any priority, nor was I forgotten in the rounds. One of the men gave me coca from his supply and I received it with two hands, as I had been taught in the rituals aboveground. I chewed enough to make my cheek feel numb, as though I had had an injection of novocaine for dental work. The men told me that coca was their gift from the Pachamama, who took pity on them in their work.

As Lino offered liquor to the Tio, he asked him to "produce" more mineral and make it "ripen," as though it were a crop. These rituals are a continuation of agricultural ceremonies still practiced by the farmers in the area. The miners themselves are the sons or grandsons of the landless farmers who were recruited when the gold and silver mines were reopened for tin production after the turn of the century.

A month after I visited level 340, three miners died in an explosion there when a charge of dynamite fell down a shoot to their work site and exploded. Two of the men died in the mine; the third died a few days later in the hospital. When the accident occurred, all the men rushed to the elevators to help or to stare in fascinated horror as the dead and injured were brought up to level O. They carried the bodies of their dead comrades to the social center where they washed the charred faces, trying to lessen the horror for the women who were coming. When the women came into the social center where the bodies were laid out, they screamed and stamped their feet, the horror of seeing their husbands or neighbors sweeping through their bodies.

The entire community came to sit in at the wake, eating and drinking in the feasting that took place before the coffins of their dead comrades. The meal seemed to confirm the need to go on living as well as the right to live.

Although the accident had not occurred in the same corridor I had been in, it was at the same level. Shortly after that, when a student who worked with me requested permission to visit the mine, the manager told her that the men were hinting that the accident had happened because the gringa (any foreign-born, fair-haired person, in this case myself) had been inside. She was refused permission. I was disturbed by what might happen to my relations with the people of the community, but even more concerned that I had added to their sense of living in a hostile world where anything new was a threat.

The miners were in a state of uneasiness and tension the rest of that month, July. They said the Tio was "eating them" because he hadn't had an offering of food. The dead men were all young, and the Tio prefers the juicy flesh and blood of the young, not the tired blood of the sick older workers. He wanted a *k'araku*, a ceremonial banquet of sacrificed animals.

There had not been any scheduled *k'arakus* since the army put the mines under military control in 1965. During the first half of the century, when the "tin barons"—Patiño, Hochschild, and Arayamao—owned the mines, the administrators and even some of the owners, especially Patiño, who had risen from the ranks, would join with the men in sacrificing animals to the Tio and in the drinking and dancing that followed. After nationalization of the mines in 1952, the rituals continued. In fact, some of the miners complained that they were done in excess of the Tio's needs. One said that going into the mine after the revolution was like walking into a saloon.

Following military control, however, the miners had held the ritual only once in San José, after two men had died while working their shift. Now the Tio had again shown he was hungry by eating the three miners who had died in the accident. The miners were determined to offer him food in a *k'araku*.

At 10:30 P.M. on the eve of the devil's month, I went to the mine with Doris Widerkehr, a student, and Eduardo Ibañez, a Bolivian artist. I was somewhat concerned about how we would be received after what the manager of the mine had said, but all the men seemed glad we had come. As we sat at the entry to the main shaft waiting for the *yatiris*, shamans who had been contracted for the ceremony, the miners offered us *chicha* and cocktails of fruit juice and alcohol.

When I asked one of the men why they had prepared the ritual and what it meant, his answer was:

"We are having the *k'araku* because a man can't die just like that. We invited the administrators, but none of them have come. This is because only the workers feel the death of their comrades.

"We invite the Pachamama, the Tio, and God to eat the llamas that we will sacrifice. With faith we give coca and alcohol to the Tio. We are more believers in God here than in Germany or the United States because there the workers have lost their soul. We do not have earthquakes because of our faith before God. We hold the crucifix to our breast. We have more confidence before God."

Most miners reject the claim that belief in the Tio is pagan sacrilege. They feel that no contradiction exists, since time and place for offerings to the devil are clearly defined and separated from Christian ritual.

At 11:00 P.M. two white llamas contributed by the administration were brought into level O in a company truck. The miners had already adorned the pair, a male and a female, with colored paper streamers and the bright wool earrings with which farmers decorate their flocks.

The four *yatiris* contracted for did not appear, but two others who happened to be staying at the house of a miner were brought in to perform the ceremony. As soon as they arrived, the miners took the llamas into the elevator. The male was on the right and the female to his left, "just the same as a marriage ceremony," one miner commented. Looking at the couple adorned with bright streamers and confetti, there was the feeling of a wedding.

Two men entered the elevator with the llamas and eight more climbed on top to go down to level 340. They were commissioned to take charge of the ritual. All the workers of 340 entered to participate in the ceremony below and about 50 men gathered at level O to drink.

At level 340 the workers guided the *yatiris* to the spot where the accident had occurred. There they cast liquor from a bottle and called upon the Tio, the Awiche, and God to protect the men from further accidents—naming all the levels in the mine, the various work sites, the different veins of ore, the elevator shaft, and the winch, repeating each name three times and asking the Tio not to eat any more workers and to give them more veins to work. The miners removed their helmets during this ritual. It ended with the plea for life, "Hallalla, hallalla, hallalla." Two bottles of liquor were sprinkled on the face of the rock and in the various work places.

The *yatiris* then instructed the men to approach the llamas with their arms behind their backs so that the animals would not know who held the knife that would kill them. They were also told to beg pardon for the sacrifice and to kiss the llamas farewell. One miner, noting what appeared to be a tear falling from the female's eye, cried and tried to comfort her. As the men moved around the llamas in a circle, the *yatiris* called on the Malkus (eagle gods), the Awiche, the Pachamama, and finally the Tiyulas (Tios of the mines), asking for their care.

The female llama was the first to be sacrificed. She struggled and had to be held down by two men as they cut her jugular vein. When they disemboweled her, the men discovered that she was pregnant, to which they attributed the strength of her resistance. Her blood was caught in a white basin.

When the heart of the dying llama had pumped out its blood, the *yatiri* made an incision and removed it, using both his hands, a sign of respect when receiving an offering. He put the still palpitating heart in the basin with the blood and covered it with a white cloth on which the miners placed *k'oa*—an offering made up of herbs, coca, wool, and sweets—and small bottles of alcohol and wine.

The man in charge of the ceremony went with five aides to the site of the principal Tio in the main corridor. There they removed a piece of ore from the image's left side, creating a hole into which they put the heart, the blood, and the other offerings. They stood in a circle, their heads bent, and asked for safety and that there be no more accidents. In low voices, they prayed in Quechua.

When this commission returned, the *yatiris* proceeded to sacrifice the male llama. Again they asked the Tio for life and good ore in all the levels of the mine, and that there be no accidents. They took the heart, blood, *k'oa*, and bottles of alcohol and wine to another isolated gallery and buried it for the Tio in a place that would not be disturbed. There they prayed, "filled with faith," as one commented; then returned to the place of the sacrifice. The *yatiris* sprinkled the remaining blood on the veins of ore.

By their absorption and fervid murmuring of prayers, both young and old miners revealed the same faith and devotion. Many of them wept, thinking of the accident and their dead companions. During the ritual drinking was forbidden.

On the following day those men charged with responsibility for the ritual came to prepare the meat. They brought the two carcasses to the baker, who seasoned them and cooked them in large ovens. The men returned at about 1:15 P.M. to distribute the meat. With the meat, they served *chicha*. Some sprinkled *chicha* on the ground for the Pachamama, saying "Hallalla," before drinking.

The bones were burned to ashes, which were then offered to the Tio. The mine entrance was locked shut and left undisturbed for 24 hours. Some remarked that it should be closed for three days, but the company did not want to lose that much time.

During the *k'araku* the miners recognize the Tio as the true owner of the mine. "All the mineral that comes out from the interior of the mine is the 'crop' of the devil and whether one likes it or not, we have to invite the Tio to drink and eat so that the flow of metal will continue," said a young miner who studied evenings at the University of Oruro.

All the workers felt that the failure of the administrators to come to the *k'araku* indicated not only their lack of concern with the lives of the men but also their disregard of the need to raise productivity in the mine.

When the Tio appears uninvited, the miners fear that they have only a short time to live. Miners who have seen apparitions say the Tio looks like a gringo—tall, red-faced, with fair hair and beard, and wearing a cowboy hat. This description hardly resembles the images sculptured by the miners, but it does fit the foreign technicians and administrators who administered the mines in the time of the tin barons. To the Indian workers, drawn from the highland and Cochabamba farming areas, the Tio is a strange and exotic figure, ruthless, gluttonous, powerful, and arbitrary in his use of that power, but nonetheless attractive, someone to get close to in order to share that power. I was beginning to wonder if the reason I was accepted with such good humor by the miners, despite their rule against women in the mines, was because they thought I shared some of these characteristics and was a match for the devil.

Sickness or death in the family can force a man in desperation to make a contract with the devil. If his companions become aware of it, the contract is destroyed and with it his life.

The miners feel that they need the protection of a group when they confront the Tio. In the *ch'alla* and the *k'araku* they convert the power of the Tio into socially useful production. In effect, the rituals are ways of getting the genie back into the bottle after he has done his miracles. Security of the group then depends upon respect toward the sacrificial offering, as shown by the following incident told me by the head of a work gang after the *k'araku:*

"I know of a man who had a vein of ore near where the bones of the sacrificial llama were buried. Without advising me, he made a hole with his drill and put the dynamite in. He knew very well that the bones were there. On the following day, it cost him his life. While he was drilling, a stone fell and cut his head off.

"We had to change the bones with a ceremony. We brought in a good shaman who charged us B$500 [about $40], we hired the best orchestra, and we sang and danced in the new location where we laid the bones. We did not work in that corridor for three days, and we spent all the time in the *ch'alla*."

Often the miners are frightened nearly to death in the mine. A rock falls on the spot they have just left, a man falls in a shaft and is saved by hitting soft clay at the bottom, a tunnel caves in the moment after a man leaves it—these are incidents in a day's work that I have heard men say can start a *haperk'a*, or fear, that can take their lives.

A shaman may have to be called in to bring back the spirit that the Tio has seized. In one curing, a frightened miner was told to wear the clothing he had on when the Tio seized his spirit and to enter and give a service to the Tio at the same spot where he was frightened. The shaman himself asked the Tio to cure his patient, flattering him, "Now you have shown your power, give back his spirit."

The fear may result in sexual impotency. At one of the mines, Siglo XX, when there is full production, a dynamite blast goes off every five minutes in a section called Glock Haven. The air is filled with smoke and the miners describe it as an inferno. Working under such tension, a shattering blast may unnerve

them. Some react with an erection, followed by sexual debilita-
tion. Mad with rage and fear, some miners have been known to
seize a knife, the same knife they use to cut the dynamite leads,
and castrate themselves. When I visited Block Haven, I noticed
that the Tio on this level had a huge erection, about a foot long
on a man-sized figure. The workers said that when they find
themselves in a state of impotency they go to the Tio for help.
By exemplifying what they want in the Tio, they seek to repair
the psychic damage caused by fear.

After feasting on the meat of the llamas and listening to stories
of the Tio, I left the mine. The men thanked me for coming.
I could not express the gratitude I felt for restoring my confidence in continuing the study.

Shortly thereafter I met Lino Pino returning from a fiesta for
a miraculous saint in a nearby village. He asked me if I would
be *madrina* at his daughter's forthcoming confirmation, and when
I agreed, his wife offered me a tin cup with the delicious cocktail
she always prepares for her husband on the days of the *ch'alla*,
and we all had a round of drinks.

Later, when I knelt at the altar rail with Lino and his daughter
as we received the wafer and the wine, flesh and blood of another
sacrifice victim, I sensed the unity in the miners' beliefs. The
miraculous Virgin looked down on us from her marbelized, neon-
lit niche, her jewelled finger held out in benediction. She was
adequate for that scene, but in the mine they needed someone
who could respond to their needs on the job.

In the rituals of the *ch'alla* and the *k'araku* the power of the
Tio to destroy is transformed into the socially useful functions of
increasing mineral yield and giving peace of mind to the workers.
Confronted alone, the Tio, like Banquo's ghost, makes a man
unable to produce or even to go on living. Properly controlled by
the group, the Tio promises fertility, potency, and productivity to
the miners. Robbed of this faith, they often lose the faith to continue drilling after repeated failure to find a vein, or to continue
living when the rewards of work are so meager. Knowing that
the devil is on your side makes it possible to continue working in
the hell that is the mines.

AMERICANA:

THE LORD'S BIDDING *

He that believeth and is baptized shall be saved . . . they shall speak with new tongues; they shall take up serpents; and if they drink any deadly thing, it shall not hurt them.

—Mark 16:16–18

T HE literal interpretation of those words has spawned some of the more bizarre sects of Christendom, and the Holiness Church of God in Jesus Name of Carson Spring, Tenn., is no more unusual than many others—a Southern Appalachian congregation whose faithful dabble in glossolalia and routinely test their faith by handling poisonous snakes. They refuse treatment when bitten; if they die, it is taken as a sign of insufficient faith.

Last week assistant pastor Jimmy Ray Williams, 34, and layman Buford Pack, 30—two spiritual veterans of snake handling —put their faith to an even sterner test. At the culmination of an evening service at the sect's little hilltop church, Williams poured a potent mixture of strychnine and water. "A perfect love casteth out fear," the preached declared. "We're just doing as the Lord has bid us to do." So saying, Williams and Pack drank the draught down, as the congregation chanted "Praise God!"

As Williams had told a reporter some months earlier, it's against the law to sell poisons for church services—and if a man told a lie to buy strychnine, "it would kill you because you lied." It wasn't clear how he had got the stuff, but outside the church after the service the two men doubled up in an agony of convulsive twitching—and by morning both were dead. They were buried at snake-handling funeral ceremonies, with Bibles opened to Mark 16:16–18 laid upon their stomachs. At the weekend, the congregation was hoping to bring them back to life with

* Copyright Newsweek, Inc. 1973, reprinted by permission from issue of April 23, 1973, p. 23.

yet another service. This time, the worshipers planned to test their faith by turning blowtorches on their own faces and arms.

Judge Bars Sect's Snakes,*

A state judge in Newport, Tenn., refused to bar members of a fundamentalist congregation from strychnine-drinking rites but ordered them to discontinue the practice of handling poisonous snakes. "If someone wants to commit suicide by drinking poison, the court is not going to interfere . . ." the judge said. He barred the snake handling because it endangered other persons. Two members of the Holiness Church of God in Jesus Name died after drinking strychnine April 8. The sect later held a service at which the ban was observed.

[A8668]

The Teachings of Don B.: A Yankee Way of Knowledge † **

W HILE doing anthropological field work in Manhattan some years ago I met, on West 11th Street, a male Yankee of indeterminate age whose name, I was told, was Don B. I found him leaning against a building in a profound torpor—perhaps the profoundest torpor I have ever seen. He was a tallish man with an unconvincing beard and was dressed, in the fashion of the Village, in jeans and a blue work shirt. After we had been introduced, by a mutual acquaintance, I explained to him that I had been told he knew the secrets of certain hallucinogenic substances peculiar to Yankee culture and in which I was professionally interested. I expressed a wish to learn what he knew and asked if I might talk with him about the subject. He simply stared at me without replying, and then said, "No." However, taking note of the dismay which must have been plain on my face, he said that I might return, if I wished, in two years. In the meantime, he would think about my proposal. Then he closed his eyes again, and I left him.

* Copyright, 1973, Los Angeles Times, Sunday April 22, 1973. Reprinted by permission.

† By Donald Barthelme.

** 1972/73 by The New York Times Company. Reprinted by permission. The New York Times Magazine, February 11, 1973, Section 6, pp. 14–15, 66–67.

I returned in the summer of 1968 and found Don B. still leaning against the same building. His torpor was now something very close to outright gloom, but he greeted me civilly enough. Again I asked him if he would consider taking me under instruction. He stared at me for a long time and then said, "Yes." But, he warned me, states of nonordinary reality could not be attained by just anybody, and if just anybody did, by accident, blunder into a state of nonordinary reality, the anybody might bloody well regret it. Yankee culture was a fearsome thing, he told me, and not to be entered into lightly, but only with a prepared heart. Was I willing, he asked, to endure the pain, elation, shock, terror and boredom of such an experience? Was I, for example, ticklish? I assured him that I was ready and was not ticklish, or not overmuch. He then led me into the building against which he had been leaning. He showed me into a small but poorly furnished apartment containing hundreds of books stacked randomly about. In the center of the room a small fire was blazing brightly. Throwing a few more books on the fire, Don B. invited me to be seated, and we had the first of what proved to be a long series of conversations. The following material, reproduced from my field notes, has been edited somewhat to eliminate the dull parts, but in the main reflects accurately what took place during the period when I was Don B.'s apprentice.

In dealing with any system of world-interpretation different from our own, it is necessary to make use of the technique of suspended judgment. This I have done, and I urge the reader to do so also.

June 11, 1968.

We were sitting crosslegged on the floor of Don B.'s apartment facing each other, with the fire, which was kept going even in summer, between us. I decided to ask Don B. about the fire, for it was markedly hot in the room.

"Why is the fire burning, Don B.? It's hot in here."

Don B. gazed at me for a time without answering. Then he said: "Fire burns because it is his nature to burn. Fire is a friend. But one must know how to treat him. He contains a thousand invisible *brillos* which, unleashed, can cause considerable harm to life and property. That is why we have fire engines. The fire engines throw water on Fire and drown the invisible *brillos*. They fear water."

"What is a *brillo*, Don B.?"

"A sort of devil who is invisible."

"But why doesn't your fire burn a hole in the floor?"

"Because I understand Fire and know his secrets," Don B. said. "When I was a boy in the city of Philadelphia, Fire seized many houses, shops and other buildings and burned them to the ground. But he never seized my house because I knew his secrets and he knew I knew his secrets. Therefore he stayed away."

"What *are* his secrets, Don B.?"

Don B. laughed uproariously.

"You are a fool," he said. "You are not a man of knowledge. Only a man of knowledge can understand secrets. Even if I told you Fire's secrets, they would be of no use to you."

"Can I become a man of knowledge, Don B.?"

Don B. fell silent. He stared at his knees for some moments. Then he gave me an intense look.

"Maybe," he said.

I went away filled with a powerful and deep sense of warmth.

June 13, 1968.

We were sitting as before on the floor of Don B.'s apartment.

"What is a man of knowledge, Don B.?" I asked him.

"A man of knowledge," Don B. replied, "is one who knows. He not only knows, he knows that he knows. He has an ally to help him know."

"What does the ally do, Don B.?"

"The ally helps the man of knowledge know and also helps him knows that he knows."

"Do you have an ally, Don B.?"

"Of course."

"Who is your ally, Don B.?"

"Turkey," he said, and laugher uproariously.

I went away filled with a sensation of not having heard him correctly.

June 17, 1968.

I had brought Don B. some food. We sat on the floor eating fettucini on rye in silence. I had noticed that although Don B.

as a rule ate very little, whenever there were two sandwiches on the floor, he ate both halves of his and half of mine, which I thought a little strange.

Without warning he said: "You feel uncomfortable?"

I admitted that I felt a bit uncomfortable.

"I knew that you felt uncomfortable," he said. "That is because you have not found your spot. Move around the room until you have found it."

"How do you mean, move around the room?"

"I mean, like sit in different places."

Don B. rose and left the apartment. I tried sitting in different places. What he had said made no sense to me. True, I had been slightly uncomfortable in the spot I had been sitting in. But no other place in the room seemed any better to me. I sat experimentally in various areas but could discover no spot that felt any better than any other spot. I was sweating and felt more uncomfortable than ever. An hour passed, then two hours. I was sitting as hard as I could, first in one place, then another. But no particular place seemed desirable or special. I wondered where Don B. was. Then I noticed that a particular spot near the south wall was exuding a sort of yellow luminosity. I painfully sat over toward it, sit by sit, a process which consumed some 12 minutes. Yes! It was true. In the spot occupied by the yellow luminosity I felt much more comfortable than I had felt in my original spot. The door opened and Don B. entered, smiling.

"Where have you been, Don B.?"

"I caught a flick. I see that you have found your spot."

"You were right, Don B. This spot is much better than my old spot."

"Of course. You were sitting too close to the fire, idiot."

"But Don B.! What is this yellow luminosity that seems to hover over this particular spot?"

"It's the lamp, dummy."

I looked up. Don B. was right. Immediately above my new spot was a light fixture containing two 150-watt bulbs. It was turned on.

I went away filled with a powerful sensation having to do with electricity.

June 18, 1968.

Once again, I had asked Don B. about the famous hallucinogenic substances used by the Yankees.

Without replying, he carefully placed another book on the fire. It was Elias Ashmole's *"Theatrum chemicum Britannicum."*

"When I sneeze, the earth shakes," Don B. said, after a time.

I greeted this announcement with a certain amount of skepticism.

"Show me, Don B.," I said.

"The man of knowledge does not sneeze on command," he said. "He sneezes only when it is appropriate and right to do so, that is, when his *brillo* is inside his nose, tickling him."

"When is it appropriate and right to sneeze, Don B.?"

"It is appropriate and right to sneeze when your *brillo* is inside your nose, tickling it."

"Does each man have his own personal *brillo*, Don B.?"

"The man of knowledge both *has* a *brillo* and *is* a *brillo*. That is why he is able to sneeze so powerfully that when he sneezes, the earth shakes. *Brillo* is nose, arms, legs, liver—the whole shebang."

"But you said a *brillo* was a devil, Don B."

"Some people *like* devils."

"How does the man of knowledge find his personal *brillo*, Don B.?"

"Through the use of certain hallucinogenic substances peculiar to Yankee culture," Don B. said.

"Can I try them?"

Don B. gazed at me for a long time—an intense gaze. Then he said: "Maybe."

I departed with a strong sense of epistemological obfuscation.

June 20, 1968.

"The four natural enemies of the man of knowledge," Don B. said to me, "are fear, sleep, sex and the Internal Revenue Service."

I listened attentively.

"Before one can become a man of knowledge one must conquer all of these."

"Have you conquered the four natural enemies of the man of knowledge, Don B.?"

"All but the last," he said with a grimace. "Those sum-bitches never give up."

"How does one conquer fear, Don B.?"

"One takes a frog and sews it to one's shoe," he said.

"The right or the left?"

Don B. gave me a pitying look.

"Well, you'd look mighty funny going down the street with only one frog sewed to your shoes, wouldn't you?" he said. "One frog on *each* shoe."

"How does having frogs sewed to your shoes help one conquer fear, Don B.?"

But Don B. had fallen asleep. I was torn inside. My most deeply held values, such as being kind to frogs, had been placed in question. I really did want to become a man of knowledge. But at such a cost?

June 21, 1968.

Today Don B. looked at me for a long time. His gaze, usually so piercing, was suffused with a sort of wet irony.

"Xavier," he said, "there is something about you I like. I think it's your credulity. Belief is very important if one wishes to become a man of knowledge—to truly 'see.' I think you might possibly be able to 'see' some day. But 'seeing' is very difficult. Only after the most arduous preparation of the heart will you be able to 'see.' Even though you are not a Yankee, it may be that you will be able to prepare your heart adequately, I don't know. I'm not guaranteeing anything."

"How does one prepare the heart, Don B.?"

"One cleanses it with either a yellow warmth or a pink luminosity. I don't know which is right in your case. It varies with the individual. Each man must choose. So we will try both. But I must warn you that the experience is dangerous and sticky. Your life may hang on how you behave in the next hour. You must do everything exactly as I tell you. This is not kid stuff."

I was filled with a sense of awe and dread. Could I, a Western man, enter into the darkest mysteries of the Yankees without putting myself and my most deeply held convictions in peril? A profound sadness overtook me, followed by an indescribable anguish. I suppressed them.

"All right, Don B.," I said. "If you really think I'm ready."

Don B. then rose and went to a cupboard. He opened it and removed two vessels which he placed on the floor, near the fire. He opened a second cupboard and produced two ordinary drinking glasses, which he also placed on the floor. Then he went into another room, returning with a sort of crock with a lid on it, a small round yellow object, and a knife. All of these he placed on the floor near the fire. He knelt alongside them and began a strange, rather eerie chant. I could not make out all of the words but they included "town," "pony," and "feather." I wondered if I was supposed to chant too, but dared not interrupt him to ask. I began chanting, tentatively, "town-pony-feather."

Abruptly, Don B. stopped chanting and began whittling at the small yellow object. Was it this, I wondered, that generated the "yellow warmth" he had spoken of? Soon there was a small pile of yellow-white chips before him. He then reached for one of the vessels he had taken from the cupboard and poured a colorless liquid, perhaps four ounces of it, into each of the drinking glasses. Then he crossed his eyes and sat with his eyes crossed for some moments. I crossed my eyes also. We sat thus for some moments, our gazes missing each other but meeting, I felt somewhere in the neutral space on either side of us. The sensation was strange, eerie.

Don B. uncrossed his eyes, blinked, smiled at me.

He reached for the second vessel and poured a second colorless liquid into each glass, but much less of it: about half an ounce per glass, I estimated. He then removed the top of the crock and took from it six small colorless objects, each perhaps an inch and one-half square, placing three of them in each glass. Next he picked up one of the yellow-white chips and rubbed it around the rim of each glass. Then he stirred the mixtures with his index finger and handed me a glass.

"Drink it down without stopping," he said, "for if you pause in the drinking of it the *brillo* which it summons, your personal *brillo*, will not appear. And the whole thing will be a bloody goddamn fiasco."

I did as Don B. bade me, and drained the glass in one gulp. Immediately a horrible trembling convulsed my limbs, while an overwhelming nausea retracted my brain. I flopped around on the floor a lot. I became aware of (left to right) a profound sadness, a yellow warmth, an indescribable anguish and a pink luminosity. Don B. was watching me with a scornful smile on his face. I was sweating, my stomach was cramping, and I needed a cigarette. I saw, on my left, the profound sadness merging with the yellow warmth, and on my right, the indescribable anguish intermingling with the pink luminosity, and suddenly, standing with one foot on the profound sadness/yellow warmth and the other on the indescribable anguish/pink luminosity, a gigantic figure half-human, half-animal, and a hundred feet tall (roughly). A truly monstrous thing! Never in the wildest fantasies of fiction had I encountered anything like it. I looked at it in complete, utter bewilderment. It was strange and eerie, and yet familiar. Then I realized with a shock of horror, terror and eeriness that it was a colossal Publisher, and that it was moving toward me, wanted something from me. I fainted. When I revived, it took me to lunch at Lutece and we settled on an advance in the low 50's, which I accepted even though I knew I was not yet, in the truest sense, a man of knowledge. But there would be other books, I reflected, to become a man of knowledge in, and if I got stuck I could always go back and see good old Don B.

*

X. The Anthropologist
at Work

In the first selection in this section, the author, Gerald D. Berreman, states that "Ethnographers have too rarely made explicit the methods by which the information reported in their descriptive and analytical works was derived." Fortunately since this article was published in 1962, there have been other articles written by anthropologists concerning the trials and tribulations of anthropological fieldwork. In the second article in this section the author, Keith H. Basso, discusses the problems involved in getting information on two topics—sex and witchcraft—that people are often reluctant to talk about. In the next article Hanna Papanek discusses the particular problems that a woman anthropologist encounters when doing fieldwork in a society where the women live in *purdah*—physical and/or social seclusion. In the final article in this section James E. Meyers describes the problems he encountered when he assigned untrained students to do fieldwork in anthropology.

"Preface and Introduction" from

Behind Many Masks: Ethnography and Impression Management in a Himalayan Village † *

E THNOGRAPHERS have all too rarely made explicit the methods by which the information reported in their descriptive and analytical works was derived. Even less frequently have they attempted systematic description of those aspects of the field experience which fall outside of a conventional definition of method but which are crucial to the research and its results. The potential field worker in any given area often has to rely for ad-

† Gerald Berreman is in the Department of Anthropology at the University of California, Berkeley, California.

* Reproduced by permission of Society for Applied Anthropology from Monograph #4—Society for Applied Anthropology, 1962 and the author.

vance information about many of the practical problems of his
craft upon the occasional verbal anecdotes of his predecessors
or the equally random remarks included in ethnographic prefaces.
To the person facing field work for the first time the dearth
of such information may appear to be the result of a conviction,
among those who know, that experience can be the only teacher.
Alternatively, he may suspect ethnographers of having established a conspiracy of silence on these matters. When he himself becomes a bona fide ethnographer he may join that conspiracy inadvertently or he may feel obligated to join it not
only to protect the secrets of ethnography, but to protect himself.
As a result of the rules of the game which kept others from communicating their experience to him, he may feel that his own
difficulties of morale and rapport, his own compromises between
the ideal and the necessary, were unique, and perhaps signs of
weakness or incompetence. Consequently, these are concealed
or minimized. More acceptable aspects of the field experience
such as those relating to formal research methods, health haz-
ards, transportation facilities and useful equipment suffice to
answer the queries of the curious. This is in large measure a
matter of maintaining the proper "front" (see below) before
an audience made up not only of the uninitiated, but in many
cases of other ethnographers as well.

As a result of this pattern "Elenore Bowen" shared the plight
of many an anthropological neophyte when, according to her
fictionalized account, she arrived in West Africa girded for
field work with her professors' formulae for success:

> Always walk in cheap tennis shoes; the water runs out more
> quickly.   [and] You'll need more tables than you think.[1]

This monograph is not an exposition of research methods or
field techniques in the usual sense. It is a description of some
aspects of my field research, analyzed from a particular point of
view. As such, it is an attempt to portray some features of
that human experience which is field work, and some of the implications of its being human experience for ethnography as a
scientific endeavor. It is not intended as a model for others to
follow. It tells what happened, what I did, why I did it and

[1] Elenore Smith Bowen, Return to
Laughter, Harper, New York, 1954, pp.
3–4.

with what apparent effect. As in all field work, the choices were not always mine and the results were frequently unanticipated. But the choices and results have proved instructive. I hope that this account will be of use to those contemplating field work and that it may stimulate more ethnographers to make available their knowledge and views of the field work experience.

Every ethnographer, when he reaches the field, is faced immediately with accounting for himself before the people he proposes to learn to know. Only when this has been accomplished can he proceed to his avowed task of seeking to understand and interpret the way of life of those people. The second of these endeavors is more frequently discussed in anthropological literature than the first, although the success of the enterprise depends as largely upon one as the other. Both tasks, in common with all social interaction, involve the control and interpretation of impressions, in this case those conveyed by the ethnographer and his subjects to one another. Impressions are derived from a complex of observations and inferences drawn from what people do as well as what they say both in public, i.e., when they know they are being watched, and in private, i.e., when they think they are not being watched. Attempts to convey a desired impression of one's self and to interpret accurately the behavior and attitudes of others are an inherent part of any social interaction, and they are crucial to ethnographic research.

My research in a tightly closed and highly stratified society will serve as a case study from which to analyze some of the problems and consequences inherent in the interaction of ethnographer and subjects. Special emphasis will be placed upon the differential effects of the ethnographer's identification with high-status and low-status groups in the community.

Data-Gathering Problems *

I T may be worthwhile here to mention some of the difficulties which confront the ethnographer in his attempt to collect data about Apache witchcraft. Most of these relate to factors which affect the appropriateness of witchcraft as a topic of conversation and as such place definite restrictions on where, when, and with whom witchcraft can be discussed.

Witches make use of *divi'* (*supernatural power*), which is potentially harmful to anyone who does not possess the knowledge necessary to control it. *Power* and all things connected with it fall into the province of adult conversation, and it is primarily because of this that all but one of my informants were over thirty years of age. There is evidence to suggest that children learn early what witches do (if not exactly how they do it), but when questioned directly on the subject they either profess complete ignorance or point out that such things are not for them to know.

Owing to its intimate association with unusual sexual activities, witchcraft is also viewed as an improper topic of discussion with members of the opposite sex. Of my 17 informants only two were female, and it is not without significance that both were in their middle sixties. On more than one occasion they explained that ordinarily women did not talk to men about witchcraft but, since their own time of sexual activity was over, discussing it with me, though not altogether correct, could do no real harm.

Witches are known to be particularly active at night when they roam freely among the people's camps and eavesdrop on private conversations; for this reason my informants consistently refused to answer questions after sundown. Older Apaches maintain that witches can arrange for lightning to strike their victims, and as a consequence, my investigations often lagged during the months of July and August when electrical storms sweep through Apache country at least once a week.

* Reproduced by permission from WESTERN APACHE WITCH-CRAFT, Keith H. Basso, Tucson: University of Arizona Press, copyright 1969.

The biggest drawback to questioning Apaches about witchcraft is that any display of knowledge on the subject may be used to infer that the speaker is himself a witch. All my informants were reluctant to talk about it at first, and they eventually agreed to do so only on the conditions that our conversations take place in strictest privacy and that I promise never to divulge the source of my information. The former demand, though met, proved endlessly frustrating. Apache camps are notoriously public places. Over-crowded with family members, they are also open to passers-by who are free to wander in and stay as long as they wish. Privacy of the sort stipulated by my informants was hard to find, but the problem was more or less satisfactorily overcome by arranging to hold discussions at my camp where, except when school was not in session, visitors were less numerous.

In *Navaho Witchcraft*, Kluckhohn (1944) reports that he had little difficulty eliciting information from total strangers, Navajos he had never seen before and in all probability would never see again. I did not find this to be the case with the Apache. Whenever I spoke of witchcraft, or even alluded to it, in the presence of Apaches previously unknown to me, they responded by acting as though nothing had been said. If I persisted and brought up the subject a second time, they simply walked away. It is significant, therefore, that my regular informants were friends of long standing. Yet I am sure there were times when even they wondered if providing me with information about witchcraft was a good thing. Said one man:

> It is dangerous for you to know about these things, and I think it is bad for me to tell you about them. What do you want with things like that? You can't use it. I could teach you about things that are good. But you want to know and I am telling you. We don't talk about it with each other except when there is sickness.

Field Methods and Techniques

The Woman Field Worker in a Purdah Society † *

IN a *purdah* society, where women are either physically or socially secluded, it goes without saying that only a woman field worker (anthropologist, doctor, teacher, village development worker, etc.) can hope to reach the women at all. The *foreign* woman field worker, however, not only has access to local women but can occupy a surprisingly flexible position in local society. She can then move with ease among local men, as well as local women, if she wishes to define her own role in this way, and if her own background enables her to do so. Western women, particularly, are often able to define their roles with a flexibility which is not available to full-fledged participants in the local culture, even when these have been influenced by Western education. This holds true only as long as the foreign woman remains truly an outsider, for on this depends her ability to maintain her local role according to a definition largely provided by herself. When she begins to conform to local mores, marries, or involves herself with a local man, the flexibility of her role-definition becomes more and more circumscribed.

The concept of role flexibility, as used here, is a way of describing a situation in which an individual can contribute a large share of the definition of his own role. The concept deals with both aspects of such a definition: the person's own ability to play a variety of roles, and the presence of ambiguities and loopholes in the social structure which permit him to do so. Where either of these two aspects is severely restricted, the opportunities for role flexibility will also be reduced.

These general reflections are the result of four years of field work in Pakistan, in the course of research among several "busi-

† Hanna Papanek is at the Radcliffe Institute for Independent Study, Cambridge, Massachusetts.

For comments and criticism she is indebted to Renée C. Fox, David Riesman, and Gustav F. Papanek.

* Reproduced by permission of Society for Applied Anthropology from HUMAN ORGANIZATION, Vol. 23, No. 2, 1964.

ness communities" (ethnic or religious endogamous groups whose main economic activities are trade, business, and industry). While my main focus was not on the problems of women, or the nature of seclusion (*purdah*), I found it impossible not to become deeply concerned with these questions. The status of women in a *purdah* society is a characteristic of major importance of the entire social system, and must be confronted at almost every turn.

In the course of gathering information about several business communities, I conducted interviews with men and women of various classes and regions in the Indian subcontinent, although the largest proportion were from the urban middle and lower-middle classes, and of western Indian origin. Since I was particularly interested in the structure of these communities, or quasi-castes, and the consequences of belonging to them, my interviews necessarily covered a wide range of topics. Interviews were generally unstructured, and usually dealt with those topics on which an individual was particularly anxious or well equipped to speak. In the case of most men, for instance, the interview centered on making a living, activity in community organizations and civic affairs, religion, finance, government, and some aspects of family life. Interviews with women usually focused on family affairs, child rearing, religion, welfare work, and civic activities, and the details of kinship and friendship. In other words, I discussed predominantly masculine concerns with the men, and topics of particular feminine interest with the women. With those individuals whose interests went beyond this traditional allocation, I often pursued a wider range of topics.

This enumeration makes it clear, however, that I had to gain acceptance among both men and women as a suitable conversational partner, in a society which traditionally restricts such partnerships to persons of the same sex. Conceivably, a women field worker whose primary interest focused on the traditional feminine concerns of the local culture might define her own role somewhat differently, and restrict its flexibility. Also a woman field worker from a non-Western background, e. g., another Muslim country, might encounter attitudes among informants and within herself which would make it impossible for her to achieve such flexibility.

In my own experience, role flexibility is strikingly illustrated by one of its external attributes: the consequences of wearing local dress—since by adopting such externals one implicitly accepts the limitations on behavior expected of women so clothed. This is particularly important on the Indian subcontinent, where women's dress is still related to social status, personal modesty, regional allegiances, and sometimes religion. For example, in Karachi I often wore a sari when attending women's celebrations or public occasions such as weddings, when I would clearly occupy a woman's role as locally defined. I never did so, however, when I sought entry where well-bred local women would not have done so. The public mourning ceremonies for Aga Khan III, in Karachi, for example, were attended by over four thousand Pakistani men, and myself, in Western dress. I was admitted without difficulty, with the comment that there was no objection—if I had none. At the women's mourning ceremonies, held inside a house of prayer, I was similarly admitted, still in Western dress, while men other than the chief religious official were not expected to enter. In another Muslim context (serving food to male mourners after a funeral in a rather conservative household) I was able to fill an essentially male role merely by virtue of being in Western dress. In a sari, I would have made the mourners feel very disconcerted. Moreover, I would not spontaneously have offered to help out in this way had I been wearing a sari along with the manner which it symbolizes.

In a deeper psychological sense, the Western woman's mobility in this kind of situation depends on a number of implicit assumptions held by local persons concerning the nature of men and women. These assumptions constitute basic aspects of the society and are likely to persist for some time despite changes in the more obvious criteria of physical seclusion. It is also in the terms presented by this substructure of expectations that the foreign woman will be able to find the loopholes which make role flexibility possible.

In a *purdah* society, the basic assumptions serve to sustain the seclusion of women by stressing the inherent aggressiveness of men and the inherent vulnerability of women. Conversely, there is an awareness of the attractiveness of women and the relative inability of men to resist. These assumptions are largely based on the Quranic recognition of natural biological drives, which cannot be suppressed within the individual, but should be socially channelled. Control over individual instances of attraction between men and women does not derive from the individual's sense of guilt. It is therefore particularly important that such attractions should not occur outside the prescribed social framework within which marriage is possible. The most important social control mechanism which is involved here centers on the arranged marriage. Such a marriage, arranged by the families of bride and groom, with some measure of consent from the prospective couple, is still the most common form in Pakistan, despite some increase in "love marriages." The arranged marriage places considerable strain on still unmarried girls, since negotiations by the older generation usually stress traditional values in assessing "suitability." Those women who are not protected by the traditional social safeguards of seclusion and chaperonage are particularly vulnerable to criticism of their behavior, and these safeguards may therefore be maintained in unexpected situations. For instance, young women research assistants in government offices in Pakistan work in rooms shared with other women, and may refuse work assignments that involve sharing an office with a male official. In such women's offices men are usually not expected to enter.

Outside the work context, the power of the assumption of feminine vulnerability shows itself also in the social context of parties, meetings, and other gatherings involving people beyond one's family circle. In many upper and upper-middle class circles in Pakistan, it has become customary to have mixed gatherings at which both men and women are present. On these occasions, as on several others, it is possible to observe the severe social uneasiness shown by many "transitional" local women not fully accustomed to free public mixing. This uneasiness both signals and reinforces their presumed vulnerability in the eyes of others. A circular process, in which initial attitudes of fear seem to be reinforced by the very feelings of social uneasiness which they produce, is present in many instances.

In the case of a foreign woman, however, judgments concerning proper behavior are more difficult to make in local terms. In the first place, she is usually not a candidate in the local marriage market, as she may already be married to a foreign husband, or may make it very obvious that she has no intentions of marrying locally. The former alternative, being safer, probably makes role flexibility somewhat easier to attain for the married woman field worker.

Furthermore, the greater social ease of Western women in mixed company, or alone with local men, makes it clear that they are less dependent on the protection of external social controls. In a situation where women are defined as inherently vulnerable, the woman who is willing to assume the risks of a protracted interview with a man can be permitted to so do, as long as she causes no damage to the existing social control mechanism. A Western woman who moves freely in a *purdah* society is, on the other hand, handicapped by the widespread belief that all Western women must be immoral, since they move about freely. The flexibility with which a particular woman can establish her own role, however, usually makes it possible to overcome these attitudes in a specific situation. An informant may be convinced that this particular foreign woman behaves in an acceptable, although unusual way—although his attitudes toward Western women in general may not change much, and a certain amount of ambivalence may remain. Not surprisingly, a frequent comment on this situation may be that it is all right for a Western woman to move around freely, since she is used to it, but it would not do for one's wife and sister.

In addition, the attitudes which a foreign woman encounters in a work context should not be confused with those encountered in a purely social setting. For example, when I attended social gatherings in Pakistan, to which my husband and I had been invited as a couple, I often encountered teasing and ambivalence among local men. Such attitudes were absent in the work context, even when my husband and I conducted joint interviews, as was sometimes the case. At a social gathering, a woman field worker's position is often defined in terms of an ambiguity already familiar from Western contexts:

she is the wife of . . . *but* she also works on her own.
By contrast, the foreign woman field worker in the work context is a much greater novelty in a *purdah* society, and, as such, has more leeway in indicating how she expects to be received.

The male field worker, on the other hand, cannot base role flexibility on elements in either the traditional or the changing social order. As the preceding discussion indicates, there are of course many modifications and ambiguities in the system of underlying assumptions as Pakistani society is being rapidly modernized. Especially in urban areas, and among the middle and upper classes, there are increasing numbers of transitional people, who illustrate in their own behavior and attitudes what some current ambivalences are. Nevertheless, it remains difficult for a male field worker to prove his lack of inherent aggressiveness which the society attributes to men in general. The foreign man may well be outside the local marriage market, but he is still in a position to injure the reputation of the local woman who intends to find or keep a local husband. For this reason, a man finds it difficult to conduct interviews with even the more Westernized and educated women, and usually does not even attempt to do so in more traditional settings. The disability facing male field workers in *purdah* societies, and analogous groups, is widely recognized, and is usually solved by enlisting the field worker's wife to make contact with the local women.

The professional status of the male field worker is also not sufficient to overcome the strong social pressures against free contacts between the sexes in a *purdah* society such as Pakistan. This is shown by existing barriers against contacts between women patients and male doctors, even though Western-trained medical men have achieved high professional status. In Pakistan, most women who use Western-trained doctors at all expect to go to a "lady-doctor," and if none is available, social pressure may force women to forego medical care. The medical profession is the major high-prestige career open to women in Pakistan today, indicating that a large market for their special services exists and may continue to expand. The woman doctor is expected to devote herself to women patients, and to specialize in relevant fields, such as obstetrics, gynecology, and family planning. Similarly, the increased demand for the education of girls has created a growing demand for women teachers, although education has traditionally been in the hands of men. It is still unusual for women teachers to work in boys' schools, especially in top positions, and it is even rarer for girls' schools to use men teachers. At the college and university level, some of these limits are less strictly observed than at the elementary one. But it is clear that professional status alone is not likely to enable the male field worker to overcome existing social prejudices.

The greater ease with which a woman field worker may move in a *purdah* society is only one of the unexpected advantages she may find. In addition, role flexibility can also be an asset in the particular interviewing situation. For example, in seeking information about masculine fields of work, such as economic and political activities, the woman researcher can try to establish herself in a predominantly male role, once she overcomes initial suspicions concerning her ability to understand these matters at all. But male informants may speak more easily and freely to a woman interviewer in some cases, since she represents no obvious competitive threat, and the novelty of the situation may have great unconscious appeal. On the other hand, if motivations and attitudes, or some other aspect of inner life are sought, it is often very fruitful to emphasize the femininity of the interviewer, since such matters are properly in the sphere of women's concerns in the local culture. Interviews of the latter type usually involve a longer time span, in the course of which an informant-interviewer relationship may take on some elements of transference. In this setting, the older cultural assumptions about the nature of women are sometimes revived, and the interviewer is faced with the very difficult problem of defining a relationship in which the advantages of a feminine approach are not lost, while her vulnerability is denied.

In short, the foreign woman working in a *purdah* society has certain unusual advantages in contributing to her own role definition in varying circumstances, whereas a man's role is much more rigidly defined. The woman field worker is able to gain entry to the world of local women as well as local men by the appropriate shifts in the definition of her own role. Since it is the woman who takes most of the risks in a situation where she is defined as inherently vulnerable, an outsider who can afford to take such risks may overcome the social disabilities of women in a *purdah* society. It is presumably these advantages of women field workers which McKim Marriott had in mind in a recent brief reference to his

> conviction that a woman in a purdah-bound society can do a better job of scientific transvestitism than can a man.[1]

My own experience in Pakistan has led me to the same conclusion, although generalizations from it must be drawn with some care. It is possible, for instance that male and female roles in some societies are so rigidly defined that even a stranger is completely bound by them. Or perhaps the crossing of these role boundaries is seen as such a threat in some societies that flexible

---

[1] McKim Marriott, "Communications," Journal of Asian Studies, XXI, No. 2 (February, 1962), 264.

role definitions cannot be attempted. On the other hand, it is very likely that societies other than *purdah* societies offer similar opportunities to women field workers—e. g., the Latin countries, and others in which an explicit dual standard applies to male and female behavior. It is also likely, finally, that the impact of modernization itself produces the kinds of social dislocations which make flexible role definitions particularly possible. In other words, the loopholes and interstices of the social structure must be sufficiently large to be useful, but they probably occur more frequently than one might expect.

Finally, the concept of role flexibility is relevant to the role of the observer in general, and the fit between certain kinds of observers and their subject of observation. To a very large extent, the ability of any field worker to elicit information from persons in a given setting depends on his ability to be simultaneously a member and a non-member of the observed group. He must be accepted enough to be tolerated and spoken to, and yet detached enough to be a permissible social contact for most local persons. The specific advantages of the woman field worker in a *purdah* society suggest that her role in this situation may be defined with greater flexibility than that of a male field worker, and that her entry into local society can be more extensive than his. In the terms of reference of a *purdah* society, a foreign woman finds it easier to remain marginal to the local social control system—and, paradoxical though this may seem at first glance, this enables her to move more easily within local society.

Unleashing the Untrained: Some Observations on Student Ethnographers † *

L IKE MANY OTHER COLLEGES and universities in the United States, Chico State College in California offers an upper division anthropology course in "Comparative Societies." As elsewhere, the course description in the College catalog is sufficiently general and ambiguous to allow a broad interpretation of what constitutes appropriate content. Most importantly for this paper, it affords the instructor considerable freedom in determining what sort of term project he wants to try to pry loose from sometimes reluctant students.

During the first week of class in the fall of 1967, and before I had made any firm decision to require what probably would have been a typical library research paper, a lively class discussion developed around the subject of gathering anthropological field data. Encouraged by what struck me as a rather cavalier attitude on the part of the more vocal members of the class toward the enthnographer's task of gathering data in his own as well as other cultures, I assigned each student the semester-long task of gathering field data on a subject of his own choice.

For practical reasons, the assignment did not follow the broad *Notes and Queries on Anthropology* format.[1] The limitations of time required that the students select, observe, and analyze a specific behavior, event, or institution on the campus or in the community. The primary goal was to give them an opportunity to experience on a microscale some of the problems confronting the anthropologist seeking information from human beings about human beings. The methodological emphasis was on the nose-to-

† James E. Myers is Associate Professor of Anthropology and Chairman of the Department of Anthropology at Chico State College, Chico, California.

This is a revision of a paper presented before the joint meeting of The Southwestern Anthropological Association and The Society for California Archaeology in San Diego, California, April 1968.

* Vol. 28, No. 2 Summer 1969, Human Organization.

1 Royal Anthropological Institute of Great Britain and Ireland, Notes and Queries on Anthropology, (sixth ed.), Routledge and Kegan Paul, London, 1951.

nose confrontation inherent in various participant-observation situations, and the students were informed that papers would be evaluated primarily in terms of evidence showing their achievement of skills directly related to various participant-observer problems. Thus, entrée into the field, structuring of the observer's role, and sequence and timing of observation took precedence over definitions of problems, generation and validation of hypotheses, control of variables, and other traditional aspects of scientific problem solving.

For three class meetings I presented lecture material to illustrate the notion that people often are not able to tell a researcher why or what they are doing or believe, either because they do not know, or (and more beguiling) because they consciously or unconsciously distort facts, withhold data, or otherwise confound the ethnographer. The students were reminded that the difference between stated belief and observed behavior may be especially difficult to sort out when the information being sought lies in an area culturally regarded as "controversial" or "sensitive." During this time I relied heavily on material from my own field experiences and from two excellent articles on field work problems by Paul and by Becker and Geer.[2]

Before describing the types of problems tackled by these intrepid ethnographers, several general points should be made:

1. During the first semester the assignment was given, there were no anthropology majors in the class of 50 students—simply because there was no B.A. program in anthropology at the time. During the second semester, after anthropology had become a bachelor's program, five anthropology majors were enrolled in the class of 48 students. These five were majors only by the fact of declaration and actually possessed a very meager background in anthropology.

2. Except for the three introductory lectures on selected field work problems, no further instruction on the problems and techniques of gathering data in the field was provided, and the students were essentially on their own.

[2] Benjamin D. Paul, "Interview Techniques and Field Relationships," in Anthropology Today, University of Chicago Press, Chicago, 1953, pp. 430–475; Howard Becker and Blanche Geer, "Participant-Observation: The Analysis of Qualitative Field Data," in Richard Adams and Jack Preiss (eds.), Human Organization Research, The Dorsey Press, Homewood, Ill., 1960, pp. 267–289.

3. It would undoubtedly appear more professional if I could report that my laissez-faire approach to the assignment was governed by a cleverly conceived pedagogical hypothesis designed to instill in students the value of independent research. The fact is, although initially harboring every intention of providing supervision for the students, I was so swamped with other academic and administrative work for the two semesters the course was given that the effect was to unleash on the college community 98 curious and enthusiastic, but notably untrained and unsupervised student ethnographers.

Categories of Research Selected

Ninety-one of the original 98 students completed the task. Of the seven who did not, three failed even to venture into the field, two gathered their data but were unable to produce a manuscript, one gathered data but claimed to have lost his "extensive" field notes to a thief, and one student failed to return from his field excursion to the Haight-Ashbury.

The problems studied fell into eight major categories:

1. *Womb-to-Tomb Critical Events.* This was the single largest category, with 21 students observing the most important ceremonies, events, and ritual behaviors occurring in an individual's life cycle (birthdays, betrothals, weddings, divorce, and funerals).

2. *The Religious World.* Seventeen students trained their energies on various religious ceremonies and beliefs (Roman Catholic mass, Jehovah Witnesses, St. Germaine Society, the priesthood, the Holy Eucharist).

3. *The Body Beautiful.* Fourteen field workers explored the mysteries surrounding the care and nurturing of the human body and the various types of attention it receives by the owner and by the spectator. (Female figure, beauty parlor, ear piercing, sorority girls and their breasts.)

4. *Fun and Games.* Thirteen people sought to understand the behavior associated with organized recreation. Reflecting their own career interests to a degree greater than any other category, all thirteen were from the Physical Education Department. (Football, surfing, golfing, automobile racing, the keg party.)

5. *The World of Work.* Nine students ventured into occupational areas, seeking to understand how and why man earns his bread and keep. (The car salesman, the life insurance salesman, the Negro hustler, the mailman.)

6. *Associations.* College fraternities and sororities, community clubs, and other nonkinship sodalities were studied by six students. (John Birch Society, the Boy Scouts, behavioral norms at a fraternity house, the Free Masons, the pledge role in the Lambda Pi fraternity.)

7. *Social Problems.* Seven papers were directed toward social problems in the community and on the campus. (The drunk, the collegiate user of marijuana, homosexuals, three juvenile delinquents, abortion.)

8. *Miscellanea.* This catch-all category comprised numerous research topics too varied to assign to any of the other areas. (Contraceptive buying, a Negro speech community, toilet behavior of the college student, seating arrangements in the College Union.)

Twenty-three students (25 percent of the class) directed their research to on-campus situations. Nine students (10 percent of the class) plunged into research areas that would be designated as culturally sensitive, i. e., they purposely selected topics demanding the utmost in observational and/or interviewing skills— for example, the papers on contraceptive purchasing, homosexuality, breasts, hustling, abortion, unmarried couples living together, pot and drugs on campus.

Fifty-nine students (54 percent) approached their problem by declaring their role of observer, 34 students (38 percent) were already members of the group they selected to study, and eight students (9 percent) decided it advantageous to pose as a member of the group being studied, although in fact they were not.

Some Sample Findings

In addition to the wide variety of research subjects chosen, the students displayed immense variation in the style, approach, and quality of their papers. The following brief excerpts and descriptions represent neither the best nor the poorest papers, nor do they represent the most seriously motivated students. They have been selected merely to convey the creativity that can be obtained from students unfettered by the restricting bonds of training and supervision.

In a paper entitled "The Keg Party," one student studied a peculiar tye of campus corroboree known as the "kegger," or keg party. Based on his attendance at thirteen keggers held during one semester, the participant-observer clearly spent more time participating than observing. However, the descriptive quality of his paper was good, and the reader emerges with a feeling that an Erik Erikson has done some reinterpreting of Allan Holmberg's happy description of a Siriono drinking bout:

> The keg is usually carried to the party site by the persons who purchased it, and there seems to be some status involved in triumphantly bringing this prize into the party area. There is an immediate uproar with the arrival of the keg, and people quickly go to work preparing for the festivities. The keg itself is a large aluminum container of some thickness which stands 2.5 feet tall with a circumference of about three feet at its widest point. It is filled with a beverage called beer, which has an alcoholic content of approximately 4.5 percent. The tapping process is usually attended to by a person who is respected because of his experience and expert handling of the process. The tapper has command and authority over the party at this point and the people follow his directions in order to finish with the work and get the beer flowing. The keg location is clearly the center of the party. The keg itself is almost given the place of a totem, notice the widespread excitement as it is brought in and made ready for tapping. This observer wonders about the possibility of the tap being a phallic symbol; witness the plunging of the cylindrical shaft into the round, awaiting container, and the cheers that go up when the liquid spurts forth.

Incidentally, this student fondness for pop-psych as an analytical tool was evident in a half-dozen papers.

Without a doubt the acme of observational skills was reached in a paper entitled "Toilet Behavior of the College Student." Recognizing that all peoples enact certain rituals to maintain their aplomb during the act of voiding, and that American society confines urination and defecation to certain rooms and fixtures, the student proceeded to analyze the behavior of males and females using first and second floor toilets in one building on the campus. Showing the advantage of having the spouse accompany the anthropologist into the field, the student ethnographer, with the unflagging and devoted aid of his wife, became privy to data that resulted in this reporter's public bathroom performance being affected forever.

The paper contained excellent diagrams of the toilet rooms observed. It included a telling analysis of urinal and stall choice, with impressive frequency distribution tables to lend statistical support to the commonly observed fact that men and women do not randomly select a stall or a urinal, as the case may be. With the sure hand of a veteran experimentalist, variable behavior was forced on the subjects by the researcher himself occupying select stall or urinals and then observing the results.

The observer concluded that self-consciousness is the major contributor to male/female toilet behavior. This was evidenced in many instances, but especially by the frequent faint-of-heart females who used the technique of waiting until one person flushed the toilet, and then urinating or defecating while the noise from the adjoining toilet drowned out the sounds of one's own relief; or, quickly relieving one's self and exiting before the stranger could see who was in the adjoining stall.

The class award for questionable motivation and hanky-panky under the guise of science, went to a fraternity lad who wrote a paper entitled, "My Cup Runneth Over: A Study of Sorority Girls and Their Breasts." Happily for science, his enthusiastic but unrealistic initial research ideas gave way to reality. After dismissing an impressive corps of eager male volunteer assistants, abandoning certain interesting techniques that had little significance to his stated problem, and enlisting the aid of female volunteer assistants to administer his questionnaire and conduct interviews, he turned out a respectable piece of research on beauty and the breast.

One student studied the activities and beliefs of ten Negro hustlers in one California metropolitan area for three months. Few students would have been able to study this subject successfully, but in this case the researcher himself came from a lower-lower class background and was familiar with his topic from prior experience. Apparently having no trouble drawing what in such a study could be an important methodological line between participation and observation, he "moved in and out of the scene with [his] hustler informants." Much of this student's success derived from the endorsement given him by two high-status hustlers, and his paper evidenced excellent observational and reporting skills in describing the hustlers' dwellings and furnishings, food, dress, grooming, violence, competition, and, of course, their women.

Methodological and Ethical Violence

Relentless in their quest for information, some of the students exhibited a blatant disregard for the rights of others and frankly startled me with the ease and willingness by which they disclosed certain data obviously not intended to go beyond the point of original reception. For example:

1. DISLOSURE OF SECRET RITUALS. Much was written about heretofore secret rites and ceremonies of various fraternities and sororities, both collegiate and community. Some of the information was wrested from its owners by devious means and in some cases was proffered to the researcher only with the understanding it would not be disclosed to anyone else.

2. VIOLATION OF ANONYMITY AND PRIVACY. One of the few caveats stressed in class in reference to the research was the great importance to be attached to informant and institutional anonymity when requested. This admonition was frequently violated and typically in those cases where anonymity and privacy was most important.

3. THE "HOMING" QUESTIONNAIRE. Another unfortunate technique was the clever design and use of the "homing" questionnaire, i. e., questionnaires that clearly indicated "do not use names," but which nevertheless were surreptitiously keyed to allow the researcher to identify who filled out a particular questionnaire. In some cases the student's reason for the subterfuge was unclear; in other cases, e. g., the study of the sorority girls' breast and brassiere beliefs, the motivation—though not condoned—can be appreciated.

4. DISCLOSURE OF ILLEGAL PRACTICES. Some reports focused on illegal practices and thus contained information that would, if made public, activate campus and/or civil authorities.

5. MISREPRESENTATION. Puzzling was the practice of some students who for one reason or another misrepresented them-

selves. Often overlooking the fact that the role of student would usually suffice to gain entrée and gather information, they proceeded under the guise of various false statuses.

6. THE AMATEUR PROFESSIONAL. Frightening was the ease with which two junior students assumed the status of experienced professionals and administered and analyzed various projective and intelligence tests in their study of a culturally disadvantaged family. One wrote: "I attempted to give her the Goodenough projective test . . . Next I attempted administering Murray's T.A.T. test . . At this time I tried to give the daughter the sentence-completion test I had devised, but I learned she was unable to read . . . Next I tried the Rorschach Inkblot test."

Unforeseen Ramifications

At least two students learned rather dramatically that social research can proceed down unintended and unforeseen avenues. Although the two examples of unplanned developments given here are a long way from DuBois' remembrances of her five unfortunate Alorese informants who were publicly decapitated by the Japanese as a warning to other informants, they are important in giving credence to her belief that "there is no end to the intricate chain of responsibility and guilt that the pursuit of even the most arcane social research involves." [3]

One student, for example, innocently set out to explore coffee-break behavior in a local county office. The result was a minor human relations catastrophe that undoubtedly involved her inexperienced approach as much as the fortuity of events that existed independent of her behavior. Thus, the study was poorly timed since a taxpayers' association was currently probing costs of county government, and was especially interested in unauthorized leaves and extended coffee breaks. The student also failed to gain approval for the study from appropriate personnel. This distressed certain administrators, who, themselves, were later charged by the taxpayers' association with not knowing what was going on under their very noses. Finally, she exhibited naiveté of organizational behavior ("I can't understand why 900 em-

[3] Cora DuBois, The People of Alor,
Harper and Brothers, New York, 1960,
p. xiv.

ployees arose in anger and indignation when only 30 were directly involved").

Before the student realized what a tempest had been stirred up,
three newspapers in the county had picked up the story ("Mys-
terious Coffee Break Survey"), the county employees' association
distributed a flier urging all employees to beware of an unauthorized survey that threatened their coffee break, and the taxpayers'
association was demanding further investigation into what appeared to be a typical county employee boondoggle of time.

The tragedy of the aborted study was summed up by an office
informant:

> It is too bad that you had to walk right into the middle of an
> already difficult situation. It is sadder because you had no
> idea of the trouble you would cause. Your intentions were
> perfectly innocent, but you sure screwed things up.

Another student gathered data on community service clubs in
a small town north of Chico. He minced few words concerning
the discrepancy between one club's stated *raison d'etre* and what
he actually observed, concluding that there was more "bulling
and boozing" in the organization than anything else. A few
weeks after he completed the study, a friend asked him if he
could read it. He did—the entire paper—to the assembled members of the club. The members did not seem to appreciate this
type of anthropological research and in fact indicated their intention of sending a formal complaint to the student, his instructor, and the college administration.

Concluding Remarks

On the credit side of the assignment, undergraduate students
at least had an opportunity to acquire an inkling of the problems
and advantages of field work as a method of gathering data. On
the debit side, some of the students probably wrought irreparable
damage to future students who may also wish to use the community and the campus as a human research laboratory.

On the whole, however, the assignment has reinforced my positive feelings toward the importance of having undergraduate
anthropology students pursue basic field training on the campus
or in the community. Whether the student is going on to graduate studies or not, we are remiss if we do not see that he has

some firsthand experience with the discipline's primary technique of gathering data.

The optimum learning experience would be an undergraduate course in field methodology, perhaps along the lines described by Bennett,[4] plus supervised work in the field with a trained ethnographer.   When either of these is not possible, as is most often the case in undergraduate programs today, an improved version of what has been described here may be the best solution.   Improvements might take many forms, but minimally, in order to avoid the problems cited in this paper, it would demand more hours devoted to classroom training and closer surveillance of the proposed studies.

[4] John Bennett, "Individual Perspective in Field Work: An Experimental Training Course," in Richard Adams and Jack Preiss (eds.), op. cit., pp. 267–289.

*

XI. Looking at Anthropology

Perhaps because there are more anthropologists today than there were several decades ago, or perhaps because anthropologists are increasingly in positions where they can influence social change if they so desire, there has been an increasing tendency in recent years for both anthropologists and non-anthropologists to take a closer look at anthropologists and anthropology.

The first article in this section represents the efforts of a non-anthropologist who has taken a careful look at the annual tribal rite of North American anthropologists—The Annual Meeting of the American Anthropological Association. In the next article by Gerald D. Berreman the author makes an articulate plea for social responsibility in social anthropology by asserting that anthropologists cannot avoid involvement in social issues. The final selection in this section is in the form of a brief letter by Donald K. Grayson who makes a strong plea for his colleagues to place the value of human life above the value of the scientific pursuits of anthropology.

Anthropologist, Study Thyself *

Richest Mine Of Research Untapped?

Army Marion, veteran hotel executive, stood in the lobby of the Olympic Hotel yesterday and voiced a common bewilderment which beset Seattle last week.

"We've had bigger conventions than this," he said, "but why does this crowd stand day and night in the entire lobby and talk and talk and talk?"

Fred Thieme, vice president of the University of Washington, who had just moderated a session of the American Anthropological Association, attempted no reply. The anthropology of anthropologists has not been undertaken, although it probably offers the richest remaining information trove in the study of man.

BEHAVIOR

When it comes to group behavior, as exemplified by the Seattle annual meeting, some light may have been shed two years ago by Harvard's Irven DeVore.

DeVore, whose work on baboon social organization is the definitive study of primate behavior circulated a paper in which he considered the structure of the group which surrounds famed Margaret Mead at any anthropological cocktail party.

With the grand dame of the art at the center, he saw her as surrounded by concentric circles of diminishing rank. At the "core area" was the central dominant hierarchy—the department chairmen, the directors of great museums, the top echelon of scholars whose works amaze the world. Far on the undulating periphery, straining to catch every drop of wisdom from the Mead lips yet spill none of their own, were the young graduate students, farther from the fountain of wisdom than from the bar.

So it was in the Olympic lobby. Margaret Mead, who unveiled the new film of her life work, "Forty Years of Margaret Mead," in a crowded session Thursday night, stood waiting for a photographer to appear.

BABBLE

She waited four minutes past the appointed time. Then, bundled in a heavy furseal coat, her right hand clutching a bifurcated staff of cherrywood she picked up in England, she set her course straight through the packed clusters of the AAA.

It was like Moses parting the Red Sea, but the hundreds of anthropologists didn't dry up. They faced about as though the Flag were passing by; then the babble rose again to the pale golden ceiling high above the mezzanine. The real work of the AAA is done once a year in conversation, not in the dozen meeting rooms which hum morning and night with oral presentations, slide shows and motion pictures.

The programmed meetings for the most part cover formal reports of work long since concluded. News, to the sophisticated, is whatever they haven't already heard via the grapevine, but the content of the written reports usually has leaked out months before.

There were two marked exceptions at the Seattle meeting—which ends this afternoon. Dr. Mead's film packed the Georgian Room, while Washington State University's team presentation of its Marmes Man—although billed at the same time as the Mead attraction—played to a full house in Ballroom B.

[A8669]

Sen. Warren G. Magnuson, who saved the Marmes site from reservoir flooding by persuading President Johnson to authorize a cofferdam complex on the Palouse, dropped in to hear Prof. Roald Frxyell's opening remarks. Dr. Richard Daugherty, co-director of the WSU dig, noted the senator's presence and the audience rose to a standing ovation.

REUNION

The annual winter meeting is a combination class reunion, tip-sheet counter, and slave market. Gathered from projects in jungles and muskeg, in ghettos and libraries, colleagues from across the world exchange information on their progress, new discoveries—and new funds. Many of the younger men are bearded; the graybeards, for the most part, wear no beards at all, but as a student of the myriad patterns of human eccentricity, the anthropologist hardly would find himself eccentric. He's just different, principally in his warmth, his enthusiasm, his dedication.

Students greet old professors, archeologists slip unpublished dig details to favored colleagues, and department heads with slots to fill in their faculties next year slip in to the formal sessions, tarry briefly and slip out. It's like scouting a baseball prospect.

"I know what a graduate student is going to say when he or she gets up to read a paper," said one graybeard shopping for an assistant professor, "I don't listen—I watch how the youngster handles himself before a critical audience."

The slave market is highly structured, formalized in second-floor bedrooms where anthropologists ready to enter the professional world file their credentials and wait for interviewers from one institution or another to tap them. Hourly, the applicants check back to see if they are named on the interview appointment list.

BAIT

Negotiations are carried on far less publicly when an older professor is sought. The bait may be more money, higher rank, better facilities for research, more travel funds. The deal is not publicized by the institution making the offer, in the hope of avoiding a bidding situation from competitors. The courted one, with a basement rate established, usually manages to be approached by other bidders, anyway, while carefully concealing from his own superiors that he's on the block.

"Prestige often is an important inducement," one experienced academic scout explained, "but I've noticed at this meeting that persistent good weather is an attraction to older people. The climate of the potential new place definitely is a factor."

Other scouts are the representatives of publishing houses. They want manuscripts and flourish contracts. The emphasis is on texts—there are no Margaret Meads available to write popular best-sellers—but anthropology is spreading into secondary schools now and texts are badly needed.

Margaret Mead, herself, hopes for a change in the present structure. The revolution of the nation's disadvantaged means that many people will be entering anthropology without the traditional formal academic preparation—but with many experiences and skills which the profession, if it is wise, can utilize. There will be people in their middle years offering their talents and their labors.

The system which now requires undergraduate and advanced degrees for professional advancement seems likely soon to select recruits for their own worth rather than letters writ on sheepskin.

[A8670]

* Reprinted by permission of the Seattle Post-Intelligencer. By Fergus Hoffman.

Is Anthropology Alive? Social Responsibility in Social Anthropology † * [1]

† Gerald D. Berreman was born in Portland, Oregon in 1930. He received his B.A. in anthropology from the University of Oregon in 1952 and his M.A. in 1953. He received his Ph.D. from Cornell University in 1959 and began teaching anthropology at the University of California at Berkeley in the same year. He is now Professor of Anthropology at Berkeley.

Berreman has done fieldwork in the Aleutians, investigating sociocultural change by means of a restudy of an isolated community 10 years after his original visit. On a Ford Foundation Foreign Area Training Fellowship, he spent 15 months in 1957–58 in a Pahari-speaking community in the Himalayas northeast of Delhi. Among the results of this experience were a monograph, Hindus of the Himalayas (Berkeley and Los Angeles: University of California Press, 1963); a paper on the problems ethnographers face in doing fieldwork, and particularly the problem of establishing a relationship with the people whose life they wish to study, Behind Many Masks (Society for Applied Anthropology Monograph no. 4); and a number of articles on caste and social stratification, among them "Caste in India and the United States" (American Journal of Sociology 66: 120–27). He is now in India, on a Fulbright-

Hays Fellowship for Advanced Research Abroad, studying intercaste and interethnic interaction in a medium-sized city.

The three papers here presented were submitted to Current Anthropology on the following dates: Berreman, 31 vii 67; Gjessing, 20 i 67; Gough, 25 vii 67. Of 51 scholars to whom the papers were sent the following responded with written comments: Olga Akhmanova, Ralph Beals, P. M. Butler, Daniel Cazés, Erik Cohen, Robert Cresswell, Andre Gunder Frank, John Gulick, T. Kawabata, Leo S. Klejn, David Levine, I. M. Lewis, Thomas McCorkle, Bruce B. MacLachlan, F. C. Madigan, Thomas Maloney, Otto von Mering, R. Mukherjee, Ethel Nurge, Sollie H. Posinsky, Cara E. Richards, Wolfgang Rudolph, Henning Siverts, and Peter Skainik. The comments are printed in full after the three papers and are followed by replies from each of the authors.

* Reproduced with permission from the author and CURRENT ANTHROPOLOGY, December 1968: p. 391–396.

[1] Proceedings of the Cultural Congress of Havana. 1968. Appeal of Havana. Reprinted in Gramna, weekly edition of January 21. [AGF*]

"The old formula for successful counterinsurgency used to be 10 troops for every guerrilla," one American specialist [in Thailand] remarked. "Now the formula is ten anthropologists for each guerrilla" (Braestrud 1967).

I

T HE notion that contemporary world events are irrelevant to the professional concerns of anthropologists was laid neatly to rest when, at the meeting of Fellows of the American Anthropological Association in Pittsburg in November, 1966, Michael Harner rose to challenge the ruling of the president-elect that a resolution introduced by David and Kathleen Gough Aberle condemning the United States' role in the war in Vietnam was out of order because it did not "advance the science of anthropology" or "further the professional interests of anthropologists." Harner suggested that "genocide is not in the professional interests of anthropologists." With that, the chair was voted down and the resolution was presented, amended, and passed.

The dogma that public issues are beyond the interests or competence of those who study and teach about man is myopic and sterile professionalism and a fear of commitment which is both irresponsible and irrelevant. Its result is to dehumanize the most humanist of the sciences, as Eric Wolf has called our discipline; to betray utterly the opportunity and obligation which he has claimed for anthropology, namely: "the creation of an image of man that will be adequate to the experience of our time". It forsakes the insights of generations of social scientists, social philosophers, and other men of knowledge who, since the Enlightenment, have been cast in the role of social critics.

That neutrality in science is illusory is a point which has been made often and well. Telling statements by social scientists in recent times have followed Robert Lynd's *Knowledge for What?*, published in 1939. That work is by now a classic, as are the writings of C. Wright Mills on the issue, most notably his articles, "The Social Role of the Intellectual" and "On Knowledge and Power" and his book, *The Sociological Imagination*. A series of recent essays on the topic appear in a volume honoring Mills entitled *The New Sociology*. Among them are: Alvin Gouldner's "Anti-Minotaur: The Myth of a Value-Free Sociology," Douglas Dowd's "Thorstein Veblen and C. Wright Mills: Social Science and Social Criticism," Sydney Willhelm's "Scientific Unaccountability and Moral Accountability," Andrew Hacker's "Power to do

What?", Kenneth Winetrout's "Mills and the Intellectual Default." Other outstanding examples of the genre are Paul Baran's "The Commitment of the Intellectual", John Bennett's "Science and Human Rights: Reason and Action", and recently Noam Chomsky's "The Responsibility of Intellectuals". Much of what I have to say here is re-emphasis of their major points—an undertaking for which I do not apologize, for I think that there are few ideas in the world that are new and exceedingly few that are both new and important. These seem to me important.

For evidence, rather than statements of the problem, of social responsibility in social science, I refer the reader to accounts of Project Camelot, to reports of the role of Michigan State University in Vietnam and its relationship to the C.I.A., and to accounts of Project Agile, "the Pentagon's worldwide counterinsurgency research program," whose anthropologists and other social scientists are said to be working hard in Thailand and elsewhere in Southeast Asia on projects of direct military relevance. I refer the reader also to our illustrious forebear, Franz Boas, who was alert to startlingly similar problems in the uses of anthropology and anthropologists during World War I, and deplored them publicly:

> . . . A number of men who follow science as their profession [including "at least four men who carry on anthropological work"] . . . have prostituted science by using it as a cover for their activities as spies.

Especially relevant to our contemporary problems are discussions of the nature and implications of the relationship between academics and universities and government sponsorship of research. This problem is posed vividly for anthropologists in reports in the *Fellow Newsletter* of our national association. For those of us in the University of California system it has been discussed at some length by students and faculty in the *Daily Californian Weekly Magazine*. Anyone who thought scientists, academics, or intellectuals could work in a value-free vacuum has been disabused of that fantasy by the revelations in the daily press and in the March, 1967 *Ramparts* of the influences of the C.I.A. in student and professional organizations and in foundations.

This should not surprise us. Scientists, we know, are creatures of culture and society like anyone else. "By the fact of his living," C. Wright Mills reminds us, every individual "contributes, however minutely, to the shaping of his society and to the course of its history, even as he is made by society and by its historical push and shove". We as social scientists are not exempt. What we do even as scientists is conditioned by our culture and has meaning in that culture. As Morton Fried has said, and as Robert Lynd said before him, science has no responsibility, but scientists do. Scientists are people. They cannot escape values in the choices they make nor in the effects of their acts.

If we choose to collect our data and make our analyses without regard to their use—leaving that choice to others—we may believe that we are adhering to the most rigorous scientific canons (and hence the most highly *valued* canons—note the word) by not intervening in society. But to say nothing is not to be neutral. To say *nothing* is as much a significant act as to say *something*. Douglas Dowd has noted:

> the alternatives are not "neutrality" and "advocacy." To be uncommitted is not to be neutral, but to be committed— consciously or not—to the *status quo*; it is, in Mills' phrase, "to celebrate the present."

Guillermo Bonfil Batalla referred to this fact when he wrote of what he called "conservative thought in applied anthropology" and its pervasiveness as a premise of our work. "The questions of human value," Lynd pointed out, "are inescapable, and those who banish them at the front door admit them unavowedly and therefore uncritically at the back door."

Our silence permits others in the society less reticent, perhaps less scrupulous, almost certainly less informed, to make their own use of the material presented. It leaves to politicians and journalists, to entrepreneurs, scoundrels, and madmen, as well as to statesmen and benefactors—but especially to the powerful—the interpretation and manipulation of matters about which they frequently know little, and nearly always know far less than those who collected the material or made the analyses. Baran notes in this regard:

> It should be obvious that society's "elections" [or choices] do not come about by miracles, but that society is guided

into some "elections" by the ideology generated by the social
order existing at any given time, and is cajoled, frightened,
and forced into other "elections" by the interests which are
in a position to do the cajoling, the frightening and the forc-
ing. The intellect worker's withdrawal from seeking to influence the outcome of those "elections" is far from leaving
a vacuum in the area of "value" formation.

It is therefore wishful thinking to assume that our work can
be put before the public without context or interpretation, there
to be judged freely and intelligently on its merits without prejudice or manipulation and acted upon accordingly. To assume
that is to contribute to misuse born of ignorance or worse. We
cannot divorce ourselves from the consequences of our scientific
acts any more than we can from those of any other of our acts
as human beings. This is a fact of existence in human society,
and it is a tenet of democracy.

II

Science—even social science—has finally arrived in our society.
The rewards to be obtained for supplying social science data and
social science interpretations of the right kinds and in the right
places are generous in the U. S. To paraphrase Kenneth Winetrout, the intellectual today can join the hired mythmakers
and harsh apologists of Madison Avenue and Washington. On
campus he can be the paid consultant or the academic en-
trepreneur and grantsman. Winetrout notes the literal applica-
bility of Carl Becker's statement that we have a society where
it pays to think likewise rather than otherwise. This results in
the contemporary prevalence of social scientists whose eyes are
on the main chance rather than on the condition of man—the
"crack-pot realists" as Mills liked to call them. This is the context within which we find social scientists whose "ideology of
non-involvement in the social effects of scientific research" simply
frees them from social responsibility, creating an "unaccountable
scientific aristocracy," closely allied to the governmental, military, and corporate elites who buy their services and validate
their heady status. Speaking of the "scholar-experts" who
abound in the academic and para-academic worlds today, Noam
Chomsky notes that they

construct a "value-free technology" for the solution of technical problems that arise in contemporary society.   .   .   .
[But] the extent to which this "technology" is value-free is
hardly very important, given the clear commitments of those
who apply it.   The problems with which research is concerned are those posed by the Pentagon or the great cor-
porations, not, say, by the revolutionaries of Northeast Brazil
or by SNCC.[3]   Nor am I aware of a research project devoted
to the problem of how poorly armed guerillas might more effectively resist a brutal and devastating military technology
.   .   .   .

Yet this is a kind of problem which would be likely to interest
social scientists who felt entirely free to follow their intellects—
at least as likely as those which have interested them under non-
scientific sponsorship.

The rationale which supports this scientific unaccountability
among moral men is the myth of a value-free social science, described by Gouldner as a Minotaur—a beast half man, half
bull, confined to a labyrinth and sustained by human victims.
This myth has been exposed to all but its most avid beneficiaries
and the most credulous in its audience by events in this country
since World War II, just as it was in Europe considerably earlier.
Gouldner holds that

.   .   .   one of the main institutional forces facilitating the
survival and spread of the value-free myth was its usefulness
in maintaining both the cohesion and the autonomy of the
modern university, in general, and the newer social science
disciplines, in particular.

Perhaps more accurately, it maintains a whole segment of the
profession—or at least the symbiotic relationship between that
segment of the profession and the sources of its funds, namely
corporate foundations and governmental agencies.   It is in the
labyrinths of those sources that the Minotaur is most welcome and
most richly rewarded.   Those whom the Minotaur has served have
used it not primarily for what it produced, but for what they *made*
of what it produced;   and they have proved to be accomplished

---

[3] SNCC is the common abbreviation
for the Student Non-violent Coordi-
nating Committee, a militant organization working for civil rights for
Negroes in the United States.

alchemists as they have turned the results of social science to their own ends. It was Alexander Leighton who said that "the administrator uses social science the way a drunk uses a lamppost, for support rather than for illumination." The uses and distortions of social scientific findings depend largely upon how amenable they are to such use and distortion, and *that* is where the social responsibility of the social scientist lies—to apply his knowledge and influence unstintingly in the attempt to insure their humane use.

If the Minotaur of value-free social science is to meet its end, it will be because we recognize that it is mythical in substance and therefore not nearly as invulnerable as its bellowing might imply or as its beneficiaries would have us believe, and because we refuse to tolerate any longer its inhumanity. Its larger and more fearsome relative in physical science disappeared in the atomic cloud. Our own is disappearing in the blood of Vietnam. That war, the policies it reflects, and the shadow of social scientific complicity have forced every American social scientist to answer anew Irving Horowitz's question, "is he a member of a human science or of an anti-human science?"

Many who applaud the end of Camelot and decry complicity with the C.I.A. seek, however, not to kill or exorcize the Minotaur but to reform it—to create a *truly* value-free social science. They ask the opportunity to forget Camelot, Vietnam, and the C.I.A., to shut out the clamor of their students and their "involved" colleagues—to retreat to an ivory tower, there to pursue their work without reference to the outside world. They seek the impossible: to become students of man who are out of touch with men and unconcerned with men. But that ivory tower is precisely where the old Minotaur was born, and the desire to avoid responsibility is what created it and led to its disastrous effects. Camelot, Project Agile, and other perversions of the concept of value-free social science are exemplifications of the truth of Wilhelm's charge that "ethical neutrality is a veneer for irresponsibility." Those adventures have done for social science in America what the atomic blasts on Japanese cities did for all science. In James Agee's words,

> When the bomb split open the universe and revealed the prospect of the infinitely extraordinary, it also revealed the old-

est, simplest, commonest, most neglected and most important of facts, that each man is eternally and above all else responsible for his own soul. . . .

This is true even for scientists.

Why is the myth of value-freedom so persistent and cherished among anthropologists and other social scientists? Mills has noted that those who exhibit

> the curious passion for the mannerism of the non-committed, . . . conform to the prevailing fear of any passionate commitment. *This,* and not "scientific objectivity" is what is really wanted by such men when they complain about "making value judgments."

Gouldner says, "the one thing [they] . . . can never abide is a lack of decorum, even if the performance is in other respects brilliant." But this is a time in which the truth is likely to be overlooked if the commitment to it is not passionately expressed; and to shrink from value, from passion, or commitment, is as inappropriate as to shrink from reason. It is a time when the specialist must forcefully announce not only his knowledge, but its implications and consequences.

III

Winetrout evinces the indecorum, the passionate commitment, which offends some of his colleagues in the closing paragraph of his essay honoring the courageous Mills:

> In our present-day world it is not enough to be scholarly; one must be concerned and angry enough to shout. It is not enough to understand the world; one must seek to change it.

The world is going to change in any case, I would argue, and our knowledge will contribute to the change whether we want it to or not. What we have a responsibility to do is see that our knowledge is used for humane changes, as we define humaneness.

Alfred Schutz suggested that "it is the duty and the privilege of the well-informed citizen in a democratic society to make his private opinion prevail over the public opinion of the man in the street." This is done not by force, but by reason. I do not advocate special powers (beyond those which come to reasoned statement) for the well-informed, but I decry special restrictions on them, whether externally imposed or self-imposed.

The late Robert Oppenheimer is quoted as having spoken before the National Academy of Sciences in 1963, "on the difficult matter of how and when scientists should speak on 'common and public questions.' " He said,

> If I doubt whether professionally we have special qualifica-
> tion on these common questions, I doubt even more that
> our professional practices should disqualify us, or that we
> should lose interest and heart in preoccupations which have
> ennobled and purified men throughout history, and for which
> the world has great need today.

Lynd maintained that

> either the social sciences know more than do . . . *de
> facto* leaders of the culture as to what the findings of re-
> search mean, as to the options the institutional system pre-
> sents, as to what human personalities want, why they want
> them, and how desirable changes can be effected, *or* the vast
> current industry of social science is an empty façade.

And Kathleen Gough Aberle has asked "who is to evaluate and suggest guidelines for human society, if not those who study it?" Our professional obligation is to present what we know and the inferences we draw from our knowledge as clearly, thoughtfully, and responsibly as we can. This is a value position with practical and humane consequences and with scientific legitimacy.

Chomsky holds that the responsibility of intellectuals is "to speak the truth and to expose lies," and he documents brilliantly the fact that this seeming truism is not manifest in the contributions of Establishment intellectuals (primarily social scientists and historians) to current and recent U.S. foreign policy.

C. Wright Mills insisted upon the application of reason and knowledge to practical problems and decried the "divorce of knowledge from power". Mills said:

> As a type of social man, the intellectual does not have any one
> political direction, but the work of any man of knowledge,
> if he is the genuine article, does have a distinct kind of politi-
> cal relevance: his politics, in the first instance, are the poli-
> tics of truth, for his job is the maintenance of an adequate
> definition of reality. In so far as he is politically adroit, the
> main tenet of his politics is to find out as much of the truth
> as he can, and to tell it to the right people, at the right time,

and in the right way.   Or, stated negatively: to deny publicly what he knows to be false, whenever it appears in the assertions of no matter whom; and whether it be a direct lie
or a lie by omission, whether it be by virtue of official secret
or an honest error.   The intellectual ought to be the moral
conscience of his society, at least with reference to the value
of truth, for in the defining instance, that *is* his politics.   And
he ought also to be a man absorbed in the attempt to know
what is real and what is unreal.

I know of no statement which speaks to the responsibility of social
scientists in our time as cogently as does that one.

Douglas Dowd says that the current American crisis is "the
chasm between reality and ideal", and he identifies the
key fact for those who oppose the status quo as *hyprocrisy*.
In this regard, as scientists and as teachers, we have a paramount
responsibility: to speak the truth, to provide "an adequate definition of reality."   Candor is a major precondition for trust and
for rational action, and this is what is lacking or threatened in our
society—in foreign policy; in race relations; in poverty programs; in support of scholarship and research; in university administration; in virtually every sphere of our national life.

The reaction of many of us is to say and do nothing about the
problems of the day; to retreat into our research, our administration, or our teaching, lulled by activity into a sense of purpose,
accomplishment, and virtue, and to hope that things will somehow
work out.   Do we need Edmund Burke to remind us that "the
only thing necessary for the triumph of evil is for good men [and,
I might add, informed men] to do nothing"?

We, as anthropologists, have not lacked outspoken champions
of truth—about race, about poverty, about professional ethics,
about the heavy hands of government and private capital in
formulating our research, about war, and especially about the
current war in Vietnam.   Probably we have more of them in
proportion to our numbers than any other academic discipline.
So far, however, we have failed to emphasize and value their contributions, and we must do this if we want to counteract the
powerful and irresponsible professionalism which belittles or con-
demns them in favor of the mindless and trivial successes obtained under the illusion of freedom from responsibility for one's
self and one's work.

In a world where anything we learn is likely to be put to immediate and effective use for ends beyond our control and antithetical to our values, we must choose our research undertakings with an eye to their implications. We must demand the right to have a hand or at least a say in the use of what we do as a condition for doing it. That demand may most often fall short of realization even when it is granted, but unless it is a minimal condition of our work we may become instruments for inhumanity in the guise of humane scientists.

We must seek to apply our knowledge and skills to real problems, defined by us and not simply accepted from the sources which provide our funds. We must ask questions which address the problems of our time rather than merely those which minimize or obscure them. *This* is the acceptance of Wolf's challenge to create an image of man adequate to our time. *This* is the acceptance of the responsibility of the social scientist, identified by Lynd as the responsibility.

> to keep everlastingly challenging the present with the question: "But what is it that we human beings want, and what things have to be done, in what ways and in what sequence, in order to change the present so as to achieve it?"

This question is as scientific as any question we might pose. Nor does the incompleteness of our knowledge disqualify us scientifically, rationally, or morally from asserting what we know. Mills pointed out 20 years ago that

> if one half of the relevant knowledge which we now possess were really put into the service of the ideals which leaders mouthe, these ideals could be realized in short order. The view that all that is needed is knowledge ignores the nub of the problem as the social scientist confronts it: he has little or no power to act politically and his chance to communicate in a politically effective manner is very limited.

Gouldner has followed logically with the statement:
> the issue . . . is not whether we know enough; the real questions are whether we have the courage to say and use what we know and whether anyone knows more.

This is why we must not be timid in asserting ourselves individually and collectively wherever we can. This is why our professional associations should not now be reluctant to express views on matters of public policy, as they have done in the past and as other professional groups do. For students of human behavior to decline comment on human behavior is irresponsible in a democracy, no matter how controversial the issues.

Most of us are teachers. As such our most immediate responsibility is to our students. We must show them by our example that, as Robert Lekachman has observed, honesty, *not* neutrality, is the prerequisite for good teaching and for good scholarship; that knowledge legitimately leads to informed opinion as well as fact, to understanding of consequences as well as causes, to commitment to act as well as to consider. We must show them that humanity is not incompatible with science; that science without humanity is a monster and social science without humanity a contradiction in terms as well; that we are proud to join Robert Redfield in placing ourselves squarely on the side of mankind, unashamed to wish mankind well; and that we will not sell our souls for money or professional advantage to the anti-human forces in society. It is not merely alarmist to take seriously the reminder that

> if today we concern ourselves exclusively with the technical proficiency of our students and reject all responsibility for their moral sense, or lack of it, then we may someday be compelled to accept responsibility for having trained a generation willing to serve in a future Auschwitz.

That day appears to be much closer now—if indeed it has not already arrived—than it was when those words were first spoken in 1961.

IV

When I asked, "Is Anthropology Alive?" I had in mind a scene in a Marx brothers film wherein Groucho, fearing for the life of a prostrate and inert Harpo, gropes for the pulse, consults his watch, and reports: "Either he's dead or my watch has stopped." The standards used by some of our colleagues to judge work in the discipline as either vital or moribund are like Groucho's watch; it is the standards that are dead more often than the work to which they are applied. The vitality of the discipline is to be judged not by the stopped watch of value-freedom, but by what it says about people—how, why, and with what effect people do what they do. This requires an anthropological version of the sociological imagination so brilliantly described by Mills, which entails a recognition of the relationship between the events—including the troubles—in the lives of people and the social, cultural, and historical circumstances in which they occur. The vitality of anthropology is in doubt only when it is humanly irrelevant or is judged by the dead measure of value-freedom.

To paraphrase the graffito—"Is God dead?" "No, he just doesn't want to get involved."—Anthropology isn't dead; it is just that many of its more nostalgic practitioners do not want to get involved. If they were to succeed, it might in fact be dead. But since their science is man, and since what they want to avoid involvement in is the affairs of men, their desire is hopeless of achievement. They are involved whether they wish it or not. The question is not "Shall I get involved?" but "How can I be involved responsibly—in a way consistent with humanity as I understand it?"

Chomsky closes his article by referring to a series of articles published 20 years ago by Dwight Macdonald on the same topic as his own—the responsibility of intellectuals. He says:

> Macdonald quotes an interview with a [German] death-camp paymaster who burst into tears when told that the Russians would hang him. "Why should they? What have I done?" he asked. Macdonald concludes: "Only those who are willing to resist authority themselves when it conflicts too intolerably with their personal moral code, only they have the right to condemn the death-camp paymaster." The question "What have I done?" is one that we may well ask ourselves, as we read each day of fresh atrocities in Vietnam . . . as we create, mouthe or tolerate, the deceptions that will be used to justify the *next* defense of freedom.

It is worth thinking at this time of the grounds for prosecution and the rules for determining guilt and punishment at Nuremberg.

I believe that we should think of these things as we teach, as we advise, as we make administrative rules and decisions in our universities upon which our male students' lives may well depend, as we undertake consultations to provide information or interpretations for agencies of the government or private beneficiaries of the war, as we accept monies from those sources—even as every man must when he pays his taxes or registers for the draft. In the context of genocide in Vietnam and the possibility of spying by our students and our colleagues, I would suggest that we think twice when we are asked to provide services which support the war or which commit ourselves, our knowledge, or our students to the war, even if only indirectly.

Each of us, in these circumstances, will choose to act differently, but I think the crucial thing is that we act as human beings and as social scientists according to our consciences and our knowledge—for the two are inseparable—and that we not be scared off by the myth of value-freedom. Our acts can have direct effect and can serve as examples to others. If we do not act, our science will die as it did in Germany in the 1930's and 1940's, and with it truth, reason, humanity, and ultimately ourselves.

James Agee's assessment of the atomic bomb written at the end of World War II has new and timely relevance. He said,

> . . . man's fate has forever been shaped between the hands of reason and spirit, now in collaboration, again in conflict. Now reason and spirit meet on final ground. If either or anything is to survive, they must find a way to create an indissoluble partnership.

We are finding, I think, that passion is not incompatible with reason; that, in fact, reason goes hand-in-hand with passion, and both with courage. The spokesmen for our current national policies are not reasonable, and few of them are impassioned; most of the dissenters from that policy are both. True, the former are currently more powerful than the latter; but power is not truth, nor, as history shows, is it even durable, while reason is.

Future history, if there is one, will bear out the reasonable men and women of our country and of the world today, and it will honor those who act on their reason, if only by bitterly regretting their lack of power. It is our duty as scientists and as human beings to be among them. This I hope we can understand and communicate to our students, our colleagues, and whatever other audiences we may reach.

I am aware that this discussion is unconventional anthropology; but these are unconventional times. We are all involved in unconventional and portentous military and political events in this country, perhaps more directly than many of us have realized until recently. These events have world-wide consequences. It is time that we accepted some unconventional responsibility for our acts, be they acts of commission or of omission.

Human Life vs. Science † *

THE April 1969 issue of the *Newsletter* seems to spell out, for those who are interested, the true state of American anthropology. In the short note, " 'Stone Age' Group Encountered," the Smithsonian Institution Center for Short-lived Phenomena reports the discovery of a "non-agricultural hunting and gathering band" in southeastern Surinam—a highly significant and very welcome addition to the anthropological realm.

But the reader is also told that "these bands will soon be decimated by disease from this contact." We are now faced with a clear dilemma: which is more important—human life, or, the scientific pursuit of anthropology? Being an anthropologist, a scientist, the author of this article, as a representative of the Smithsonian Institution, seeks to ensure that these people, the Akuri, will indeed be short lived. Instead of pleading that anthropologists, as humans, mobilize all the economic and political resources at their command to provide proper medical treatment for the Akuri and their neighbors, we see a request for anthropological help in the study of a people which we are to let die.

I cannot help but be reminded of the WWII Nazi physician dissecting live persons in the interest of his science. Luckily, the Nazi doctor is no longer permitted to perform his atrocities, and I suggest that anthropologists, too, should realize that it is far more important to save life than to record its passing.

It is immoral and inhumane to take "support funds" for this anthropological study when these funds could be used to provide medical help for the Akuri people. I suggest that we make known

† By Donald K. Grayson, University of Oregon.

* Reproduced by permission of the American Anthropological Association from AAA Newsletter, Vol. 10, No. 6, 1969, and the author.

to William Crocker, Priscilla Reining, as well as to all those who feel otherwise, that the objective study of anthropology has no right to exist when it denies the right of existence to the living. And, by making no attempt to help the Akuri, by cheerfully taking funds which could be spent for medical aid, we are denying this right.

I hope that the attitude which spawned the requests in the Smithsonian's note will itself be short lived. If the Institution's Center for Short-lived Phenomena is to be characterized by such attitudes, then I also hope that it will soon qualify as one of those phenomena which it purports to study. Right now, however, our concern must be for the Akuri.

*

INDEX

†